Prof. Weinstein

The New Authoritarianism in Latin America

Sponsored by the Joint Committee
on Latin American Studies
of the Social Science Research Council
and the American Council of Learned Societies

The New Authoritarianism in Latin America

David Collier, *Editor*

CONTRIBUTORS

Fernando Henrique Cardoso
David Collier
Julio Cotler
Albert O. Hirschman
Robert R. Kaufman
James R. Kurth
Guillermo O'Donnell
José Serra

PRINCETON UNIVERSITY PRESS

PRINCETON, NEW JERSEY

Acknowledgments

The research reported in this book has been sponsored by the Joint Committee on Latin American Studies of the American Council of Learned Societies and the Social Science Research Council. These studies are part of the Research Planning Program of the Joint Committee, and the support of the Ford Foundation and the Tinker Foundation for this Program is gratefully acknowledged. In addition to writing the chapters in this volume, all participants in the project made significant contributions to planning and executing our collaborative effort. Albert Hirschman, in particular, played an important role, ranging from his support for the project while Chairman of the Joint Committee, to valuable suggestions regarding problems of compiling and editing this volume. Louis Wolf Goodman, as Staff Associate of the Social Science Research Council, greatly facilitated the administration of the project. Both he and Alfred Stepan, in his role as a member of the Joint Committee, played an important part in shaping the intellectual content of our efforts. The translations from Spanish and Portuguese were done by Richard C. Miller and David Collier, and Miller served ably as research assistant for the project. Finally, Philippe Schmitter and Abraham Lowenthal provided valued advice and encouragement in the planning stage of the project.

Table of Contents

The New Authoritarianism in Latin America

Introduction

In 1964, Brazil had a military coup. Two years later, the military also seized power in Argentina. These coups inaugurated periods of rule by the military as an institution, during which the armed forces sought to promote accelerated industrial growth based on massive new foreign investment. They also eliminated or drastically controlled elections of all kinds; introduced important new restrictions in labor unions; and adopted economic austerity programs which imposed wage controls on the urban "popular sector"—i.e., the working class and the lower middle class. These austerity programs were widely interpreted as an important part of the effort to create an investment climate presumed to be attractive to potential foreign investors. Since austerity programs had often been vigorously opposed by the popular sector, in part through such channels as labor organizations and elections, the controls over these forms of political expression appeared essential to the effort to sustain the new economic policies and to achieve economic growth.

The resurgence of military rule in these two major, industrially advanced countries, which contain roughly 65 percent of the population of South America and produce roughly 75 percent of the region's industrial output,[1] occurred in the context of the erosion of earlier expectations of the first two decades of the post-World War II era that greater economic and social equality and a more democratic form of politics would emerge in Latin America.[2] It also called into question the hypothesis of modernization theory that more advanced industrialization is associated with the emergence of democracy and equality[3] and stimulated a

[1] Calculated from data presented in James W. Wilkie, ed., *Statistical Abstract of Latin America*, Volume 17 (Latin American Center, University of California at Los Angeles, 1976) and Robert R. Kaufman, "Mexico and Latin American Authoritarianism," in José Luis Reyna and Richard Weinert, eds., *Authoritarianism in Mexico* (Philadelphia: Institute for the Study of Human Issues, 1977).

[2] An excellent analysis of these expectations is provided in Robert A. Packenham, *Liberal America and the Third World* (Princeton: Princeton University Press, 1973).

[3] Within the large literature dealing with different aspects of this relationship, three crucial initial studies are: Seymour Martin Lipset, "Some Social Requisites

fundamental reassessment of this relationship within the Latin
American context.[4] In place of this earlier hypothesis, a new set
of hypotheses emerged which suggested that in late developing
nations more advanced levels of industrialization may coincide
with the collapse of democracy and an increase in inequality.

In the course of this reassessment, a new term came into use.
Argentina and Brazil were ruled by the military as an institution,
rather than exclusively by individual military rulers. In addition,
the military appeared to adopt a technocratic, bureaucratic
approach to policy making (as opposed to a more "political" approach through which policies are shaped by economic and
political demands from different sectors of society, expressed
through such channels as elections, legislatures, political parties,
and labor unions). This approach to policy making in these regimes has led scholars to join the adjective "bureaucratic" with
the term "authoritarian" and to call these systems "bureaucratic-authoritarian."[5] This label has come to be an important
addition to typologies of national political regimes.[6]

The events of the 1970's in Latin America have greatly in-

---

of Democracy: Economic Development and Political Legitimacy," *American Political Science Review*, 53 (March 1959), pp. 69-105; James S. Coleman, "Conclusion:
The Political Systems of the Developing Areas," in Gabriel A. Almond and James
S. Coleman, eds., *The Politics of the Developing Areas* (Princeton: Princeton University Press, 1960); and Phillips Cutright, "National Political Development: Measurement and Analysis," *American Sociological Review*, 27 (April 1963), pp. 253-64.

[4] Three of the most important statements that reflect this reassessment and
that are accessible to the English-language reader are Fernando Henrique Car-
doso and Enzo Faletto, *Dependency and Development in Latin America* (Berkeley and
Los Angeles: University of California Press, 1978), which was originally pub-
lished in Spanish in 1969; Philippe C. Schmitter, *Interest Conflict and Political
Change in Brazil* (Stanford: Stanford University Press, 1971); and Guillermo
O'Donnell, *Modernization and Bureaucratic-Authoritarianism: Studies in South
American Politics* (Institute of International Studies, University of California,
Berkeley, Politics of Modernization Series No. 9, 1973).

[5] Important examples of the initial use of this term are found in O'Donnell,
Modernization and Bureaucratic-Authoritarianism and Fernando Henrique Cardoso,
"Associated Dependent Development: Theoretical and Practical Implications,"
in Alfred Stepan, ed., *Authoritarian Brazil: Origins, Policies, and Future* (New Haven: Yale University Press, 1973).

[6] A major recent study that discusses the concept of bureaucratic-authoritarianism within the framework of a broad typological analysis of political regimes
is Juan J. Linz, "Totalitarian and Authoritarian Regimes," in Fred Greenstein
and Nelson Polsby, eds., *Handbook of Political Science*, Volume 3 (Reading, Mass.:
Addison-Wesley, 1975).

creased the importance of understanding bureaucratic-authoritarianism. This type of military rule has persisted in Brazil, and it reappeared in Argentina in 1976. In 1973, well-institutionalized competitive regimes collapsed in two other economically advanced Latin American nations—Chile and Uruguay—and were also replaced by bureaucratic-authoritarian systems. In Argentina, Chile, and Uruguay both the level of violence employed in suppressing political parties, trade unions, and labor protest and the decline in the real income of the popular sector went far beyond that experienced in Brazil and Argentina in their initial bureaucratic-authoritarian periods in the 1960's. In Brazil the degree of repression had also become notably more intense, beginning roughly in 1969. These new developments dramatically called attention to the need to push further the rethinking of the relationship between industrial modernization and political change that had begun a decade earlier. The goal of this book is to contribute to the rethinking of this relationship.

Apart from the understandable importance to scholars particularly concerned with Latin America of the attempt to explain bureaucratic-authoritarianism, research on this topic is also important because of the contribution it has made to the critique of modernization theory. A number of the most important lines of argument advanced by scholars concerned with modernization theory—such as the hypothesized relationship between democracy and industrial modernization—have long been seriously questioned.[7] Yet, scholarly debate continues regarding how one can reasonably go about developing useful and appropriate hypotheses concerning the interaction among the political, eco-

---

[7] Important examples of the critique of modernization theory include Samuel P. Huntington, "Political Development and Political Decay," *World Politics*, XVII, No. 3 (April 1965), pp. 386-430; Reinhard Bendix, "Tradition and Modernity Reconsidered," *Comparative Studies in Society and History*, 9 (April 1967), pp. 292-346; Joseph R. Gusfield, "Tradition and Modernity: Misplaced Polarities in the Study of Social Change," *American Journal of Sociology*, 72 (January 1967), pp. 351-62; C. S. Whitaker, "A Dysrhythmic Process of Political Change," *World Politics*, 19 (January 1967), pp. 190-217; Lloyd I. Rudolph and Susan Hoeber Rudolph, *The Modernity of Tradition: Political Development in India* (Chicago: University of Chicago Press, 1967); Packenham, *Liberal America and the Third World*; and Dean C. Tipps, "Modernization Theory and the Comparative Study of Societies: A Critical Perspective," *Comparative Studies in Society and History*, 15 (March 1973), pp. 199-226.

nomic, and social spheres that occurs in the course of industrial modernization. There is also a debate over the specific hypotheses that adequately characterize this interaction.

Research on Latin America has contributed to both parts of this debate. With regard to the first issue, it has criticized the presumed universality of earlier assumptions about political change and has pointed to the need to develop distinctive hypotheses for the analysis of different historical and cultural contexts.[8] Such critiques do not reflect an antitheoretical bias, but rather a concern with specifying the characteristics of the particular context one is analyzing in terms of theoretically relevant variables.[9] For researchers concerned with contemporary Latin America, one of the most salient characteristics is the relatively late industrialization of this region as compared with most of the North Atlantic countries. This, it is argued, has led to a series of distinctive economic, social, and political problems.[10] A related characteristic is the economic dependence of the Latin American region, involving a heavy reliance on foreign capital, technology, and managerial expertise in order to promote industrialization. A third characteristic is that this external dependence has largely involved dependence on nations and firms operating in the international capitalist economic system.[11]

[8] These issues are addressed in O'Donnell, *Modernization and Bureaucratic-Authoritarianism*, Chapter 1; Philippe C. Schmitter, "Paths to Political Development in Latin America," in Douglas A. Chalmers, ed., *Changing Latin America: New Interpretations of Its Politics and Society* (New York: Academy of Political Science, Columbia University, 1972); and Glaucio Dillon Soares, "The New Industrialization and the Brazilian Political System," in James Petras and Maurice Zeitlin, eds., *Latin America: Reform or Revolution?* (Greenwich, Conn.: Fawcett World Library, 1968).

[9] This approach corresponds to that recommended in Adam Przeworski and Henry Teune, *The Logic of Comparative Social Inquiry* (New York: John Wiley and Company, 1970).

[10] See Albert O. Hirschman, "The Political Economy of Import-substituting Industrialization in Latin America," *Quarterly Journal of Economics* 82, 1 (February 1968), pp. 2-32.

[11] A major initial statement that emphasizes the aspects of dependency analysis that are relevant here is Cardoso and Faletto, *Dependency and Development*. For a recent warning by Cardoso regarding the misuse of dependency analysis, see his "The Consumption of Dependency Theory in the United States," *Latin American Research Review* 12,3 (1977), pp. 7-24. Another valuable recent discussion of this perspective is Richard R. Fagen, "Studying Latin American Politics: Some Implications of a Dependencia Approach," *Latin American Research Review*, 12,2 (1977), pp. 3-27.

Research on Latin America has also made a theoretical contribution by developing new hypotheses about political change within this particular setting. These suggest why the interactions among the patterns of economic, social, and political change that have occurred in this context of late, dependent, capitalist development have not consistently led to democracy, but rather appear, at least in some cases, to be linked to the emergence of bureaucratic-authoritarianism. These hypotheses, which for the sake of convenience may be referred to as the bureaucratic-authoritarian "model," are a central concern of this book. They are reviewed in detail in Chapter 1.

These hypotheses about the emergence of bureaucratic-authoritarianism attracted wide scholarly attention.[12] This occurred not only because they seemed to provide a suggestive explanation for an important set of contemporary political events but also because they represented a "respecification" of the models of political change offered earlier by modernization theorists. In the context of the 1970's, when the central thrust of political research on the Third World had shifted from a concern with analyzing democratization and "Westernization" to a concern with the difficult issues of a national political economy faced by these societies, this respecified model was a welcome addition to the literature.

Though these hypotheses made an important contribution toward understanding bureaucratic-authoritarianism, there has been a growing sense of dissatisfaction with a number of elements in this bureaucratic-authoritarian model. The model unquestionably addresses important issues and adopts a valuable approach to explaining political change in the context of late, dependent, capitalist development. Yet even in the first phase of the evolution of this literature, in which analyses were focused on Brazil and Argentina, scholars began to raise questions regarding the degree to which bureaucratic-authoritarianism, which was clearly a new phenomenon in relation to the political patterns of the 1950's and early 1960's, in fact represented a "restoration" of a type of authoritarianism that had existed in the 1930's and 1940's. They also questioned the economic arguments employed in explaining its emergence.[13]

[12] See note 6 in Chapter 1 of this volume.

[13] Thomas E. Skidmore, "Politics and Economic Policy-Making in Authoritarian Brazil, 1937-71"; Philippe C. Schmitter, "The 'Portugalization' of Brazil?";

Beginning in the mid-1970's—in the context of the attempt to understand bureaucratic-authoritarianism in Chile and Uruguay, as well as in Brazil and Argentina—scholarly dissatisfaction with this model became even more widespread.[14] The political-economic model pursued by these authoritarian governments increasingly appeared to be considerably less consistent and coherent than was initially thought. These four countries were not at comparable levels of industrialization, and the initial hypotheses noted above regarding the role of problems of industrialization in the emergence of bureaucratic-authoritarianism therefore came under increasingly critical scrutiny. It was also not clear that increased inequality was in fact an economic prerequisite for the success of the development policies adopted by these governments. There was an increasing sense of a need to place greater emphasis on political explanations of these economic policies and of the rise of authoritarianism. For instance, it appeared that the structure of the party system and the political strength of the popular sector were important determinants of the degree to which polarized class conflict emerged in each country. In certain countries, the ideological polarization that occurred prior to the appearance of bureaucratic-authoritarianism could not be explained simply as a consequence of the interplay of economic forces.

Finally, bureaucratic-authoritarianism has not, at least to date, appeared in all of the industrially more advanced countries of Latin America.[15] In Mexico, one finds a milder form of authori-

---

Albert Fishlow, "Some Reflections on Post-1964 Brazilian Economic Policy"; and Samuel A. Morely and Gordon W. Smith, "The Effect of Changes in the Distribution of Income on Labor, Foreign Investment, and Growth in Brazil," all in Stepan, ed., *Authoritarian Brazil*. See also Mario S. Brodersohn, "Sobre 'Modernización y Autoritarismo' y el estancamiento inflacionario argentino," *Desarrollo Económico*, 13, 51 (October to December 1973), pp. 591-605.

[14] This and the following paragraph summarize the issues raised in the initial discussions among members of the working group which is described below.

[15] In terms of the overall level of industrial production, a variable stressed by authors such as O'Donnell, Latin American countries could be placed in three broad groups, with Argentina, Brazil, and Mexico at the highest level; the other five of the eight countries discussed below at an intermediate level; and the remaining countries at a considerably lower level. For a discussion of classifications of socioeconomic modernization in South America, see O'Donnell, *Modernization and Bureaucratic-Authoritarianism*, Chapter 1. Supplementary data on these groupings of countries was derived from the two sources cited in note 1, above.

tarianism involving the rule of a political party, rather than military rule. Competitive regimes persist in Colombia and Venezuela. The military rule experienced in Peru since 1968—both in its initial reformist phase and in its current more conservative phase—is likewise distinct from the military rule of the south. For the scholar concerned with the hypothesis that there is an inherent association between advanced industrialization and bureaucratic-authoritarianism in Latin America, the challenge was thus to extend the analysis beyond the countries where this form of authoritarianism has appeared—i.e., Argentina, Brazil, Chile, and Uruguay. It was essential to achieve a broader understanding that also encompassed these other relatively advanced countries in which, at least so far, it has not appeared. This larger comparison could yield new insights both into the experience of other countries and into the four cases of bureaucratic-authoritarianism.[16] Although certain elements of this larger comparison had begun to appear in studies of Latin American authoritarianism,[17] this comparison had not yet been employed in a systematic reassessment of explanations of bureaucratic-authoritarianism.

In 1975 the Joint Committee on Latin American Studies of the American Council of Learned Societies and the Social Science Research Council established a working group in order to consolidate and build upon these dissatisfactions and criticisms.[18] The goal of the working group, which has been coordi-

[16] The use of this broader comparison to refine arguments about the emergence of bureaucratic-authoritarianism reflects the use of the "constant comparative method" advocated in Barney Glaser and Anselm Strauss in *The Discovery of Grounded Theory: Strategies for Qualitative Research* (Chicago: Aldine Publishing Company, 1967).

[17] See Thomas Skidmore, "The Politics of Economic Stabilization in Post-War Latin America," in James M. Malloy, ed., *Authoritarianism and Corporatism in Latin America* (Pittsburgh: University of Pittsburgh Press, 1977); Kaufman, "Mexico and Latin American Authoritarianism"; and "Corporatism, Clientelism, and Partisan Conflict: A Study of Seven Countries," in Malloy, ed., *Authoritarianism*; David Collier, *Squatters and Oligarchs: Authoritarian Rule and Policy Change in Peru* (Baltimore: The Johns Hopkins University Press, 1976); David Collier and Ruth B. Collier, "Who Does What, to Whom, and How: Toward a Comparative Analysis of Latin American Corporatism," in Malloy, ed., *Authoritarianism*; Alfred Stepan, *The State and Society: Peru in Comparative Perspective* (Princeton: Princeton University Press, 1978), Chapters 3 and 4; and Juan J. Linz and Alfred Stepan, eds., *The Breakdown of Democratic Regimes* (Baltimore: The Johns Hopkins University Press, 1978).

[18] An initial report on the activities of this group is found in David Collier,

nated by David Collier and Julio Cotler, is to broaden the debate on the nature and causes of bureaucratic-authoritarianism by bringing together the often contrasting perspectives of scholars from both the Southern and Northern Hemispheres, as well as from different academic disciplines. The working group included political scientists, sociologists, and economists from Peru, Argentina, Brazil, and the United States, all of whom had previously contributed to this area of research and all of whom felt that these dissatisfactions and criticisms could form a useful starting point for building a more complete understanding of Latin American authoritarianism. Members of the group met informally a number of times in 1975 and 1976 and held a formal, two-day meeting in early 1977, at which preliminary papers were presented. On the basis of a wide-ranging exchange of comments and criticisms—both at this meeting and in extensive subsequent correspondence among a number of the authors—these papers have all been substantially revised. The essays published in this volume are a product of this collaborative effort.

Part I of this volume provides an overview of the issues of social science analysis raised by the recent emergence of authoritarianism in these industrially advanced countries of Latin America. The chapter by David Collier reviews the basic arguments contained in the bureaucratic-authoritarian model and poses some initial critical questions about these arguments. Because other chapters focus particularly on the form these arguments took as they crystallized in the work of Guillermo O'Donnell, his formulation receives central attention in Collier's chapter.[19]

The chapter by Fernando Henrique Cardoso then opens the discussion of bureaucratic-authoritarianism by proposing a major conceptual clarification. He opposes the use of this term as a global characterization of the political system, a usage followed in the initial formulation of the bureaucratic-authoritarian model. He stresses the need to distinguish between the

---

"Industrialization and Authoritarianism in Latin America," *Social Science Research Council Items*, Vol. 31/32, No. 4/1 (March 1978), pp. 5-13.

[19] As a further introduction to the subject matter of this book, readers not familiar with contemporary politics in Brazil, Argentina, Chile, and Uruguay may find it helpful to consult the brief sketches of the recent political history of these four countries presented as part of Robert Kaufman's extended analysis of explanations of authoritarianism in Part II of this volume (see pp. 170 ff.).

core characteristics of bureaucratic-authoritarian *regimes* and the type of *state* with which they are associated—in the neo-Marxist sense of the state as the larger system of economic and political "domination," which in the Latin American context he characterizes as "dependent" and "capitalist." He argues that the relationship between regime and state is more complex and variegated than is implied by the bureaucratic-authoritarian model. One cannot adequately analyze the differences, and similarities, among such important cases as contemporary Brazil, Mexico, and Venezuela—all of which he considers dependent capitalist states—unless one distinguishes carefully between regime and state. Cardoso also analyzes the political institutions of bureaucratic-authoritarianism, drawing attention to the variegated features and internal contradictions of these systems. In order to place the experience of the countries of the Southern Cone of South America in clearer perspective, he points to a series of contrasts, as well as similarities, with the non-military authoritarianism of Mexico, the recent reformist military government in Peru, and the democratic regime in Venezuela.

Part II addresses the problem of explaining the rise of bureaucratic-authoritarianism. In the first chapter in this section, Albert O. Hirschman—an economist—reminds researchers not to stress economic explanations of political phenomena to the point of neglecting political explanations. Placing his discussion within the larger tradition of social thought regarding the political consequences of industrialization, he critically surveys various economic explanations of the rise of authoritarianism and finds them all inadequate. Hirschman argues that different phases of industrialization have important consequences for politics, in part because of the expectations they create in the minds of policy makers regarding the likelihood of sustained economic growth. It appears that the relative ease with which the initial expansion of consumer goods production occurred in Latin America generated unrealistic expectations about opportunities for growth, and hence for economic reform, which in turn played a role in the sequence of events that led to bureaucratic-authoritarianism. Hirschman then broadens his analysis of the role of ideas in shaping political change and proposes a new approach to explaining the rise of authoritarianism. He analyzes the way in which political ideas and political action interact in the evolution of the "entrepreneurial" and "reform"

functions in society. This perspective, which focuses on differences in what may be called the "political culture of capitalism,"[20] is used to provide a partial explanation of the contrast
between the recent pluralist experience of Colombia and Venezuela and the authoritarian experience of Argentina, Brazil,
Chile, and Uruguay.

The chapter by José Serra critically analyzes three hypotheses
regarding the relationship between economic development and
the emergence of bureaucratic-authoritarianism. These hypotheses focus on the "superexploitation" of the working class, the
attempt to achieve a "deepening" of industrial production, and
the idea that this form of authoritarianism promotes a certain
type of economic "rationality" that contributes to economic
growth. Devoting most of his attention to Brazil, but also drawing on the Chilean and Mexican cases, Serra finds that available
evidence does not support these hypotheses. His close analysis of
Brazil is of particular importance to this volume because the
special conjunction in Brazil of economic and political crisis, followed by harsh authoritarianism, regressive economic policies,
and successful economic growth has made Brazil in a sense the
"paradigmatic case" for the bureaucratic-authoritarian model.
Other countries, by contrast, are only partial approximations. In
Argentina, the coherence of authoritarian rule has been limited;
in Chile and Uruguay, the idea of the deepening of industrialization may be irrelevant because of the small scale of their
economies; and Mexico involves a rather different pattern,
based on non-military authoritarianism which did not result
from the "triggering" political crisis experienced in the other
cases and which is based on quite a different political coalition.
Hence, by disconfirming these hypotheses for the case that presumably fits the bureaucratic-authoritarian model most closely,
Serra makes a particularly useful contribution to the larger debate on explanations of the rise of authoritarianism.

The chapter by Robert Kaufman provides a detailed review of
the fit between the bureaucratic-authoritarian model and the
recent experiences of Brazil, Argentina, Chile, Uruguay, and
Mexico. After presenting an extended critique of the "deepening" hypothesis that is parallel to that of Hirschman and Serra,

---

[20] This term was proposed by Walter Dean Burnham in correspondence with
Albert O. Hirschman regarding Hirschman's chapter.

Kaufman broadens the model to include an analysis of the implications—for the evolution of political coalitions and political regimes—of five different development strategies that might be adopted in order to promote economic growth in these societies. These include, in addition to the deepening of industrialization, the alternative strategies of promoting consumer durables, industrial exports, and primary product exports, and the expansion of the domestic market for consumer goods. Within this modified framework, Kaufman finds that the transitions among different phases of industrialization have narrowed the range of policy alternatives open to Latin American societies in a way that contributed to the emergence of bureaucratic-authoritarianism. He thus finds an important fit between the underlying argument contained in the bureaucratic-authoritarian model and the experience of these five countries.

The final chapter in Part II, by Julio Cotler, focuses on the need to explore more systematically the ways in which the developmental experience of Argentina, Brazil, Chile, and Uruguay differs from that of many other countries in Latin America. Cotler builds on the distinction between these "Southern Cone" countries, in which export-led growth earlier in this century was in important measure nationally controlled, and the "enclave" societies in which export-led growth occurred primarily in isolated enclaves of economic activity which were directly controlled by foreign corporations. Concentrating his attention on the contrast between these Southern Cone countries and Mexico and Peru, he argues that throughout most of this century these enclave cases have followed a very different pattern of political change. However, within the present decade he notes an important shift in this pattern, and he speculates about the possibility that these alternative patterns may now converge.

The final section of the volume probes the likely direction of future change in bureaucratic-authoritarianism, as well as appropriate directions for further research. The opening chapter by Guillermo O'Donnell takes an important step toward developing a *political* theory of the dynamics of authoritarian rule by exploring the generic political predicaments inherent in bureaucratic-authoritarianism. He argues that political society is conventionally held together by two underlying forces—domination and consensus—and that bureaucratic-authoritarianism involves an emphasis on domination to the virtual exclusion of

In order to promote the consensus Weber?

consensus. This is due in part to the heavy emphasis placed by these governments on maintaining economic and political conditions that are attractive to foreign investors and to international lending agencies. This encourages the neglect of traditional symbols often used to generate internal consensus such as economic nationalism and patriotism—both particularly relevant to the popular sector. In addition, the attempt to destroy the political parties and labor organizations that previously served to mediate the relationship between the state and society undermines the structures of representation that are another fundamental channel through which consensus is conventionally achieved. O'Donnell notes that this rejection of consensus in favor of domination leads to severe tensions and contradictions, and he suggests that these tensions may ultimately be resolved only through the creation of a new political formula that permits some form of democratization.

The chapter by James Kurth broadens the discussion by exploring the relationship between the problems of industrialization emphasized in the bureaucratic-authoritarian model and the concerns of research on industrialization and political change in Europe. Kurth first places the argument about Latin American industrialization within the larger framework of research on the timing of industrialization that has grown out of the work of Alexander Gerschenkron.[21] This literature argues that the patterns of economic, social, and political change that accompany industrialization are not the same in all countries, but differ in important—and to some degree predictable—ways according to the degree to which industrialization occurs "early" or "late" in relation to the first historical cases of industrialization in Western Europe. Kurth then analyzes the politics of industrialization in a number of European countries, using an approach that combines these arguments about the timing of industrialization with the approach of the bureaucratic-authoritarian model that emphasizes different sectors of industry (e.g., consumer goods versus intermediate and capital goods). He shows that by analyzing simultaneously differences between "early," "late," and "late-late" industrializers (involving Western,

[21] Alexander Gerschenkron, *Economic Backwardness in Historical Perspective* (Cambridge, Mass.: Harvard University Press, 1962); and "The Typology of Industrial Development as a Tool of Analysis," in Gerschenkron, ed., *Continuity in History and Other Essays* (Cambridge, Mass.: Harvard University Press, 1968).

Eastern, and Southern Europe, respectively) and differences among distinct sectors of industry, one can discover striking regularities in the politics of European industrialization. Kurth concludes his chapter by showing how the patterns that emerged in his analysis of Europe can suggest new insights into some of the Latin American countries considered in other chapters in this volume. Kurth's analysis thus illustrates some of the improvements in theory that can derive from applying arguments about Latin American authoritarianism to other regions. Yet he makes it clear that one cannot rely on a mechanical extension of these arguments. Rather, it is essential to specify with great care a series of theoretically relevant characteristics in each context one analyzes in order to apply the theory to that context in an appropriate way.

The final chapter by David Collier synthesizes the issues raised in the volume and points to priorities for future research. Collier stresses five issues. First, terms such as bureaucratic-authoritarianism are used in somewhat different ways by different authors, leading to an inconsistent classification of cases. How can one deal with this problem of description? Second, there is considerable disagreement among the authors regarding the relative importance of economic, political, ideological, and other factors in contributing to the rise of authoritarianism. How can one begin to sort out these alternative explanations? Third, several authors attempted to extend the bureaucratic-authoritarian argument to additional Latin American nations as a starting point for modifying the argument so as to account for the non-appearance of bureaucratic-authoritarianism in some countries, and also to provide a better explanation of the cases where it has appeared. As a first step toward consolidating the insights derived from this extension of the argument, Collier presents a preliminary, unified version of the argument in order to illustrate how one might begin to integrate economic and political explanations in an analysis that includes eight Latin American countries. Fourth, he reviews the explanations that have been advanced to account for different patterns of change once authoritarian rule has been established and explores the possibility that these explanations might ultimately be incorporated into an integrated model that could help to understand long-term patterns of national political change in Latin America. Finally, he suggests that extending the argument to other world regions can yield similar intellectual gains, pointing particularly to ways in which Kurth's chapter serves as an example of how such an extension might be carried out.

Collier also stresses a major theme that underlies the entire volume. Apart from contributing to social science theory, efforts to understand bureaucratic-authoritarianism have practical implications. The contributors to the volume share the belief that the importance of analyzing bureaucratic-authoritarianism derives in part from the possibility that a more complete understanding of the economic, social, and political problems that gave rise to this authoritarianism can contribute to the discovery of better solutions to these same problems. It may thus contribute to the effort to bring to an end the current era of harsh authoritarianism in Latin America.

David Collier

PART ONE

The New Authoritarianism in Latin America

CHAPTER 1

OVERVIEW OF THE BUREAUCRATIC-AUTHORITARIAN MODEL

*David Collier**

The prevalence of authoritarian and military governments in the economically more advanced countries of contemporary Latin America poses a major analytic challenge to the student of Latin American politics, as well as to scholars more broadly concerned with understanding political change. The earlier hypotheses of the development literature that suggested a positive association between socio-economic modernization and democracy can hardly serve as a guide to understanding this new authoritarianism.[1] How, then, is one to explain it?

A substantial body of literature has sought to address this question. One of the principal lines of analysis that has emerged focuses on the social, economic, and political tensions generated in recent decades by the particular type of dependent, capitalist modernization being experienced in Latin America. These tensions are seen as contributing to a fundamental reorientation of national politics. More concretely, they are seen as having led to the collapse of the earlier pattern of "populist" politics in which the "popular sector" (i.e., the working class and lower middle class) was an important participant in the dominant national political coalition in several countries and an important beneficiary of public policy. There has emerged instead a period of "post-populist" politics characterized by the appearance of re-

* The helpful suggestions of Ruth Berins Collier, Guillermo O'Donnell, Albert O. Hirschman, Benjamin Most, Louis Goodman, Abraham Lowenthal, Philippe Schmitter, Alfred Stepan, Robert Kaufman, Alfred Diamant, Jean Robinson, Lila Milutin, Robert Packenham, Peter Evans, Peter Cleaves, and Richard Stryker aided in revising both this chapter and Chapter 9 in this volume. Portions of this chapter and an early version of portions of Chapter 9 previously appeared in *World Politics* (1978). These chapters are part of a larger study of political change in Latin America which has been supported by National Science Foundation Grant No. SOC75-19990, the Social Science Research Council, and the Tinker Foundation.

[1] See notes 3 and 7 in the Introduction for citations of this literature and of critiques of these hypotheses.

1- Modernization
Lead to Democratization
2. Late Modernization leads to
Bureaucratic Authoritarian
Regime
inequalities &

pressive authoritarian governments that seek to resolve these earlier tensions by eliminating the popular sector as an important participant in the national political arena and by enforcing a regressive movement of income away from this sector.[2] More advanced levels of industrialization are thus seen as linked to a turn away from democratic, competitive politics and to an increase in inequality—quite the opposite from the pattern hypothesized in much of the earlier literature.

One of the most important formulations of this "populist/ post-populist" argument is found in the work of the Argentine political scientist Guillermo O'Donnell.[3] Explicitly building on

[2] A small sampling of the literature in which various forms of this argument have appeared might include Fernando Henrique Cardoso and Enzo Faletto, *Dependencia y desarrollo en América Latina* (Mexico City: Siglo Veintiuno Editores, S.A., 1969); Fernando Henrique Cardoso, *Ideologías de la burguesía industrial en sociedades dependientes* (Argentina y Brazil) (Mexico City: Siglo Veintiuno Editores, S.A., 1971); and "Associated Dependent Development: Theoretical and Practical Implications," in Alfred Stepan, ed., *Authoritarian Brazil: Origins, Policies, and Future* (New Haven: Yale University Press, 1973); Octavio Ianni, *Crisis in Brazil* (New York: Columbia University Press, 1970); and *A formação do estado populista na America Latina* (Rio de Janeiro: Editora Civilização Brasileira, 1975); Alfred Stepan, *The Military in Politics: Changing Patterns in Brazil* (Princeton: Princeton University Press, 1971); and *The State and Society: Peru in Comparative Perspective* (Princeton: Princeton University Press, 1978), Chapter 3; Helio Jaguaribe, *Economic and Political Development: A Theoretical Approach and a Brazilian Case Study* (Cambridge, Mass.: Harvard University Press, 1968); and *Political Development: A General Theory and a Latin American Case Study* (New York: Harper and Row, 1973); Thomas Skidmore, *Politics in Brazil, 1930-1964: An Experiment in Democracy* (New York: Oxford University Press, 1967); and José Luis de Imaz, *Los Que Mandan* (Albany: State University of New York Press, 1964).

[3] See *Modernization and Bureaucratic-Authoritarianism: Studies in South American Politics* (Institute of International Studies, University of California, Berkeley, Politics of Modernization Series No. 9, 1973); also published in Spanish as *Modernización y Autoritarismo* (Buenos Aires: Ediciones Paidos, 1972); "Reflexiones sobre las tendencias generales de cambio en el Estado burocrático-autoritario (initially presented to the "Conference on History and Social Science," Universidad de Campinas, Brazil, 1975, and published as Documento CEDES/G.E. CLACSO/No. 1, Centro de Estudios de Estado y Sociedad, Buenos Aires, 1975 and as Procesos Políticos Latinoamericanos, No. 3, Universidad Católica del Perú, Lima, 1975. A revised version has been published in English as "Reflections on the Patterns of Change in the Bureaucratic-Authoritarian State," *Latin American Research Review*, XIII, No. 1 [1978], pp. 3-38); "Estado y alianzas en la Argentina, 1956-1976," *Desarrollo Económico*, XVI (January-March 1977), pp. 523-54; and "Corporatism and the Question of the State," in James M. Malloy, ed., *Authoritarianism and Corporatism in Latin America* (Pittsburgh: University of Pittsburgh Press, 1977), pp. 47-88. See also his "Modernización y golpes mili-

the research of Fernando Henrique Cardoso and Enzo Faletto, Octavio Ianni, Luciano Martins, Philippe Schmitter, Albert Hirschman, Alfred Stepan, Thomas Skidmore, Helio Jaguaribe, Juan de Imaz, Marcos Kaplan, Celso Furtado, Candido Mendes, Torcuato di Tella, and others,[4] O'Donnell attempted to bring into sharper focus the network of arguments developed by these authors concerning the consequences of dependent capitalist industrialization and of associated changes in social structure for national political change. He deliberately sought to stress the impact of economic and social factors on politics as a means of clarifying certain basic conceptual and empirical issues that arise in the study of Latin American societies. His goal was to provide a better "conceptual map" of social reality which could serve as a starting point for future research that would also consider the impact of political factors on economic and social change and the interactions among all of these dimensions.[5]

O'Donnell's formulation of the populist/post-populist argument has received considerable attention in the work of other scholars, stimulating numerous efforts to elaborate, refine, and criticize his argument.[6] It has become an important point of ref-

---

tares: Teoría, comparación, y el caso Argentino," *Desarrollo Económico*, XIII (October to December, 1972), pp. 519-66 (published in English in Abraham F. Lowenthal, ed., *Armies and Politics in Latin America* [New York: Holmes & Meier Publishers, Inc., 1976]).

[4] See the references in *Modernization*, Chapter 2, especially note 2.

[5] *Modernization*, p. 113. The innovations in O'Donnell's work in relation to this broader literature include: his presentation of a highly detailed and elaborately conceptualized political analysis; his attempt to organize the argument into systematic propositions; his attempt to move toward greater theoretical parsimony by devoting close attention to a small number of critical variables; and his elaborate critique of existing modernization theory and detailed discussion of how the types of comparative analysis commonly employed in tests of modernization theory must be modified if they are to deal meaningfully with the new theoretical perspectives emerging out of research on Latin America.

[6] For examples of research that address issues raised by O'Donnell, see Mario S. Brodersohn, "Sobre 'Modernización y Autoritarismo' y el estancamiento inflacionario argentino." *Desarrollo Económico* 13, No. 51 (October-December 1973), pp. 591-605; Juan J. Linz, "Totalitarian and Authoritarian Regimes," in Fred Greenstein and Nelson Polsby, eds., *Handbook of Political Science*, Vol. 3, *Macro Political Theory* (Reading, Mass.: Addison-Wesley Press, 1975); Robert R. Kaufman, "Notes on the Definition, Genesis, and Consolidation of Bureaucratic-Authoritarian Regimes" (unpublished manuscript, Department of Political Science, Douglass College, 1975) and "Mexico and Latin American Authoritarianism," in José Luis Reyna and Richard S. Weinert, eds., *Authoritarianism in*

· erence in analyses of the political economy of Latin American authoritarianism and has explicitly served as a starting point or "base line" for most of the chapters in this book.

Because of the importance of O'Donnell's analysis to the rest of this book and because his analysis is scattered over various articles and books that have appeared over a period of several years, it seemed appropriate to present here a brief synthesis of his argument.[7] As is evident in the following chapters, O'Donnell's analysis in no sense represents an accepted interpretation of Latin American politics. It is summarized here in the same spirit in which he originally presented it—as a conceptual framework and a set of hypotheses intended to stimulate scholarly debate.

Mexico (Philadelphia: Institute for the Study of Human Issues, 1977), pp. 193-232; Susan Kaufman Purcell, *The Mexican Profit-Sharing Decision: Politics in an Authoritarian Regime* (Berkeley and Los Angeles: University of California Press, 1975), Chapter 1; William C. Smith, "The Armed Forces and the Authoritarian-Bureaucratic State in Argentina" (paper presented at the Inter-University Seminar on the Armed Forces and Society, Tempe, Arizona, 1976); Kenneth P. Erickson and Patrick V. Peppe, "Dependent Capitalist Development, U.S. Foreign Policy, and Repression of the Working Class in Chile and Brazil," *Latin American Perspectives*, III, No. 1 (Winter 1976), pp. 19-44; David Collier, "Timing of Economic Growth and Regime Characteristics in Latin America," *Comparative Politics*, VII, No. 3 (April 1975), pp. 331-59; and *Squatters and Oligarchs: Authoritarian Rule and Policy Change in Peru* (Baltimore: The Johns Hopkins University Press, 1976); James M. Malloy, "Authoritarianism and Corporatism in Latin America: The Modal Pattern," in James M. Malloy, ed., *Authoritarianism and Corporatism in Latin America* (Pittsburgh: University of Pittsburgh Press, 1977), pp. 3-19; David Collier and Ruth B. Collier, "Who Does What, to Whom, and How: Toward a Comparative Analysis of Latin American Corporatism," in Malloy, ed., *Authoritarianism*, pp. 489-512; Silvio Duncan Baretta and Helen E. Douglass, "Authoritarianism and Corporatism in Latin America: A Review Essay," in Malloy, ed., *Authoritarianism*, pp. 513-24; and Alfred Stepan, *The State and Society: Peru in Comparative Perspective* (Princeton: Princeton University Press, 1978), Chapter 3. At least four doctoral dissertations are currently in progress at Stanford University, Yale University, and Indiana University that focus on central elements of O'Donnell's argument. An example of the application of this perspective to East Asian politics can be found in Sungjoo Han, "Power, Dependency, and Representation in South Korea" (paper presented at the 1977 Annual Meeting of the American Political Science Association, Washington, D.C.).

[7] It should be emphasized that O'Donnell himself has introduced many refinements in the argument. To the extent possible, these refinements are incorporated in the synthesis presented here, thereby avoiding a pointless debate over issues that have already been resolved. His numerous suggestions for improving this summary of his analysis are gratefully acknowledged.

Three dimensional
political structure (regime)
who governs (coalition)
who benefits (public policies)

TYPES OF POLITICAL SYSTEMS

O'Donnell's approach to describing different types of political
systems is similar in many ways to that employed in the more
general populist/post-populist literature. He in effect focuses on

excluding or
incorporating

three distinct dimensions, involving: the structure of the national political *regime* (including freedom of electoral competition, freedom of interest associations, and level of repression);
the class and sectoral composition of the dominant political *coalition*; and certain crucial public *policies* (particularly as they relate
to the distribution of resources among different class groups and
sectors of the economy). He thus combines a concern for political structure with a concern for who governs and who benefits.
A central distinction derived from these three dimensions is
whether the system is "incorporating" or "excluding," in the
sense that it "purposely seeks to activate the popular sector and
to allow it some voice in national politics" or deliberately
excludes a previously activated popular sector from the national
political arena.[8]

O'Donnell identifies certain recurring "constellations"[9] in
which different patterns of regime, coalition, and policy have
appeared in Latin America.[10] On the basis of these constellations, he describes three types of political systems that he sees as
representing an historical sequence.[11]

1. Oligarchic.[12] The scope of political competition is limited. The
elite of the primary-product export sector (based on minerals

---

[8] *Modernization*, pp. 53 and 55.   [9] *Ibid*., p. 68.

[10] Although in *Modernization* O'Donnell explicitly restricts the analysis to South
American countries (pp. viii to ix), in "Reflexiones" he adds Mexico to the
analysis (pp. 44-53), thereby implicitly including Latin America more broadly in
his framework. Following the emphasis of this more recent study, the present
discussion treats his framework as applying to Latin America rather than South
America.

[11] *Modernization*, Chapter 2. In suggesting that these different constellations of
regime, coalition, and policy represent different types of "political systems," I am
following O'Donnell's usage in *Modernization*. In more recent writing he has spo-
ken of these constellations as involving different types of "states" (see Chapter 7
and the Glossary). Because this usage may be unfamiliar to many readers in the
United States, it seemed simpler in the present introductory chapter to retain the
earlier usage.

[12] In *Modernization* O'Donnell refers to these as "traditional" systems (pp. 112
and 114). However, this usage could lead to the incorrect conclusion that his
analysis is oriented around the widely criticized tradition-modernity distinction.
I have substituted the expression "oligarchic" system, which corresponds to the

and agricultural products) dominates the state and orients public policy around its needs. Such systems are neither incorporating nor excluding, because the popular sector has not yet become politically activated.[13]

2. *Populist.* While there is considerable variation in the degree to
which these systems are competitive and democratic, they are
clearly "incorporating." They are based on a multi-class coalition
of urban-industrial interests, including industrial elites and the
urban popular sector. Economic nationalism is a common feature of such systems. The state promotes the initial phase of industrialization oriented around consumer goods. It does so both
directly, through support for domestic industry, and indirectly,
through encouraging the expansion of the domestic market for
consumer goods by increasing the income of the popular sector.[14] O'Donnell gives particular attention to two widely discussed examples of populism—the governments of Vargas in
Brazil (1930 to 1945 and 1950 to 1954) and of Peron in Argentina (1946 to 1955).

3. *Bureaucratic-Authoritarian.* These systems are "excluding" and
emphatically non-democratic. Central actors in the dominant
coalition include high-level technocrats—military and civilian,
within and outside the state—working in close association with
foreign capital. This new elite eliminates electoral competition
and severely controls the political participation of the popular
sector. Public policy is centrally concerned with promoting
advanced industrialization. The cases of bureaucratic-
authoritarianism considered by O'Donnell are the post-1964 period in Brazil, the period from 1966 to 1970 and the post-1976
period in Argentina, the post-1973 period in Chile and
Uruguay, and contemporary Mexico.[15] Important examples
from other regions include the later Franco period in Spain and
the authoritarian systems that emerged in several Eastern European countries between the two world wars.[16] O'Donnell emphasizes that bureaucratic-authoritarianism should not be con-
fused with German and Italian Fascism, which he sees as a

---

standard usage of Latin American scholars who refer to this as the period of the
"oligarchic" state, as well as to O'Donnell's usage in "Corporatism," where he refers to it as the period of "oligarchic domination" (p. 66).

[13] *Modernization*, pp. 112 and 114.   [14] *Ibid.*, p. 57.

[15] *Ibid.*, Chapters 2 and 3; "Reflexiones," p. 6; and "Estado y alianzas," p. 1.

[16] *Modernization*, pp. 92-93 and "Reflexiones," p. 51.

different political configuration that emerges in a different economic and social context.[17]

ECONOMIC AND SOCIAL CHANGE

O'Donnell attempts to explain the transitions from one system to another, particularly to bureaucratic-authoritarianism, and to explore the dynamics of bureaucratic-authoritarianism. He argues that these political transformations derive from the social and political tensions produced by industrialization and by changes in social structure at both the elite and mass level. He sees these socio-economic changes as linked to the growth of the *absolute* size of the modern sector, rather than the size of the national economy in *per capita* terms, which was emphasized in many earlier comparative studies.[18] The focus on absolute size locates large countries with lower levels of income, such as Brazil and Mexico, among the highly modernized countries of Latin America and provides a new perspective for explaining their political evolution.

O'Donnell devotes particular attention to the dialectical interplay among three crucial aspects of socio-economic modernization. These are: (1) industrialization, particularly the initial transition to the production of consumer goods and the subsequent "deepening" of industrialization to include production of intermediate and capital goods;[19] (2) increased political activation of the popular sector;[20] (3) growth of "technocratic occupational" roles in public and private bureaucracies.[21]

1. Industrialization. O'Donnell suggests that different phases of industrialization are linked to political change in part because they alter the economic payoffs to different class groups. The transition to the initial phase of industrialization involving the production of consumer goods is associated with the transition from an oligarchic system to populism. Domestically owned enterprises, often enjoying substantial tariff protection and other forms of state subsidy, begin to produce for an existing local market previously supplied by imported goods. Because indus-

[17] "Reflexiones," p. 50.
[18] *Modernization*, pp. 16 ff. Three well-known studies within the earlier "requisites of democracy" tradition that used per capita indicators are cited in note 1.
[19] *Modernization*, pp. 37 ff. and Chapter 2.
[20] *Ibid.*, pp. 74 ff.   [21] *Ibid.*, pp. 79 ff.

trial production may initially expand rapidly as it seeks to satisfy this newly protected market, this phase of industrialization is often referred to as the "easy" phase of "import-substitution." Tariff protection and state subsidy reduce the pressure for production to be internationally competitive, and the leeway enjoyed by economic and political elites regarding wage policy and other worker benefits may therefore be moderately large. This leeway, combined with the interest of industrialists in expanding working class income in order to enlarge the domestic market for consumer goods, may create an opportunity for an "incorporating" populist coalition. Workers receive important material benefits and support for labor unions as organizations in exchange for their political support, thus strengthening the position of industrialists in relation to the previously dominant export elite. From his initial examination of the emergence of populism in Argentina and Brazil, O'Donnell generalizes his findings by noting a broader tendency toward more open competitive political systems at the intermediate level of industrial modernization in Latin America.[22]

Bureaucratic-authoritarianism derives, according to O'Donnell, from a complex set of reactions to the problems that emerge with the completion of the consumer goods phase of import-substitution. Once the domestic market for simple manufactured products is satisfied, opportunities for industrial expansion become considerably more limited. In addition, though the initial phase of industrialization may reduce dependency on imported consumer goods, the cost of importing the intermediate goods and capital equipment needed for the production of consumer goods is high, producing or increasing deficits in the balance of payments, foreign indebtedness, and inflation. These problems lead to a "zero-sum" economic situation which undermines the multi-class character of the earlier coalition. Policy-making elites commonly attempt to shift to more austere "orthodox" developmental policies that de-emphasize distribution to the popular sector. They see a long-term solution in the "vertical integration" or "deepening" of industrialization through domestic manufacture of intermediate and capital goods. However, the levels of technology, managerial expertise, and capital needed in this phase require large, more efficient,

[22] *Ibid.*, pp. 113-14.

highly capitalized enterprises—often the affiliates of multi-national corporations. The concern with attracting this type of foreign investment encourages the adoption of orthodox economic policies in order to deal with the economic crisis and to create conditions of long-term economic stability that meet the often exacting requirements imposed by multinational corporations and international lending agencies.[23]

2. *Activation of the Popular Sector*. The increasing political activation of the popular sector which resulted from its growing numerical and economic importance complemented the orientation of the populist coalition and was in fact encouraged through public policies supported by this coalition. With the completion of the first phase of industrialization and the shift to orthodox economic policies, however, the increasingly powerful popular sector is likely to challenge the new policies. The result is a gap between demands and performance, widespread strikes, stalemate of the party system, and severe political and economic crisis.[24] The popular sector is in some cases strong enough to bring a temporary return to the policies of the earlier populist period, and populist and orthodox developmental policies may follow each other in rapid succession as the economic crisis continues.

3. *Technocratic Roles*. Higher levels of social differentiation which accompany industrialization also lead to a greatly enlarged role of technocrats in society—both in the private sector and in civilian and military bureaucracies in the public sector. The technocrats have a low level of tolerance for the ongoing political and economic crisis and perceive high levels of popular sector politicization as an obstacle to economic growth. Within the military, this new technocratic orientation is reflected in what another author has called a "new professionalism" oriented toward active military intervention in political, economic, and social life.[25] The increasing communication among the military and civilian technocrats and their growing frustration with existing political and economic conditions encourages the emergence

[23] *Modernization*, p. 62, and "Reflexiones," passim.
[24] *Modernization*, pp. 70 ff.
[25] *Ibid.*, 154 ff., and Alfred Stepan, "The New Professionalism of Internal Warfare and Military Role Expansion," pp. 46 to 63 in Stepan, ed., *Authoritarian Brazil: Origins, Policies, and Future* (New Haven: Yale University Press, 1973).

of a "coup coalition" that ultimately establishes a repressive "bureaucratic-authoritarian" system in order to end the political and economic crisis. This complex set of interactions among industrialization, popular sector activation, and the spread of technocratic roles is summarized schematically in Figure 1.

FIGURE 1

SELECTED ELEMENTS OF O'DONNELL'S
ARGUMENT CONCERNING THE EMERGENCE
OF BUREAUCRATIC-AUTHORITARIANISM

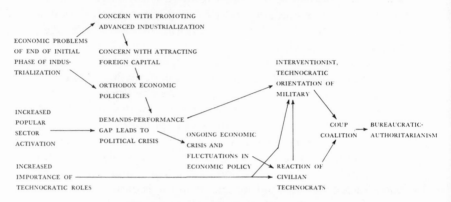

EMERGENCE AND EVOLUTION OF BUREAUCRATIC-AUTHORITARIANISM

O'Donnell argues that these crises have played a central role in the emergence of bureaucratic-authoritarianism in most of the advanced countries of Latin America: Brazil in 1964, Argentina in 1966 and 1976, and Chile and Uruguay in 1973. In addition, he identifies an alternative trajectory of change—exemplified by Mexico—that leads to a contemporary political pattern which has many traits in common with these South American cases. In Mexico, the end of the initial phase of industrialization occurred within the context of firmly established authoritarian control, with the result that the transition to more advanced industrialization was accompanied by a much greater continuity of political institutions.[26]

Bureaucratic-authoritarianism varies both over time and across countries. Internal tensions produced by the effort to create political and economic conditions conducive to renewed foreign investment are an important source of these variations.

---

[26] *Modernization*, p. 95, note 77, and "Reflexiones," pp. 45 ff.

Groups that initially supported the coup, including national entrepreneurs and elements of the middle class, suffer from the orthodox economic policies and from the preoccupation with orienting industrial expansion around foreign and state investment. This preoccupation leads to a "denationalization" of the coalition that supports the state, in that the principal economic "class" that sustains the state is foreign capital. This denationalization appears difficult to sustain over a long period of time. Strong internal pressure eventually emerges for a transformation from the coalitional "duo," involving the state and foreign capital, to a subsequent "trio" in which national entrepreneurs once again come to play a larger role.[27]

The way this transition occurs, O'Donnell suggests, is crucial in influencing the success of these systems in their own terms, as in the contrast between the post-1964 Brazilian experience and the post-1966 Argentine experience. Where the pre-coup crises are fairly intense and the new technocratic coalition perceives these crises as a major threat to the established order, as was the case in Brazil, the new coalition is more cohesive and better able to maintain political control in the face of these internal pressures. An enlarged role for national entrepreneurs eventually emerges, but only after the long-term guarantee of political and economic stability has insured large infusions of foreign capital.

In Argentina in the 1960's, by contrast, the immediate pre-coup crisis was less severe than in Brazil and the perception of threat more limited. Elite cohesion after the coup was consequently not sufficient to resist pressure from the popular sector and other groups within society. The result was a collapse of bureaucratic-authoritarianism, a reemergence of a populist-type coalition of disaffected groups, renewed economic and political crisis, and a failure to attract foreign investment on a long-term basis and to sustain growth.[28] The case of Chile suggests that levels of pre-coup crisis even higher than those experienced in Brazil may not further enhance the likelihood of success. In Chile the crisis was so intense, the economic disruption so severe, and the post-coup repression so violent that for a substantial period the government had difficulty in attracting foreign investment in spite of extreme economic orthodoxy.

With regard to other Latin American countries which may

---

[27] "Reflexiones," pp. 31 ff.
[28] *Modernization*, pp. 99-103, and "Reflexiones," pp. 36 ff.

face crises of advanced industrialization, O'Donnell urges caution in assuming that earlier patterns will recur.[29] First, the context of modernization for later modernizers within Latin America may be different. Second, special economic or political resources may be available, such as oil revenues in Venezuela or special patterns of party competition in Colombia. These may make it possible to avoid the political transformations that occurred in the first countries that achieved advanced industrialization. Third, through purposive political action, leaders may find alternative political solutions to the problems and crises of advanced industrialization. O'Donnell suggests that there is thus not just an "affinity" between advanced industrialization and bureaucratic-authoritarianism in Latin America, but, borrowing a phrase from Weber, an "elective affinity."[30]

CONCLUSION

This line of argument, which for the sake of convenience may be referred to as the bureaucratic-authoritarian "model,"[31] provides the analytic framework around which the chapters in this book are organized. At a relatively general level, this framework focuses on the interaction between certain crucial features of national politics in Latin America—particularly the nature of the dominant coalition, the political regime, and the class and sectoral orientation of public policy—and the social and economic tensions that have arisen in the course of industrialization within the region. At a more specific level, the framework focuses on a series of topics crucial to the study of this interaction: the economic and social problems that arise at different points in the industrialization process; the political and economic crises that grow out of these problems; the reaction of different elites to these crises and the degree of "perception of threat" on the part of these elites; the emergence of new types of authoritarian rule and new types of military intervention in politics in the context of these crises; the striking variations in the ways in which this new authoritarianism has evolved; and the widely differing

---

[29] *Modernization*, pp. 110-11.   [30] *Ibid.*, pp. viii and 196.
[31] This term is used here in the informal, non-mathematical sense of a verbal argument organized around an interrelated set of explanatory statements or hypotheses.

impacts of the economic and social policies adopted by these governments.

The purpose of this book is to scrutinize, modify, and elaborate the concepts and hypotheses that have been developed within this larger framework. In order to anticipate the issues raised in these chapters, it is appropriate to provide here a brief overview of the principal questions they address.

The first set of questions concerns the characterization of authoritarianism itself. What are the most useful ways of conceptualizing the similarities and differences among the authoritarian experiences of these countries? What are the alternative ways in which a concept such as bureaucratic-authoritarianism can most usefully be employed—both in the analysis of contemporary authoritarianism and in exploring the contrasts, as well as possible areas of similarity, in relation to earlier patterns of authoritarianism?

Second, on the basis of a growing body of new case study material and of further analysis of previously available evidence, what progress can be made in refining the explanation of the new authoritarianism? Is the original argument concerning the links between the emergence of authoritarianism and the tensions produced by the transitions among different phases of industrialization, the spread of technocratic roles, and the attempt to achieve a deepening of industrialization consistent with this evidence? Can a "respecified" form of the model provide a more complete explanation? What was the impact of major differences among countries in the structure of the party system and the political strength of the popular sector? Did public policies in earlier periods shape patterns of industrialization in ways that may have intensified or eased the crises experienced in this more recent period? Did ideologies and political ideas play an independent role in shaping these events?

Third, can the extension of the analysis to other Latin American countries where bureaucratic-authoritarianism has not occurred provide new insights into the cases in which it did occur—as well as advancing the understanding of these other countries? Is it possible to incorporate more systematically into the model cases of formally democratic regimes, such as Venezuela and Colombia, and of reformist military governments, such as that which appeared in Peru in 1968? Can Mexico be more fully incorporated into the model?

Fourth, how does bureaucratic-authoritarianism evolve once it is established? Though it is appropriate to characterize these systems as authoritarian, it is essential to recognize that they often face grave problems of authority and legitimacy. What are the implications of these problems for the dynamics of change under authoritarian rule? What consequences do they have for the degree of success experienced by these governments in promoting economic growth? What are the prospects for an eventual reemergence of competitive regimes in Latin America? If such a reemergence occurs, how would the new priorities for research that it raises be related to the concerns of the studies in this book?

Finally, can elements of the bureaucratic-authoritarian model usefully be extended to other world regions, and can such extensions of the analysis lead to improvements in the model as it applies to Latin America?

This book addresses these questions.

CHAPTER 2

ON THE CHARACTERIZATION OF AUTHORITARIAN REGIMES IN LATIN AMERICA

Fernando Henrique Cardoso

In recent years there has been an accentuated tendency toward authoritarianism in Latin America. In itself, authoritarianism is hardly a new phenomenon. For a long time, *caudillismo* and militarism have been dominant features of political life in the region, and in this context democracy has been more an exotic plant than the expected result of a long-term trend. However, traditional *caudillismo* and militarism were a product of societies in which the hacienda and the agrarian or mineral export economy was predominant. By contrast, what strikes us today is precisely the resurgence of authoritarianism in societies which could broadly be described as in a process of "modernization."

What are we to conclude from the fact that a whole region is becoming simultaneously both more modernized and more politically authoritarian? Did not the theory of modernization postulate a discontinuous but global process of democratization stimulated by the spread of democratic and egalitarian attitudes and values in all spheres of social activity? There is clearly a contradiction between the political consequences of economic growth postulated by this theory and the actual course of political history marked by military coups and flourishing authoritarian regimes.

If the theory of modernization provides little help in explaining this new authoritarianism, how is one to explain it? Another approach is historical. We must not forget that in the history of Latin America respect for political rights—or even the subjective existence of such a notion—and for the formal rules of political participation has been far more an ideology for the use and enjoyment of dominant oligarchies than a common practice. However, the recognition of a history of arbitrary rule does not serve as an explanation for contemporary authoritarianism.

Still another approach to explanation, and for some people to moral justification, focuses on the specific needs of rulers and of the state. Yet even those people most disposed to accept the facts of life as if they were moral rules and to believe that the politics of princes necessarily implies the exercise of violence have difficulty in recognizing torture and kidnapping as legitimate means in the defense of the established order. If their doubts do not arise from a healthy human reaction against such practices, at least they know that obedience without consent is a weak foundation for a stable and durable political order.

Others who are not inclined to justify the new authoritarianism take still other approaches to explaining it. Yet they do not face such an easy task either. Even a brief survey of the already ample bibliography on Latin American authoritarianism leaves the reader perplexed. The state is defined with a whole range of adjectives such as "dependent," "bureaucratic," "corporative," "fascist," "bonapartist," "militarist," "police state," and so on. Needless to say, this proliferation of adjectives is hardly a substitute for coherent explanation.

In light of this state of the literature, I must make a plea for clemency. If the character of the authoritarianism dominant in Latin America has not yet even been precisely defined, it would be presumptuous on my part to produce a detailed theory of authoritarianism now. I can do no more than suggest in a very schematic way some of the problems outlined by the authors who have dedicated themselves to the subject and perhaps put forward some ideas arising from my own direct experience of one or another of the authoritarian situations. I shall therefore examine a number of issues concerning contemporary authoritarianism in Latin America, without suggesting that by so doing I shall have exhausted the subject or even touched upon all the central points.

BUREAUCRATIC-AUTHORITARIANISM

When one looks at Chile since the fall of Allende, at the Uruguay of Bordaberry and more recently, or at contemporary Brazil—which has already experienced a decade-and-a-half of military government—one should not be surprised that some social scientists have proclaimed the existence of a new and homogeneous form of regime: a military and authoritarian regime. The temptation to do this is even further reinforced by the recent history of Argentina, which has seen both the resurrection of Perón and his death, together with the fleeting days of magic and terror of Lopez Rega, only to be replaced by generals who, although eager to exorcise the magicians of Isabelita's court, did not flinch from using the rack and dungeon against the threat of subversion of the existing order.

But the Southern Cone of South America does not have the dubious privilege of a monopoly of military regimes. Though in other parts of Latin America the influence of the military and its bureaucratic efficiency may not be as great as in the south of the continent, there is the long-standing military regime in power in Paraguay, as well as the self-proclaimed revolutionary military government that came to power in Peru in 1968, although in the latter case there has been little or no torture. Moreover, military men control Ecuador, Bolivia, Panama, Honduras, and El Salvador. And even though the government of Guatemala has called elections, it is hardly possible to characterize it as other than a military regime. To do otherwise would mean that the Brazilian regime (always ambivalent in dealing with the difficult problem of legitimation) would cease to be a military regime with every controlled election that it holds.

Though military regimes rule in most of Latin America, it is essential to make distinctions among them. In classifying such diverse situations we must avoid a confusion between the *caudillismo* of the old Latin American militarism (as in the case of Paraguay) or family-based *caudillismo* (as in the case of Nicaragua), and the more institutional control of power by the officer corps as a whole which exists in some other countries.

It was in order to make effective distinctions of this type that the social scientists who first tried to characterize the new South American militarism added another adjective: "bureaucratic." It has been argued that the characteristic feature of the types of regimes implanted in Latin America in more recent years has been precisely the fact that in these regimes it is not a single general or a colonel who, like the *caudillos* of the nineteenth century, imposes a personal order by decrees. Rather, it is the military institution as such which assumes the power in order to restructure society and the state.

We must not underestimate the importance of this contrast. The bureaucratic-authoritarian regime *is* different from the old forms of *caudillo* domination—whether civil or military. A new phenomenon has emerged in contemporary Latin America. The armed forces take power not as in the past to maintain a dictator in power (such as Vargas or Perón) but rather to reorganize the nation in accordance with the "national security" ideology of modern military doctrine. In contrast with the traditional forms of military domination in Latin America, contemporary militarism likewise stands out because of the already mentioned rule by the military institution as an organization. In the past, this phenomenon was not possible, given the less fully developed professional structure of the armed forces and the much greater power of the civilian oligarchies, which needed only occasional military intervention in order to exercise their domination.

The initial preoccupation of the authors who have tried to characterize the new authoritarianism in Latin America has been to distinguish it not only from authoritarian regimes of the past, but also from European fascism and corporatism. With regard to this second contrast, the differences are more subtle. In the first place, Latin American authoritarianism is different from the typical forms of fascism because it aspires, above all, to produce apathy among the masses. It fears the mobilization of followers, even if they could be recruited from the middle, rather than from the lower, strata of society. In consequence, it dispenses with political parties as organizational links between civil society and the state. The army, as guarantor of the authoritarian order, prefers a "technical," supportive relationship between the state and social groups, rather than a relationship based on alliances with broad social groups. Thus bureaucratic-authoritarianism diverges not only from the democratic model of bonds between representatives and electors, but also from Italian or German fascism, in which the mobilization of the party and the use of its extremist members as a repressive force was essential. It does not fully approach the form of Spanish corporatism either, for in the sphere of civil society it allows the representative organizations of liberal-capitalist classes to survive without organic bonds with the state, declarations from Onganía or Pinochet in favor of corporatism notwithstanding. The state tends to exclude class organizations (although not class interests) from the decision-making process, preserving a rigid hierarchical structure that is bureaucratically controlled by various national security agencies and by the commanders of the armed forces. As in the past, corporative links are established within the trade unions (between workers and management)

and between them and the state, and where these links were historically weak (as in Chile), the military regimes encourage
them. But the state does not adopt a corporative form. It does
not try to stimulate class organization, to promote a doctrine of
organic harmony among social groups, or to establish corporative links among them that could form a base for *political* domination. Rather, the links between civil society and the bureaucratic-authoritarian regime are achieved through the cooptation
of individuals and private interests into the system. Under these
circumstances, stable pressure groups are unlikely to mate-
rialize, and a truly corporatist network of links between society
and the state is unlikely to emerge.

Regarding ideology, we may observe in typical fascist regimes
an ideology of national superiority based on a belief in the virtues of the race and in the people's destiny. This "ideological
cement" was in accord with the orientation toward economic and
territorial expansion. Such nationalism could not be an ambition
of Latin American authoritarian regimes, given their economic
dependency. Instead, official ideologies favor a conservative and
hierarchical mentality whose vision of grandeur has been confined to the reinforcement of the state apparatus. Hence, the
ideological claims made in Latin America differ from those prevailing under classic European fascism.

Apathy and lack of mobilization; a mentality that is statist and
hierarchical, rather than a broadly nationalistic ideology; state
but not party; hierarchy and no representation—these all form
part of the particular ideological and organizational instruments
of contemporary military authoritarianism in Latin America. It
would appear, therefore, that the characterization of the emerging forms of political domination in Latin America as bureaucratic-authoritarian has something new to offer the typology of
political regimes in general.

In thinking about this new type of regime, we must note differences and similarities in relation to other regimes in Latin
America which have many bureaucratic-authoritarian characteristics, but are not military regimes. Some authors have extended the term bureaucratic-authoritarian beyond the cases of
strictly military regimes to include countries such as Mexico. Yet,
if *all* these regimes are bureaucratic-authoritarian, what is the
value of such a concept? If this term covers such a range of regimes, from the Chilean junta (or any military junta for that

matter), through Peru, Panama, Ecuador, and even to Mexico, what is the analytical content of this concept? Its degree of abstraction may be too great.

I would argue that the notion of bureaucratic-authoritarianism should not be used in such a wide sense. I would restrict it to situations in which military intervention occurred in reaction against leftist movements and in which the policies which served to reorganize the state and the economy in such a way as to guarantee the continued advance of capitalist industrial development were implemented by *military* regimes, as in Argentina and Brazil. The reason for this restricted application of the concept is not an analytical whim but rather the need to underline the crucial fact of the militarization of the state. It is essential to differentiate these decidedly *military* authoritarian regimes from others such as the Mexican regime, which, although not completely bereft of bureaucratic-authoritarian traits, is undoubtedly civilian in its mode of control. How are we to conceptualize these obvious differences between Mexico and the military regimes of the Southern Cone?

POLITICAL REGIME AND STATE

To clarify the characterization of contemporary authoritarian politics, it is essential to distinguish between the concept of political regime and the concept of the state. By "regime" I mean the formal rules that link the main political institutions (legislature to the executive, executive to the judiciary, and party system to them all), as well as the issue of the political nature of the ties between citizens and rulers (democratic, oligarchic, totalitarian, or whatever).

The conceptualization of the state is a complex matter, but there does exist a certain degree of agreement that at the highest level of abstraction the notion of state refers to the basic alliance, the basic "pact of domination," that exists among social classes or fractions of dominant classes and the norms which guarantee their dominance over the subordinate strata. When Marx and Engels referred to the state as the "committee for the management of the common interests of the whole bourgeoisie," they characterized it at this level of abstraction: the capitalist state is the "expression" of the capitalist mode of class domination. To avoid metaphysics, this "expression" ought to be conceived of in organizational terms; that is to say, the dominant classes must make a continuing effort to articulate their diverse and occasionally contradictory objectives through state agencies and bureaucracies.

The need to distinguish between regime and state in this sense becomes quickly evident if one begins to compare Latin American countries. It is commonly argued that bureaucratic-authoritarian regimes enforce rules of political exclusion for the benefit of the private sector of the economy. It is understood that the predominant economic interests that support these regimes favor accelerating capital accumulation through controlling the labor force—a measure that appears to be an important concomitant of successful capitalist development. But, in this respect, there are obvious similarities between the Mexico of the PRI and the Brazil of Institutional Acts imposed by the army. In both cases the policies aim to achieve rapid capitalist development, while the governments feel in the long run that continuing worsening of income inequality and dependency do not affect the historic destiny of their respective nations. Indeed, using these criteria, even such democratic countries as Venezuela and Costa Rica have the same type of capitalist state. In these two countries there is likewise a socio-economic exclusion of the majority. There are similar models of economic accumulation (control of wages, patterns of income distribution) and even similar favorable policies toward multinational corporations. Thus the state, when seen as a basic pact of domination, is a comparable capitalist state in all of these countries.

A major shortcoming in the discussions of authoritarianism is that they have not focused adequately on this distinction between the state and the political regime. An identical form of state—capitalist and dependent, in the case of Latin America—can coexist with a variety of political regimes: authoritarian, fascist, corporatist, and even democratic. One line of economic reasoning looks for a one-to-one causal relation between state and regime. It presupposes that for each "stage" of accumulation there is an appropriate type of regime. However, the same historical difficulty that this reasoning produces in the case of mature capitalist countries (i.e., the absence of fascism in Anglo-Saxon countries, which made the most substantial contributions to the early development of capitalism) occurs in its application to Latin America as well. Brazil's growth under Kubitschek and the present Venezuelan boom are clearly cases in which dependent capitalist states have sustained democratic regimes.

Nevertheless, though the idea of a simple economic determination of politics is best discarded, there is room for exploring the degree of "compatibility" between different forms of dependent capitalist states and different types of regime. For example, what are the conditions under which a democratic regime can coexist with class domination based on a form of economic accumulation which imposes increasing inequality among social classes? Are not the roots of the crisis of all three Southern Cone democracies (Argentina, Chile, and Uruguay) to be found in the contradiction between a system of wide participation and political representation of the masses and the need for accumulation and control over the work force? I doubt that one can answer this question affirmatively, much less generalize an affirmative answer to the whole of Latin America. As I pointed out, the economic achievements of contemporary Venezuela and of Brazil during the Kubitschek period, among others, remind those who hastily proclaim the inevitability of military dictatorship in opening the way to the "current phase" of capitalist development that history is more capricious than it may appear. Further, it is hard to believe that exclusively economic motives were behind the right wing political and military mobilization against the Allende government or the post-Peronist administration. There is therefore a need for more careful analysis and further interpretation in the study of the relationship between a dependent capitalist state and different forms of political regime. To date, most of the gap created by the lack of research on this relationship has been filled by highly polemical interpretations generally insensitive to the variety of historical experience.

At this point, it should be obvious that I find it most useful to use the term bureaucratic-authoritarianism to refer, not to the form of the state as such, but to the type of political regime. The relationship between the two is far from clear and, given that this is a complex and rather controversial subject, it might be wiser to advance modestly along the unambitious path of the political description of the institutions of bureaucratic-authoritarian regimes.

THE INSTITUTIONS OF AUTHORITARIANISM

Almost by definition, bureaucratic-authoritarian regimes organize the relations of power in favor of the executive. It is the strengthening of the executive and the reinforcing of its technical capabilities (of its formal "rationality") that stands out in these regimes. The strengthening of the executive involves increased centralization which undermines the federal tradition, where it existed before. It also involves the elimination or sharp reduction in the role of the legislature. Moreover, the judiciary is controlled in practice, if not in theory, by the executive.

The non-democratic procedures for selecting the president and the bureaucratic expansion of the central administration in these regimes are, nonetheless, subject to a counterbalancing system. On the one hand, formal rationality requires the strengthening of a bureaucratic body of technicians, especially in the economic field; on the other hand, these regimes express the political will of the armed forces as an institution. In this way, the executive depends on the technocratic bureaucracy and on the only real party, the armed forces.

The institutionalization of mechanisms to solve conflicts between the executive and the techno-bureaucracy is relatively simple. The relationship between the executive and its real base of power, the military, is more complex. One might think that in these regimes the distinction between the executive and the armed forces is nonexistent. However, as soon as the military-bureaucratic systems become stable, the armed forces as such do not determine state policies or implement them. The military have veto power over the "big decisions"—the most important being control of political succession—but they are not necessarily involved in decision making regarding the economy or other important issues. It is for this reason that problems arise regarding the functioning of these regimes and lead to clashes between the executive and the armed forces. Once civilians who are independent of the armed forces begin to play a part, however small, in the decision-making process, the executive becomes the center of these decisions, and clashes with military "hard liners" are inevitable.

The success of the regime depends in part on the type of delegation of military authority to the executive that is adopted.

There have been cases of military juntas and military presidents that are directly responsible to the officer corps. When the president is a general, the alternatives regarding the length of his mandate are few. These range from situations—transitory in general—in which the president is the commander of the armed forces, to the pretense of a presidential legitimacy defined by rules which are not exclusively military. In the Brazilian case there is an attempt to preserve something of the electoral presidential tradition: the president is a general nominated by the supreme command of the armed forces, but ratified by congress. He receives a mandate for a limited number of years. In other cases, the question of the presidential term is left open, provoking crises within the high command concerning the limits of the mandate and the course of succession. In Brazil the succession is a traumatic event, but rival military factions have time and hope on their horizon, given the limited mandate of the general-president. It may be due to this factor that military crises just prior to the completion of the presidential terms have been avoided, despite the fact that, to this date, Brazilian military presidents have been unable to have any of their own candidates nominated as successors.

The appearance of a strong, near dictatorial presidentialism sometimes hides the effective control that the military institution exercises over those in government, whether they are civilians or generals. There is, however, great tension between the strengthening of the executive and the control by the armed forces. In regimes controlled by military establishments that are less professional, and therefore less apt to accept the rules of the hierarchy, as in Bolivia or Ecuador, the threat of new clashes is constant. But extreme tension between the armed forces and the presidency has also occurred in Argentina, while in Uruguay the crisis between Bordaberry and the high command exemplifies the lack of institutionalization of such regimes. In a more discrete way, presidential power in Brazil has sometimes been opposed by the power of the high command. Paradoxically, the strengthening of the executive, combined with its lack of an institutional base, continues a characteristic feature of bureaucratic-authoritarianism in its military form. This is an important difference between such a form of government and the type of civil authoritarianism prevailing in Mexico, where the president has perhaps more power than any general-president of a military government in the Southern Cone countries.

Another important dimension of authoritarian regimes relates to the question of political parties. The official ideology (or mentality) accentuates the non-party character of military governments, as well as the aim of putting an end both to "politics" as an expression of conflicting ideologies and to the existence of parties which undermine the "national unanimity" desired by the military governments. Yet it is obvious that in practice the activity of political factions reappears. The relationship between interest groups in civil society and the state is based more on the criteria and mechanisms of cooptation than on the mechanisms of representation. In other words, those who control the state apparatus select various people to participate in the decision-making system, a selection process that will be extended to include even the most powerful of social forces, and even sectors of the lower classes. But they will never subscribe to the idea of representation. The delegation of authority from below is not encouraged. On the contrary, the decision regarding who will be called to collaborate, and for how long, is made at the apex of the pyramid of power.

The interest groups within civil society will naturally attempt to penetrate the decision-making circles. Once they have achieved this, they seek to further their own interests. However, they are not legitimized as representatives of their own constituents. It is the bureaucrats or people controlling top positions in the state apparatus who decide that this or that person may participate. The people who are selected may occasionally speak on behalf of other persons or groups, but they do not form a delegation as such. Hence, they are never recognized formally as "representatives" or delegates. Thanks to this mechanism, civil servants can "defuse" any pressure simply by dispensing opportunities to participate by their own selective means. In other words, in bureaucratic-authoritarian regimes, the representation of groups or factions—the political parties—is not legitimate per se. The interests that social groups manage to articulate in authoritarian regimes have to be defined inside the state machinery, while political parties in democratic systems tend to be rooted in civil society. The mechanism of cooptation allows private interests to establish their roots within the state, but only through committees or special advisory groups controlled by state officials (civilian and military). These may later become the leaders of semi-political organizations which I have described elsewhere as bureaucratic clusters or "rings" that constitute the links between the interests of civil society and the state, involving bargaining between private and state interests. Even though they may resemble the classic format of the lobby, these bureaucratic rings are different in that they do not involve genuine, autonomous pressure groups, but rather are part of the state apparatus itself and normally are under the formal leadership of a state official.

We cannot apply this characterization to all authoritarian regimes or even to all phases of a single regime. The degree of liquidation of representative mechanisms and parties depends on the degree of distrust that these institutions inspired in the dominant classes and especially in the military establishment during the phase preceding the rise of authoritarianism. Populism, as much as democracy, permitted the existence of left-wing parties and also permitted alliances between them and reformist forces. In the climate of the Cold War of the 1950's, the Cuban revolution in 1958 and the spread of guerrilla movements in subsequent years generated a political challenge at the local and international level. It was the reaction against the possibility of socialism that culminated in the present "Thermidor" in Latin America. The armed forces adopted and adapted the Franco-American doctrines of internal warfare and became increasingly preoccupied with internal repression. They also became preoccupied with the necessity of implementing policies that promoted accelerated economic growth in order to pass quickly through the initial phase of economic "take off" in which, according to counterrevolutionary strategies inspired by the writings of W. W. Rostow, there is a greater likelihood that social revolution will occur.

The timing of the implantation of contemporary authoritarian regimes, as well as the degree of their economic and political achievements, have varied greatly among countries. The gradual establishment of a military bureaucratic order in Brazil carried with it the inheritance of a multi-party system. A second coup in 1965 created the present two-party system. In Chile and Uruguay bureaucratic-authoritarianism emerged with more devastating force than in Argentina and developed an emphatically anti-party orientation. It was no coincidence that before the arrival of militarism in these countries, a wide range of left-wing groups, from the violent revolutionaries to the supporters of the peaceful road to socialism, had constituted themselves into a powerful threat to the established order. To the dominant classes and to the armed forces in these countries, "representative democracy" sounds only marginally less frightening than opening the front door to the devil, an appropriate metaphor, given that the military see themselves as the defenders of Christian and occidental values against the world wide menace of communism.

To the disappointment of collectors of neat labels and monocausal explanations, the characteristics of the purest bureaucratic-authoritarianism are not always found in the most reactionary political and economic regimes. For example, from a formal point of view, the so-called "Peruvian model" of reformist tendencies has some similarities to countries governed by the military authoritarianism of the south. It would be wrong, therefore, to believe that the formal characteristics I have been discussing will always appear in an orderly and predictable fashion in conjunction with other important features of authoritarian regimes.

THE FUNCTIONING OF AUTHORITARIANISM

It seems obvious that the presence or absence of a party system will open alternative paths to authoritarian regimes. It indicates, at least, a different degree of relative autonomy in the political organizations controlled by social classes. As far as I know, there are no studies concerning the way in which pre-existing political parties have survived under military authoritarian regimes. In the case of Peru, if there is some form of party still surviving, it is APRA, some of whose program and ideology were adopted by the post-1968 government in an apparently successful attempt by the military to neutralize this party. To assure success, the military added to their movement a tinge of nationalism and reformism, and even attempted certain forms of political mobilization through the Sistema Nacional de Apoyo a la Mobilización Social. However, because of the inherent difficulties that bureaucratic-authoritarian regimes have in developing any form of popular mobilization, this has now been diluted.

In Chile the prevailing militarism, having destroyed left-wing organizations, went on to dismantle the other political alternative in civil society, the Christian Democrats, but it is likely, given the Chilean social and political tradition, that the parties will just hibernate and eventually reemerge almost intact. The same can be said of Argentina under Onganía and Lanusse, and in the state of near civil war which is evident in Argentina today there is a withdrawal from political life toward a pre-political society: "man is wolf to man" once more. However, although in these circumstances it is difficult to imagine how political parties can be reconstituted, I do not believe that either the trade union organizations or the political parties of the popular sector and the middle classes (previously semi-organized under Peronism and Radicalism) will simply be eradicated. I would not be surprised if, in the not too distant future, the armed forces in Argentina have to face political demands too great for the narrow limits of militarism.

In the analysis of Latin American authoritarianism, one of the most interesting contrasts would appear to be between Brazil and Mexico. In these countries, it might be said that civil society is rather weakly organized in comparison to the civil societies of the Southern Cone countries. A tradition of a strong state plus elitist political control (in the case of Brazil) and of a bureaucratic hierarchy (in the case of Mexico) increases the likelihood of success for these authoritarian regimes—despite differences between them in form and content. Nevertheless, we have recently seen in Brazil how the one of the two parties created by the military regime to fill a purely formal role of opposition has actually become an effective opposition party. In the general elections of November 1974 the opposition won sixteen of the twenty-one seats for the senate. In the following months, the strong resulting impact gave the ironic impression that this military regime had made a rather original contribution to modern forms of authoritarianism by creating a party system almost exclusively based on the opposition. It is true that the dominant political system soon reacted, using whatever tools were available to deny the opposition any possibility of gaining power through the electoral system. In any case, the significant point is that the goals of the military have by no means been fully accomplished. In civil society there is an awareness of the illegitimacy of the regime and a conviction that sooner or later the political organization of society will have to be reconstituted.

Mexico, a civilian regime, provides an example of great stability, a stability that has much to do with the origins of the regime. The Mexican regime was born of a revolution that partially incorporated broad sectors of society into national life and established a political system more open to pressures and suggestions from the bottom, although still controlled from the top. Moreover, the Mexican bureaucratic elite has a capacity for control regarding economic and social matters which secures a certain hegemony within society. An extensive system of bargaining with regard to economic interests, along with efficient financial and economic performance since Cárdenas, turned the Mexican state into an effective instrument of domination and political control. Consensus without democracy was the logical outcome, in spite of the continuing use of the instruments of repression to stifle any threat to the political or social order. The repressive aspects of Mexican politics have been diluted by the well-known mechanism of massive cooptation of the opposition practiced by the state and by a tolerance of violations of the boundaries between private interest and public office. In consequence, it is a non-military and "inclusionary" type of regime that has achieved a greater capacity for endurance by giving social roots to an authoritarian system.

What factors affect the degree of autonomy of civil society in the face of authoritarian rule? One is clearly the presence or absence of a preexisting party system. Others include the degree of effective control that authoritarian regimes exercise over everyday life (and over the mass media as well as the peoples' reaction to this control). For example, Peruvian military authoritarianism is markedly different in this regard from the Argentine or Uruguayan regimes: Peru has not implemented a system of terror within society. Although it is true that in Peru there is state control of the press, the formation of public opinion does not face the obstacles that are characteristic in Uruguay, not to mention in Chile, or in Brazil during the more repressive phases of the Brazilian regime.

Political science in Latin America has advanced little in the study of the control capacity of authoritarian regimes—perhaps due to a certain repugnance at having to investigate the different types of malignant tumor that these forms of authoritarianism are considered to be. This capacity for control varies among different authoritarian regimes due to multiple factors. The first of these involves the circumstances under which the regimes came to power. In some cases the military overthrew the constitutional order by means of a blood bath. In others a radio announcement was sufficient to depose the previous president. In the second place, the degree of weakness or strength of civil society must also be considered in order to explain the capacity of the regime to control it. Obviously, it is more difficult for the regime to deal with autonomous and therefore potentially more defiant social groups (Chile) than to keep itself in power in a society where politics is the exclusive preserve of an elitist bureaucracy (Brazil). In the third place, there are technical factors that either expand or narrow the control capacity of these regimes. We must bear in mind that we are not analyzing cases that resemble Nazi Germany, which was able to implement and maintain much more complete forms of control. Latin American authoritarianism is still "underdeveloped": it may kill and torture, but it does not exercise complete control of everyday life. The state is sufficiently strong to concentrate its attention and repressive apparatus against so-called subversive groups, but it is not as efficient when it comes to controlling the universities, for example, or even the bureaucracy itself. It would be unwise, however, to underestimate the recent advances made in this field, although the lack of a party to monitor and denounce the enemies of the regime makes this control rather difficult. Up to now, repression has been a task for the police rather than for the politicians.

An additional word on the functioning of authoritarian regimes is in order. Authoritarian regimes which are not based on a political party (again, the Mexican situation based on an effective party does not correspond to the pure bureaucratic-authoritarian regimes in this respect) are sometimes too weak to cope with complex societies. Moreover, it would be incorrect to suppose that the state apparatus operates as a unified whole in authoritarian regimes in Latin America. The absence of a party that could bind the system together and of a truly totalitarian ideology prevents the techno-bureaucracy and office holders from becoming committed to the military ideology of state grandeur. On the contrary, a considerable degree of privatization of the state apparatus occurs in such regimes. The coherence of the regime exists more at the top level, through the ideological discourse of ministers and generals, than in the routine behavior of the state officials. Quite frequently, the latter control parts of the state apparatus almost independently of the government, pursuing personal objectives of an economic or bureaucratic nature.

These features make the functioning of bureaucratic-authoritarian regimes less consistent than it looks at first glance. Potentially destabilizing factors are almost always present, diminishing the capacity of the regime to absorb pressures. This leads to a continuing use of repression, with all the demoralization and alienation produced by the widespread use of violence, even in the name of the security of the nation against its hidden internal enemies. When these regimes face situations in which actual "subversive" groups are few, the reiteration of the same arguments about threats to national security will become less convincing to the entrepreneurs and dominant groups that support the regimes, and opposition from these groups may increase greatly.

Many forces may thus tend to undermine these regimes, including the eroding factors mentioned above, the possibility of a political reaction against authoritarianism, plus changes in the actual degree of censorship and in the degree of repression. Variations in the effectiveness of repression sometimes occur in the same political regimes with the change of governments, if not within the period of any one government. It is obvious that the form of regime does not solely depend on the mood of people in power; yet this is important. The chances that political action aimed at the transformation of authoritarian regimes will in fact succeed may shift with every particular conjuncture.

And, Finally, the Socioeconomic Bases

At this point we must turn to another difficult theoretical question in social science: the relationship between structure and conjuncture. I prefer to avoid theoretical statements that would with difficulty escape pedantry, and would simply like to address two or three basic issues that have arisen in recent discussions of authoritarian regimes.

After more than a decade of military authoritarianism in

many countries of the continent and of various decades of civilian authoritarianism in some others, most earlier interpretations of its social bases have been superseded by history. The tradition of a militarism conceived as the armed hand of landlords and *latifundistas* was displaced in part by the economic policies consistently oriented toward industrialization that bureaucratic-authoritarian regimes have themselves undertaken. Sometimes these policies have even damaged agrarian interests, and almost always the military regimes have preferred to receive support from agro-business than to preserve ties of close friendship with the *latifundia*.

It seems less clear which groups have been favored by the industrialization policies of these authoritarian governments. To whom have the military addressed their policies and where have they looked for support? The immediate effects of monetary stabilization policies usually implemented by the military after the take-over (normally after a period of political crisis, inflation, and economic uncertainty) demonstrate clearly which social groups have *not* been taken into account: workers and wage earners in general, as well as people living on fixed incomes. However, when the two critical economic variables—inflation and capital formation—are controlled, it is difficult to argue that these bureaucratic-authoritarian regimes have adopted a significantly different set of wage or income distribution policies from those launched in Latin American societies by democratic regimes. Moreover, in Peru the ruling militarism, which clearly did not adopt socialist policies, at least cannot be envisaged as a deliberate supporter of an "income concentration" pattern. Apparently what counts in these matters is the character of the state rather than that of the regime, as well as the level of development of the economy and, above all, the strength of social pressures from below. It is to control these pressures and thus to facilitate capital accumulation that bureaucratic-authoritarianism becomes repressive and depresses the living standard of the workers and of the masses. Alliances between big capital and the state are often implicit, but they exist even in situations such as Peru, where the ruling groups explicitly seek to be perceived as the people's defenders. The consequences of such an implicit pact are, of course, the same as if it had an explicit character: after all, bureaucratic-authoritarianism was not launched to assure the well-being of the people. Even though sociological inquiries have found a low level of political consciousness among the lower strata, there is one thing that people do know: this type of regime does not correspond to the political model of their dreams. Whenever it is possible, the masses make their dissent known to the regime: voting against it, rioting, or just keeping to themselves.

It is likewise difficult to identify the beneficiaries of authoritarianism simply by looking at the industrial and development policies of the regime. Initial hypotheses stressed the affinity between authoritarianism and big business, and to my knowledge there is no strong evidence to reject this hypothesis. Nonetheless, we should not give a mechanistic interpretation of these links such as to argue, for instance, that only a military regime can be successful in setting up the production of capital goods and in assuming the control of modern technology in a developing country. The economic policies implemented in Venezuela, Mexico, Argentina, and Brazil are quite similar, but their political regimes are clearly distinct. Again, behind such a hypothesis there lies a confusion between political regime and types of state.

Given these reservations, and taking for granted that all capitalist states must facilitate and guarantee the process of capital accumulation, the appropriate questions with respect to this problem are probably the following: which groups have gained advantages from the current authoritarianism? Which centers of capital accumulation benefited from authoritarian rule—the local private enterprise sector, the state productive sector, or multinational enterprises? It has taken some time to render the obvious answer acceptable: bureaucratic-authoritarianism is politically profitable for the civilian and military bureaucrats that hold state office. The difficulty in arriving at such a truism comes from a theoretical analysis that sees the state just as the *expression* of class interests, without recognizing that such an expression requires an *organization* which, since it cannot be other than a social network of people, exists in its own right and possesses interests of its own. The answers to the second question are more complex. It is not correct to deduce from the formal character of authoritarian regimes what type of economic growth policies they will pursue. The acceptance of such an interpretation would involve precisely the opposite error from that which occurs when one ignores the fact that the state is a principal beneficiary of bureaucratic-authoritarianism. It would

imply that the state and its bureaucracy are the only real historical actors. The fact is that even in authoritarian situations the
state is linked in various ways to social classes and to their interests.

Another important variation in the economic orientation of
these regimes involves the relative emphasis on promoting enterprises in the public, as opposed to the private, sector. The
Chile of today (under the direct influence of the so-called
"Chicago boys") is making considerable efforts to undermine the
state sector of the economy. The Chilean leaders are attempting
to establish a peculiar kind of "liberal" economy in the sense that
the state redistributes wealth to those groups of private interests
that economically control the regime. The Peruvian generals, at
the opposite pole, strengthened the state organization and increased its capacity for economic decision making. This state
building occurred much earlier in other countries, under the
political control of the entrepreneurs and professional groups,
but in Peru a military intervention was necessary to strengthen
the state. Subsequently, from a position of greater strength, the
military regime attempted to renegotiate the terms of dependency. The Brazilian generals, initially enamored of an economic ideology oriented toward private interests and eager to
expand relationships with foreign capital, have in the end enlarged the sphere of state production and even clashed with the
American government on the issue of nuclear technology.
Thus, it seems impossible to identify a one-to-one correspondence between forms of authoritarian regimes and a set of
homogeneous economic interests.

Obviously, the range of alternatives has some limits. Though
there are important differences among cases, the fundamental
character of this type of authoritarian state is nonetheless
capitalist. Similarly, the decisions taken by state bureaucracies
occur within well-defined limits. Up to now they have not tried
to "change the model." That is to say, the general rules of the
local and world capitalist system of production are maintained.
However, it would be incorrect to replace the cliché that the military are the bodyguards of landlords with the cliché that they
now form a militia to protect the interests of multinational corporations. Authoritarian regimes try to accommodate themselves within the international environment by taking advantage
of occasional fissures in the world's economic system. They make
deals with multinational enterprises that in some cases involve

renegotiating the terms of dependency within narrow limits—
though, in some cases, as in Chile, they do simply accept local
and eventually international private interests as if they corresponded to the needs of the nation and of the people. Yet as a
rule, at the ideological and sometimes at the practical level, they
try to reinforce not the nation, but the state—if not for other
motives, then at least to protect their own interests as a bureaucracy.

In the space available, it is not possible to spell out in detail the
implications of this formulation. Nevertheless, it is worth stressing that if in recent years there has been a significant feature in
the behavior of civilian and military public bureaucracies, it is
their role in the creation of a self-sustained economic basis for
their own power. State enterprises are expanding in most countries, and bureaucratic-authoritarianism has been an important
factor in this trend. I am not referring to the formation of an
ideal "state capitalist" mode of production, but to the use of state
enterprises to facilitate capitalist development and to reinforce
the position of those in power. However, a trend toward nationalistic and anti-imperialistic ideologies and practices is not
likely. On the contrary, in recent years joint ventures between
state enterprises and multinationals have been widely encouraged.

The immediate result of this process in terms of the composition of the state has been the creation of bureaucratic strata en-
dowed with entrepreneurial capacity. Sometimes the top executives of state enterprises clash with a government which has to
cope with interests and pressures that come from different social
groups, and sometimes the government as such has to enforce
policies that are not in conformity with the expansionist interests
of the state enterprises. Thus there emerges a social stratum
which is created within the state and yet which, paradoxically,
achieves to some degree a separate basis of power and can eventually clash with the government under given circumstances.

The point of this argument is not to minimize the significance
of the growing links between Latin American economies and the
international productive system. But it is difficult to believe that
dependency derives from the military authoritarian form of
these regimes. If it is true that these regimes make possible new
agreements with multinational enterprises, they paradoxically
encourage as well aspirations toward more autonomy among the

military and among the executives of state enterprises. Further, the few countries still ruled by representative democracies in Latin America can hardly be presented as a proof of the argument that democracy by itself preserves a country from foreign penetration.

Some Inconclusive Conclusions

I am afraid that this short incursion into complex matters may have provoked not just doubts—which would not be a bad consequence—but more perplexities and ambiguities than clarifications. I started by trying to emphasize the utility of the notion of bureaucratic-authoritarianism for describing, though not explaining, contemporary political realities. However, I fear that I may have contributed to the belief that factors of differentiation among Latin American regimes are so deep that the broad notion of bureaucratic-authoritarianism is almost useless. Furthermore, I have not been successful in identifying a one-to-one link between authoritarian regimes and particular economic policies. It is true that some military regimes have strengthened economic systems based on multinational enterprises, as well as on state corporations, which they themselves control. But it is also true that multinational enterprises managed to survive and expand under democratic systems (not to speak of their achievements under civilian authoritarian ones), while they were weakened under military government in Peru, for instance.

It may well be that the inconclusiveness of my argument about the relation between economics and politics reflects some anxiety that my intellectual inclinations prevent me from expressing more clearly. Yet I do not think that we search in vain when we look for sequences and coherence in history, provided that we keep in mind that there is no greater irrationality than the belief that history can be fully understood through formal rationality. The character of the state—i.e., the structure of class domination and the economic system upon which this structure rests—imposes some limits on the form of the political regime. For instance, the bureaucratic features of these authoritarian regimes (civilian or military) cannot prevent the emergence of the entrepreneurial function that the capitalist economy imposes on them. Yet it is a hopeless effort to look at political events from the narrow point of view of economic factors alone.

It is simplistic to imagine that a dependent capitalist process of industrialization can take place only through authoritarianism. A military junta may not even open new roads to economic growth, as recent events in Chile or Uruguay demonstrate. But, whatever the regime, the dominant classes, given the increasing internationalization of production, are forced to make deals with foreign interests and to reorganize the internal system of economic exploitation in order to cope with new realities. This requires the establishment of an economic system based on state and private corporations and demands state policies to promote capitalist expansion. The assessment made by the dominant classes of the value to them of any authoritarian regime, and hence the actual support that they will give to it, depends primarily on the regime's effective capacity to enforce development policies. The Mexican and Brazilian political systems are similar in this respect. Both have up to now been successful in reorganizing society to cope with more complex forms of capitalist growth. To achieve this, relatively stable forms of labor control have been established and state bureaucracies and public enterprises have been expanded, thus laying a base for the peculiar links already described between private interests and the state. The state as a "pact of domination" thus shows similar traits in both countries. However, it would be quite misleading not to take into consideration the political differences between the two regimes: the military form of the Brazilian system represents a crucial contrast to the party structure that underlies the Mexican regime.

Less marked but still important variations are found among the military regimes in different countries. These variations are primarily the product of differences in the development of the class struggle in each case. In general, the current period of military rule is a response to the crisis provoked in the state by political movements and social struggle before the military takeover. In several Latin American countries, ruling classes have been unable to control the political pressure launched by workers and radicalized sectors of the middle classes. In such circumstances, the dominant classes cannot maintain their power without open military intervention and support. The price to be paid for this "help" depends on the extent of the political disintegration prior to military intervention, as well as on the capacity of the armed forces to control revolutionary groups.

Above all, when leftist political forces were strong and well rooted in society, the initial phases of the military regime are highly repressive. It is in this initial stage that the fascist components of militarism stand out. The entrepreneurial role of these governments, on the other hand, evolves gradually. Attempts to solve the economic and social problems faced by these countries, as well as the emergence of alliances between multinational, domestic private, and state enterprises, progressively confer upon the authoritarian regimes their peculiar entrepreneurial features. Repression continues to be a significant component of political life, but attempts have to be made to justify the regime in the name of a rapid process of accumulation. High rates of output growth are as important as repression in the process of creating and projecting the image of the regime and in its acceptance by dominant classes. Social order with economic progress is the slogan used to hide any questions about "progress for whom?"

A final word might need to be said about the economic achievements of authoritarian regimes and their capacity to impose political conformity on society. It is commonly said that these regimes are "strong." If what is meant by strength is a capacity for violence, then this is tautologically true. But it does not necessarily follow that authoritarian regimes are by themselves able to resist any kind of political challenge. The most dramatic evidence that they are not is the "Cordobazo" that put an end to Onganía's attempt to build a stable authoritarian order. Apart from their "internal conflicts," the authoritarian regimes cannot avoid the elements of uncertainty which pervade all political life. The present difficulties of Brazilian authoritarianism exemplify this. Hence, in explanations of change, it is necessary to take into consideration two different levels of analysis. The first refers to the interplay between structural possibilities for action and the actual behavior of social groups and leaders. Structural possibilities and actual behavior do not necessarily coincide. The second refers to the fact that the actual results of political action do not necessarily coincide with intended results. For example, sometimes military coups are launched in order to preserve private enterprise, but eventually they give rise to governments which—in spite of themselves—expand state enterprise, creating unexpected contradictions.

It is better, therefore, to recognize frankly the ambiguous character of historical situations than to proclaim nostalgia for the logic and coherence of explanations which ignore the unexpected and contradictory aspects of real political life and thus reinforce the image that authoritarian military regimes are likely to cope successfully with any new demands.

The ambiguities of politics give ground for hope. Sometimes they open roads favorable to change by generating forces within an established order that eventually undermine authoritarian rule. The very functioning of authoritarian regimes and the achievement of proposed economic goals create new challenges to the military and new forms of opposition. The military will not necessarily be able to overcome these difficulties. To a large extent, the likelihood of change may depend on the political capacity of opposition groups to propose creative alternatives of power that address these same challenges by offering different, and better, solutions.

PART TWO

Explaining the Emergence of
Bureaucratic-Authoritarianism

THE TURN TO AUTHORITARIANISM IN LATIN AMERICA AND THE SEARCH FOR ITS ECONOMIC DETERMINANTS

Albert O. Hirschman[*]

INTRODUCTION: EIGHTEENTH-CENTURY HOPES AND TWENTIETH-CENTURY REALITIES

"Economic development of underdeveloped areas" emerged as a new and eminently "exciting" field of studies in the late 1940's and early 1950's. The task was truly formidable, but the promise of tackling it with success was held out by two concurrent developments. Theoretical advances in the economics of growth, together with a number of new insights into the specific nature of underdeveloped economies, provided economists, so it was thought, with the tools they needed to give effective advice to governments wishing to steer their countries onto a path of rapid economic expansion. Secondly, the success of the Marshall Plan in Western Europe seemed to confirm the possibility of rapid economic transformation of non-socialist economies provided two conditions were present: (1) appropriate amounts of foreign aid would supplement domestic capital formation and (2) beneficent, "indicative" planning would supplement market signals in making sure that available capital resources would be productively invested.

Some twenty-five years later, that early optimism has largely evaporated, for a number of reasons. Growth, while substantial, has by no means overcome the division of the world into the rich "north" and the underdeveloped "south." In the south itself, moreover, the fruits of growth have been divided more unevenly than had been anticipated. And there is another, often unacknowledged, reason for the disenchantment: it looks increasingly as though the effort to achieve growth, whether or not

* Acknowledgments: Walter Dean Burnham, Bruce Cumings, Marcelo Diamand, Carlos Díaz-Alejandro, Jorge Dominguez, Clifford Geertz, Peter Gourevitch, Sarah Hirschman, James Kurth, Paul Streeten; and, very specially, David Collier, José Serra and Judith Tendler.

successful, brings with it calamitous side effects in the political realm, from the loss of democratic liberties at the hand of authoritarian, repressive regimes to the wholesale violation of elementary human rights. Many economists, cozily ensconced in their ever-expanding discipline, were unconcerned about the possibility of such connections between economic and political events.[1] Others gave vent to their dismay over political developments by looking for weak points in the economic performance of the disliked regimes, such as alleged "structural stagnation" or regressive income distribution. Only a few were so troubled by the course of events that they were anxious to probe whether it was the quest for economic development that had wrought political disaster, but they found that they lacked the conceptual tools needed to investigate the problem.

My own reaction was to withdraw into history, and more specifically into the history of ideas. Since little light had been shed on the connections between economic growth and political disaster by my contemporaries, I decided to dwell for a while among the political philosophers and political economists of the seventeenth and eighteenth centuries, to find out what they had to say about the likely political consequences of the economic expansion then taking place under their eyes. This retreat into the past resulted in my book *The Passions and the Interests: Political Arguments for Capitalism before Its Triumph* (Princeton, 1977). The most surprising, almost bizarre, idea I came across—and whose intricate genealogy is traced in the book—was the speculation that the expansion of commerce, of industry, and of the market economy would serve to restrain, for various reasons and through various mechanisms, the "passions" of the sovereign and would therefore result in less arbitrary and more humane government. Economic growth would bring constraints that would put an end to abuses of power, to unjust exactions—in short, to "despotism." Put positively, a thriving market economy would be the basis for a political order in which the exercise of individual rights and freedoms would be insured. Or, as Tocqueville was to express it epigrammatically: "A close tie and a necessary relation exist between these two things: freedom and

---

[1] An exception must be made for John Sheahan whose thoughtful paper "Market-Oriented Economic Policies and Political Repression in Latin America," forthcoming in *Economic Development and Cultural Change*, came to my attention as the present chapter was going to press.

industry.["2] Yesterday's hopeful doctrine and today's dismal reality could not be farther apart and Tocqueville's sentence would seem to be more applicable to the current Latin American experience if it read instead: "A close tie and a necessary relation exist between these two things: torture and industry." This contrast between the two statements, or between expectation and reality, can usefully serve as a starting point for our discussion.

First of all, it should be noted that the contrast is not so much between European hopes and Latin American disappointments. Not only were there plenty of disappointments in Europe, but hopes similar to those expressed by European thinkers from the seventeenth to the early nineteenth century can be found in late nineteenth- and early twentieth-century Latin America. The idea that an expanding and industrialized economy would discipline the excesses of power-seeking and of passionate politics in general appears in a classic work on Colombian economic history which comments in the following terms on the period of political consolidation and economic expansion subsequent to the termination of the Thousand-Day Civil War in 1902:

"The ultimate foundation of this policy [of industrial protection] was not really or mainly economic. The stimulus (*fomento*) given to industrial firms was an element, and a very important one, in the change of direction which Reyes and the group around him wanted to impart to the political and social life of the country. What mattered was to find a way of reducing the intensity of political infighting which had become unbearable, of making sure that politics would not absorb all of the nation's energies and attention. . . . The formula of the Radicals was being inverted: no longer was liberty to bring us progress; to the contrary, progress was expected and was supposed to bring us liberty."[3]

The idea that an expanding economy and its insertion into the world market would serve as a check against political passions is

[2] Through this synthetic formulation, Tocqueville actually paid only lip service to the prevailing doctrine, which he then proceeded to criticize. See *Passions and Interests*, pp. 122-24.

[3] Luis Ospina Vásquez, *Industria y protección en Colombia, 1810-1930* (Medellín: E.S.F., 1955), pp. 326-27. The author goes on to say that industrial development, with its favorable political consequences of "order and liberty," was also expected to make the country less vulnerable to attacks against its territorial and political sovereignty, obviously a matter of great concern to Colombia after the loss of Panama.

strongly affirmed, by another Colombian writer, not only for a growing industrial establishment, but in reference to the increased production of an export staple such as coffee:

"[In the pre-coffee era, policy makers] are lyrical and romantic because they cannot yet defer to a product whose output is constantly on the increase. It is a time of childhood and play. Coffee will bring maturity and seriousness. It will not permit Colombians to continue playing fast and loose with the national economy. The ideological absolutism will disappear and the epoch of moderation and sobriety will dawn. . . . Coffee is incompatible with anarchy"[4]

It is particularly interesting that the participation of Colombia in the world economy through the coffee trade is viewed here quite positively, as a way of imposing a much-needed discipline on domestic politics and on policy making, rather than as a threat to the country's autonomy, and as a manifestation of its "dependencia."

History has of course largely disappointed the hopes expressed in these eloquent passages. In my book I have tried to explain some of the reasons why the identical optimistic expectations of such eighteenth-century figures as Montesquieu and Sir James Steuart have remained unfulfilled in the advanced industrial countries.[5] By drawing on some of the critics of their ideas, such as Adam Ferguson and Tocqueville, I showed that the very characteristics of the "modern economy" which were supposed to constitute a bulwark against "despotism" could, from an only slightly different perspective, *justify* something close to that abhorred form of government. For the principal point and insight of Montesquieu and Steuart, as of the just cited Colombian authors, was that a more complex economy is a delicate mechanism with exigencies of its own that must not be tampered with. In the mind of a Montesquieu (or of Nieto Arteta) this tampering could emanate only from the government or its head, the capricious sovereign. But the argument cuts several ways; to quote myself, "If it is true *that the economy must be deferred to*, then there is a case not only for constraining the imprudent actions of the prince but for repressing those of the people, for limiting

---

[4] Luis Eduardo Nieto Arteta, *El café en la sociedad colombiana* (Bogotá: Breviarios de orientación colombiana, 1958), pp. 34-35. This posthumously published essay was written in 1947.

[5] *Passions and Interests*, pp. 117-28.

participation, in short, for crushing anything that could be interpreted by some economist-king as a threat to the proper functioning of the 'delicate watch.' "[6]

The principal "economic" explanations of authoritarian rule in Latin America today run along these same lines. The economy and its growth, so it is said, have certain intrinsic exigencies, which are sometimes blatantly ignored by the rulers or ruled, or both. When this happens, regime change becomes likely, and lately such change has meant a move in the direction of a more authoritarian government.[7]

The emphasis of these explanations—which shall soon be examined at greater length—is on the structural characteristics of the economy and on the complex and imperative conditions for its continued growth. These are the to-be-deferred-to exigencies: the *deferenda*. The problem arises from the clash between these deferenda and those who are supposed to do the deferring, but sometimes refuse to abide by the disciplines of the "delicate watch." In this fashion, the differential *propensity to defer* of the policy makers could be an important element in the story we are trying to understand. Latin American policy makers have on occasion shown a particularly low propensity to defer. Sometimes they seem to revel in violating the most elementary constraints of the economic system. The best expression of this attitude is the well-known 1953 advice Perón gave to Carlos Ibáñez, then President of Chile:

"My dear friend:

"Give to the people, especially to the workers, all that is possible. When it seems to you that already you are giving them too much, give them more. You will see the results. Everyone will try to scare you with the specter of an economic collapse. But all of this is a lie. There is nothing more elastic than the economy which everyone fears so much because no one understands it."[8]

A similar refusal to believe in the existence of the "delicate

[6] P. 124. The watch metaphor was repeatedly used by Sir James Steuart in his analysis of the expanding modern economy.

[7] Regime change in the opposite direction has been known to occur and has often been explained along similar lines; important examples are the overthrow of Perón in 1955 and of Rojas Pinilla in 1957.

[8] Quoted from Alejandro Magnet, *Nuestros vecinos argentinos* (Santiago de Chile: 1956), p. 14, by Fredrick B. Pike, "Freedom or Reform in Latin America," Occasional Paper, Graduate Center for South American Studies, Vanderbilt University, Nashville, Tennessee, August 1963, p. 3.

watch" and a similar impatience with any of its constraints were evident in the more ill-considered—and ill-fated—economic and monetary policies of a number of Latin American countries in recent decades. So perhaps it is not, after all, that the economy poses at some point particularly difficult problems for the policy makers at certain moments. Rather, the policy makers may be given, every once in a while, to testing the "elasticity" of the economy with utter recklessness and simply to revolting against the constraints in which Sir James Steuart as well as Nieto Arteta had deposited their hope for an end to despotism and to *mal gobierno* (a term whose meaning ranges from poor administration to misrule).

Actually Sir James Steuart gives us a clue as to why such a revolt is almost to be anticipated. He notes the contradiction between the increasing power that is expected to accrue to the sovereign as the economy expands and the simultaneous increase in the constraints on the *use* of that power, with the constraints originating precisely in the increasing vulnerability of the economy, that is, in the non-existence of that elasticity which Perón had affirmed. Sir James Steuart says that the statesman, faced with this disconcerting situation, "looks about with amazement," but concludes that in the end he will submit to the unexpected and irritating constraints because "he finds himself so bound up by the laws of his political economy, that every transgression of them involves him into new difficulties."[9] Obviously, Sir James Steuart did not foresee the modern Latin American sovereign or policy maker, who, meeting with the same contradiction, will refuse to be "bound up by the laws of his political economy" and will not be deterred by the prospect of "new difficulties."

To put the accent on the nature of the policy maker rather than on the nature of the problems he has to deal with seems a personalistic and therefore rather old-fashioned interpretation. But it can readily be given a more modern social scientific flavor. The policy makers' recurrent illusion about the "elasticity" or non-vulnerability of the economy could be related to a number of characteristics of "late late" industrialization in Latin America. In the first place, industrialization was expected, not

---

[9] For references and a more extended treatment, see *Passions and Interests*, pp. 81-87.

just to increase income and employment, but to reduce dependence, to "transfer decision centers" from abroad and thus to lead to greater autonomy for the policy makers. Moreover, while *desarrollo hacia afuera*—development based on the export of primary products—had taken place under the aegis of laissez-faire, that phase, together with the ideology that had presided over it, was now considered to have come to an ignominious end. The new phase of industrialization, in contrast, was supposed to require a great deal of guidance and intervention from an activist state. Thus the "statesman"—to use Sir James Steuart's term—was not only expecting to become more powerful; he also felt justified by the newly prevailing ideology in using his power to the hilt. Finally, the unexpected early successes of the "easy" phase of import-substituting industrialization may have led to an overestimate of the economy's "elasticity." This was the hypothesis I put forward in an earlier paper:

". . . the 'exuberant' phase of import substitution was accompanied by flamboyant public policies which badly overestimated the tolerance of the economy for a variety of ventures, be they income redistribution by fiat, the building of a new capital, or other extravaganzas . . . it may be conjectured that in their very different ways, Perón, Kubitschek, Rojas Pinilla, and Pérez Jiménez could all be considered victims of the delusions of economic invulnerability fostered by the surprising early successes and rapid penetration of industry into a supposedly hostile environment."[10]

The point of view here presented can be related to Guillermo O'Donnell's paper on the economic phenomena underlying the rise of authoritarianism in Latin America.[11] This paper, whose principal thesis is to be discussed in the next section, makes a great deal of the unpredictability of policy making in Latin America prior to the establishment of authoritarian regimes, and views it as an important obstacle to accumulation and long-

[10] "The Political Economy of Import-Substituting Industrialization in Latin America," *Quarterly Journal of Economics*, 82 (February 1968), reprinted in my *A Bias for Hope: Essays on Development and Latin America* (New Haven: Yale University Press, 1971), p. 100.

[11] Guillermo O'Donnell, "Reflexiones sobre las tendencias generales de cambio en el Estado burocrático-autoritario," CEDES Document No. 1, Buenos Aires, August 1975 (mimeo). A somewhat different English version was published in *The Latin American Research Review* 13, No. 1 (1978), pp. 3-38.

term investment planning. O'Donnell connects the "higher" phase of industrialization in which intermediate inputs and capital goods are to be produced with a greater need for predictability. But it is obvious that some degree of predictability is needed for any sort of development in countries where a large portion of savings, investment, and production decisions are made by private economic agents. To the extent, then, that O'Donnell identifies the lack of minimal predictability of economic policy as an important factor in the retardation of development and in the establishment of authoritarian regimes, he invites us to seek out the reasons for this lack—something that, coming from a rather different perspective, I have attempted to do here.

Perhaps I can claim by now that my recent absorption in seventeenth- and eighteenth-century thought was not entirely a matter of escaping from an unpleasant reality. That expedition into the ideological past has yielded at least one contribution to the understanding of Latin America's turn toward authoritarianism. It has led me to stress the low propensity of the policy makers to defer to *normal* economic constraints. This is in contrast to the more common explanations, which have emphasized the *unusually* difficult economic tasks that were encountered. But I certainly do not wish to imply that the latter explanations are all wrong. In fact, a discussion along the lines of the traditional explanations will occupy the larger part of this essay. Toward its end, I shall return briefly to the argument just presented.

I. ECONOMIC ARGUMENTS: SPECIFIC EXIGENCIES OF INDUSTRIALIZATION AS DETERMINANTS OF AUTHORITARIANISM

The "Deepening" Conjecture of O'Donnell

Over a century after Marx, the *general* proposition that important political change can best be explained by economic factors is neither particularly novel nor wholly convincing. Nevertheless, considerable intellectual excitement is still apt to be generated—quite legitimately so—when a *specific* turn of the political tide is shown or alleged to originate in a *precise* feature of the underlying economic terrain. Guillermo O'Donnell's just-mentioned paper is a good example. Its principal thesis is that the emergence of authoritarian regimes in the major Latin American countries since the 1960's is largely, if indirectly, due to the difficulties of "deepening" (*profundización*) that are apt to beset the industrialization process. "Deepening" is defined as the putting into place, through backward linkage, of the intermediate input and capital goods industries once the "last-stage" industries turning out consumption or final demand goods are established.[12] Written in 1974-1975 and presented to a variety of audiences in the course of 1975, this thesis succeeded in dominating the discussion within a very short span of time. Naturally, the intellectual terrain was well prepared for the O'Donnell thesis by the notion of "exhaustion of import substitution," a phrase that had been more or less current in economic discussions for over ten years.[13] It took only one further step to relate the alleged difficulties of import-substituting industrialization (ISI) in Latin America to the rise, in several countries, of authoritarian regimes. The bare bones of the idea can indeed be found elsewhere, without much explanation and as though it needed none.[14] But O'Donnell's formulation, which he had foreshadowed in his earlier work,[15] was particularly rich, timely and persuasive.

Since I have been a participant in the debate on the industrialization process, I naturally have some feelings about the O'Donnell thesis.[16] These feelings are ambivalent. What is worse, I now realize that my own writings have been ambiguous.

[12] I shall use "deepening" throughout this paper as a translation of O'Donnell's "profundización." Economists should be put on notice that the meaning of "deepening" in O'Donnell's sense is distinct from that of "capital deepening," which refers to an expansion of production achieved in conjunction with an increase in the capital-labor ratio, in contrast to "capital widening," which achieves such an expansion without stepping up capital intensity.

[13] That is, at least since the well-known article of Maria da Conceição Tavares on "Rise and Decline of Import Substitution in Brazil," *Economic Bulletin for Latin America*, 9 (March 1964), pp. 1-65.

[14] A good example is Celso Lafer's analysis of the Brazilian political system, where the "exhaustion of the import-substitution model" is invoked several times to explain the crisis of the "populist republic" and the installation of a new political regime. See Lafer, *O sistema político brasileiro* (São Paulo: Perspectiva, 1975), pp. 69, 76.

[15] Already in his *Modernización y autoritarismo* (Buenos Aires: Paidós, 1972), pp. 170 ff., O'Donnell related the difficulties of achieving "vertical integration" and of establishing "basic industries" to the trend toward authoritarianism.

[16] O'Donnell generously refers to my work at the start of his own inquiry, "Reflexiones," p. 11. My article "The Political Economy," built on Chapters 6 and 7 of *The Strategy of Economic Development* (New Haven: Yale University Press,

On the one hand, the central purpose of my 1968 article was
to question the notion of "exhaustion" of ISI. I therefore have
an immediate critical reaction to a thesis which attributes a most
momentous political outcome to an economic phenomenon
about whose very existence I tried to raise some doubts.

Yet, while arguing that ISI was not necessarily bound to grind
to a halt all over Latin America in the absence of profound structural change, I also pointed out: (a) that industrialization in
Latin America was more of a sequential, "tightly staged" affair
than it had been among the earlier industrializers; (b) that there
are a number of resistances to the backward linkage dynamic,
that is, to "deepening" (as well as several ways of overcoming
them); and (c) that there is such a thing as an "exuberant" or
"particularly easy phase of import substitution when the manufacturing process is entirely based on imported materials and
machinery while importation of the article is firmly and effectively shut out by controls."[17]

Jointly, these observations could lend support to the idea that
the deepening of industrial structure in the direction of intermediate inputs and capital goods represented some crucial
threshold after all.

I have now bared the intimate reasons for which I may either
like or dislike the O'Donnell thesis. But the question is obviously
not whether the thesis conforms to ideas and opinions previously expressed by me, but whether it is true or false; or, more
modestly, whether it is a sustainable generalization considering
the historical evidence so far before us.

Attempts to answer that crucial question are made elsewhere
in this book by Robert Kaufman and José Serra. Their work
raises doubts about the empirical foundation of O'Donnell's
thesis with respect to crucial countries such as Brazil and Chile.
Only in Argentina is it at all plausible that difficulties of deepening the industrial structure, and the need to do so by bringing in
complex foreign technology through multinational firms, have
been experienced as real problems before the first, unsuccessful

---

1958; New York: Norton, 1978) and the concepts of backward and forward linkages there introduced. Further thoughts are in my recent paper "A Generalized
Linkage Approach to Development, with Special Reference to Staples," in *Economic Development and Cultural Change*, 1977, Supplement (Essays in Honor of
Bert F. Hoselitz), pp. 67-98.

[17] *Bias*, p. 99.

(Onganía) attempt in 1966 to implant an authoritarian regime.[18] But similar correspondences are difficult to establish elsewhere.

It appears, therefore, that O'Donnell's attempt to explain political developments on the basis of economic phenomena is running into trouble. His thesis must be either discarded or reformulated. I would like to advocate the second course: O'Donnell's search should be widened rather than abandoned. As everyone knows, purely political factors, and in particular the reactions to the Cuban revolution—the "great fear" of the Latin American ruling groups, the spread of guerrilla tactics on the Left, and the determination of the United States to prevent a "second Cuba"—have contributed mightily to the installation of authoritarian regimes in one Latin American country after another since 1958. Nevertheless, the quest for economic development has been so dominant a theme during the last thirty years throughout Latin America that the existence of a systematic connection between the course of this quest—its successes and disappointments, on the one hand, and major political trends, on the other—has an inherent intellectual appeal. The reason for the wide acceptance of O'Donnell's thesis is precisely that appeal. I shall now discuss some alternative ways of establishing such a connection.

But first a methodological point. To establish the connection of some puzzling events—say, regime change in the authoritarian direction in a number of countries—to some underlying causal factor, such as the difficulty of "deepening" the productive structure, it is not enough to show that the latter systematically preceded the various regime changes. There is a need to demonstrate a plausible, meaningful connection between the two series of events. In the case at issue here, this need is particularly strong because, as a result of the Marxian thinking of our time, the appeal to economic causes for non-economic phenomena carries an excessive aura of a priori plausibility. O'Donnell is clearly aware of these matters: he does not tie the installation of authoritarian regimes directly to the "exhaustion" of ISI, as is

[18] In Chapters 14 and 15 of his well-known book *La economía argentina* (Mexico-Buenos Aires: Fondo de Cultura Económica), first published in 1963, Aldo Ferrer spoke of the "lack of integration" of Argentine industry as one of the major obstacles to a satisfactory growth experience for the country. The meaning of Ferrer's "industrial integration" is very close to that of O'Donnell's "deepening."

done in the more "vulgar" presentations. Instead, he brings in as an intermediate link of the causal chain the already mentioned lack of and need for predictability. At one point, moreover, he attempts to show that his cause became an actual motive for the actors by affirming that the various military coups proceeded (a) from an understanding that the political and social disturbances which had to be quelled were in part caused by the recurring inflationary and balance-of-payments crises; *and* (b) from the awareness that these crises in turn derived from the lack of vertical integration of national industrial structures.[19] The fact that this sort of statement came under O'Donnell's pen shows that he felt—quite appropriately—the need to prove his thesis by more than just establishing the existence of a temporal sequence leading from his alleged cause to the establishment of authoritarian regimes.

Now proposition (a) is certainly correct: high inflation rates and recurrent balance-of-payments crises are widely understood as both symptoms and propellents of sociopolitical disintegration; perhaps the policy and coup makers traced these ills even farther, but if they did so they could not have attributed them to the lack of a deepening process that did not even exist as a problem in a number of the countries in question.

This is a good point of departure for the previously announced effort to widen the O'Donnell search. If the deepening thesis does not hold, is there anything, within the sphere of economic development, that can be put in its place? Which, if any, are the economic problems and the ideologies through which such problems were interpreted that have, directly or indirectly, made a number of countries "ripe" for the installation of authoritarian regimes? If the question is asked in this form, one is inquiring both about economic problems as such and about the way in which they have impinged on the consciousness of various social and political groups. In the following I shall touch on both these matters.

The Transition to More Orthodox Economic Policies

There does exist a serious alternative candidate for the role that O'Donnell has attributed to deepening. This is the need for a set of more orthodox economic policies after ISI has been pur-

[19] "Reflexiones," p. 16.

sued for some time through the well-known, but quite unorthodox, combination of inflation, overvaluation of the currency,
tight quantitative import controls, and some foreign finance in
the form of both aid and private capital.[20] As has often been
pointed out, this combination of policies had the virtue of
achieving a transfer of income from traditional exporters of
primary products to the expanding industrial sector, and of
doing so indirectly, even deviously, without actually taxing the
exporters. From the point of view of the state, the arrangement
worked better and longer in some countries (such as Brazil) than
in others (such as Argentina), largely because the ability of the
traditional exporters to fight back by shifting into non-penalized
activities differed considerably from country to country—that
ability was much greater for breeders of cattle in Argentina than
for growers of coffee in Brazil and Colombia, for the simple reason that cattle, unlike coffee trees, can be slaughtered, where-
upon the proceeds from their sale can be invested in non-
penalized activities.[21] But eventually this particular pattern of
promoting industrialization ran into trouble everywhere because one or another of the several conditions essential for the
functioning of the pattern as a whole came to falter: traditional
exports lost ground (some sooner and some later, as just noted);
inflation proved difficult to keep within reasonable bounds; resources that had originally been devoted to industrialization
were diverted to other purposes (e.g., building of Brasilia); and,
partly as a result of these various developments, the providers of
foreign capital and aid became skittish.

The slowing down of industrialization that occurred in various countries at different times during the 1950's and 1960's was
occasioned more by such difficulties than by any "exhaustion" of

[20] In the English literature, the two phases have frequently been labeled
"outward-looking" and "inward-looking," respectively. I dislike this terminology
because of the positive value judgment "outward-looking" carries in comparison
to the supposedly deleterious "inward-looking" phase (note that in Spanish *desarrollo hacia adentro* has a positive connotation because, instead of autarchy and
introversion, it evokes the image of opening up the interior and the domestic
market). My own value judgments about these two phases will become apparent
in the course of the next few pages. But, quite apart from this point, "outward-
looking" refers only to one aspect of the new policies, that is exchange rates,
tariffs, etc., and disregards the new fiscal and interest-rate policies that can be
just as important.

[21] See *Bias*, pp. 11-12, for an elaboration of this point.

ISI, that is, by some intrinsic barrier to further industrial expansion. What happened was that ISI was carried forward under an institutional pattern which at one time represented a brilliant social invention to get around structural obstacles, such as the difficulty of directly taxing the exporters of primary products and the weakness of the domestic bourgeoisie. As frequently happens, the invention was the more brilliant the less conscious or planned it was—that is, during its first phases—and lost in efficacy soon after policy makers realized what had been happening. As in the myths that demonstrate the dangers of wresting secrets from the gods, the policy makers abused their newly discovered knowledge and applied to excess the magic formula that had paid such handsome early dividends.[22]

Moreover, while the original institutional pattern for the promotion of ISI declined in effectiveness, a number of new opportunities arose as a result of the intervening industrialization, though they went often unnoticed for a considerable time. With the world economy in rapid expansion, export possibilities emerged for some of the new manufactures (as well as for non-traditional primary products), but they were hidden from view by the overvalued exchange rate which made domestic prices appear non-competitive.[23] Secondly, industrial investment could increasingly be financed out of the profits earned by the new industries, so that the intersectoral transfers that had originally served this purpose became dispensable. Finally, and particularly in the larger countries, industrialization and the expansion of the domestic market laid the economic basis for broadening income taxation, and for borrowing by the state and state agencies from an incipient capital market.

As a result of these new developments and opportunities it actually became promising to dispense with the deteriorating original pattern for the promotion of ISI. This meant the establishment and maintenance of a non-overvalued exchange rate, combined with greater reliance on direct taxation for public ex-

[22] See, for example, "The Goldfish" in *Russian Fairy Tales* collected by A. Afanas'ev (New York: Pantheon, 1973), pp. 528-32.

[23] Marcelo Diamand and Daniel Schydlowsky have called attention to this situation. See Diamand, *Doctrinas económicas, desarrollo e independencia* (Buenos Aires: Paidos, 1973), Chapters 10 and 11; Schydlowsky, "Latin American Trade Policies in the Seventies: A Prospective Appraisal," *Quarterly Journal of Economics* 86 (May 1972).

penditures, on realistic prices for public services, and on capital markets, rather than on inflationary finance and profits from foreign exchange operations.

This sort of transition to a more orthodox, market-oriented set of policies—in the following I shall on occasion just use the term "transition"—was by no means easy to achieve, because of a large number of vested interests that had a stake in the old arrangements. In some cases, in Latin America and elsewhere, the transition came about in a discontinuous way, by combining devaluation with the rapid dismantling of certain exchange controls as well as through enactment, within a brief span of time, of various reforms in the fields of taxation, public service pricing, and capital markets. Because of these characteristics of the transition—opposition to it from various powerful quarters and possible need for discontinuous policy decisions—it *seems* an excellent candidate for taking the place of "deepening" as the underlying economic problem that led to the installation of authoritarian regimes.

Before this hypothesis is considered, it is of interest to examine how it differs from the O'Donnell conjecture. In "Reflexiones . . ." O'Donnell speaks repeatedly of the need for exports of manufactures, as though such exports were part and parcel of "deepening" (for example, p. 17). But this is hardly legitimate, at least without a great deal of further explanation. The turn toward exports of manufactures means first of all that some *existing* industries acquire new outlets for their products—it represents widening rather than deepening. And, as Serra shows, this widening took place in Brazil *after* the advent of authoritarianism, along with an increase in the import coefficient for a number of basic industrial products, that is, just the opposite of deepening. Finally, the transition I have been talking about involves a number of other policies besides export promotion, and these other policies—tax and capital market reform, among others—have once again very little to do with deepening.

From one point of view it can nevertheless be argued that deepening and the export of manufactures are closely related: an overvalued exchange rate penalizes not only export of manufactures but also the backward linkage or deepening process. The reason is simple. Overvaluation of the domestic currency means that what imports are let in by the control machinery carry an attractively low price tag. With imports of capital goods being given priority in the allocation of scarce foreign exchange, the low domestic cost of imported machinery is apt to act as a deterrent to the domestic manufacture of capital goods, just as overvaluation discourages exports. The establishment of a realistic exchange rate can therefore be important for the development, in due course, of a domestic capital goods industry. But this is an unintended (and usually much delayed) *effect* of the transition.

The economic problems and resulting turning point in economic policy here delineated become even more distinct from deepening once ideological matters are taken into account. As was mentioned earlier the economic problems of which the "policy and coup makers" were most conscious were, first, inflation and, second, balance-of-payments disequilibrium, especially when foreign exchange reserves were threatening to run out. Those who have been responsible for turning Latin American politics in the authoritarian direction, partly under the impact of these twin crises, had some notions about the political and economic problems that were in turn responsible for the immediate emergency. But, as far as I am aware, the lack of deepening played only a very minor, if any, role in such notions except perhaps, once again, in Argentina.

Inflation was first of all attributed to the incompetence, profligacy, and incapacity to resist populist pressures of the pre-coup governments. But a belief in deeper, more "structural" factors was also at work. In all authoritarian regimes the top economic policy-making positions were first occupied by a certain type of person—one who professed a greater trust in market forces and who denounced, and set out to correct, some of the more serious distortions in relative prices that were the usual legacy of inflation, particularly with regard to exchange, interest, and public utility rates. The ideological influence to which these policy makers were primarily responding was an anti-planning, anti-ISI, and anti-ECLA backlash. As is well known, the most absolutist component of this movement was a group of Latin American economists who had received graduate training at the University of Chicago, in whose department of economics strict neo-laissez-faire views had long been dominant.

But other, seemingly less doctrinaire, influences worked in the same direction. In the middle to late 1960's, the policies that had served to promote ISI were criticized in detail by a group of economists, primarily from the developed countries and with the influential support of such organizations as the Brookings Institution, the World Bank, and the Organization for Economic Cooperation and Development.[24] The principal technical concept developed in these various reports, accompanied by a large outpouring of articles in the professional journals, was that of the "effective protection rate," which can differ substantially from the nominal rate defined by customs duties.[25] By relating the duty to value added rather than to the total value of the protected article, the effective rate expresses the *actual* protection granted by customs duties to the local producer—that is, the extent to which the costs of his own manufacturing operation may exceed world competitive standards. Given the typical phasing of industrialization in the developing countries, with import substitution of consumer goods occurring long before that of intermediate and capital goods, which were imported and paid low duties, the effective protection rates for consumer goods in these countries were often a multiple of the already high nominal rates.

There are two principal ways of bringing down the effective rate: one is to slash the nominal rates on domestically produced consumer goods; the other is to *increase* the rates on intermediate inputs and machinery—as long as these goods are not produced locally but are needed by domestic industry, they usually pay low or zero rates. An increase in such rates is a foregone conclusion once domestic production of these items gets under-

[24] See Harry G. Johnson, *Economic Policies Toward Less Developed Countries* (Washington, D.C.: Brookings, 1967). This book was written as a critical analysis of the first UNCTAD conference in 1964. The OECD sponsored a large multi-country research project on industrialization and trade policies covering Brazil, India, Mexico, Pakistan, the Philippines, and Taiwan. The principal outcome of the project was *Industry and Trade in Some Developing Countries* by Ian Little, Tibor Scitovsky, and Maurice Scott (published for the OECD by Oxford University Press in 1970). This general report was often far more critical of ISI than the country studies on which it was supposed to be based. This is particularly evident when it is compared with the study by Joel Bergsman, *Brazil: Industrialization and Trade Policies* (OECD-Oxford University Press, 1970). Another large-scale study, sponsored by the World Bank and the Inter-American Development Bank, is by Bela Balassa and Associates, *The Structure of Protection in Developing Countries* (Baltimore: The Johns Hopkins University Press, 1971).

[25] The actual calculation of effective rates required input-output statistics which by the mid-1960's were becoming available for a number of developing countries.

way. Deepening of the industrial structure is thus another way
of bringing down effective protection rates. It is, to be sure,
more roundabout than the straightforward cutting of nominal
rates. Nevertheless, one might have expected at least some of the
numerous publications on the subject to pay attention to it. But,
except for an important early article that did make the point,[26]
no such suggestion can be found, and the whole weight of the
criticism of ISI was in one direction only: if you want to reduce
the allocative inefficiences (including such horrors as "negative
value added") resulting from high levels of effective protection,
you must reduce your nominal rates. Through this unilateral
policy advice, the effective protection literature revealed its anti-
industrialization bias. It also becomes apparent that deepening
was not part of the ideological climate that prepared the ground
for transition policies: logically the effective protection analysts
should have recommended, at least occasionally, deepening of
the industrial structure, but they never did so because such a
recommendation did not fit their ideological premises and intent. Quite clearly, that literature attacked industrialization, not
because it had accomplished too little, but because it was thought
to have been carried too far.

Is it, then, in order to proclaim that the rise of authoritarian
regimes in Latin America was linked to the need for accomplish-
ing, at a certain phase, the transition to a set of more orthodox
economic policies? At first sight, this explanation seems in line
both with some of the observed facts and with the declarations
and ideologies of the policy makers. In fact, the authoritarian
governments that have come to power have often adopted the
new set of policies with considerable fanfare and have stuck to
them with extraordinary obstinacy even when they were far
from successful. In this way the impression has been created that
it takes an authoritarian government to accomplish the transition. On a closer look, however, considerable doubts arise on this
score.

The fact is that in various cases the transition has been or is
being achieved without the presence of an authoritarian regime.
Colombia is perhaps the clearest illustration. Here, a number of
measures typical of the transition have been taken. First export

[26] See Max Corden, "The Structure of a Tariff System and the Effective Protection Rate," *Journal of Political Economy*, 74 (June 1966), p. 229.

subsidies and later mini-devaluations have successfully promoted new agricultural and industrial exports; the average level
of protection has been lowered; interest rates have been raised
substantially, so that the bulk of credit transactions no longer
takes place at negative real interest rates; and a substantial income tax reform has been enacted. All of this occurred without
the prior establishment of an authoritarian regime. In pre-
Allende Chile, similarly, transition policies, particularly with respect to the establishment of more realistic exchange rates
through mini-devaluations and export subsidies, made their appearance in the 1960's, during the Frei Administration. Brazil is
obviously the country whose recent history best fits the hypothesis that it takes an authoritarian regime to accomplish the transition. But this is so only, it now appears, because authoritarianism
came so early to Brazil. Policies which look in Brazil as though
they are due to the regime change that took place in 1964 were
subsequently adopted elsewhere under diverse political auspices.

Accelerating Industrial Growth through
Increased Income Inequality[27]

I shall deal briefly with a third possible connection between
economic development and the installation of authoritarian regimes. It can be pieced together from a number of writings,
mostly by Brazilian authors.[28] Put as succinctly as possible, here
is the thesis: when industrializing countries with the income distribution typical of Latin America move into the phase of stressing the domestic manufacture of automobiles and other durable
consumer goods, their politics is likely to move in the authoritarian and repressive direction.

That sectoral patterns of growth have some relation to the nature of the political regime is not really a new idea. The following statement, for example, sounds both familiar and plausible:
a government that wishes to pour all of its investment resources
into armaments and capital goods for heavy industry must keep
consumption down and is therefore likely to be more repressive
than a government that lets part of the economy's growth take
the form of increased consumption. This sort of reasoning has

---

[27] This subsection has been added in response to a suggestion from José Serra.

[28] Parts of the argument are due to Celso Furtado's *Análise do "Modelo"
brasileiro* (Rio de Janeiro: Civilização brasileira, 1972).

often been used in explaining the maintenance of authoritarian policies in the Soviet Union; and, at one time, many analysts tied the prospects for political liberalization in that country to changes in economic policies that would favor the long-delayed expansion of consumer goods industries. Events have not precisely confirmed these conjectures, as more consumer goods are now being produced in the Soviet Union, while the authoritarian nature of the Soviet regime is not noticeably on the wane. As a result, not too much has been heard along these lines lately.

For Latin America, an interesting variant of the idea has been proposed. Here it is not the compression of aggregate consumption, designed to make room for an expansion of the capital goods sector, that is held responsible for repressive and authoritarian politics. Rather, the accent is on the *uneven expansion of consumption*, uneven with respect to both kinds of articles and categories of consumers.

The argument goes about as follows. At one stage of Western-style industrial development, the easiest way to foster rapid growth is through an expansion of the automobile and consumer durable industries, with the latter being aided by a boom in the construction of middle- and upper-income housing, which can itself make a fine contribution to overall growth. As long as it is primarily oriented to the domestic market, this sort of expansion can take place only if there is an adequate bloc of middle- and upper-income receivers who will want to sustain the consumer durables (and housing) boom through new purchases. Since only the better-off people are in a position to acquire the automobiles, houses, or apartments, and many of the consumer durables, the increase in income that comes with economic expansion must be channeled to them. The poorer sections are at a hopeless distance from being customers of the expanding industries and would merely "waste" any increased earnings on rice and beans; their income must therefore be kept from increasing, the more so as the latter items are in inelastic supply. But in order to achieve that sort of consumption profile (also designated as "excluding and concentrating development"—*desarrollo excluyente y concentrador*), political repression and authoritarianism are required.

There is something intriguing about these propositions. But two critical observations are immediately in order:

1. None of Latin America's authoritarian regimes were estab-

lished *in order to* pursue the growth strategy that has just been outlined. As with deepening, the idea of that sort of strategy never became an actual motive for the generals and politicians who ushered in those regimes.

2. As in the case of the transition to more orthodox policies, booms or boomlets of automobile and consumer durable industries have taken place in a number of Latin American countries over the past twenty years or so, before as well as after the establishment of authoritarian regimes and also in their total absence.

The argument just presented has nevertheless its convincing side, for it describes rather well what has been going on for a number of years in Brazil, the country with the most spectacular boom in automobile and consumer durable production. From the mid-1960's to about 1973, Brazilian economic policy has indeed funneled massive amounts of consumer credit for automobile and consumer durable purchases to anyone who could claim to be a serious customer, has widened wage and salary differentials, and has held down wages at the low end of the scale, at least until 1974. It is likely that these policies could not have been pursued so consistently in the absence of a "strong" government.

What we have here, therefore, is not an economic explanation of authoritarianism, but a political explanation of a turn in Brazilian economic development: prior existence of an authoritarian government facilitated the shaping of economic policy strongly oriented toward the expansion of a special category of consumption. Much else could be said about the economic and economic-policy *consequences* of authoritarian regimes, but this does not happen to be the subject of the present essay, which deals with their economic *determinants*.

II. Stress on Ideology: An Overdose of Proposed Problems?

Having found fault with O'Donnell's "deepening" conjecture and also with the two alternative hypotheses, am I returning empty-handed from the expedition of the preceding section? I do not think so. Rather, on the basis of that expedition, it is possible to suggest that the relationship between unsolved economic problems and regime change is of a somewhat different nature. The search for a single, specific structural economic difficulty underlying the rise of authoritarianism in Latin America seems

to me unpromising. But there is obviously a relationship between the rise of authoritarian regimes and the generalized consciousness that the country is facing serious economic problems
(which may differ from country to country) without being able to
solve them.[29] The greater and more widespread the feeling of
incapacity to solve problems, the greater will be the propensity
to undertake regime change as well as the readiness on the part
of large groups to accept and perhaps hail it. And the greater
the number of real or alleged unsolved problems at the moment
of the establishment of an authoritarian government, the
greater will be the temptation and justification for that government to install itself in power for a long period of time, and the
greater are the chances for such a government to legitimate itself, provided some of these problems are capable of being
solved or ameliorated. If the matter is put in this general way, it
is possible to salvage something from the various hypotheses
that have been examined. Awareness of the problems of deepening, say in Argentina, and of transition, say in Brazil, may well
have contributed in both countries to the regime change in the
authoritarian direction and even more to the determination of
the new authoritarian regimes to stay in power and to their potential for legitimization. But with this formulation our inquiry
changes in nature, as attention is focused not so much on the
hidden problems to be detected by the penetrating eye of some
social scientist as on the tasks that are *openly* and loudly proposed
to a society by influential spokesmen from within or without.

This leads me in a new direction. Often it is taken for granted
that there is some strict proportionality between the problems a
society experiences and the problems proposed to it by its intellectuals, policy makers, and other influentials. But this assumption can be questioned. It is conceivable for the articulation of
problems and the elaboration of proposals for their solution to
increase at times quite independently of what actually goes on in
economy and society. Such an autonomous increase in prob-
lem-and-solution proposing could obviously have important
political consequences, and I am now going to argue, as an an-

---

[29] The process through which some state of affairs comes to be defined as a
problem that ought to be solved or ameliorated by public policy is discussed in my
Journeys Toward Progress: Studies of Economic Policy-Making in Latin America (New
York: Twentieth Century Fund, 1963, and The Norton Library, 1973),
pp. 229-38.

tithesis to the preceding section, that a phenomenon of this sort was strikingly in evidence in Latin America during the past decades.

Some years ago I professed to see considerable value in the structuralist school of thought in Latin America and in its search for the "deep" problems—such as certain land tenure conditions—that were believed to underlie the surface problems of inflation and balance-of-payments disequilibrium. My argument was that in this way the surface problem acts like a searchlight and helps in the early detection of social ills that, if neglected for too long, might be much more difficult to cure. From the point of view of the present essay it appears, however, that the structuralist strategy of problem solving can be and probably has been overdone: in recent decades Latin American societies have been subjected to an unceasing and unprecedented barrage of proposed structural reforms. It is as though the inflation of the price level has produced in the ideological realm an inflation in the generation of "fundamental remedies." When the policies that are thus proposed are considerably beyond the capabilities of a society, a pervasive feeling of frustration is easily generated.

We are dealing here with the counterpart of the remarkable ferment, excitement, and creativity that has been so notable a feature of the Latin American intellectual scene during the last thirty years. It was in this period that Latin American social science, while not quite achieving the triumphs of contemporary Latin American literature, gained wide recognition for its vitality. New ideas were constantly generated and often became dominant themes in international discussions. The outstanding contribution of Latin Americans to the analysis of the problems of the poorer countries was recognized, for example, in the nomination of Raúl Prebisch as first Secretary of the United Nations Conference on Trade and Development (UNCTAD).

But there was a counterpart to these achievements that can only now be perceived in retrospect, somewhat similar in nature to that of other such periods of intellectual ferment, from the French Enlightenment to the extraordinary cultural flowering in Vienna at the turn of the nineteenth to the twentieth century. This counterpart was the frustration resulting from the widening gulf between the reality of Latin American societies and the tasks proposed to them.

As we look back at the sequence of these tasks, it appears that they were proposed in order of increasing difficulty. The task proclaimed a few years after World War II was industrialization, when efforts in this direction were already well underway. As an ongoing activity, industrialization was an undertaking clearly within the reach of Latin American societies. But this relatively easy task was soon supplemented, in the 1950's, by the call for planning; it came not only from ECLA but, powerfully backed by loanable funds, from such unimpeachable "establishment" quarters as the World Bank. Planning for economic development was supposed to set targets for the economy as a whole and for the balanced growth of its various sectors, and to indicate how these targets could be achieved by coordinated investment on behalf of both the public and the private sector. This was a more complex undertaking and one that went against the grain of much of the institutional structure of Latin American government and society.[30] Attempts to set up planning agencies and to produce planning documents were duly made in many countries, but the extent to which these efforts had any bearing on the course of governmental action and of economic development differed widely among countries and fluctuated wildly from one period to another, even within those countries where there was an impact. Strangely, the planning agencies which had been set up to impart greater stability to governmental action in the economic field were themselves subject to considerable instability, swinging from hectic bursts of activity and real influence to near total somnolence and impotence. Eventually a certain consolidation of the new bureaucratic structures was achieved; but their accomplishments were decidedly modest in comparison with the ambitious notions which had inspired their creation.

The next task to be proclaimed—in the early 1960's—was for a yet more ambitious undertaking: the economic integration of the various Latin American economies. Plausibly enough, it was pointed out that efficient and full industrial development could not be achieved by the Latin American countries in isolation because of limited markets and economies of scale. Enormous intergovernmental negotiations were launched, and full-fledged

[30] See, in this connection, the papers submitted to a conference organized by the Latin American Institute for Economic and Social Planning (ILPES) and the Sociedad de Estudios Colombianos in Bogotá, June 10-12, 1976, on the political aspects of economic planning in Latin America (to be published).

international machineries and bureaucracies were established. The framers of the agreements were not satisfied with the goal of a customs union, but felt that, because of differences between Latin America and Western Europe, it was imperative to attempt the difficult task of apportioning industries to various countries on a complementary basis. Ten to fifteen years later, the various efforts that were undertaken—the Central American Common Market, the Latin American Free Trade Association, and the Andean Pact—had very unequal achievements to their credit, but all of them had fallen far short of their original goals.

Roughly speaking, the tasks of industrialization, planning, and integration can be considered as comparatively "non-antagonistic." As policy goals, they do not explicitly threaten any important class or sector of society, and can be presented as being in the long-run interest of all. But having made an increasingly poor showing at these successively proclaimed tasks, Latin America was summoned by its intellectuals in the middle and late 1960's to do battle on the terrain of *antagonistic* tasks that involved quite another order of difficulty: now it was widely proclaimed, in a final escalation, that Latin America must solve its problems by redistributing wealth and income domestically and by overcoming "dependence," that is, by reordering its international economic relations in what could only be a conflictive process with the major powers, and particularly with the United States. Unsurprisingly, the response to this latest, most demanding, call to action has not been overly impressive.

An ancient myth must be appealed to once again, this time to convey how odd the process just described really was. Everyone is familiar with the story of the wanderer or pretender to the hand of the king's daughter who is given increasingly difficult questions to answer or increasingly complex tasks to accomplish before he is granted access to the coveted prize. In these stories, the easier questions must be *solved* before the next more difficult question is posed. In Latin America, on the other hand, new, more difficult tasks were continuously presented to the state and society *whether or not* the previous task had been successfully disposed of. Indeed it would almost seem that the less satisfactorily a previous task had been grappled with, the bigger was the jump in difficulty of the next task and the sooner was it introduced.

This strange process of ideological escalation may well have contributed to that pervasive sense of being in a desperate predicament which is a precondition for radical regime change. Some Latin American countries were more exposed to this sense than others during the recent past. Among the larger ones, Colombia and Venezuela were probably least affected by the ideological climate just described. In Colombia, there is a tradition of self-conscious intellectual isolation from outside ideological currents and a conviction that the country's problems can somehow be handled by home-grown, savvy members of the country's political elite. Venezuela, with its petroleum wealth, was evidently a special case and ideas elaborated in countries (and by citizens of countries) permanently subject to inflationary and balance of payments pressures were here prima facie suspect.[31] Interestingly, these two countries are also the ones that have so far proved most resistant to the authoritarian wave.

It is with some reluctance that I have put forward the thoughts of the preceding pages, if only because they may offend some of my closest friends. Nevertheless, when a series of disastrous events strikes the body politic, everyone's responsibility must be looked at, including that of the intellectuals. Having done just that, I must promptly add some caveats. To begin with, it is not easy to say what, if any, policy conclusions should be drawn in consequence. Obviously it would be folly to wish that the flowering of Latin American social thought of recent decades had not taken place, because this thought may have contributed to an ideological climate of frustration which in turn may bear some responsibility for certain deplorable political events. In other words, it would be ludicrous to draw the conclusion that intellectuals should stop being intellectuals and refrain from analyzing the problems of their countries. One might suggest, however, that they ought to be more fully aware of their responsibility, which is the greater because of the considerable authority they are apt to wield in their countries. Because of this authority, the process that in the realm of science and technology is known as the protracted sequence from invention to innovation often takes remarkably little time in Latin America

[31] It is perhaps significant in this connection that the ECLA group of political economists who gathered around Raúl Prebisch and elaborated the various ECLA doctrines in the 1950's did not contain a single Colombian or Venezuelan of stature. For some remarks on the comparative isolation of Colombia from the currents of social science thinking in Latin America, see Francisco Leal Buitrago, "Desarrollo, subdesarrollo y ciencias sociales" in F. Leal Buitrago et al., *El agro en el desarrollo colombiano* (Bogotá: Punta de Lanza, 1977), pp. 27-28.

with respect to economic, social, and political ideas. With social thought turning so rapidly into attempted social engineering, a high incidence of failed experiments is the price that is often paid for the influence intellectuals wield.

My second caveat relates to the weight that ought to be given to the preceding observations. In stressing developments in the ideological realm, I have no wish to claim that they ought to wholly supersede those explanations of the turn to authoritarianism that focus on some soft spot in economic structure or policy. It seems likely, in fact, that behind the occurrence of the remarkable intellectual activity of the last decades there lurk in turn "real" economic and political factors that might be encompassed by a more general analysis. An attempt in this direction is made in the next and last section of this essay.

III. A More General Framework: The Entrepreneurial and Reform Functions and Their Interaction

The following notes are exploratory and fragmentary. Their intent is to suggest that the conceptual framework to be proposed has promise.

So as not to have to think up everything *ex nihilo*, I shall start out with the by now almost obvious-sounding observation that growth creates imbalances and inequalities. It does so in many dimensions: in *The Strategy of Economic Development* I had stressed the sectoral and geographical imbalances, but increasing social and income inequalities are an important part of this picture. In time, pressures will arise to correct some of these imbalances, both because the continuation of growth requires such correction at some point and because the imbalances bring with them social and political tensions, protest and action. This formulation leads immediately to the definition of the two principal tasks or functions that must be accomplished in the course of the growth process, and also, as will soon be apparent, to an appreciation of several typical ways in which the process as a whole may run into economic or political trouble.

The first of the two tasks is the unbalancing function, or the *entrepreneurial* function, or, as James O'Connor calls it in *The Fiscal Crisis of the State*,[32] the *accumulation* function. It can be per-

---

[32] New York: St. Martin's Press, 1973. For my definition of the disequilibrating and equilibrating functions, see the section "The Two Functions of Government" in *The Strategy of Economic Development*, pp. 202-05.

formed by private domestic enterprise, foreign capital, the state, or by any combination thereof. At some point after this function has had its run there will be efforts at catching up on the part of lagging sectors and regions, at social reforms to improve the welfare and position of groups that have been neglected or squeezed, and at redistribution of wealth and income in general. This is the "equilibrating," distributive, or *reform* function. Like the entrepreneurial function, it can be performed by different actors, that is, by the interested parties themselves through collective action or by the state ("reform from above").[33]

How well these two functions are performed and coordinated is crucial for both economic and political outcomes of the growth process. Some of the trouble that can arise is no doubt traceable to characteristics of the two functions taken in isolation.[34] But the present formulation intends to draw attention to their perhaps more crucial interaction.

From a somewhat Olympian point of view, it is easy to see that

[33] The term *legitimation function* used by O'Connor seems unnecessarily restrictive since it refers only to such performances of this function as are carried out by the state. Moreover, the term is misleading: it implies something about the objective which actors aim at when they engage in reform activity; quite often, however, nothing could be further from their minds than to seek "legitimation" for the state even when that is the outcome. And now a brief note on my own terminology: I chose *entrepreneurial function* in preference to *accumulation function* because, in talking about those who perform it, the term *entrepreneurs* is less awkward than *accumulators* (or *capitalists*), especially in a developmental context. As to the term *reform function* I chose it in preference to *distributive* (or *redistributive) function* because the latter, like O'Connor's legitimation function, implies that the state alone can perform it. The term *reform function* is not totally satisfactory to me, since it does not seem to include those corrective actions or policies that are designed to help a lagging economic sector catch up with the others in the process of growth. However, a more inclusive term, such as "corrective," would have been too flat. Also, the term *reform function* has the advantage that its performers can simply be referred to as "reformers." However, use of this term in the text is not meant to imply that these people are "reformists" in the sense of having foresworn any idea of revolution; to my mind, they include anyone determined to correct imbalances and inequities that have arisen in the course of growth, no matter what the consequences; in other words, they can be entrepreneurs, state agencies, reformists, reform-mongers, or revolutionaries.

[34] With respect to the entrepreneurial function (in isolation), see Fernando Henrique Cardoso, *Empresario industrial e desenvolvimento econômico* (São Paulo: Difusão Européia do Livro, 1964) and "The Industrial Elite" in S. M. Lipset and A. Solari, *Elites in Latin America* (New York: Oxford University Press, 1967), pp. 94-116. For case studies of the reform function (in isolation), see my *Journeys Toward Progress*.

the reform function has an essential role to play in making it possible for growth to be sustained after a powerful, yet disequilibrating, push by the entrepreneurs. This is borne out by the famous historical examples of comparatively successful reform experiences—such as the 1832 Reform Act in England, the New Deal in the United States, and the accomplishments of Lázaro Cárdenas in Mexico. But these examples also illustrate that, with the possible exception of sectoral imbalances,[35] those who are performing the entrepreneurial function are ordinarily not only unaware of the emerging need for complementary action but are often strongly opposed to the reform function being performed at all. That function, whether undertaken from below or above, has of course its own interested carriers, performers, or protagonists, but their appearance on the stage at the right time and with the right strength is not in any reliable fashion coordinated with the entrepreneurial function and its performance. In fact, while the performance of both functions (in some proper sequence) may be "objectively" essential for the growth process, their protagonists are more often than not determined adversaries, and perhaps must be just that up to a point if they are to accomplish their respective purposes.

I shall now try to spell out some characteristics of the entrepreneurial and reform functions in Latin America, and of their interplay, in comparison to the advanced industrial countries. Later some important differences among Latin American countries will be discussed.

Take, first, the strength of the entrepreneurial function. Here we are on fairly familiar terrain. That strength depends both on the pull of opportunities for profitable investment and on the push of ideological forces. For the European latecomers the powerful impetus of ideology, with its borrowings from diverse sources such as Saint-Simonism in France and Marxism in late-nineteenth-century Russia, has been memorably brought out by

---

[35] Sectoral imbalances come to the attention of entrepreneurs through emerging shortages and relative price rises and, if capital markets function properly, the manifestation of this kind of imbalance is the beginning of its cure, *with the participation in that cure of the entrepreneurs responsible for the imbalance*. With regard to regional disequilibrium, correction is less prompt and predictable and much more political. In the absence of strong, state-sponsored incentives, the imbalance is here unlikely to be redressed by those who caused it. What holds for regional disequilibrium applies even more strongly to social or income inequalities arising or widening in the course of growth.

Alexander Gerschenkron.[36] Moreover, the effort to build up industries with which one would then proceed to conquer leading positions in world markets for manufactures was often advocated, viewed, and sensed as part and parcel of the competition for national power; just as the desire to recoup such positions after a military defeat had overtones of a national crusade. While the loss of the northern provinces by Mexico and that of Panama by Colombia had a somewhat similar "mind-concentrating" impact on these two countries, the ideological forces propelling industrialization in Latin America were on the whole not nearly as potent. Finally, though, as a result of the Great Depression and then of World War II, there arose considerable unhappiness and soul-searching in Latin America about its economic role in the world. This travail culminated after the war in the Prebisch manifesto of 1949 and its call for industrialization. The subsequent calls for planning and integration can (with some qualification) be considered additional ideological props for industrial development. In Brazil, a particularly determined and temporarily successful attempt to fashion a national ideology for development and industrialization was spearheaded by Kubitschek and a number of his ideological, political, and institutional allies in the 1950's.

But now comes another peculiarity of the Latin American sequence: the postwar push for industrialization lasted a mere decade or so and was followed by a very different ideological phase during which pleas for redistribution predominated. What is most interesting is that these pleas came from essentially the same quarters which had issued the earlier calls for a vigorous assertion of the entrepreneurial function. These quarters had become convinced that development now required redistribution rather than continued accumulation along traditional lines.

The ideological forces behind the entrepreneurial function, then, were weaker in Latin America than in Europe. But from the point of view of political outcomes it is perhaps more important that in Latin America major intellectual voices which had at one time come out in support of the entrepreneurial function rallied soon thereafter behind the reform banner. The older

[36] *Economic Backwardness in Historical Perspective* (Cambridge, Mass.: Harvard University Press, 1962), pp. 22-26.

aims of development and industrialization were now denounced and the term *desarrollismo* ("developmentalism"), previously a badge of honor and progress, was strangely but effectively turned into a term of opprobrium![37] A number of reasons can no doubt be found for this reversal—a particularly important one was probably the leadership assumed by foreign capital in the course of the industrialization process. In any event, this sort of reversal has no counterpart in Europe or North America—at least not during the early stages of industrialization—where the support for the entrepreneurial function was far from evaporating when the reform function made its appearance. Here the two functions had distinct ideological constituencies. At most, as more recently with a certain type of Keynesianism, there was simultaneous support for both.

In Latin America the ideological mutation just discussed—the withdrawal of intellectual support from one function and its shift to the other—was particularly evident in Chile, Argentina, and Brazil. Strongly entrenched social groups were left in these countries without any ideological fig leaf, an uncomfortable and perhaps precarious position. In this manner it may be possible to account for the readiness of these groups to use force, which served to make up, as it were, for the lost ideological support. For, as Rousseau pointed out long ago in his *Essay on the Origin*

---

[37] The same reversal can be noted with respect to industrialization, which, after a brief period of praise, was surrounded by terms that conveyed either contempt or impending trouble. A series of extravagant metaphors, with derogatory or pessimistic connotations, came into use. Again and again, industrialization is alleged to have reached an "impasse," to have come to a "dead end" (*callejón sin salida*), even a "chromium-plated (*cromado*) dead end," and is said to suffer from both "exhaustion" (*agotamiento*) and "strangulation" (*estrangulamiento externo*, a term routinely used for the balance-of-payments difficulties typically accompanying a strong industrial spurt). Take even "import-substituting industrialization," a term that is consecrated by now and sounds almost value-free. Obviously all industrializations, with the exception only of England's, were import-substituting to a degree. Why, then, was this term picked to characterize Latin America's industrialization? Could it be because it subtly downgrades that effort? A substitution or *Ersatz* is, as we all know, never quite as good as the real thing. Moreover, the term *import-substituting industrialization* implies, quite wrongly in the case of most newly established industries no matter which product they turn out, a total absence of creative adjustment and problem-solving.

It is worth noting that the criticism of ISI from within Latin America and from the Left came at about the same time as the criticism of "inward-looking industrialization" that originated primarily within the developed countries as reported above (pp. 71-77).

of Languages, force is a substitute for "eloquence" and "persuasion."[38]

Various points can be made about typical differences, among Latin American countries, with regard to our two functions and their interplay. It is apparent, for example, that the reform function appears at widely different dates and with very different lags behind the emergence of the entrepreneurial function.

An obvious way of beginning to account for these differences is to look at the ownership of the economic activities and resources that are shouldering the bulk of the entrepreneurial function. If that ownership is foreign, ideological support for the entrepreneurial function can be expected to be particularly weak, and demands for reforms and redistribution ought to be heard sooner and more powerfully than if ownership of the dynamic economic sector were in domestic hands. In Chile, for example, foreign ownership of the nitrate (and later copper) mines led to early demands on the part of middle-class groups for taxation of the foreign investors and for a consequent strengthening of the state apparatus.[39] On the other hand, an even earlier and more determined attempt at redistribution in the wake of export-led economic development took place in Uruguay, where important components of the dynamic economic sector (land, cattle, sheep) were owned by nationals. Moreover, in Venezuela, where the exploitation of petroleum resources was in foreign hands, the demand that arose, perhaps because of the temper of the times after World War II, was less for redistribution than for the state itself to take on or promote entrepreneurial functions that would complement or rival those of the foreigners. It is therefore necessary to look for additional criteria if the timing of reform tendencies in relation to entrepreneurial activities is to be understood.

In an attempt to appraise why there may be prolonged ideological support for the entrepreneurial function in a society,

[38] "In ancient times, when persuasion took the place of public force, eloquence was necessary. What would it be good for today when public force is substituted for persuasion?" (Chap. 20) Rousseau saw force driving out eloquence. But it is also possible that the departure of eloquence (that is, of ideological support) contributes to the bringing in of force. This remarkable passage was brought to my attention by Bento Prado, Jr. See his "O Discurso do Século e a Crítica de Rousseau" in *Almanaque*, 1 (1976), p. 12.

[39] See various writings of Aníbal Pinto, for example his *Tres ensayos sobre Chile y América Latina* (Buenos Aires: Solar, 1971), pp. 67 ff.

Gramsci's influential notion of hegemony comes to mind.[40] Gramsci affirmed that, up to the point when an effective counter-ideology takes over, the ideology of the ruling class permeates and shapes the world view of all other classes and groups of society, even that of the most exploited—herein, rather than in naked force, resides the essence of stable social and political arrangements. When the capitalists rule, hegemony would presumably be reflected by the fact that all classes of society support capitalist growth, even though that growth may favor some classes, groups, and regions far more than others. But why should this happen? For Gramsci, hegemony was an insight of great importance for revolutionary politics. But he rather tends to treat it as an axiom and, unlike Machiavelli with regard to the state, he does not tell us much about the processes through which hegemony is established, maintained, or lost.[41]

An attempt to look, from one particular vantage point, into some of these processes, is made in my article "The Changing Tolerance for Income Inequality in the Course of Economic Development."[42] I argued there that, during a first phase of rapid economic development, even those who are left behind will feel encouraged and will tend to support the existing order for a while because of the hope that their turn will surely come; and that this tolerance for inequality (the "tunnel effect") will last longest when those who are left behind are able to empathize with those who are moving ahead socially and economically. Thus tolerance will be comparatively short-lived and appearance of the reform function accordingly prompt in societies where economic progress is restricted to one particular group that is perceived by the rest as distinct and closed. This argument can account for the early appearance of the reform function in *both* Chile and Uruguay, since the group of large landowners in Uruguay who prospered during the period of

[40] A review of Gramsci's widely scattered notes and observations on this topic is in Thomas R. Bates, "Gramsci and the Theory of Hegemony," *Journal of the History of Ideas*, 36 (1975), pp. 351-66; see also Perry Anderson, "The Antinomies of Antonio Gramsci," *New Left Review* Number 100 (November 1976 to January 1977), pp. 5-80.

[41] To give an account of "how [states] are acquired, how they are maintained, and how they are lost" is Machiavelli's intent in the *Prince* as defined by himself in a famous letter to Francesco Vettori of December 10, 1513.

[42] *Quarterly Journal of Economics* 87, No. 4 (November 1973), pp. 543-66 (with a mathematical appendix by Michael Rothschild).

export-led growth were just as alien to the emerging urban middle class as the foreign mine owners in Chile.

I also argued that a shared historical experience—such as war,
revolution or the achievement of important reforms—can act as
a strong homogenizing influence on society so that, after such
events, the stage is set for highly uneven development and prolonged tolerance thereof, even and perhaps particularly in
countries where the reduction or elimination of inequalities was
one of the principal aims of revolution or reform. With equality
proclaimed as the essence of nationality, and with social barriers
and cleavages supposedly overcome, the return of inequality will
either be long unrecognized or, once recognized, will be tolerated for a long time. Mexico after Cárdenas is a case in point:
under the cover of the accomplishments of the revolution, development proceeded here in a sharply uneven way, with political stability remaining unimpaired until the student uprising of
1968.

One point I did not make in the article is that tolerance for
inequality may well be stronger when growth is rapid than when
it is slow. This may seem a surprising statement: normally, the
more rapid growth is, the greater are the inequalities that arise
in its wake. But with rapid growth, economic change and the
concomitant physical transformation of the country and its cities
are more apparent, so that the expectation or possibility of improvement is persuasively communicated to various groups and
individuals. It is perfectly conceivable that this communication
effect of rapid growth can outweigh its unequalizing effect with
the paradoxical result that the country where inequality has
widened *more* is actually *less* subject to reform pressures. It would
be interesting to look at the recent history of Brazil and Argentina in the light of this proposition.

The early or late appearance of pressures toward reform in
relation to entrepreneurial forces is a topic of considerable intrinsic interest. It is tempting to establish a relation between it
and the breakdown of pluralist regimes along the following
lines: if reform appears "too early," it will paralyze the entrepreneurial forces ("kill the goose that lays the golden eggs") and
this will lead to stagnation, discontent—and an attempt to secure
the process of accumulation and growth by means of an authoritarian regime. If reform appears "too late," the pressures for it,
long held back, will explode with violence—and in its wake the

identical political configuration is to be expected unless a successful revolution (presumably with its own authoritarian stamp) has been able to take over. But this result should give us pause: since no country is likely to achieve just the right timing, it looks as though there is hardly any escape from authoritarianism in the course of capitalist development. Clearly additional factors must be considered.

The obvious candidates are the identities of the *carriers* of the two functions. As was said at the outset of this section, both functions, entrepreneurial and reform, are essential for the successful achievement of development under capitalist auspices, even from the point of view of the longer-run interests of this process itself. But, at the same time, the reformers are unlikely ever to appear as "little helpers" of the entrepreneurial groups. When they enter the stage, they may well be full of invective against the latter, who will return the compliment. The breakdown of pluralist forms may then be related to the degree and nature of this hostility between the protagonists of the two functions.

This approach was suggested to me by what is almost received doctrine about Colombian politics: that political stability and maintenance of limited pluralism in that country has depended on some elements of the country's durable elite ("oligarchy") being able to take on the role of reformers while others pushed on with their entrepreneurial activities. Considerable hostility was often generated in the process between the two groups and there were some serious "accidents"—the *violencia* in the late 1940's and 1950's and the Rojas Pinilla dictatorship (1953-1957). Yet, the resilience of pluralist forms during the critical 1930's or during the current authoritarian wave is remarkable and may have something to do with the ability of the elite to assure some minimal performance of both functions by splitting into two groups. Communication between the two groups was often strained, but was never quite cut off, in part because of personal relationships and in part because, after a while, it became obvious that the reformers, whatever their phraseology, were by no means revolutionaries, but were acting in the best interests of their brethren.

In Venezuela the two functions are carried out in a very different way, but the outcome has been similar, for the past twenty years at least. Here it is the state and its bureaucracy, rather than a "private" ruling group dominating both the economy and the state, that carries out both functions. Because of the petroleum-based wealth of the state, major impulses toward the founding of new economic activities originated with it and so did efforts to improve social services such as health and education, attempts at greater regional balance and agrarian reform, and similar reform ventures. There was little probability here that the activity of one part of the bureaucracy would paralyze that of the other. A modus vivendi with the private sector was comparatively easy to establish since the state was so obviously an important partner in virtually any major economic activity.

So much for the two major surviving pluralist regimes in Latin America. What of the others?

There is an old, and still useful, distinction between reform "from below" and "from above." The prototype of "reform from above" has long been the institution by Bismarck in the 1880's of various social security schemes in Germany. Probably as a result of this paradigmatic historical experience the idea has become firmly established that reform from above has the effect of stabilizing the political order, at least in the short run, and of preventing the social and political turmoil that would ensue if the reforms were achieved through the determined actions of workers or other claimant groups.

This notion needs to be thoroughly revised in the light of the experience of Latin America.[43] Because of the weakness of trade unions and similar mass organizations, reform from above (often combined with mobilization from above) has been the rule rather than the exception here, but in many cases the result has been instability and eventually political disintegration followed by authoritarianism. One reason may be that the reform-minded social groups that capture the state on occasion are totally out of sympathy with the traditional elites, domestic and foreign, who are manning the entrepreneurial function and are in turn determined not to yield anything if they can help it. The reforms attempted under these conditions are therefore not conceived by the reform elites in the spirit of making the system work better, nor are they accepted by the entrepreneurial elites in the spirit of "giving up something in order not to lose everything." Moreover, not being hammered out in a direct confron-

[43] Actually, all that needs to be done is to show that in Latin America reform from above does not bring stability even in the short run; in the long run it did not do so in Germany either, as has been brought out by a number of studies connecting the advent of National Socialism with Bismarck's domestic policies.

tation between opposite classes (as would be the case with "reform from below"), the reforms imposed from above often turn out to be unrealistic, easy to emasculate, and sometimes not particularly helpful to their intended beneficiaries. The result can be the worst of both worlds: the enervation of the entrepreneurs, combined with an absence of real advances for the disadvantaged groups on behalf of whom reforms are introduced.

Viewing the development process in Latin America as the sequential unfolding of the entrepreneurial and reform functions appears to have its uses. The changing ideological support for the two functions, their timing in relation to one another, and the group identity of the reformers in relation to that of the entrepreneurs—all of these topics have yielded some understanding of the interaction between economic development and politics, although we are obviously far from any unified theory. One claim that can be made for the approach that has been sketched here is that it brings together "structural" and "ideological" factors in a way that has been missing from the attempts at explanation that have been considered earlier in this essay.

The conceptual framework that is suggested here can also be used to make contact with some of the earlier propositions of this essay. For example, it may well be that it is the impasse or *desencuentro*—an extraordinarily apt term coined in Argentina—between the entrepreneurial and the reform elites that acts as an irresistible invitation to the intellectuals to come forward with their own proposals and solutions. That impasse, then, may be responsible for the intellectual ferment of recent decades which was the topic of Section II.

From our new vantage point, it is also possible to achieve a better understanding of the introduction to this paper, where a good deal was made of policies that overestimate the "elasticity" of the economy. It now appears that to the extent that those policies are pursued by reformers, they may not be rooted in misperceptions, but could proceed from basic incompatibilities in outlook and values with other elites. In this manner, these policies become less wanton and more intelligible.

ENVOI

This chapter has become something of a critical survey of possible approaches to an understanding of the turn to authoritarianism in Latin America. In addition to purely economic interpretations, others that stress ideology, politics, culture, and even personality have been presented. And in the end, a more general framework has been sketched that incorporates economic, political, social, and ideological forces. I believe that each of the attempts at explanation has something to contribute to the understanding of the disagreeable phenomenon that is being studied.

Two types of critiques can be leveled at the manner in which I have proceeded: first, that I have nibbled at my topic from too many sides, that I have been excessively eclectic; second, that by supplying so large a number of explanations I have made authoritarianism in Latin America appear as totally inevitable and perhaps even justified.

The first criticism does not really bother me: I would rather be eclectic than reductionist, and it is hard to say where the golden mean lies between these two alleged vices. But the second criticism is a serious matter. Fortunately it is wrong, because of a fundamental theorem about the social world which can be formulated as follows: as soon as a social phenomenon has been fully explained by a variety of converging approaches and is therefore understood in its majestic inevitability and perhaps even permanence, it vanishes. The existence of this basic law first dawned on me thirty years ago when, at a conference on France, all the reasons for French industrial and economic retardation were cogently set forth and substantiated, at the precise moment when that country was setting out on its remarkable postwar economic modernization and recovery.[44] Numerous other examples of the theorem in operation could be given. Why things should work this way is left to readers to figure out; just in case they find the proof of my theorem troublesome, they can take heart from the fact that Hegel expressed the same thought less paradoxically and more beautifully when he wrote "the owl of Minerva spreads its wings only with the falling of dusk."

It follows that the more thoroughly and multifariously we can account for the establishment of authoritarian regimes in Latin America, the sooner we will be done with them.

[44] For the proceedings of the conference, see Edward M. Earle, ed., *Modern France* (Princeton: Princeton University Press, 1951).

CHAPTER 4

THREE MISTAKEN THESES REGARDING THE CONNECTION BETWEEN INDUSTRIALIZATION AND AUTHORITARIAN REGIMES

*José Serra**

INTRODUCTION

Many analysts argue that the bureaucratic-authoritarian regimes that have emerged in the more industrialized countries of South America, as well as in Mexico, are the political configuration which the capitalist system of domination tends to assume in the Latin American periphery in the era of the "internationalization of production" or, as others would say, in the period following the end of the "easy" phase of import substitution. Some authors, entangled in a linear analytic framework, have come to posit a more or less direct and necessary causal relationship between this form of regime and these economic conditions. Within this analytic framework, these regimes allegedly arise as a result of the implacable logic of the underdevelopment and dependency that characterize the economy of this region.

My point of departure in writing this chapter derives from an uneasiness with this type of approach. The problem is not a lack of correlation between this type of regime and a certain pattern of economic development which has been labeled socially "perverse" and which is integrated in an extremely dependent fashion into the international capitalist system. But, at times, this approach employs an analytic scheme reminiscent of the Comintern of the 1930's. Just as this earlier perspective viewed European fascism as the result of the domination of finance capital, the bureaucratic-authoritarian regime is now posited to be the result of a dependency on international monopoly capital. Yet this perspective fails to explain why some countries where the internationalization of production has taken place—such as Co-

* I am indebted to David Collier, Paulo Renato C. Souza, and specially to Albert Hirschman for helpful comments and suggestions. This chapter was written during the fall of 1977, when I was a visiting member of the Institute for Advanced Study, Princeton. Partial support of the Social Science Research Council is acknowledged.

lombia and Venezuela—do not, to date, have bureaucratic-authoritarian regimes. Nor does such a limited analytic perspective permit an adequate analysis of the often important differences among the bureaucratic-authoritarian regimes that have emerged. It also makes it more difficult to perceive new patterns of political and social change and, as Cardoso suggests, to discover ". . . contradictions and tensions which can, by the very force of their existence, transform social outrage into an organized force capable of expressing the viewpoint of those who are socially and politically oppressed."[1]

In certain instances this approach simplifies reality to the point of transforming the socioeconomic process into a continuum that is free from internal contradictions. Alternatively, it reduces the existing contradictions to those between the dominant classes in each country (which are subordinate to international capitalism), on the one hand, and the dominated masses, on the other.

A typical example of this perspective can be found in an article in which James Petras analyzes what he calls "the death of democratic capitalism" and the "experiment with a new totalitarianism" in Latin America. He argues that the emergence of a homogenous type of repressive regime is an irreversible trend which is a requirement of North American capitalism and is guaranteed by the armed forces, which, this author suggests, represent the true "political party of multinational corporations."[2] This homogenization, according to Petras, involves, among other things, "the transfer of public enterprises to the private sector" as a natural concomitant of the "market economy model based on the encouragement of foreign capital, the raising of prices, and the compression of wages that is implemented by these regimes."[3] It also involves a process of "proletarianization" which occurs "through the dislocation of white collar workers" and "the general reduction in the standard of living," which diminishes "the differences between the distinct social strata."[4] And, as a consequence, the "combined effects of economic policy and social repression eliminate the intermediate

---

[1] Fernando Henrique Cardoso, *Autoritarismo e democratização* (Rio de Janeiro: Editora Paz e Terra, 1975), p. 27.

[2] James F. Petras, "L'Amerique Latine, banc d'essai d'un nouveau totalitarisme," *Le Monde Diplomatique* (April 1977), p. 4.

[3] *Ibid.*, p. 4.   [4] *Ibid.*, p. 4.

strata that have traditionally had the function of mediating social conflicts."[5]

If one adopts this type of perspective, it is obviously difficult
even to begin to understand the means of reproduction, the
internal dynamic, and the likely future direction of change of a
regime such as that in Brazil, under whose tutelage public enterprises have continued the pattern of expansion initiated prior
to 1964 and whose evolution, in the words of Florestan Fernandes, has had as its "principal characteristic . . . the rapid
differentiation and the enormous growth of the middle classes
on a national scale."[6] It would be even worse to use this type of
perspective as a basis for developing proposals for political action on the part of the dominated classes.

In this chapter, I will explore some of the complexities of the
relation between economics and politics by focusing mainly on
the economic analyses that underlie certain explanations of
bureaucratic-authoritarianism. I am convinced that the problems with these interpretations are not totally due to the
difficulties—which are in fact enormous—of capturing dialecti-
cally the connections between economic and political processes. I
believe that these problems also derive, in part, from certain errors in the economic analyses themselves.

I will critically examine three hypotheses that deal with the relationship between economic development and the emergence
of bureaucratic-authoritarian regimes. The first of these emphasizes, in an effort to explain the existence of these regimes,
the inevitability of the "superexploitation" of the working class.
The second hypothesis posits an "elective affinity" between the
emergence of these regimes and the *deepening* of industrial
capitalism in the more diversified economies of Latin America.
The third hypothesis views "modern" authoritarianism as a kind
of incarnation of economic rationality which is presumed to be
necessary for the development of capitalism in the region.

I will limit myself principally to the case of Brazil, making
brief references to other countries of Latin America when dealing with the second hypothesis. With respect to the first hypothesis, which I will address only briefly, the argument is presented
at a level of generality such that it may easily be extended to all

[5] *Ibid.*, p. 4.
[6] Florestan Fernandes, *A revolução burguêsa no Brasil* (Rio de Janeiro: Zahar,
1975), p. 363.

of the more industrialized economies of Latin America. By concentrating the analysis on a single case—Brazil—I avoid the risk of excessive generalizations and an overly high level of abstraction. The selection of this particular case seems especially appropriate, given the fact that the Brazilian bureaucratic-authoritarian regime is perhaps (or at least has been) the "paradigmatic" case of bureaucratic-authoritarianism. The Brazilian case lacks the ambiguities of the Mexican regime and is characterized by sufficient longevity and a significant period of "stability," as well as having been the most successful economically in terms of its rate of economic growth. Indeed, it is the only one of these regimes, except for Mexico, that has achieved rapid growth.

I. "SUPEREXPLOIT OR PERISH"?[7]

The theory of superexploitation is extremely ambitious, claiming to constitute a kind of philosopher's stone for understanding the laws that govern dependent capitalism and that explain the existence of the authoritarian regimes currently found in some countries of Latin America. If one follows the reasoning of one of the principal formulators of this theory, Rui M. Marini, the "superexploitation" of the working class appears to be a *necessary* condition for capitalist development in Latin America.[8] In this context, authoritarianism is an essential instrument for guaranteeing capitalist accumulation, i.e., a means of preventing the working class from jeopardizing or frustrating the realization of superexploitation through its organizations and its protests.

But, why the *necessity* of superexploitation? Analyzing the Brazilian case, Marini, in a book published in 1969, argued that the

[7] This section draws heavily on part of an article which I wrote with Fernando Henrique Cardoso, entitled "As desventuras da dialética da dependência" (Princeton: Institute for Advanced Study, mimeographed, 1978).

[8] Rui M. Marini, *Dialéctica de la dependencia* (Mexico City: Nueva Era, 1973), pp. 92-93. According to Marini, "superexploitation" does not simply involve a high rate of exploitation (i.e., a high rate of surplus value). It implies more. It means a "greater exploitation of the physical strength of the worker, in contrast to the exploitation resulting from the increase in his productivity. This normally is reflected in the fact that the labor force is paid less than its actual value." Probably, by "remuneration for less than the actual value of the labor force," Marini means "wages lower than the cost of reproducing the labor force." (Marini, *Dialéctica*, pp. 92-93.)

rate of surplus extracted from the country by foreign capital compels the bourgeoisie to compress the wages of the workers so as to ensure their own share of economic output.[9]

Another answer given by Marini in a subsequent work, though not excluding this initial explanation, attempted to be more comprehensive and sophisticated. Its point of departure was a truly elementary Marxist economic analysis, which is in fact valid at a certain level of abstraction.[10] According to this analysis, within the framework of any given level of real wages and any given length of the work-week, the rate of surplus value can be increased only by means of cheapening the wage goods consumed by workers. Taking this conclusion as a premise, Marini identifies, in this same study, two variants:

(a) The first argues that because Latin American industrial production is: "Dedicated primarily to the production of goods which rarely if ever become items of popular consumption, the level of workers' wages is not an important factor in the evolution of Latin American industry. This is true in two senses. First, because they are not an essential element in the individual consumption of the worker, the value of manufactured goods does not determine the value of the labor force that produces them. *Therefore, a reduction in the cost of manufactured goods will not affect the rate of surplus value. This makes it unnecessary for the industrialist to concern himself with increasing the productivity of the workers*, making the cost per unit of production drop in order to decrease the cost of labor. Inversely, it involves seeking ways to increase the value of the product through greater exploitation—intensive and extensive—of the worker, as well as the reduction of his wage below its normal level [emphasis added]."[11]

(b) The other variant is somewhat more complicated. It argues

---

[9] Rui M. Marini, *Subdesarrollo y revolución* (Mexico City: Siglo Veintiuno Editores, 1969), p. 89. See also André Gunder Frank, "Latinoamérica: Subdesarrollo capitalista o revolución socialista," *Pensamiento Crítico* 13 (February 1968), p. 28. Another cause of superexploitation also discussed by Marini is the problem of marketing manufactured products that results from the low wages of the workers. This forces domestic industry to seek external markets, which in turn requires reduced labor costs in order to increase the competitiveness of these exports. Marini sees this need to compete in the external market as the starting point for the phenomenon of "subimperialism."

[10] Marini, *Dialéctica*. It involves, for example, the assumption that the problem of transforming value into prices does not exist.

[11] Marini, *Dialéctica*, p. 64.

that the industrial goods that the workers do not consume are consumer durable goods which represent in turn the most dynamic sector of the economy in terms of its rate of technological innovation.[12] However, this innovation, by not adding to surplus value, does not allow the entrepreneurs of this sector to increase their profits. This leaves them with the alternative of doing so only "by increasing the total value of production."[13] Thus, Marini concludes: "The diffusion of technical progress in the dependent economy will . . . coincide . . . with a greater exploitation of the worker, precisely because *accumulation continues to depend more on the increase in total value and therefore surplus value—than on the rate of surplus value*."[14]

On the other hand, the problems involved in the marketing of consumer durable goods (due to the fact that they are produced by industrial sectors which absorb technical progress at a greater rate and whose products are not wage goods) only reinforce the necessity of superexploitation, since these problems can be avoided only by transferring purchasing power from the workers to higher income groups. Given this necessity, wage-goods production will suffer, since the reduction of the workers' capacity for consumption leads to a slow rate of growth (or even stagnation) of the demand for these goods. This will therefore discourage ". . . any possibility of attracting technological innovation in the sector of production destined to fill the needs of popular consumption."[15]

Marini derives important political implications from this analysis. As we indicated, authoritarianism is treated as a fundamental condition for the development of capitalism in Latin America, in that it is indispensable for guaranteeing the superexploitation without which the system would stagnate, or might not even survive. Moreover, in the face of the problem of marketing industrial products that arises in this situation, the more industrialized countries of the region will find themselves impelled toward a "subimperialistic" expansion.[16]

Before critically examining the reasoning behind this argument, I should note that two of its premises are correct for the Brazilian case, though they are hardly original with Marini.

---

[12] *Ibid.*, p. 72. [13] *Ibid.*, p. 72.
[14] *Ibid.*, p. 72. [15] *Ibid.*, p. 73.
[16] See note 8. For an analysis which refutes this thesis, see Serra and Cardoso, "As desventuras."

First, the authoritarian regime did indeed inaugurate a policy of severe wage compression,[17] whose effects can be seen in Table 1. Second, according to ECLA and the structuralist economists: (a) the consumer durables sector was indeed one of the two principal leaders of industrial growth in the postwar era, especially since the middle of the 1950's (see Table 4 for the case of Brazil), and (b) there is indeed a significant disparity between the level of income required by the pattern of consumption needed to sustain the production of these goods and the per capita income of the Latin American economies, at least in comparison with the developed capitalist economies.

Where, then, do the first flaws in the "theory" of superexploitation appear? In my view, the source of its fundamental errors are the problems that I mentioned in the introduction, which involve the inability of this approach to capture the contradictory character of all socioeconomic processes and the tendency to exaggerate the importance of certain trends which do in fact appear in certain phases of this process, elevating them to the status of rigid, iron-clad "laws." I will now show how these deficiencies affected Marini's actual analysis.

One theoretical defect should be emphasized from the start which, among the many elements in this analysis, is one of the

[17] This policy consisted, on the one hand, of ending the freedom of labor unions and of reducing job security. On the other hand, it consisted of government wage setting, including wages in the private sector, based on an index formula. In practice, due to the first factor and to the manipulation of many of the coefficients in the formula, the wages of the workers declined in absolute terms from 1964 to 1968, after which they began to rise slowly and irregularly, and always at a lower rate than the increase in productivity. Productivity in the industrial sector rose 75 percent between 1959 and 1970 and by approximately the same proportion between 1964 and 1974. In this latter period, the per capita gross domestic product increased by nearly two-thirds. (These figures should be contrasted with the data in Table 1.) Ironically, one of the creators of the wage policy of the Brazilian authoritarian regime, Mario H. Simonsen, affirmed that the formula for wage readjustment ". . . establishes an objective criterion for collective wage negotiations, resolving mathematically what in many countries is resolved through strikes and political pressures." See Mario Henrique Simonsen, "Brasil e suas perspectivas econômicas," Brasilia: Ministerio de Fazenda—mimeo, 1976. The government of General Geisel (1974-1979) corrected some of the more extreme distortions that resulted from the application of the formula, with the goal of granting higher wage readjustments. However, the practical effect of this policy on the level of real wages ended up by being offset by the acceleration of inflation (which was not due, it should be pointed out, to the newly increased wage levels).

TABLE 1
Real Wages[a]
(1960 = 100)

	Wage Index for 18 Unions	Minimum Wage, City of Rio de Janeiro
1957	98[b]	114
1958	103[c]	99
1959	94[d]	113
1960	100	100
1961	105	115
1962	105	96
1963	107	89
1964	103	89
1965	98	82
1966	92	76
1967	89	73
1968	92	74
1969	94	71
1970	95	70
1971	98	69
1972	102	71
1973	98	68
1974	107[d]	69

[a] Deflated by the Rio de Janeiro cost of living index.
[b] Based on 8 unions.
[c] Based on 10 unions.
[d] Based on 15 unions.
Source: E. Bacha and L. Taylor, "Brazilian Income Distribution in the 1960's: Facts, Models, Results, and the Controversy" (Cambridge, Mass., 1977, mimeographed). Their data are taken from Departamento Intersindicial de Estatísticas e Estudos Socio-Economicos, *Dez anos de política salarial* (São Paulo: Estudos Socio-Econômicos 3 [August 1975]). For 1973 a correction has been made taking into account the new data on the Rio de Janeiro cost of living in that year.

more important. Marini seems to ignore the fact that, for capitalist accumulation, the fundamental issue is the rate of profit and not the rate of surplus value. The former, of course, depends upon the latter, but not exclusively, since the rate of profit is also a function of the output-capital ratio, which means that profits can rise without a simultaneous rise in the rate of surplus value.[18] Therefore, the stagnation of the rate of surplus value

[18] Algebraically, $r = \propto (1 - n)$, with r being the rate of profit, $\propto$ the output-

does not necessarily mean the stagnation of capitalism, and an increase in the length of the work day or a reduction in the number of workers is not the only means of achieving capitalist development.[19] It is clear that in certain contexts within this development, this reduction might appear to be indispensable. But on the basis of this, deriving an inexorable law from the dilemma that one must choose between having to superexploit or perish involves an enormous step that involves both theoretical and empirical errors. We shall enumerate some of them here:

1. Since the industrial sector has been the most dynamic within the entire economy and since within this sector the most dynamic subsector has been consumer durables, it is reasonable to say that the capital saving innovations that occurred in this sector are particularly important, just as are the impact of rapid growth and of economies of scale on the output-capital ratio. And this seems to have occurred in Brazil. But if one recognizes that the output-capital ratio calculated on the basis of current prices is not the same as when it is calculated on the basis of value, it is interesting to note that for the production of consumer durables, this coefficient, measured in current prices, increased significantly between 1959 and 1970: approximately 12 percent in the electrical and transportation industries[20]—having played an impressive role in the maintenance or increase of the rates of profit.

2. To conclude that the industrialists were uninterested in increasing worker productivity on the basis of the erroneous assumption that the workers do not consume manufactured goods (or consumer durables) does not merely represent a theoretical

---

capital ratio, and *n* the proportion of the product represented by wages, which varies inversely with the rate of surplus value.

[19] This is not only due to the possibility of the reduction of the cost (in real value) of fixed capital and its consequent effect on the output-capital ratio. The cheapening (in real value) of producer's goods that are used in wage-goods production could bring a reduction of the unit value of these goods, thus increasing the rate of surplus value (assuming that the value "depreciation" is always translated into a reduction of market prices).

[20] Regis Bonelli, "Growth and Technological Change in Brazilian Manufacturing Industries during the Sixties" (doctoral dissertation, University of California, Berkeley, 1975), Appendix. This percentage certainly underestimates the increase because many of these sectors also produce capital goods, whose performance during this decade was much less dynamic than that of consumer durables.

error. In Brazil, between 1959 and 1970, productivity increased by 75 percent in the industrial sector and, though Marini would consider it to be counterproductive, it in fact increased by an even greater percentage in consumer durables.[21]

3. In the same period there was a 4.4 percent increase in the length of the work week of the industrial sector that could not alone explain more than a small part of the increase obtained in the rate of exploitation.[22]

4. It is erroneous to assume, as does Marini, that industrial products are not part of the consumption of the masses. A study of working-class consumption patterns in São Paulo found that in 1969-1970, nearly 32 percent of the expenditures of families whose income was less than 3.1 times the minimum wage were devoted to goods and services other than food and shelter, with clothing and domestic appliances accounting for 13.6 percent of these expenses. For those families whose income was between 3.1 and 6.2 times the minimum wage, these percentages were 37 and 15.5 respectively.[23] It should be noted, in addition, that many foodstuffs are industrially processed and those which are not still require industrial inputs in their production, transport, and marketing.

5. Even though wage compression has occurred, it is not necessarily the case that "*all possibilities* for attracting investment" were closed to the wage-goods producing sector, a circumstance that would have prevented the industrial sector from increasing its rate of surplus value through the reduction of labor costs, thus completing the vicious cycle of superexploitation. Between 1959 and 1970, productivity in wage-goods sectors (textiles, clothing and footwear, food, beverages, and tobacco) increased by 46 percent, capital stock by nearly 90 percent, and the real output by 80 percent (all unweighted averages). Also, during the most recent cycle of expansion, due to growing employment

[21] Bonelli, "Growth and Technological Change," Appendix. In the automobile industry the product per worker increased by almost 50 percent between 1966 and 1972. See E. Suplicy, "A política salarial e o indice de preços" (Brasilia: Comissão de Economia do Senado, 1977).

[22] This assumes that the additional hours did not add to the cost of the industrial entrepreneurs, in that they were offset by a reduction in the hourly wage of the workers.

[23] Departamento Intersindicial de Estatísticas e Estudos Socio-Econômicos (DIESSE), *Família Assalariada: Padrão e Custo de Vida* (São Paulo: *Estudos Socio-Econômicos* 2, janeiro, 1974).

(between 1966-1967 and 1972-1973 the increase in the work force engaged in manufacturing was 9 percent per year) and rising wage rates,[24] as well as the increase in exports, the production of consumer non-durable goods expanded rapidly—nearly 12.3 percent between 1969 and 1973—[25] which would lead one to assume that investment and productivity also rose at an accelerated pace. There was, therefore, neither a technological "freeze" in the wage-goods sector nor stagnation in terms of growth of productivity in this sector.

One could argue that, in any event, wage-goods producing activities were always below the average in the industrial sector with respect to growth, investment, and productivity. This is true but not surprising, given the secondary role of these sectors within the process of capitalist accumulation (the expansion of which depends, in great measure, on investment decisions), the income elasticity of demand (given the present pattern of income distribution), *and* the wage compression that has occurred. At the same time, a substitution effect has occurred with the consumption of some non-durable goods having been replaced by the consumption of durable goods, even among the lowest income sectors. This is due to the demonstration effect, to the relative cheapening of consumer durables in relation to consumer non-durables, and to credit facilities.[26] All of this evidently limited the modernization of wage-goods production. Yet, as we saw, it did not prevent it entirely.

[24] This was due to the acceleration of demand, since the suppression of union rights continued, along with the policy known as the "arrocho salarial" (wage squeeze).

[25] The data for the period 1959-1970 are taken from the *Censos Industriais* and were derived from various tables in Bonelli, "Growth and Technological Change." The data on employment was obtained from the *Boletins do SEPT do Ministério do Trabalho*. The rate of growth of the consumer non-durables sector is presented in Table 4.

[26] For data on this substitution process in the 1960's, see the study cited above on the consumption patterns of the working class in São Paulo (DIESSE, *Família assalariada*). As this study indicates, this substitution took place despite the fact that the average real income of these families in 1969-1970 was more or less the same as in 1959. With regard to relative prices, between 1969 (the first six months) and 1976, the mean price of consumer durable goods rose by a factor of 3.4 while the mean price of consumer non-durable products increased by a factor of 5.3. (*Conjuntura Econômica*, October 1977.) It is clearly evident that the difference in relative prices constitutes a recurring phenomenon: it limits the demand for consumer non-durable goods, which, in turn, limits the growth of this sector and therefore its modernization (in relative terms).

Rather than closing this section of the chapter by trying to offer an alternative interpretation of the evolution of workers' wages and of the shape of the productive structure, I will try to suggest some further questions regarding this topic that should be considered. I do not believe that wage compression, in the proportions in which it occurred, derived from an iron-clad logic of "dependent capitalism." Likewise, the political repression which did occur and which effectively blocked the possibility of popular sector organization and protest was not carried out solely because of the necessity of imposing that supposed logic. Granted, given the configuration of forces that seized power in 1964, there were "structural" limits to the possible solutions to the economic crisis of 1963-1964. But I believe that it was the reactionary character of those forces, and the considerable weakness of the unions and other popular sector organizations, that led to the wage squeeze and to the far-reaching "anti-social" economic policies. And, once the economy was on the road to recovery, with these lower levels of wages already "programmed in" to the plans for capitalist accumulation,[27] it proved much more difficult to change the previously adopted policy, especially through changes initiated from above. Even between 1968 and 1973, in the midst of the "miracle" and with inflation practically stabilized and the GDP growing annually at a double digit rate, the official policy of severe wage restraint was maintained. Any improvement in the position of wage earners was left to "market forces" and was not made a goal of government policy. Instead, government policy continued to be restrictive, both in dealing with union activities and with social protest more generally. These continued to be repressed as much, or even more, than before.

I do not deny that in an underdeveloped economy a pattern of growth that emphasizes consumer durables will tend to restrict the possibilities for direct or indirect income redistribution (in this case through the "social expenditures" of the state), or that it will contribute to a greater concentration of income. Yet considering the case of Brazil, there is no reason to suppose that, simply because of its capacity to change demand curves and to

[27] An example of this phenomenon was the opportunity created by wage compression to make it easier for productive activities to absorb the greater financial costs which derived from the reorganization and development of the financial sector after 1964.

create new financing for consumption, the consumer goods sector *had* to grow at an annual rate of 20 percent. It seems to me that, in large part, the growth of this sector also responded to the concentration of income that derived from "exogenous" factors, such as the repression of unions and the political weakness of the popular sector. That is to say, it derived in large measure from the dynamic of the class struggle and from the characteristics of the political process in the years immediately prior to the 1964 coup, which fostered within the dominant classes and the military a perception of the existence of an extreme threat to the established order.[28] And there was no reason to suppose that the survival or restoration of political freedoms, including those relating to the contractual power of the unions, is *necessarily* an impediment to the survival of the system because of the implacable logic of certain "laws" that govern "dependent capitalism"—laws which, as long as this system endures, would leave us with no option other than living under a bureaucratic-authoritarian regime.

I hope that the observations presented in this section have served to cast serious doubt on the more simplistic, deterministic features of the "law" of superexploitation. I hope in this way to make possible a less "economistic" analysis of wage compression and of the style of growth that has occurred in recent years. And, rather than revising the analysis in light of the problems that have been noted, I tried merely to demonstrate the need for such revision. I have sought thereby to warn against explanatory models—of which Marini's analysis served as an example—that, like all economistic constructions, attempt to achieve the degree of integration and coherence of an elegant geometric construct, but that in fact are based on dubious metaphysical assumptions.

II. Import Substitution and "Deepening"

According to the analysis of Latin American industrialization which became prevalent in the early 1960's, involving particu-

[28] For an analysis of the importance of this threat for the emergence of bureaucratic-authoritarian regimes more generally in Latin America see Guillermo O'Donnell, "Reflexiones sobre las tendencias generales de cambio en el Estado burocrático-autoritario" (Documento CEDES/G.E. CLACSO/No. 1, Centro de Estudios de Estado y Sociedad, Buenos Aires, 1975), pp. 7-8. This was also published in English in *Latin American Research Review*, 13: 1 (Spring 1978), pp. 3-38.

larly the work of ECLA and of the structuralists, the manufacturing sector in the most developed countries of the region had, after several decades of growth, undergone an excessive degree of "horizontal" diversification—that is, an excessive diversification in the production of finished consumer goods. This was due to the fact that the highly regressive distribution of income, which had not been significantly reduced by industrialization, generated an unusually diversified pattern of demand for consumer goods in relation to the prevailing average income. This, in turn, influenced the pattern of import substitution and led to avoiding or delaying investments oriented toward the "deepening" of industrial production, i.e., the production of intermediate and capital goods.[29] This also led to: (a) a greater demand for modern technology and the concentration of resources to produce these goods; (b) less inclination on the part of entrepreneurs to run the risk of expanding production in this direction,[30] given that they could import these goods at more favorable prices, with better quality, and with more favorable financing (in the case of machinery and equipment); and (c) the "closed" character of industrialization in relation to the export markets—i.e., the lack of concern with exporting industrial products. The implications of the features outlined above are obvious: (a) aggravation of the problems of scale and of market barriers for numerous products; (b) a fragmented and rigid pattern of imports; and (c) a large portion of the "backward linkages" from the growth of internal production were channeled abroad. It can be said in passing that these difficulties, rather than the problems of increasing exports at a sufficiently high rate or of the high capital-labor ratio implicit in the prevailing investment patterns (that would supposedly lead to a reduced level of employment to the extent of causing a decline of the product-capital ratio) were the focus of the most important theories of stagnation that emerged in the middle 1960's.

[29] For example, at the beginning of the 1960's Chilean industry, in terms of a two-digit classification of types of industrial production, was more diversified than that of six *developed* countries. See José Serra, "Economic Policy and Structural Change in Chile, 1970-1973" (doctoral dissertation, Department of Economics, Cornell University, Ithaca, New York, 1976), Chapter 1.

[30] "The Political Economy of Import Substituting Industrialization in Latin America," Chapter 3, in Albert Hirschman, *A Bias for Hope* (New Haven: Yale University Press, 1970).

The Deepening Hypothesis

It was out of this analytic framework that Guillermo O'Don-nell seems to have derived the idea of an elective affinity be-tween bureaucratic-authoritarian regimes and the necessity, for the capitalist development of the countries in the region, of the "vertical integration" or "deepening" of their industrial sectors in the direction of producers' goods that have a high capital-labor coefficient and high technological requirements. This appeared to be the alternative to the stagnation which had been caused by inadequate vertical integration of the industrial sec-tor.[31]

In an attempt to identify the "intimate and systematic" rela-tionship between the bureaucratic-authoritarian regime and the development of capitalism in Latin America,[32] O'Donnell begins by asserting that the bureaucratic-authoritarian regimes: ". . . correspond to a stage of important transformations in the mechanisms of capital accumulation in these societies, transfor-mations that are, in turn, part of a process of *"deepening"* of a form of capitalism which, while peripheral and dependent, is also characterized by extensive industrialization [emphasis added]."[33]

This process of deepening does not simply involve "any change in a capitalist economy, *but instead involves the achievement of a higher degree of vertical integration of the productive structure*, in close association with international capital, of capitalist econo-mies which had already been characterized by extensive and diversified industrialization . . . [emphasis added]."[34]

O'Donnell argues that *deepening was necessary for the very sur-vival of capitalism* because of the problem of external bottle-necks.[35] O'Donnell thus argues:

"If the external bottlenecks that limited the growth of the na-

[31] O'Donnell, "Reflexiones."

[32] ". . . the rise, social impact, and dynamics [of the modern form of authoritar-ian political domination that BA represents] cannot be understood or explained without exploring its intimate and systematic relationship with the structure and transformation of a particular type of capitalism which has a set of specific char-acteristics that must be appropriately identified." O'Donnell, "Reflexiones," p. 4.

[33] *Ibid.*, p. 6.   [34] *Ibid.*, pp. 48-49.

[35] Evidently, and with good reason, he took for granted that the nature of the social and political forces that promoted the authoritarian regime precluded at-tempts at "nationalist-redistributivist" solutions.

tional economy . . . were exacerbated by acute inflationary problems, and if these contributed to an increasingly acute sociopolitical crisis, then the next step in the development process *had* to
have one central goal: the domestic production of those goods
(industrial inputs, capital goods, and eventually technology) the
imports of which had increased so rapidly [emphasis added])."[36]

"This should ease the problems of the external sector in two
ways. On the one hand, the emergence of a *new phase of import-
substitution* (after the earlier, premature declarations that this
process had been 'exhausted') would eliminate the need to import items that represented heavy balance of payments liabil-
ities. On the other hand, by creating a more 'mature' industrial
structure, it would create possibilities for new industrial exports
that had a high value added [emphasis added]."[37]

". . . given the conditions of international trade—which make
it difficult to feel confident about the consequences of failing to
increase significantly the domestic production of intermediate
inputs and capital goods; given the terms on which foreign investments and technology are available; and given the fact that it
was politically and ideologically impossible for the classes and
sectors that consolidated their domination by means of BA to
consider any non-capitalist approach to development—*deepening
appeared to be the only possible direction to take*. It also seemed politically indispensable, since the constant balance of payments difficulties and poor vertical integration of industry had unquestionably contributed to the economic crises that had nourished the
'threatening' political and social upheavals that the implantation
of BA sought to eliminate [emphasis added]."[38]

This last paragraph adds a new idea: that the actors in the
inner circle of power in the authoritarian regime (and therefore
at least a large part of its backers) considered the supposedly
imperative need to *deepen* as the *central* task of economic policy.
This is made explicit later on: "The leaders who in the first stage
of BA are situated in the highest positions of institutional power
. . . clearly perceive and approve of these same priorities: *the emphasis on deepening*, the indispensable role of international capital
in achieving deepening, and the need to create the conditions to
attract this investment [emphasis added]."[39]

[36] O'Donnell, "Reflexiones," p. 15.   [37] *Ibid*., p. 15.
[38] *Ibid*., pp. 15-16.   [39] *Ibid*., p. 28.

It is important to note that deepening, according to O'Donnell, would have to be principally the responsibility of the state and of the multinational corporations, in part for the two reasons—(a) and (b)—indicated in the first paragraph of this section. Deepening would require: (a) "large organizations that are financially, and otherwise, capable of waiting out the long periods required for the maturation of their investments"; (b) a "complex process of modification of the manufacture of finished industrial products," due to the fact that the inputs and equipment employed in the manufacture of these products will be supplied by the new industries created by deepening; and, (c) to the extent that an attempt is made to link deepening with the "expansion of industrial exports, it was necessary to guarantee stability in some of the institutional mechanisms—typically, promotion systems and exchange rates—that had varied most erratically in the previous period." All of this would require "a high degree of *future certainty* concerning the factors decisive for determining the final results of investment decisions."[40]

The above paragraph seems to suggest some of O'Donnell's reasons for positing the "elective affinity" between bureaucratic-authoritarian regimes and deepening: (a) the necessity of increasing the rate of investment (and therefore of freezing or reducing popular consumption); (b) the necessity of achieving institutional-political stability in order to guarantee the presence of multinational enterprises, the degree of future certainty needed for the type of investment required, and the growth of industrial exports. This is made clear when the author asserts:

"It is obvious that the political and economic upheaval prior to BA made it impossible to guarantee such certainty and predictability. [In] the years prior to BA [it was] *clearly impossible to guarantee the continuity of public policy and to control the underlying economic fluctuations.* A state which was buffetted by the upheavals of civil society could not initiate a program of deepening, nor could it attract the international capital that would have made it possible to do so [emphasis added]."[41]

"In sum, such a situation [in the period prior to BA] was incompatible with the objective needs of stability and social predictability of any complex economy."[42]

"Bureaucratic-authoritarianism involves an attempt to put the

[40] *Ibid.*, pp. 16-18.   [41] *Ibid.*, p. 18.   [42] *Ibid.*, p. 7.

state 'in shape,' to develop its capacity to control and process information, as well as to select and implement policies that serve to quickly reduce the socioeconomic fluctuations that preceded its emergence, and provide the infrastructure *needed for future investments in deepening*. It also involved a need to develop a capacity to negotiate the terms under which the new inflows of international capital would occur [emphasis added]."[43]

Moreover, O'Donnell suggests that the policy makers of bureaucratic-authoritarianism indeed *pursued deepening as a fundamental objective*, and, perhaps also (this is not clear in the text) that there have been more or less significant advances in the direction of deepening, depending on the country.[44]

To conclude, O'Donnell summarizes his argument as follows: ". . . given (a) the prior crisis of this type of capitalism and (b) its resulting tendency to generate threatening processes of popular activation and assuming (c) the defeat of non-capitalist alternatives, we can, with slightly more confidence, hazard the conclusion that (d) *the economic changes that will tend to occur will be in the direction of deepening*, which in turn (e) will be associated with the emergence and expansion of BA, and (f) in the first stage of BA one will find an orthodox approach to economic policy oriented around the *recognition and approval of the objective necessity of achieving a deepening of these capitalist economies* [emphasis added]."[45]

It may be added, finally, that from O'Donnell's analysis there appears to flow the logic which supports the following assertion: "[In Mexico] deepening advanced as much or more than in Brazil, having begun earlier and continuing more uninterruptedly."[46] This would be expected, in that Mexico has had a bureaucratic-authoritarian regime for quite some time. An essay inspired by the work of O'Donnell has affirmed this by suggesting that in Mexico "The early consolidation of authoritarian corporatist controls does much to explain why . . . *the new challenges of capital accumulation were more successfully and smoothly resolved*."[47]

[43] *Ibid.*, p. 21.   [44] *Ibid.*, p. 27-28.
[45] *Ibid.*, p. 29.   [46] *Ibid.*, p. 47.
[47] Robert R. Kaufman, "Mexico and Latin American Authoritarianism," in José Luis Reyna and Richard S. Weinert, eds., *Authoritarianism in Mexico* (Philadelphia: Institute for the Study of Human Issues, 1977), p. 195.

Assessing the Hypothesis

O'Donnell's study unquestionably represents one of the most valuable attempts to interpret, within the limits of an essay, the emergence of these authoritarian regimes in the most industrialized countries of Latin America. Nonetheless, on the basis of an analysis of the Brazilian, Chilean, Uruguayan, and Mexican experiences, I find no basis for considering deepening to be one of the "intimate relationships" between bureaucratic-authoritarian regimes, on the one hand, and the structure and transformation of capitalism in these countries, on the other. Moreover, I think that on the basis of this hypothesis it is difficult to understand the formation, the dynamic, and the contradictions of these regimes.

Hence, in the case of Brazil:

a. The deepening process advanced considerably during the 1950's—especially in the second half of the decade—and at the beginning of the 1960's. It was actively promoted by the administrations of the pre-BA regimes, which would clearly be considered democratic.

b. Pursuing deepening, as described by O'Donnell, was not the crucial problem faced by Brazilian capitalism in the years immediately prior to the installation of the bureaucratic-authoritarian regime; a new stage of *deepening did not appear necessary for the survival of capitalism* within the political parameters that came to prevail.

c. The concern with deepening was not a matter of particular importance for the promoters of the authoritarian regime nor for the actors that emerged among them to occupy positions of power. This holds true even if one discounts the inevitable preoccupation in the first stage of the authoritarian regime with inflation and the resulting concentration of effort on stabilization policies.

d. Deepening was not the core of economic policy nor the engine of growth in the first two "economic phases" of the regime (the 1964 to 1967 stabilization period and the 1967 to 1971 period of recovery); it was pursued only to a limited extent in the third phase (the period of rapid growth from 1971 to 1974); and became a primary concern only in the fourth phase (involving the decline in the rate of growth that began in 1974), after some

ten years of authoritarianism. The difficulties which characterized the entrance of the economy into the fourth phase were
due principally to imbalances in the earlier growth, which derived from the relative backwardness of the production of intermediate and capital goods and which led to disequilibria in
the vertical integration process which had a widespread impact
on the economy (see Tables 2 and 3). In fact, the regime did not
exhibit any special orientation toward deepening. On the contrary, one could even say, stretching the terms slightly, that: (a)
during the decade, instead of deepening, the economy was "un-
deepened," at least in relative terms; (b) the concern with
deepening and the attempt to achieve it did not appear at the
beginning of the regime, but ten years later, as a result of the
very problems and contradictions generated from pursuing the
development strategy that was initially adopted; (c) these recent
attempts to achieve deepening have been among the principal
factors that contributed to the recent "destabilization" of the regime. I will now try to elaborate each of the above points.

Import Substitution

It is worthwhile to observe at the start that, in attempting to
establish commonalities among the more industrially advanced
countries of Latin America, many analysts have come to attribute the problems of the Brazilian economy at the beginning of
the 1960's to the difficulties encountered during the shift from
the so-called "easy phase" of import-substituting industrialization (ISI) to the "difficult" phase.[48] In fact, in the 1950's and particularly between 1956 and 1961, a substantial part of the most
"difficult" ISI was completed and the problems that emerged
derived more from the difficulty of "digesting" the results of this
ISI than from the limitations on the extent of ISI. Naturally, this

---

[48] This is not the case with O'Donnell in his "Reflexiones" article, as his comments on p. 13 demonstrate, although he may have *underestimated* the extent of
deepening which was already achieved before 1964. In an earlier work this underestimation is clearer, for example when O'Donnell asserts that: "What happened in the Argentine and Brazilian economies came to be known as the
'exhaustion' of the 'easy' stages of industrialization—i.e., the end of the period of
extensive, horizontal industrial growth based on the substitution of imports of
finished consumer goods." See Guillermo A. O'Donnell, *Modernization and
Bureaucratic-Authoritarianism: Studies in South American Politics* (Institute of International Studies, University of California, Berkeley, Politics of Modernization
Series No. 9, 1973), p. 60.

TABLE 2
Growth of the Brazilian Gross Domestic Product,
Selected Periods
(percentages)

Period	Annual Average Growth
1947-1961	7.1
1947-1952	7.0
1952-1956	5.6
1956-1961	8.3
1961-1974	7.0
1961-1967	3.7
1967-1974	10.0
1974-1977	
1975	5.6
1976[a]	9.2
1977[b]	5.0

[a] Provisional data.
[b] From government press release.
Source: Data provided by the Centro de Contas Nacionais da Fundação Getulio Vargas.

TABLE 3
Annual Inflation in Brazil
(percentages)

Year	Price Increase[a]	Year	Price Increase[a]
1962	54.8	1970	18.2
1963	78.0	1971	17.3
1964	87.8	1972	17.4
1965	55.4	1973	20.5
1966	38.6	1974	31.5
1967	28.8	1975	32.7
1968	27.8	1976	41.3
1969	20.3		

[a] Gross Domestic Product Implicit Deflator
Source: Data provided by the Centro de Contas Nacionais da Fundação Getulio Vargas.

did not mean that the country had achieved some form of quasi self-sufficiency in the manufacture of producers' goods. A *cycle* of ISI was completed, in which the production of intermediate and particularly capital and consumer durable goods expanded rapidly (see Tables 4 and 5). Automobiles, naval construction, heavy electrical goods, and other capital goods industries were installed during this period. Basic industries such as metallurgy, petroleum, non-ferrous metals, cellulose and paper, and chemicals expanded considerably. As can be seen in Tables 7 and 8 and Figures 1 and 2, the share of imports in the total supply of industrial products dropped drastically until the early 1960's. There is no doubt that, even considering the tensions and contradictions that accompanied this process, it would be an exaggeration to say that "this system of capitalism performed poorly in terms of deepening." On the contrary, within the historical context in which it was placed, the pre-authoritarian regime promoted the "large and complex investments involved in deepening" with reasonable efficiency. In addition, this occurred despite the prolonged stagnation of exports which, in current dollars, grew only *0.85 percent per year* between 1947-1948 and 1961-1962, while imports grew by *1.6 percent* and gross domestic product rose on the average of *7 percent* annually in real terms. This was a striking feature of what can be called *late, introverted industrialization.*

I referred above to the completion of a *cycle* of ISI, and I feel that it would be appropriate to elaborate this point, both to indicate more clearly the limitations of O'Donnell's hypothesis and to indicate some of the misconceptions that persist concerning the nature of ISI.

I think that if one accepts the idea that in certain periods in Latin America the dynamic of industrial growth derives from the process of import substitution, it is reasonable to speak of the exhaustion of this process in a specific period (which of course varies according to the country), provided that at least two qualifications are made.

First, this idea of exhaustion refers to a specific *cycle* of ISI. That is, ISI is not exhausted forever, but reaches a certain stage, which may be different in each country, beyond which it is difficult for it to continue in its role as the *principal stimulus* for industrial growth, at least until the expansion of the internal market and changes in the balance of payments once again lead it to as-

TABLE 4
Annual Real Growth Rates of Manufacturing Output
by Major User Groups

	Capital Goods	Intermediate Goods	Consumer Goods Durable	Non-Durable
1949-1955[a]	10.8	10.5	18.4	6.7
1956-1959[a]	21.9	9.7	16.2	5.5
1959-1965[b]	9.4	5.4	8.4	5.1
1966-1969[b]	7.1	10.2	21.0	7.8
1969-1973[b]	22.5	15.5	22.0	12.3
1974[b]	13.6	6.7	17.3	5.2
1975[b]	5.9	4.1	3.1	2.4
1976[c]	8.5	—	—	—

Sources: [a] M. C. Tavares, *De substituição de importaçoes ao capitalismo financeiro* (Rio de Janeiro: Zahar, 1972).
[b] Regis Bonelli and Pedro S. Malan, "Os limites do possível: Notas sobre balanço de pagamentos e indústria nos anos 70," *Pesquisa e Planejamento Econômico* 6, No. 2 (1976).
[c] Data provided by the Instituto Brasileiro de Geografia e Estatística.

TABLE 5
Average Annual Rates of Growth for Selected Processing Industries
during Three Periods

Industry	1957-1962	1962-1967	1967-1972
Non-metallic Minerals	5.9%	0.5%	13.9%
Metallurgy	15.6	6.2	12.5
Mechanics	16.5	1.4	20.5
Electrical Materials	27.0	8.1	15.4
Transportation Materials	27.0	0.0	19.3
Paper and Cardboard	9.1	6.3	7.1
Rubber	15.0	6.2	13.7
Chemicals	16.7	6.0	15.2
Textiles	8.8	−5.0	6.3
Foodstuffs	7.5	1.8	8.7
Beverage	4.1	0.9	7.9
Tobacco	6.6	−1.0	5.5
Total	11.9	2.7	12.1

Source: Instituto do Planejamento Econômico e Social do Ministerio de Planejamento. *Crescimento Industrial no Brasil* (Rio de Janeiro, Relatorio de Pesquisa No. 26, 1974).

TABLE 6
Imports of Capital Goods:
Annual Real Growth Rates
(1970 cruzeiros)

1966-1969	20.5
1969-1973	23.0
1974	47.5
1975	5.0
1976	−17.4

Sources: For 1966—1975, Regis Bonelli and Pedro S. Malan, "Os limites do possível: Notas sobre balanço de pagamentos e indústria nos anos 70," *Pesquisa e Planejamento Econômico* 6, No. 2 (1976). For 1976, Banco Central.

TABLE 7
Share of Imports in Total Supply
According to Use of Manufactured Goods[a]

Year	Consumer Durable Goods	Consumer Non-Durable Goods	Intermediate Goods	Capital Goods
1949	64.5%	3.7%	25.9%	63.7%
1955	10.0	2.2	17.9	43.2
1962	2.4	1.1	8.9	12.9
1965	1.6	1.2	6.3	8.2
1965[a]				14.5
1967				22.3
1970				24.5
1974				28.4

[a] The 1949-1965 figures are based on 1955 indices of physical volume and prices. The 1965-1974 figures are based on 1970 indices of physical volume and prices. It should be noted that 1965 is an atypical year in that the import of capital goods diminished drastically due to a sharp reduction in the rate of investment.

Sources: For 1949-1965, Instituto de Planejamento Econômico e Social do Ministerio do Planejamento, *Diagnóstico da Industrialização Brasileira* (Rio de Janeiro, 1968). For 1965-1974, R. Bonelli and P. S. Malan, "Os limites do possível: Notas sobre balanço de pagamentos e indústria nos anos 70," *Pesquisa e Planejamento Econômico* 6, No. 2 (1976).

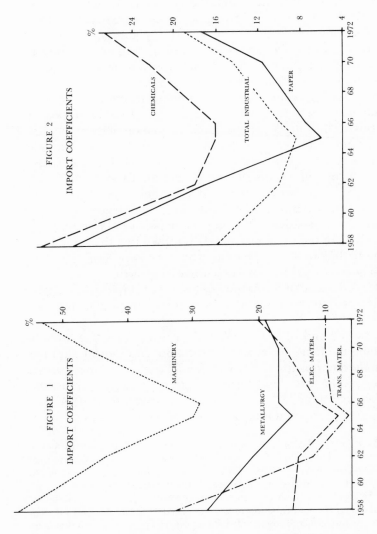

FIGURE 1

IMPORT COEFFICIENTS

MACHINERY

METALLURGY

ELEC. MATER.

TRANS. MATER.

FIGURE 2

IMPORT COEFFICIENTS

CHEMICALS

TOTAL INDUSTRIAL

PAPER

Source: Instituto do Planejamento Economico e Social do Ministerio de Planejamento, *Crescimento Industrial no Brasil* (Rio de Janeiro, Relatorio de Pesquisa No. 26, 1974).

sume this role. And, in fact, there would be no reason to discard
the idea that, having found alternative "sources of expansion"
(the stimulation of demand and the possibility of taking advantage of them by means of profitable investments) and, eventually, resolving problems of external restrictions *after* a certain
period of growth, the economies could undergo new substitution cycles,[49] i.e., periods in which these restrictions are converted into the *principal* stimulant for growth.

From this perspective, the error of many structuralists lies, not
in calling attention to the decline of ISI, but rather in supposing
that this decline implies an inevitable stagnation of the industrial
sector (and of the economy) and, therefore, that the domestic
market will not expand—or will do so very slowly—unless "structural reforms" of a redistributive nature are carried out.[50] It is
worth noting, in passing, that they were not alone in this "pessimism." For example, others who were not structuralists en-
dorsed the thesis that industrial stagnation would accompany
the decline of the ISI, *except that* they argued that this stagnation
would be followed by a phase in which the export of manufactured goods would be a dynamic force of growth.

This is the case of Sir Arthur Lewis, for example, who asserts,
with respect to the industrialization in the "tropical countries,"
that:

". . . by the end of the 1960's the early starters were already
reaching the limits of import substitution, and industrialization
began to slow down. . . . If 70 percent of the labor force consists
of low productivity food farmers, with only a tiny surplus, the
market for domestic manufacturers is strictly limited. As the
limits are approached the pace of industrialization can be main-

---

[49] As we indicated earlier, this possibility re-emerged in Brazil after 1974. The
belief in the definitive end of ISI was so widespread that an issue of the journal
World Development (Vol. 5, Nos. 1 and 2, January-February 1977) dedicated to
Latin America was entitled "Latin America in the Post Import-Substitution Era."

[50] The logic of this outline of reforms, in relatively simplified terms, would be
the following: the redistribution of income would stimulate demand for non-
durable consumer goods, thereby benefiting the areas of production that (supposedly) have a higher output-capital ratio; on the other hand, the increased size
of the market for these goods would indirectly create a demand for producers'
goods sufficient to make it profitable to have further import substitution in this
area or to achieve a more efficient scale of production for producers' goods
which were already being produced domestically.

tained only by exporting manufactures. And this is what happened."[51]

The second qualification has to do with the fact that, when speaking of the exhaustion of ISI, the structuralist authors thought, and in my view with some justification, that the decline of ISI as the *principal stimulus* for industrial growth occurred because, for the bulk of the imported items that could be substituted, the limited domestic market did not allow them to be substituted profitably.

These observations suggest the existence of a twofold error underlying O'Donnell's hypothesis. First, there is an idea that ISI can and should continue to be the dynamic force behind rapid industrial growth (provided that the political-institutional modifications associated with the emergence of bureaucratic-authoritarian regimes are carried out). However, the most elaborate critique of the supposed exhaustion of ISI was made by Hirschman,[52] and was one which O'Donnell explicitly took into account in elaborating his hypothesis. This critique centered mostly around the idea that, *given* the problems of the market and the small size of factories (the importance of which Hirschman sought to deemphasize), as well as the foreign exchange situation, the means were available (for example, overcoming the resistance of the entrepreneurs to deepening) which

---

[51] W. A. Lewis, "The Evolution of the International Economic Order" (Princeton: Janeway Lectures, mimeo, 1977), p. 22. In a similar vein, Grunwald asserts: "There are two broad strategies of industrialization to lead emerging nations toward economic maturity. One is through the development of labor intensive manufactures for export to advanced countries. The other is through import substitution industrialization." See Joseph Grunwald, "Some Reflections on Latin American Industrialization Policy," *Journal of Political Economy*, Vol. 78, No. 4 (August 1970), p. 848.

With regard to the Lewis citation, it should be noted that the logic of his reasoning apparently does not depend on the percentage of the population engaged in agriculture, since in this "dual" economy, given the level of per capita income, the size of the market would be a function of the *absolute* number of urban dwellers. On the other hand, this was not what happened. In Latin America there was significant growth of industry and of the domestic market even during the period when ISI ceased to be the (or even a) dynamic factor in economic growth. The export of manufactures, though having grown rapidly, was not sufficient to explain the rate of industrial growth (see Table 8 for the case of Brazil).

[52] Albert O. Hirschman, "The Political Economy."

could have made possible the continuation of import substitution. But he did not attempt to discuss the problem of whether or not ISI could continue to be the principal source of stimulus for industrial growth, and under what circumstances this could occur.

Second, with reference to the Brazilian case, it is undeniable that O'Donnell, as I indicated earlier, underestimated the degree to which industrialization had advanced by the beginning of the 1960's, when the level of import substitution which had already been achieved suggested the possibility of a new cycle of expansion supported principally by growth in internal demand. In fact, in the 1950's, especially in the second half of the decade, industrialization in Brazil had actually made a significant step toward more advanced activities—in terms of concentration, capital density, and technology—including the manufacture of producers' goods.

Along these same lines, it is worth noting Hirschman's idea, also taken into account by O'Donnell, that industrialization in Latin America (which is experiencing what he calls "late-late" industrialization) had a "highly sequential" and "tightly phased" character in comparison with the "late" industrializers analyzed by Gerschenkron (Germany, Italy, Russia). They lacked "some of the essential characteristics of Gerschenkron's 'great spurt.' " However, in the case of Brazil, this contrast could be considered valid only until the beginning of the 1950's.[53]

[53] Hirschman, "The Political Economy," pp. 93-95. From a "revisionist" ECLA perspective it could be argued that, although formally there had been an accelerated process of import substitution during this decade, which was reflected in the notable reduction in the import coefficients as part of the total supply of numerous producers' goods and consumer durable goods (and this despite the accelerated increase in supply), the industrial expansion which took place could not be explained solely by the stimuli provided by external restrictions and by the favorable domestic market, since the investment by the state and the MNCs in these areas occurred before the introduction of these stimuli. On the other hand, the installation of a significant producers' goods sector meant that the cyclical movement of the economy responded to a much more endogenous factor than had been the case in the previous decades.

All of this would explain the greater similarity of the Brazilian case to the model outlined by Gerschenkron for the late industrializers, and would support the argument that already in the 1950's the principal dynamic source of growth was not ISI, as is conventionally believed. In the other countries of Latin America this greater degree of autonomy also emerged, though, as one author put it: "In Brazil [more than in Argentina, Venezuela, Chile, and other coun-

Hirschman recognizes this when he notes that: ". . . at least one experience in Latin America, that of Brazil during the 50's, came fairly close to the picture drawn by Gerschenkron [for the late-industrializers]."[54]

"Orthodox" Economic Thought and Deepening

Even if deepening was not the central or crucial problem for the development (not to mention the survival) of capitalism in Brazil, did the promoters, ideologues, beneficiaries, and the actors of the regime think it was the crucial problem? I do not believe so, and indeed the contrary was the case. Examine, for example, the Plan of Economic Action of the Castelo Branco government or the books written by the economist ideologues most representative of the forces that took power in 1964— Eugenio Gudin and Mario Simonsen—[55] whose orientation was clearly inspired by those who, as Hirschman says in his chapter in the present volume, "attacked industrialization not because it had accomplished too little but because it had been carried too far."

Actually, one could not logically infer any deepening ideology from the thought of the economists identified with the regime, who basically adhered to "orthodox" economic thought. We may take, for example, the relationship which O'Donnell posits be-

---

tries] the government was anxious to promote maximum vertical integration, i.e., to promote both final consumer goods industries and intermediate and capital goods sectors." See Werner Baer, "Import Substitution and Industrialization in Latin America: Experiences and Interpretations," *Latin American Research Review*, Vol. 7, No. 1 (Spring 1972), p. 98.

Perhaps Chile is where this autonomous investment went the furthest (in relation to the small size of its economy) not only before but also after the exhaustion of the "easy" phase of ISI. In this case it occurred principally under the Christian Democratic government. The success of the experience, at least in the short run, was very modest, in part due to the small size of the domestic market and the decision to *simultaneously* pursue large investments in the consumer durables sector (including automobile production), producers' goods, export industries, agrarian reform, and "redistributive" social services.

[54] Hirschman, "The Political Economy," p. 95. This observation suggests that it would be worthwhile to critically examine an argument that has been made in a number of studies. The literature on populism has stressed the affinity between this type of regime and the supposedly smooth and tightly staged character of industrialization. Yet, if this were true, in the Brazilian case populism should not have lasted beyond 1945.

[55] Eugenio Gudin, *Análise de problemas brasileiros* (Rio de Janeiro: Agir, 1965); and Mario Henrique Simonsen, *Brasil 2001* (Rio de Janeiro: APEC, 1969).

tween external bottlenecks and the need to deepen. Nothing is further from orthodox thought than the idea that deepening would be the way to alleviate balance of payments problems, for at least four reasons. First, no one, neither orthodox nor heterodox thinkers, believed that the solution to the shortage of foreign exchange was to reduce imports (the Brazilian import coefficient in the early 1960's was extremely low—about 5 percent in 1964). Nor did they believe that a new phase of ISI would achieve this reduction. Second, nothing is more alien to the orthodox perspective than to be concerned about "the consequence of failing to significantly increase the local production of intermediate capital goods" that results from "the conditions of international commerce" and "the terms on which foreign investments and technology are available."[56] Third, it was simply not true that it was "politically and ideologically impossible for the classes and sectors that consolidated their domination by means of the BA state to seriously explore the alternatives [to deepening]."[57] Fourth, the solution to external bottlenecks which the orthodox thinkers always defended involved, in order of importance, increasing exports (including non-traditional primary products), incentives for direct foreign investment, and external financing. It is interesting to note in passing that the "deepening" accomplished before 1964, which was considered excessive by orthodox thinkers because it did not promote "efficiency," was viewed as one of the restraints on the expansion of exports because it supposedly reduced the international competitiveness of industrial products or ignored the idea that foreign trade is a "two-way street." In Simonsen's words: "the inordinant increase of the indices of nationalization (i.e., of deepening) often led to the waste, rather than the saving, of foreign exchange."[58]

[56] O'Donnell, "Reflexiones," p. 16. If this doubt did indeed exist and if deepening were the only escape, the orthodox thinkers could even be considered to be "antidepentistas." This would be true to the extent that one accepts Cardoso's definition: ". . . a dependent economy . . . is an economy where the process of accumulation does not develop autonomously. Because of the absence of a producers' goods sector—or its weakness—any initiative to increase the production of capital must come from the central economies [i.e., of the developed countries]." Fernando Henrique Cardoso, *O modêlo político brasileiro* (São Paulo: Difel, 1972), p. 43. From this perspective, the bureaucratic-authoritarian regime, if it were to pursue deepening and was successful, could within limits lead to the weakening, at the very least, of the ties of dependency.

[57] O'Donnell, "Reflexiones," p. 16.   [58] Simonsen, *Brasil 2001*, p. 290.

Crisis and the Recovery of Growth

On the basis of these considerations, it is thus clear, in my view, that starting in the early 1960's deepening did not necessarily constitute an alternative for stimulating economic growth. I will now develop this point, briefly analyzing the crisis of 1962 to 1964, the policy alternatives which appeared, and the trajectory subsequently followed.

The contraction of industrial growth and of the economy in general had clearly begun by 1962, lasting until 1967 (see Tables 2, 4, and 5). Between 1964 and 1967, this contraction was reinforced by the stabilization policy, so that the question of major interest lies in the reason for the initial decline.[59]

One plausible explanation for this decline focuses on two sets of circumstances. The first involves a cyclical phenomenon. Indeed, the beginning of the 1960's saw a declining rate of growth that resulted from the interaction of a variety of factors. In the first place, the wave of massive investments that was initiated in 1957 reached its ebb, and the powerful linkage effects that it created, which in turn had a strong impact on investment, employment and consumption, began to lose their intensity. Second, in addition, many of the "new" sectors of producers' goods and consumer durables had become overextended because of the investment incentives provided by the state, and the expectations created by the period of rapid expansion and/or because of problems of the minimum scale of production in relation to the size of the market.[60] In the third place, the producers of consumer durables had saturated the market, which had previously been supplied with imports and had been expanded by the multiplier-effects of the overall increase in investment. Thus, the subsequent expansion of consumer durables came to depend on lowering prices and providing financing for consumers, as well as on a change in income distribution and in the income-elasticity of demand of different groups. Fourth, the production of non-durable consumer goods, long since heavily dependent

[59] A similar interpretation is found in M. C. Tavares, "Acumulação de capital e industrialização no Brasil" (Rio de Janeiro: Faculdade de Economia e Administração da UFRJ, mimeo, 1975).

[60] Regarding capital goods, studies by ECLA indicated that idle capacity in the capital equipment and metallurgy sectors had already risen by 1960. To a lesser but still significant degree there was also underutilization in the heavy electrical equipment sector.

upon the increase in demand due to population growth, did not exhibit great dynamism, partly due to the slow growth of employment and the increasing inflation that since 1959 had eroded the purchasing power of the wage-earning masses. Fifth, the capital goods sector tended to be strongly resentful of the consequent disincentives to invest which resulted from these conditions. The public sector, in turn, encountered enormous difficulties in expanding and even in maintaining its level of investment because of problems of financing, which made it difficult to compensate for the weakness of the induced component of investment through increasing the autonomous component.[61] Finally, the hesitancy of international financial institutions and the balance of payments situation (involving the heavy burden of external debt and the stagnation of exports) made it impossible to resolve the problem through aid from the external sector.[62]

But this deceleration of growth would not necessarily have led to a crisis if it had not coincided with another set of related circumstances: political instability and the failure to control inflation.[63] These conditions increased the disincentive for private and in particular foreign investment,[64] especially after measures aimed at controlling foreign profit remittances were adopted. On the other hand, the government, without freezing wages, tried in 1963 to apply a stabilization program by reducing public investment and private credit, and the economy entered into a phase of open crisis. Nature also contributed to the crisis, in that the drought in south central Brazil led to a rationing of electric

[61] Until 1962 this latter component grew significantly, thereby, in effect, achieving this compensation.

[62] For some authors the crucial factor that slowed growth involved external bottlenecks. See, for example, Nathaniel H. Leff, "Import Constraints and Development: Causes of the Recent Decline of Brazilian Growth," *The Review of Economics and Statistics*, Vol. 49, No. 4 (November 1967), pp. 494-501. For a convincing critique of this article, see Joel Bergsman and Samuel Morley, "Import Constraints and Development: Causes of the Recent Decline of Brazilian Economic Growth. A Comment," *The Review of Economics and Statistics*, Vol. 51, No. 1 (February 1969), pp. 101-04.

[63] It was obviously hardly a coincidence that these two phenomena occurred in conjunction with the decline of growth, but it would be risky on the basis of this to view them solely as dependent variables or, at the other extreme, as independent variables.

[64] About one-third of industrial production was based on foreign investment. See Bonelli, "Growth and Technological Change," Appendix.

energy and, together with widespread frosts, led to a drop in agricultural production.

Given the political consequences of the crisis, what alternative means were available for reestablishing economic growth? One way out of the crisis which evidently was precluded was any attempt to carry out a redistribution of income or any other measures which, some believed, could inject greater dynamism into the light consumer industries. A renewed and intensive process of deepening could also have been pursued, but this would have involved not only a form of discrimination against the consumer durables sector—one of the two dynamic sources of growth in the previous decade—but also declining income in the short run, due to the problems of scale and maturation of investments. It would also have met with strong external resistance from financial institutions and from the MNCs.[65] It should be understood that this did not mean that there was not a need for new deepening investments which might have eliminated certain bottlenecks, thus permitting the use of the productive capacity installed during the previous years, or that there was no room for new areas of expansion involving intermediate and capital goods production—for instance, in petrochemicals.[66] But it would seem that, given the political parameters which came to prevail and the belief of those in power in the need to open and internationalize the economy, as well as the enormous potential for accumulation that already existed in the consumer durable sector, it was reasonable to suppose that consumer durables could begin (or continue) to play a central role in the next phase of growth.

This potential for accumulation derived from a variety of sources: the volume of the productive capacity already installed in the consumer durables sector; its degree of monopoly; and the possibility of benefiting from significant increases in the product-capital ratio by means of utilizing external economies and economies of scale in general, as well as through its strong

[65] The financial institutions resisted because of the protectionist and "autarkic" policies that such a program implied; the MNCs resisted because of their desire to continue supplying their local subsidiaries from abroad.

[66] It should be emphasized, as was noted in a study done in that period, that "The fact that the expansion of the industrial sector has been disturbed provoked a series of disequilibria [such as] insufficient installed capacity in the intermediate goods industry: metallurgy and basic chemicals, rubber, paper, etc." See M. C. Tavares, *De Substituição de Importações ao Capitalismo Financeiro* (Rio de Janeiro: Zahar, 1972), p. 165.

linkage effects in relation to the urban economy. Because of these factors, the consumer durables sector was in an excellent position to secure financing for the acquisition of its products, both because of the extent of available resources and because of the strong stimulus to the economy that would result from its expansion—a factor which is always very persuasive to the authorities responsible for credit policy.

On the other hand, the large firms of the consumer durables sector had an exceptional capacity for influencing internal demand to their own benefit. This derived from the type of goods produced, the availability of extensive resources for advertising, and their affiliation with the multinational corporations, which guaranteed them a constant flow of innovations derived from the investment in research and development of the parent companies.

The "new" phase required a profound reorganization of public, private, and external systems of financing, which had been in shambles since the end of the 1950's. This reorganization involved institutional changes (involving tax legislation, the public debt, financial policy, foreign capital, and foreign trade), as well as policies concerning the distribution of income, both among individuals and between sectors. Much was done in this direction in the first years, as can be seen in the substantial rise in public revenues, the rapid growth of the public debt (intended at first to finance the deficit and afterwards to "absorb" liquidity), the organization of an effective system of consumer credit and of financing for home construction, the relaxation of regulations pertaining to foreign capital, the progressive liberalization of import restrictions, and the introduction of an expanding set of incentives for exports, as well as the violent compression of wages of less skilled blue and white collar workers.

The post-1964 growth trajectory is well known. Among the fundamental factors in the economic recovery were the resurgence of consumer durable production and of the construction industry—which occurred principally because of the establishment of a system of financing centered in the National Housing Bank—[67]as well as, somewhat later, the capital goods sector (ini-

---

[67] The greater part of the resources of this bank come from a fund based on a tax which is the equivalent of eight percent of salaries and which is controlled by the enterprises. Deposits are made in the name of the employees, who have the right to withdraw their deposits in the event that they are dismissed from their jobs.

tially stimulated by the resurgence of public investment) and non-traditional exports. With regard to supply, the idle capacity[68] and the existing "potential for expansion" played a decisive role, as did the increase in the import capacity.[69] Thus, while the industrial product increased by more than 75 percent between 1967 and 1972, the stock of capital did so by only 45 percent between 1966 and 1971 and the share of imports in the industrial supply grew from 10 to 15 percent between 1966 and 1972.

What happened to deepening in the first years of the economic recovery? It clearly did not play a central role either in economic policy or in the evolution of the economy. There is no doubt that industrial investment rose in absolute terms, but the rate of investments of this sector in 1970 was still lower than in 1962; in addition, the rate of overall investment hardly increased at all (see Tables 10 and 11). The *level* of public investment (in petroleum, energy, and in communications) also rose considerably and large projects promoted principally by the state and multinational corporations were initiated—for example, in the area of petrochemicals. But these initiatives did not play a predominant role as the source of growth.

On the other hand, it is essential to keep in mind that the actual recovery between 1967 and 1970 did not stimulate a comparable expansion in the domestic capital goods sector, and this was not principally due to the idle capacity or to the lack of supply in this sector. The fact is that in response to the pressure from, and to the advantages associated with, external sources of financing, and because of the preferences of multinational corporations and of the desire to maximize the rates of short-term growth, economic policy began to discriminate against the industries that produced machinery and equipment, granting fiscal incentives only for the purchase of *imported* capital goods. As Tables 4 and 6 show, between 1966 and 1969 capital goods imports grew 20.5 percent annually, while domestic production

[68] One indicator of the existing margins of idle capacity is the fact that in 1965 the levels of production of eleven of the eighteen sectors of Brazilian manufacturing, representing more than two-thirds of the industrial value added (in 1955 prices), were below the levels of 1962. This estimate was made on the basis of data provided by the Instituto do Planejamento Econômico e Social do Ministerio do Planejamento (IPEA), *Diagnóstico da Industrialização Brasileira* (Rio de Janeiro, 1968), p. 218. And this despite the fact that the productive capacity in these sectors continued to expand, though at a decreasing rate.

[69] This is due to the growth of exports and to external indebtedness.

TABLE 8

Industrial Production, Industrial Imports and Exports,
and Share of Imports in Total Supply, 1965-1975
(millions of 1970 cruzeiros)

Year	Industrial Production (a)	Industrial Exports (b)	Industrial Imports (c)	Total Supply (d)=(a)−(b) + (c)	Share of Imports in Total Supply (c) / (d) %
1965	57,366	1,105	4,130	60,391	6.8
1966	64,456	982	5,721	69,195	8.3
1967	65,552	1,303	6,430	70,729	9.2
1968	76,630	1,363	8,819	84,086	10.5
1969	84,600	1,774	9,424	92,250	10.2
1970	95,513	2,459	11,869	104,923	11.3
1971	109,076	2,790	15,631	121,917	12.8
1972	128,927	3,887	19,109	144,149	13.3
1973	149,298	4,023	22,812	168,087	13.6
1974	160,645	4,046	32,304	188,903	17.1
1975	166,589	4,484	28,822	190,927	15.1

Source: Regis Bonelli and Pedro S. Malan, "Os limites do possível: Notas sobre balanço de pagamentos e indústria nos anos 70," *Pesquisa e Planejamento Econômico* 6, No. 2 (1976).

TABLE 9

Foreign Trade and Terms of Trade Indices
(1970 = 100)

Yrs.	EXPORTS Pr.	Qua.	IMPORTS Global Pr.	Qua.	Crude Oil Pr.	Qua.	TERMS OF TRADE Tot.	Oil Excl.
1966	87	78	95	60	95	72	92	91
1967	87	74	97	65	106	67	90	91
1968	86	85	100	80	104	79	86	85
1969	88	97	98	83	98	84	90	89
1970	100	100	100	100	100	100	100	100
1971	96	106	104	122	126	118	92	94
1972	109	135	111	148	138	145	98	98
1973	150	155	139	179	173	203	108	108
1974	189	158	214	242	576	207	88	105
1975	196	165	217	222	582	217	90	96
1976	226	162	220	218	617	248	103	111

Source: Data provided by the Banco Central.

TABLE 10
Brazilian Exports
(in millions of U.S. Dollars—
annual percentage change)

	PRIMARY PRODUCTS		MANUFACTURED PRODUCTS		TOTAL	
	Value	*Change*	*Value*	*Change*	*Value*	*Change*
1964	1,340.5		89.3		1,429.8	
1965	1,466.5	9.4	129.0	44.5	1,595.5	11.6
1966	1,598.6	9.0	142.5	10.5	1,741.4	9.1
1967	1,490.2	−6.8	163.8	14.9	1,654.0	−5.0
1968	1,706.3	14.5	175.0	6.8	1,881.3	13.7
1969	2,066.5	21.1	244.7	39.8	2,311.2	22.9
1970	2,373.2	14.8	365.7	49.4	2,738.9	18.5
1971	2,381.0	0.3	522.9	43.0	2,903.9	6.0
1972	3,160.9	32.8	830.3	58.8	3,991.2	37.4
1973	4,864.8	53.9	1,334.4	60.7	6,199.2	55.3
1974	5,804.5	19.3	2,146.7	60.9	7,951.2	28.3
1975	6,165.1	6.2	2,504.8	16.7	8,669.9	9.0
1976	7,579.8	22.9	2,550.6	1.8	10,130.4	16.8

Source: Data provided by the Secretaria do Planejamento.

rose only 7.1 percent. Thus, a large part of the powerful accelerating effects which derived from the higher rates of investment and from the decrease in the margins of idle capacity were channeled outside the country. Apart from wasting part of the already installed capacity for accumulation, this had the effect of limiting the expansion of the capital goods sector and increasing its relative technological backwardness.[70]

With regard to intermediate inputs, the problem consisted mostly in the fact that, contrary to what some analysts assume, the post-1964 government actually does not seem to have assumed a "more pervasive planning role" very adequately, in that the investments in this sector—which are the most complex and which require the greatest planning and long periods of maturation—fell notably behind in relative terms. Thus, by the beginning of the 1970's the economy had to import, for exam-

[70] Evidently, the producers' goods sector could not have expanded more rapidly after 1967 without inhibiting, at least in some measure, the accelerated expansion of the consumer durables sector. This inhibition would involve, other things being equal, a different style of growth—slower and, of course, more oriented toward deepening.

TABLE 11
Gross Fixed Capital Formation in Brazil
(as a percentage of GDP)

1955	18.4
1956	20.2
1957	21.9
1958	23.3
1959	23.8
1960	22.8
1961	22.4
1962	22.1
1963	20.5
1964	19.8
1965	16.1
1966	17.6
1967	17.6
1968	19.8
1969	19.8
1970	21.0
1971	22.0
1972	24.4
1973	26.5
1974	28.5
1975	25.3

Source: For 1955 to 1974, Regis Bonelli and Pedro S. Malan, "Os limites do possível: Notas sobre balanço de pagamentos e indústria nos anos 70," *Pesquisa e Planejamento Econômico* 6, No. 2 (1976). For 1975, this is my estimate based on official unpublished data.

ple, steel, aluminum, and fertilizer and suffered from increasing shortages of a wide range of basic inputs. With respect to steel, the well-documented programming error made by the Ministry of Planning under the management of Roberto Campos should be mentioned. This involved a serious underestimation of the installed capacity of this sector, creating problems which lasted for many years. This represents one of the best examples of a lack of any special talent on the part of the technocrats of the bureaucratic-authoritarian regime for promoting deepening.

In 1971, upon recognizing the difficulties that would result from the backwardness of the producers' goods sector, the government, among other measures, offered incentives for the purchase of domestically produced capital goods and also initiated or accelerated various programs of investment in basic inputs.

TABLE 12

Fixed Investment and Income in Processing Industries

1962-1972

(in billions of 1969 cruzeiros)

Year (t)	Investment (I_t)	Income (Y_t)	I_{t-1}/Y_t (%)
1962	3.11	17.69	—
1963	2.64	17.64	18
1964	2.41	18.53	14
1965	2.46	17.66	14
1966	2.89	19.84	12
1967	2.77	20.18	14
1968	3.32	23.59	12
1969	3.85	26.05	13
1970	4.81	28.77	13
1971	6.01	31.67	15
1972	7.51	35.77	17

Source: Instituto do Planejamento Econômico e Social do Ministerio de Planejamento, *Crescimento Industrial no Brasil* (Rio de Janeiro, Relatorio de Pesquisa No. 26, 1974).

TABLE 13

Deficit of the Brazilian Balance of Payments

(in current account)

	As a Percentage of Total Capital Formation	As a Percentage of Gross Domestic Product
1967	5.0	1.0
1968	6.1	1.3
1969	2.8	0.7
1970	5.4	1.3
1971	9.9	2.5
1972	9.5	2.4
1973	7.7	2.1
1974	21.1	6.7
1975*	21.2	5.4

* Provisional data.

Source: Calculated from "Contas Nacionais," *Conjuntura Econômica*, July 1977.

FIGURE 3

IMPORT COEFFICIENT*

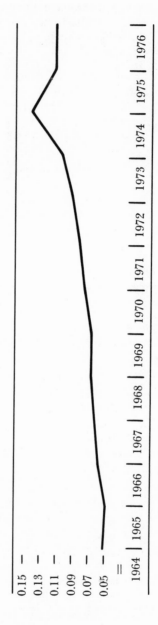

*Imports of Goods and Services divided by Imports of Goods and Services plus GNP
Source: Banco Central

But, this was done with the goal of stimulating an increase in the rate of investment which would help to maintain the dramatic expansion of consumer durable production, luxury housing construction, and related public investments, not to mention the projects that were initiated in connection with the triumphal extravagances of the Medici government (e.g., football stadiums, the trans-Amazonian highway, and the Rio-Niteroi bridge). In this way, a rapid increase in the import coefficient became necessary, which was in turn reinforced not only by means of greater incentives for exports but also through a major increase in foreign indebtedness, an eloquent demonstration of the external sector's blind confidence in the regime, which had not been shaken by the major disturbances in the international economy which at that point were already evident. Thus, the attempt at deepening was initiated without halting horizontal expansion. As I have written elsewhere, "bridging the gap between demand and the domestic production of intermediate and capital goods by means of imports, at the same time that there is an attempt to increase the domestic production of these goods, could make it possible to avoid entering the ISI cycle in its declining phase, or could at least help to avoid some of the problems of this phase."[71]

Nevertheless, even before the precariousness of the scheme became evident, the deepening program of the Medici government left much to be desired, at least in terms of efficiency. As a document of the IPEA (an agency of the Ministry of Planning) put it cryptically, with reference to the Council of Industrial Development (CDI) which was then the principal instrument for executing the industrial policy:

"Actually, the CDI has not complied with the objectives which it set for itself. Limiting itself to summarizing the projects which are proposed, it proceeds to grant concessions indiscriminately. With the exception of some sectors whose market is controlled directly by the government, the CDI approves practically all of the projects presented to it, ignoring market problems, sectoral priorities, absorption of technology, costs and efficiency, and the sectoral and regional compatibility of the projects, as well as the goal of linking industrial policy with the overall objectives of

[71] José Serra, "El milagro económico brasileño: realidad o mito?" *Revista Latinoamericana de Ciencias Sociales*, Vol. 1, No. 3 (1972), p. 38.

economic policy. Because it has no effect on the orientation of investments, it fails to serve as an organ of economic policy, draining the instruments of policy which it administers of their efficiency. The relative backwardness of the domestic capital goods industry (especially until 1970) and the actual shortage of intermediate goods are merely two examples of the effects to which this 'non-policy' contributed."[72]

For instance, in 1973, notwithstanding the deepening program initiated by the Medici government, no less than 50 percent of the projects approved by the CDI involved consumer goods. An extreme illustration of the waste and irrationality that characterized the government's orientation in this period, and that further calls into question the reputation of the regime for successfully promoting deepening, was the decision to permit the state government of Minas Gerais to promote the installation of a Fiat automobile factory in that state. This involved an extraordinary and, probably until that time, unequalled mobilization of incentives, inducements, and tax exemptions, which reduced the total contribution of the Italian firm to a minimum. The proposed factory was to be built at a cost of six hundred million dollars, at a point when the country already had no less than seven automobile enterprises. Because of problems of demand as well as of supply of inputs (already clearly perceptible), the belief that the production of automobiles could continue at its annual growth figure of 20 percent appears to have been pure fantasy.

The difficulties of implementing the strategy adopted at the beginning of this decade were quite evident in 1974, when inflation shot up and the balance of payments problems reached a critical point (see Tables 3 and 13), leading to a period of economic difficulties. Indeed, the policy of deepening soon required a major increase in the rate of investment. This increase in fact did occur (see Table 11) and had a notable accelerating effect on the domestic capital goods and intermediate inputs industries, as well as on the imports of these goods (see Tables 4 and 6). This effect was, moreover, reinforced by the fact that deepening was pursued simultaneously with the ongoing program of massive public works (such as those referred to above), with a rapid expansion of consumer durable production, and

---

[72] IPEA, *Crescimento industrial no Brasil* (Rio de Janiero: Relatorio de Pesquisa, No. 26, 1974), p. 207.

with a boom in luxury housing construction, duly sanctioned by government policy and stimulated by the euphoric expectations of the private sector. These expectations played, moreover, an important independent role in the rise of the rate of investment, which is reflected in a tendency to overaccumulate—including stocks of intermediate goods—which was also reinforced by speculation stimulated by the uncertainties of the external sector.[73]

Within this context, since petroleum imports (and overall imports) started growing at a dizzying pace after 1967, and particularly after 1970 (see Tables 8 and 9), the quadrupling of oil prices came to represent a virtual *coup de grace*, precipitating a balance of payments crisis.

The earlier development program had already generated inflationary pressure before the petroleum "crisis," involving the over-heating of the economy and the increase of international prices starting at the end of the previous decade.[74] This pressure was visible in 1973 and could be mitigated only by the reapplication of price controls, the overvaluation of the *cruzeiro* (whose price in relation to that of the dollar was not altered during this entire year) and a dubious manipulation of the official price indices (which was later recanted), which began to skyrocket in 1974, when the rate of inflation rose to one and one-half times that of 1973 (see Table 3), a proportion well above that which could have been caused by increases in petroleum prices alone.

On the other hand, this development program had been viable only due to an enormous external indebtedness which was necessary despite the pronounced growth of exports. By 1973, the deficit in the current account of balance of payments had been equivalent to more than 2 percent of GDP and almost 8 percent of the level of gross capital formation in the economy. In 1974, with the further rise of petroleum prices and the sharp increase of imports of producers' goods, these percentages rose to almost 8 and 21 percent respectively, creating a situation which could not be sustained (see Table 13).

It was in this context that the new government which was in-

[73] According to the national accounts recently published (*Conjuntura Econômica*, July, 1977), the increase of these stocks in the economy in 1973 and 1974 was, respectively, 95.4 and 91.3 percent in real terms, with the level reached in each year being approximately 4 and 7.4 percent of the GDP.

[74] These pressures were due as much to the increase in the prices of imports as to the rise in the prices of Brazilian exports.

stalled in 1974 tried to embark upon a program of deepening which could be considered more "classic," i.e., based on a reduction of the import coefficient in a manner more conventionally associated with the "difficult" stage of ISI.[75] Important sectors of the government came out in support of this strategy, which was now indeed perceived as necessary and which was implemented with the explicit purpose of shifting the dynamic source of growth from consumer durable goods to producers' goods. The import substitution program, which focused on basic inputs and capital goods, was also accompanied by a vast energy program and by the attempt to expand considerably the production of primary product exports (cellulose, iron, aluminum, and even steel) by means of enormous investments in the form of joint ventures between the state, multinationals, and, to a lesser degree, private national capital. There was also an attempt to end the exponential growth of consumer durable production, principally automobiles. On the supply side, the CDI's incentives for this sector of production were eliminated, and, with regard to demand, the maximum time limits for consumer credit were reduced.

It should be noted that the implementation of this deepening program, which was undertaken by the authoritarian regime in Brazil, has not been characterized by any particular imagination or rationality that are more original or superior to those exhibited during the previous deepening cycle which preceded the bureaucratic-authoritarian regime. This recent program has, in fact, weakened the structure of the BA regime which, stretching the terms a bit, even seems to exhibit a certain *disaffinity* for deepening. This is because deepening, under the conditions in which it has taken place, has in fact required the abandonment of assumptions that were fundamental for the stability of the regime during its most authoritarian period (the period of the Medici government). On the one hand, they have in large measure limited the expansion of consumption. On the other hand,

[75] During 1974, in the midst of the repeated declarations that in the context of the world crisis the Brazilian economy represented an "island of tranquility," those responsible for economic policy still did not believe that it was necessary to reduce the import coefficient. No type of effective control over imports had been established, which was partially responsible for the 35 percent increase in imports over 1973. Only beginning in the middle of 1975 were more decisive steps taken in this direction.

this has taken place in the context of a decline in the growth of demand, which greatly reduces the likelihood of success. This factor, along with growing inflation and a major change in the patterns of investment, reduces the predictability of economic policy and considerably increases the conflict of interests among the different sectors of the bourgeoisie, including its internationalized—or directly international—fractions and the directors of state enterprises. Moreover, what remained important—in terms of its implications for the ideological weakness of the regime—was the fact that it was not always possible to find some "guilty" party that was responsible for the economic problems. These problems arose and worsened, even though all the conditions that the ideologues of the right claimed as necessary and sufficient for sustained economic growth were met: the absence of an effective organized labor movement, of free and direct elections, and of any trace of national populist (i.e., nationalist and distributive) tendencies at the core of the government; an absolute guarantee and all manner of stimuli and incentives for the so-called business community, national as well as international; and repeated and effective "votes of confidence" for the good health of Brazilian capitalism.[76]

Returning to the O'Donnell hypothesis, I would like to emphasize, as Tables 6 and 7 and Figures 1 and 2 indicate, that during the growth phase observed between 1966-1967 and 1973-1974, the economy considerably increased its degree of "structural dependence" in relation to the international economy.[77]

---

[76] I do not pretend to suggest a simple causal relationship between the economic difficulties and the political opening, both of which occurred during the Geisel government. Indeed, in other contexts, they have been negatively correlated. It should be recalled that Geisel's project of "decompression" was conceived *before* the economy entered into this period of instability, and that the decompression occurred after there had been a liquidation of opposition political groups, both armed and unarmed.

[77] Regarding this greater structural dependence, it is appropriate to mention the results of a regression analysis between the annual commercial balance as a proportion of exports (BAL) and the difference between the potential product and the actual product (GAP), for the period of 1952 to 1974. The potential product has an annual rate of growth of 7 percent, which was uniform throughout the period. According to this analysis, for the economy to operate at "full" capacity, i.e., with a GAP of zero, the commercial deficit would have to be equivalent to *11 percent* of exports in 1952 to 1963 and *45 percent* of exports from 1964 to 1974. For BAL to equal zero—that is to say, in order to achieve equilibrium in the commercial balance—the GAP have to be equal to less than *3 percent* in

Import substitution and deepening certainly occurred during this period, but at a rate and to a degree that fell far short of representing an "opening" of the economy. Thus, the role of imported goods as a proportion of the total supply of the majority of producers' goods increased significantly. It is quite true that if one employs a highly disaggregated classification of industrial activities, there would be a substantial reduction of the import coefficients for many of them. But in no case could such a reduction, to the extent that it occurred, begin to refute the existence of a larger pattern of increased dependence and even "undeepening," understood in relative and dynamic terms.

Indeed, reflecting upon what has occurred in the Brazilian economy in relation to O'Donnell's essay would suggest that if the bureaucratic-authoritarian regime does indeed achieve (a) the stability which the MNCs desire, (b) a "certificate of good conduct" from the centers of international finance, and (c) the expansion of exports; and given the exclusion of the working masses (which leads to income concentration, in both functional and personal terms), the tendency with regard to deepening is the opposite from that suggested by O'Donnell. On the one hand, the relaxation of foreign exchange controls, the growing importance of the subsidiaries of the MNC's, and the acceleration of technology and product obsolescence, all tend to facilitate and to "force" greater imports of capital goods, intermediate inputs, and technology.[78] On the other hand, these same factors contribute to high rates of growth, concentration of income, and diversion of substantial resources to finance "modern" consumption and its support activities, which further accentuate the disparities in sectoral growth and, consequently, the need for imports to compensate for them. In this context, the elasticity of imports in relation to GDP tends to increase sharply.[79] And this is *not* due to requirements of *deepening* which was taking place prior to the process and which, therefore,

---

1952-1963 and close to *12 percent* in 1964-1974. See Edmar Bacha, "Issues and Evidence on Recent Brazilian Economic Growth," *World Development*, Vol. 5, Nos. 1 and 2 (January-February 1977), pp. 47-68.

[78] This is also true for expenditures on tourism and imports of unnecessary consumer goods which are largely caused by this relaxation of foreign exchange controls.

[79] It is interesting to note that, on the average, the elasticity of imports in relation to GDP rose from 0.32 in the period 1954-1962 to 1.9 in the period 1965-1973. In the latter period the Latin American average (including Brazil) was 1.3.

would end not only by stopping the growth of elasticity but by reducing it as well.

Chile and Mexico

What can be said of the relation between bureaucratic-authoritarian regimes and deepening in other Latin American countries? I will now refer briefly to the cases of Chile and Mexico. Concerning the first, it seems extraordinarily difficult to observe any deepening attempt on the part of the military regime—even at the level of rhetoric, not to mention in practice.

It is true, on the other hand, that the Chilean economy was considered a *locus classicus* with respect to the evils of excessive horizontal expansion. However, I question the notion that in the 1960's deepening, in the sense intended by O'Donnell, was perceived as absolutely indispensable by the political right, or that it was the *only* solution for capitalism or even, perhaps, a viable solution. In fact, the military regime seemed to want to carry out a reduction of horizontal expansion, not by means of a greater degree of integration of domestic (or even regional) production, but rather through the elimination of some productive activities and through a greater opening of the economy.

The examination of the Mexican case, which has a relatively industrialized economy, as well as what is probably the oldest and most stable bureaucratic-authoritarian regime of Latin America, could also be considered a relevant test of O'Donnell's hypothesis. In fact, since the period prior to industrialization, the Mexican state has not been "at odds" with civil society. For this reason, one could argue, the Mexican state would have been able to guarantee the social stability and future predictability necessary both for assuring the infusion of foreign capital and for pursuing deepening in such a way that "this capitalism" could most effectively fulfill the "essential function of transforming accumulation into productive investment."

Nevertheless:

a. Deepening in Mexico has not advanced farther than, or even as far as, in Brazil, or even in the long-suffering Argentine economy. Tables 14, 15, and 16 reflect this fact. Actually, the well-established bureaucratic-authoritarian regime notwithstanding, Mexico has progressed less than pre-1964 Brazil, according to the data in these tables.

b. There is no doubt that the Mexican regime was always more

TABLE 14
Imports as a Percentage of Internal Demand, 1970

	Argentina	*Brazil*	*Mexico*
Non-Electrical Machinery	25	40	80
Electrical Machinery	18	16	32
Metal-Mechanics	12	12	31

Source: Data provided by the Economic Commission for Latin America.

TABLE 15
Productive Structure of the Manufacturing Sector
(percentages)

| | *1969* | | | *1971* | | |
	A	B	C	A	B	C
Argentina	44.5	26.8	28.7	33.9	31.9	34.2
Brazil	41.2	29.4	29.4	30.3	32.7	37.0
Mexico	53.7	35.5	10.8	47.6	38.4	14.0
Colombia	63.4	27.2	9.4	58.8	29.1	12.1
Chile	61.2	29.1	9.7	57.8	33.2	9.0
Peru	63.6	28.7	7.7	60.3	28.0	11.7
Venezuela	63.5	29.4	7.1	49.9	40.6	9.6
Latin America	56.5	26.1	14.4	50.8	30.0	19.2

Notes:

A Principally industries which produce goods of current consumption: food, beverage, cloth, clothing, footwear, furniture, publishing, sundries.

B Principally industries which produce intermediate goods: chemicals, petroleum and coal by-products, non-metallic minerals, basic metallurgy.

C Principally industries which produce consumer durable and capital goods: metal processing, electrical machinery, transportation materials.

Source: Economic Commission for Latin America, *El proceso de industrialización en América Latina en los primeros años del segundo decenio para el desarrollo* (Santiago, 1971).

"efficient" in its role in internal social arbitration and that, with regard to economic policy and direct intervention in the economy, it was the most innovative in Latin America in the 1930's and 1940's. Mexico's ability to control the social mechanisms which generate inflation and the early (within the Latin American context) organization of a centralized system of financial in-

TABLE 16
Share of Metal Manufacturing and Machinery Industries
in the Generation of Industrial Production
(percentages)

	1960-1969	1965-1969	1970	1971	1972	1973	1974
Argentina	33	33.9	35.9	37.3	39.7	41.9	42.0
Brazil	31.5	31.4	32.2	34.3	35.1	35.7	36.6
Mexico	18.5	19.8	20.4	19.7	20.0	20.9	22.7

Source: Date provided by the Economic Commission for Latin America.

termediation, which was without parallel in the region, permitted it simultaneously to guarantee relative price stability,[80] also unique among the more diversified Latin American economies, and to orient the allocation of resources in a way which was more conducive to sustained growth.

But this did not mean that Mexico placed any particular emphasis on the task of deepening. It is important to note that starting in the mid-1950's, the Mexican state began reducing its role as the "engine of growth" (a tendency which would only be reversed starting in the mid-1960's and again in the 1970's),[81] reducing its role in providing external economies to private capital and in regulating the financial system. This change occurred precisely when deepening became the order of the day for industrial development in the larger countries of Latin America and when the Mexican regime was becoming "more" authoritarian. One of the indicators of the lesser relative importance of the state is, for example, the level of taxes in relation to the GDP. In 1970, this came to only 8.8 percent, in contrast to a Latin American average of 14.3 percent and 20.6 percent in Brazil.[82] Concerning public investment, Brazilian public investment represents approximately three-fifths of total investment and in the

[80] The more limited restrictions on the external sector were also crucial in insuring this price stability.

[81] On this topic, see the data compiled by E. V. K. Fitzgerald, "The State and Capital Accumulation in Mexico" (paper presented to the Society for Latin American Studies at York, April, 1977).

[82] This data was obtained from the Economic Commission for Latin America (ECLA). Contributions to the social security system are not included as taxes, and the above figures were calculated at 1970 prices.

Mexican case this proportion is only two-fifths, which is lower than the level of pre-1964 Brazil.

It seems to me that two ideas regarding differences between Mexico and Brazil in their performance in the area of deepening should be abandoned. First, the relatively sound capacity of the Mexican economy to import during the decisive 1950's and the early 1960's permitted the maintenance of an open economy at the same time that there were high rates of growth. Second, Mexico had less room for maneuver in relation to external centers of decision making, due to a lesser "diversification" of its dependency relations. Thus, more than three-fourths of Mexico's export earnings in 1958 came from the United States, a percentage that in 1968 was still two-thirds. With regard to the origin of imports, similar proportions hold. It is interesting to note that both these factors were, on the other hand, essential for the greater stability of the regime (except for the formation of the regime, in the case of the second factor). The success of the external sector in contributing to the control of inflation and the proximity and "threat" of the United States can be viewed as crucial factors contributing to social cohesion, in that they gave rise to the formation of a strong nationalist sentiment which had important ideological and political implications.

Thus, just as there is not a necessary link between the bureaucratic-authoritarian regime and deepening, there is likewise, in my view, no link between the existence of an older and more stable bureaucratic-authoritarian regime in Mexico, with a greater capacity for maintaining internal social cohesion, and the greater or lesser degree of strengthening of the state as an "engine of growth" or at least as an "engine of deepening."

III. THE AUTHORITARIAN REGIME AND ECONOMIC RATIONALITY

In the previous section, within the framework of analyzing the deepening hypothesis, I summarized some of the principal features of the evolution of the Brazilian economy since the middle 1950's, especially beginning in 1964. This will now form the basis for discussing another type of connection—in this case involving a direct causal link that has been widely discussed with reference to Brazil—between the bureaucratic-authoritarian regime and economic growth. This argument has been presented not only by the ideologues of the regime but also by others who, although unhappy about the suppression of democracy, the repression, and the social consequences of economic growth that have occurred, nonetheless extol the supposed virtues of authoritarianism as an agent for promoting development.

This position is reflected in the writings of two authors who, analyzing the emergence of new military regimes in Latin America, argue that: ". . . the military in Latin America functions as a pivot, guaranteeing state autonomy and creating the same conditions of state power that obtain in older industrial powers. The military creates the conditions for growth, even though the price is sometimes extremely harsh in parliamentary and democratic terms."[83]

In the case of Brazil, one of the causes of this presumed talent of authoritarianism for stimulating the economy would seem to be in the association between this type of regime and a type of "pragmatism" and "rationality" in the economic policy-making process, an association which is extolled by the Brazilian policy makers[84] and which has also been emphasized by scholars concerned with Brazil:

"What have been the accomplishments of the military regime since 1964? Certainly they have succeeded in great measure in further centralizing the central government. Decision making is more efficient, resources are allocated more rationally, and economic growth goals are no longer subverted by the turmoil of the civilian political process. It is the economic record of the regime that stands as its one positive accomplishment."[85]

On closer examination, what does this talent for managing the

[83] Irving Louis Horowitz and Ellen K. Trimberger, "State Power and Military Nationalism in Latin America," *Comparative Politics*, Vol. 8, No. 2 (January 1976), p. 233.

[84] Thus, after saying that "The Revolution of March 1964 opened a new phase in the Economic History of Brazil" (capital letters in original) Simonsen emphasizes that the first aspect of this new phase involved ". . . the identification of economic development as the primary national objective, within a stable political setting which contributed to the continuance of the initial economic advances and which permitted economic decisions to be formulated on the basis of technical criteria, free from electoral pressures." Mario H. Simonsen and Roberto Campos, *A nova economia brasileira* (Rio de Janeiro: Livraria José Olimpio Editora, 1974), pp. 1-2.

[85] Riordan Roett, "A Praetorian Army in Politics: The Changing Role of the Brazilian Military," in Riordan Roett, ed., *Brazil in the Sixties* (Nashville: Vanderbilt University Press, 1972), p. 49.

economy really consist of? The arguments seem to be the following:

1. Authoritarianism impedes the eruption of "premature"
social aspirations caused by the demonstration-effect that accompanies the development of the mass media and by electoral
competition under democratic regimes. These phenomena lead
to distributivist policies which are incompatible with the rates of
investment necessary for rapid growth, or to inflation, which has
disruptive effects on economic activity.[86]

2. The social and political "tranquility" guaranteed by the iron
hand of the regime is essential for attracting foreign capital and
for satisfying international financial institutions, as well as for
carrying out large-scale investment projects which require a
high degree of future predictability with regard to the economy.

3. The authoritarian regime not only permits an increase in
capital formation by providing the resources and the demand
incentives for necessary investments, but also allocates resources
more efficiently and contributes to more balanced growth. This
is because, sheltered from the instability that is inherent in democracy in a country of low per capita income, it facilitates careful planning on the part of "dispassionate and pragmatic" state
technocrats. It reestablishes the healthy functioning of the price
system and replaces the inflationary mechanisms of financing
with an efficient system of financial intermediation.

How can one assess, in practical terms, this superior rationality? According to the criteria established by economic orthodoxy,
the basic method would be to consider the performance of the
economy with regard to overall growth, balance of payments,
inflation, rate of investment, and allocation of resources. The

---

[86] Simonsen asserts: "Organizing the aspirations of society into a feasible program of action is the great challenge to government officials of the modern
world, and it is unfortunately necessary to admit that many of them have been
unable to accomplish this task. It is also unfortunate but true that universal suffrage frequently rewards those candidates who promise to divide resources into
parts whose sum is greater than the whole. This leads to an excessive emphasis
on 'distributive' policies whose consequences include rapid inflation, external indebtedness, the failure of growth, and social disorder."

Mario Henrique Simonsen, "Preface" to M. Millo Filho, *O modelo brasileiro* (Rio
de Janeiro: Bloch Editores, third edition, 1974), p. 2. He then goes on boastfully:
"While a large part of the world continues to struggle with these problems, Brazil
has stood apart, since the Revolution of 1964, as an island of rationality." See
Simonsen, *ibid.*, p. 2.

performance of the last four variables is not an end in itself, but it is a relevant indicator of the possibilities of sustaining growth. These five variables will now each be examined in turn.

Growth

The rate of growth of the GDP between 1968 and 1974 was quite vigorous: about 10 percent per year (see Table 2). It is helpful, however, to analyze this dynamism within a larger time horizon. Thus, from 1962 to 1967 (which includes four years of the military regime) the rate was only 3.7 percent per year, which gave rise to the conjecture that the subsequent rapid growth could be interpreted as part of an upswing in the economic cycle that followed six years of limited overall growth of the GDP—and actual stagnation in per capita terms. During these years it was thought that considerable margins of idle capacity and potential for accumulation were created which contributed to the strong subsequent expansion (at least in its first phase, until 1970-1971). From this perspective, the performance of 1968 to 1974 simply brought the economy back to its overall level of growth in the postwar era, which is approximately 7 percent annually, as can be seen in Table 2 and in Figure 4. Between 1947 and 1961, a period in which the country had a reasonably democratic regime (especially between 1956 and 1961), the rate of GDP growth was 7 percent annually, an average which equals that of the 1961 to 1974 period. After this last year, as Figure 4 shows, the rate of growth of the GDP dropped to a level below the average level of the postwar era.

I believe, at the very least, that these facts persuasively underscore the uncritical character of assertions of the following type:

"The political agreement [that grew out of the 1964 coup] meant an abandonment of political democracy . . . and direct imposition of military rule *in order* to achieve a high gross national product. In an earlier political/democratic phase Brazil showed less growth in the economic sector. . . . After power was seized by the military, the gross national product rose annually by 11 to 12 percent and plateaued off at the latter level of 1974. Thus, we see that the military rule, by its impositions on all social classes of a coercive factor . . . began to spark an economic takeoff in very much the way that Europe managed economic gains with civilian rule [emphasis added]."[87]

[87] Horowitz and Trimberger, "State Power," p. 35.

FIGURE 4

REAL GAP IN BRAZILIAN GDP, 1947-1977
(Based on index with 1939 = 100; semi-log scale)

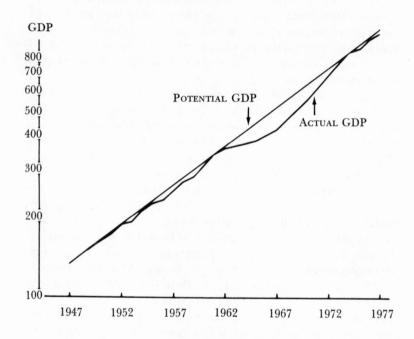

Sources: For 1947 to 1975, E. Bacha, "Issues and Evidence on Recent Brazilian Economic Growth," *World Development* 5, Nos. 1 and 2 (1977). For 1976 to 1977, it is based on my own calculations.

Balance of Payments

With regard to balance of payments, the most striking development is certainly the high rate of export growth, both in value and in quantity, especially after 1968 (see Table 17). There

TABLE 17
Annual Growth of Exports and International Reserves
(percentages)

	WORLD EXPORTS		BRAZIL EXPORTS		TOTAL RESERVES (SDRs)
	Value	Quantum	Value	Quantum	
1952/53-1958/59	1.5	1.8	-2.6	3.6	1.6
1958/59-1966/67	5.6	4.7	3.8	3.2	3.2
1966/67-1972/73	16.5	10.3	20.0	12.4	12.5

Source: Basic data from *International Financial Statistics*, 1977 Supplement (May).

has also been a significant diversification of exports, with industrial products in particular playing a larger role. There has also been a diversification among the non-industrial products, to the extent that coffee has lost the prominent position that it occupied until the beginning of the 1960's.

The brilliant performance of exports is frequently one of the principal triumphs held up to justify the merits of authoritarian governments in contrast to those which are elected democratically since, after the war and until the middle of the past decade, as we indicated above, exports remained practically stagnant. To what extent can this success be attributed to the regime?

It is undeniable that the set of export incentives first inaugurated in 1964 and developed principally after 1968, including the policy of mini-devaluations initiated in August of that year, played a fundamental role in this success. But we must not overlook the exceptionally favorable conditions of external demand during this period. We should recall that between 1952-1953 and 1958-1959 world exports grew at a rate of only 1.8 percent per year, in comparison with a growth of 10.3 percent in the period 1966-1967 to 1972-1973. Evidently economic policy makers knew how to take advantage of this changing situation, but, as Albert Fishlow carefully puts it, "Policies to exploit the external market are reactive to perceptions of generalized demand and cannot be presumed independent of it."[88]

On the other hand, was an authoritarian regime a necessary condition for the adoption of these export policies? Thomas Skidmore seems to suggest a positive response:

"Before 1964, Brazil had conspicuously failed to expand exports and thus created a serious 'import bottleneck.' One might wonder whether any elected government could have undertaken such a vigorous export promotion policy. . . . One might reasonably doubt whether they [Campos and Bulhões] could have sold such a policy [export promotion] to an elected government in 1964, when the animus against the export sector was still great among politicians who remained under the influence of the ECLA thesis."[89]

Apart from this extravagant hypothesis, which posits the supposed influence of ECLA[90] as a link between export promotion

[88] Albert Fishlow, "Development Policy: Some Lessons from the Past." Paper presented at the Annual Meeting of the American Economic Association, New York, 1977. It is interesting to point out, with regard to industrial exports, that together with the favorable conditions of external demand and the stimulus of the government export policy, there is no doubt that the crucial factor was the prior development of the industrial productive base, including the accompanying development of infrastructure, which was achieved in the expansive cycle of the 1950's and the early 1960's. During this period the dynamism of internal demand, the limited external demand, and the incipient state of development of the industrial sector, which had only recently begun to be more diversified, made it impossible to achieve dynamic growth in the export of manufactured products.

[89] Thomas E. Skidmore, "Politics and Economic Policy Making in Authoritarian Brazil, 1937-1971," in Alfred Stepan, ed., *Authoritarian Brazil: Origins, Policies, and Future* (New Haven: Yale University Press, 1973), pp. 24-25.

[90] ECLA's pessimism concerning exports can be traced back to the 1950's, when it was based on a not wholly incorrect perception of the conditions of the international market, as well as on the initial need to promote industrialization vigorously. With regard to this last aspect, as the secretary of ECLA says, referring to the decade of the 1950's: "[The] concern [with the export of manufactured goods] was outside the historical and objective framework within which the problem was posed. What was really in question was the very purpose of industrialization." See F. Iglesias, "Situación y perspectivas de la economía latinoamericana en 1975," *Revista CEPAL* (Primer Semestre, 1976), p. 87.

and the authoritarian regime, other types of links could be suggested. One is the hypothesis presented by Marini that "low wages increase the competitiveness of exports"; or that there is a need for "political stability in order to guarantee the stability of exchange policy, the stimulation of exports, and the future predictability required by the investments in the exporting industries" which is stressed by Robert Kaufman in Chapter 5 of this volume. These hypotheses, which are more relevant to industrial exports, are more reasonable than that of Skidmore, but they do not appear to me to be convincing. Regarding wages, it would be difficult to demonstrate that their compression in the post-1964 period explains the growth of manufactured exports to any significant degree, especially in comparison with the importance of the government's export incentives.[91]

As for the other hypotheses, it is appropriate to recall that, on the one hand, the export of manufactured goods mainly involved the shipping abroad of part of the output of industries that were primarily oriented toward the domestic market. There were no separate, large-scale investments that had been aimed primarily at developing this production for export. On the other hand, it has yet to be demonstrated that the guarantees of future predictability—and the related need for political stability required for investments in exports—is any higher than that for investments which aim at the domestic market.[92] Finally, it is difficult to believe that a consistent policy of export promotion could not have been carried out by more democratic governments, which might also have responded to the favorable conditions of external demand, as well as to the favorable conditions of internal supply, as occurred in Colombia and Chile in the 1960's.[93]

Another striking aspect of the evolution of the balance of payments, i.e., the major increase in foreign indebtedness, was also in part a result of the state of the world economy in the 1960's and 1970's, which was characterized by a notable expan-

[91] In the case of certain products, the combination of fiscal, credit, and exchange incentives reduced export prices more than 50 percent in relation to domestic prices.

[92] It may be said in passing that the investments in exports are always more uncertain, since they depend on external demand, which is an exogenous factor that is beyond the control of internal economic policy. But this has nothing to do with the question at hand.

[93] In Colombia between 1960 and 1970 non-traditional exports grew from one-eighth to one-third of total exports.

sion of international credit. Between 1966-1967 and 1972-1973, international reserves grew at an average rate of 12.5 percent annually, compared with only 1.6 percent in the period 1952-1953 to 1958-1959. The conjunction of export growth and this external financing allowed (and induced) imports to grow still more rapidly, as Tables 8 and 9 indicate. And it was only beginning in 1974, when the current accounts deficit reached a critical proportion of the GDP (see Table 13), that it became evident that it would not be possible to strike a balance between the rapidly growing payments for external goods and services, on the one hand, and receipts from exports and capital flows, on the other.

Indeed, the Brazilian experience in this area points to an interesting paradox that could, *mutatis mutandis*, be extended to the other Latin American countries with more diversified economies. This experience seems to suggest that the pattern of domestic growth tends to be readjusted in response to the possibilities for the external opening of the economy in that the demand elasticity for imports increases rapidly as these export opportunities increase, until the problem of external disequilibrium again returns.

It cannot be emphasized enough that this problem recurred in spite of the pronounced growth of exports (and despite generous external financing) which, at the rate at which it took place, should have been more than sufficient to avoid this disequilibrium if the earlier orthodox and structural diagnoses of the Brazilian economy were correct.[94]

Inflation

On this front, the success was more modest than is usually believed. It is quite true that the annual increase in prices was reduced from more than 80 percent in 1963 to a level close to 20 percent after 1968 (see Table 3). But this level is too high to allow one to say that inflation has really been "stabilized," even if

[94] Along with the disequilibrium, external dependency would have been increased—at least if one accepts the definition of Simonsen, writing as Minister of Fazenda: ". . . the true measure of the external dependency of a country is in the volume of imports essential to the functioning of economic activity and to the maintenance of an adequate level of investment. It may be asserted that the pattern of industrial development followed until 1973 increased Brazil's external dependency." See the *Gazeta Mercantil*, July 9-11, 1977, p. 6.

one takes into account the fact that two factors which orthodox economics always pointed to as the principal causes of the sustained high prices—the governmental deficit and union pressure—had disappeared.[95]

The fact that inflation had been reduced to one-fourth of its original level reflected the capacity of the regime to compress the income of the wage earner and of the popular classes in general, but the levelling of the inflation rate at this relatively high level reveals the difficulty faced by the regime in finding other means of resolving horizontal distributive conflicts—between the different sectors of the bourgeoisie and between the bourgeoisie and the public sector. This illustrates quite well, on the other hand, that authoritarianism is not necessarily an optimal substitute for more democratic regimes with regard to eliminating inflation.[96]

Indeed, the supposedly pragmatic and rational technocrats who were placed in control of economic policy by the bureaucratic-authoritarian regimes and who did not have to deal with any competition in the political sphere or with union opposition, do not necessarily represent a sure guarantee against inflation and may even exhibit objective behavior similar to that of the economic authorities of an ordinary democratic regime. This is exemplified by the acceleration of price increases which began in 1973,[97] under the influence of a heightened pressure of demands that resulted from the overheating of the private sector at the peak of the cycle of expansion, and which was further stimulated by a strong expansion of credit to the private sector.

[95] See José Serra, "El milagro económico brasileño."

[96] See Albert O. Hirschman, "The Social and Political Matrix of Inflation: Elaborations of the Latin American Experience" (Princeton: The Institute for Advanced Study, mimeo, 1978). The above assertion seems plausible to me provided that the authoritarian regime does in fact pursue high rates of growth, as in the case of Brazil.

[97] It should be reiterated that in 1973 (and to a certain extent in 1972) the technocrats themselves applied an anti-inflationary measure that was hardly orthodox: they underestimated the rise in the cost of living by basing their estimate on official prices instead of market prices. In fact, the official figure for the increase in the cost of living in 1973 (in Rio de Janeiro) was initially 12.3 percent, which was used as the basis for making wage adjustments, as well as for the calculation of the increase of the general price index. Subsequently, during the Geisel government, it was recognized that the increase had been 22.5 percent. The DIEESE index for the city of São Paulo reflected an even greater increase (26.5 percent).

Rate of Investment

At first glance, one of the most surprising characteristics of the performance of the economy after 1964 was the fact that the rate of investment, after declining in 1965 and rising in the following years, only in 1972 surpassed the levels reached in the period of 1958-1963. The data for industry reveal that in 1971, the rate of investment was still below that of 1962 (see Tables 11 and 12).

If the calculations of these trends are correct,[98] it is necessary to modify the idea that the authoritarian regime had a special talent for promoting productive accumulation (as if it were a type of Stalinism of the right), given that this accumulation rose above the maximum levels obtained in the 1950's only in the last three years of the expansive cycle of 1968-1974 and this, in large measure, because of the extremely high deficit in current accounts (see Table 13).

On the other hand, the attainment of this rate of investment calls into question the hypothesis that either income concentration (personal or functional) between 1960 and 1970 or the critical compression of workers' wages really represented a price that had to be paid by the popular sectors in order to allow society to invest a larger proportion of its resources. On the contrary, the popular sectors seem to have provided resources for the more affluent classes in society, in part for their consumption and in part so that they could finance the purchase of consumer durable goods by the better paid sectors of the middle class and the working class.

Resource Allocation

There is no evidence that the allocation of resources in the post-1964 period, or particularly after 1968, was more efficient than that, for example, during the previous cycle of expansion in 1956-1961. Assertions to the contrary are usually based on the idea that the economic policy of the authoritarian regime reestablished a freer price system and that the introduction of corrections in the monetary system neutralized a good part of the distortions generated by inflation. However, even if we admit

[98] The data on capital formation in Brazil are of questionable reliability (for discussion of this problem see Wilson Suzigan et al., *Crescimento industrial no Brasil: incentivos e desempenho recente.* Rio de Janeiro: IPEA/INPES, 1974). These conclusions should therefore be viewed with caution.

that both phenomena could have occurred, it is hard to conclude that the allocation of resources really "improved," if considered from a dynamic and macro-economic point of view. As we saw above, the prevailing pattern of investments and growth[99] tended to generate external disequilibrium, accelerated inflation, and imbalances among the three principal macro-sectors (producers' goods, consumer non-durables, consumer durables), thereby forcing the economic policy makers of the regime to resort to procedures which in the past would have offended the orthodox economists (we will return to this below).

That the efficiency of allocation of resources in the 1956-1961 period was not significantly inferior to that in the post-1964 years is clearly evident in the reflections of the individual orthodox economists. Thus, referring to the distortions that have accompanied the growth of the economy after 1950, Simonsen, in a book published in 1969, mentions that the "structurally most important" distortion that resulted from sustained development was the "artificial exploitation of the capital-output ratio."[100] Such exploitation would have been achieved through a pattern of investments which neglected the capitalization of agriculture and of social services, as well as through the abuse of the exchange subsidies for imports of equipment. Therefore, Simonsen argues, the "artificial" mechanisms used to reduce the capital-output ratio (i.e., to raise the output-capital ratio) ". . . beyond a doubt contributed to brilliant economic growth in the decade of the 1950's, but none of these could establish a stable, long-term policy of development."[101] What does Simonsen tell us about the period of 1968 to 1974?

". . . the automobile industry and the consumer durable sector in general grew at extremely high rates, which were not matched by the metallurgical industries or by the production of basic inputs and capital goods. Placing ourselves in the perspective of that period, there is no reason to criticize this pattern of development. The growth of the finished goods industry requires

[99] This growth included, as we already indicated in the previous section, heavy investments in unnecessary public works (much like those for which the right had criticized national-populist governments), not to mention the waste of foreign exchange due to the importation of unnecessary products that were in competition with domestic products, expenditures for tourism, and interest payments resulting from the excessive accumulation of reserves.

[100] Simonsen, *Brasil 2001*, p. 60.   [101] *Ibid.*, p. 61.

fewer investments and produces more rapid results, in terms of the increase in real product, than does the expansion of basic industries."[102]

That is, there was ample recourse to a pattern of investments that also "exploited" high product-capital ratios, but at the cost of backwardness in the producers' goods industries, of generating external disequilibrium, and of the acceleration of inflation. This hardly represented "a stable long-term policy of development."

The Vicissitudes of Economic Policy

It is always fascinating to observe in these quotations how orthodox thinkers focused so critically on the "artificialities" of the trajectory of the pre-1964 economy, whereas in their analyses of post-1964 development they began to view such artificialities—through a benevolent sociology of knowledge—as reasonable and logical. And indeed, they would seem to claim that their policies should be beyond any censure, principally because ill luck, and not the type of growth which took place, was the factor responsible for the economic difficulties which emerged beginning in 1964:

"Since it was not possible to anticipate that the price of petroleum would quadruple at the end of 1973, it seemed natural to accelerate economic development by the easiest route, leaving the more difficult part for an era in which the country would already have achieved a reasonable level of per capita income. The unhappy coincidence was the occurrence of the petroleum crisis precisely at the moment in which we were reaching the highest point of international dependency."[103]

Placing the "blame" on the hazards of the international economy is a predictable argument for the policy makers of the regime to make. For them, economic booms are always explained by the policy makers' virtues and economic failures by bad luck. This is understandable but not very persuasive, since it was precisely the phenomenon of "un-deepening"—in other words, the sectoral imbalance which accompanied the expansive cycle of 1968-1974—that was the starting point for the disturbances that began to affect the economy beginning in 1974. The first

[102] Mario H. Simonsen, lecture at the Escola Superior de Guerra, July 9-11, 1977.

[103] *Ibid.*

symptoms of these disturbances were already visible before the oil crisis, as in the shortage of basic primary materials and of labor and the acceleration of inflation. The oil crisis was an aggravating factor, rather than a cause, of the problems that occurred. Actually, the economic policies that accompanied the 1968-1974 cycle, based on unlimited confidence that the international economy would sustain its rapid expansion almost indefinitely, fell victim to a problem similar to that which Albert Hirschman called the "foreign exchange illusion."[104] Trying to attribute the principal responsibility for the decline of the cycle of expansion to the external sector is equivalent to trying to blame reality for not having behaved according to the requirements of an illusion.[105]

Finally, it is worth emphasizing that the experience of the Brazilian economy since 1974 magnificently illustrates how changes in objective conditions force those responsible for economic policy to adopt new measures that in the recent past would have horrified the orthodox economists: negative taxation on activities considered strategic to import substitution, compulsory deposits for imports, slower readjustments of public utility rates, and price controls for basic consumer goods. In the same way, characteristic dilemmas of the past are repeated (although there are also new types), as in the case of the difficulty

---

[104] Albert O. Hirschman, *The Strategy of Economic Development* (New Haven: Yale University Press, 1958). According to Hirschman: "The user of imported products immediately reacts to an increase in his needs by putting through more orders, and the importer transmits them abroad with gay abandon, not realizing that the real supply limitation consists in the ability of the country to earn additional foreign exchange through exports. This supply limitation is never perceived in advance and must therefore be brought home to the economic operators entirely through rise in price of foreign exchange or through exchange controls resulting from excess demands for foreign currency." Hirschman, *Strategy*, p. 168. It is obvious that this perception occurred much later than one would have hoped, since, as I indicated in note 75, only in the middle of 1975 was some control over imports first established.

[105] It should be noted that the adverse consequences of the changes in the international economy have been overestimated. For example, in the period following the petroleum "crisis," Brazil's terms of trade index did not worsen as much as is customarily alleged. This index in 1975-1976 was practically the same as 1970 to 1972 (see Table 9). It would not be correct to take 1973 as a base, since it was an exceptionally good year for Brazilian export prices. Nor would it be accurate to compare it with 1974, when the expected reactions of other international prices to the price of petroleum did not occur.

of further devaluating the *cruzeiro* (which is considered over-valued) because of the high levels of indebtedness in foreign currency on the part of enterprises; or of the need to halt or considerably reduce large investment projects in the primary product export sector, owing to the defections of the foreign partners who are discouraged by the poor prospects for the evolution of the international economy. And one also finds major errors in the planning and execution of these and other projects, including infrastructure projects, as is illustrated by the problems which arose in the execution of the railroad project.

CONCLUSION

It is appropriate to emphasize that we are not concerned with making value judgments about the appearance of stumbling blocks and disequilibria in the progress of the economy which, in the end, are simply inherent to capitalist development.[106] It suffices to note that, first, the bureaucratic-authoritarian regime in no sense created the conditions for enlightening its "state planners," even to the point of allowing them to rationalize their goals, not to mention to the point of allowing them to control the course of events through ignoring or overcoming the cyclical and contradictory character of capitalist development. Second, such problems as accelerated inflation, external bottlenecks, and the fact that cycles of expansion come to an end can also occur in the absence of effective competitive electoral processes and of any possibilities of organization and protest by the popular sectors. Third, dynamic economic growth and important transformations in the productive structure did occur, in the postwar Brazilian experience, under more democratic regimes. Fourth, the rapid growth observed between 1968 and 1974 was not the result of some superior skill of the authoritarian regime at capitalist accumulation, but rather of a particular combination of favorable conditions of the domestic economy and of trade and capital conditions in the world market. Fifth, it does not appear that the implementation of some of the more fundamental measures of economic policy—such as the promotion of ex-

---

[106] And these stumbling blocks and disequilibria, in a dialectical sequence, can have the end result of increasing (as has actually occurred) the chances for a fundamental reorientation in the economic sphere and even the emergence of a more democratic political system.

ports—required an authoritarian regime. Finally, it likewise does not appear that the style of growth observed (for example, regarding the distribution of income) was, for technical-natural reasons, inevitable. Actually, there is no convincing evidence that different political conditions, which responded to the very different dynamic of the class struggle, might not have been compatible with a satisfactory performance of the economy.

CHAPTER 5

INDUSTRIAL CHANGE AND AUTHORITARIAN RULE IN LATIN AMERICA: A CONCRETE REVIEW OF THE BUREAUCRATIC-AUTHORITARIAN MODEL

*Robert R. Kaufman**

Why are so many of the industrially advanced South American countries dominated by governments which express strong commitments to economic development and simultaneously trample so thoroughly on human rights? To what extent can such governments be usefully understood in terms of contradictions characteristic of delayed, dependent industrialization? This chapter addresses these questions through a comparative analysis of Brazil since 1964, Chile and Uruguay since 1973, and Argentina between 1966 and 1970: four instances of what has been labeled bureaucratic-authoritarian (B-A) rule.[1] "Authoritarian" Mexico, though less repressive than its South American counterparts, will also be considered at certain points, to broaden the comparison. The principal focus will be on the economic and social problems to which these governments appear to be a response. Though this is obviously only one perspective from which the origins of these governments may be viewed, it is clearly an essential perspective, both for a complete understanding of these cases and in terms of the larger set of theoretical arguments that are the concern of this book.

Militarism is, of course, a common Latin American phenomenon. Nevertheless, the South American governments referred to above have employed public instruments of surveillance, repression, and torture with unusual ruthlessness and efficiency.

* The research for this paper was supported by the Center for International Affairs, Harvard University, and by grants from the Social Science Research Council. Thomas Bamat provided extremely useful research assistance. I would also like to acknowledge the valuable suggestions of David Collier, Eric Davis, James Kurth, Guillermo A. O'Donnell, José Serra, and Alfred Stepan.

[1] Guillermo A. O'Donnell, *Modernization and Bureaucratic-Authoritarianism* (Berkeley: Institute of International Studies, University of California, 1973).

They have emasculated or suspended electoral and legislative processes, purged and demobilized the labor movement, and carefully monitored the activities of the media and the universities. Moderate and even rightist politicians, as well as leftists and guerrillas, are included among their victims. It may be that some traditionalist dictatorships—those, for example, of Duvalier, Trujillo, or Stroessner—have matched this record of systematic repression; but such men ruled over far less modernized societies, exercising power and extracting wealth for their personal benefit and for that of their families. The governments with which we are concerned display a rhetoric and intent which is modernizing and impersonal. Their "arbitrary" rule over workers, politicians, students, and intellectuals is accompanied by attempts to establish pragmatic and predictable relations with the private entrepreneurial sector, particularly international business, and to rationalize and advance the economy as a whole. It is this combination of repression and "rationality" which warrants empirical exploration and theoretical explanation.

In one sense, it is not difficult to understand why these forms of authoritarianism emerged in relatively advanced industrial societies. Any government which seeks to demobilize and control such societies for long periods must apply rather large doses of coercion. These governments are also more likely to possess the necessary technological and bureaucratic resources. A closer look, however, reveals some theoretical puzzles about why these South American regimes emerged where and when they did— puzzles which are particularly intriguing for those who are interested in uncovering systematic connections between socio-economic and political change.

Authoritarian modernization, for example, has often been viewed as a phenomenon associated with the earliest phases of industrialization.[2] The principal right-wing models are the nineteenth-century German and Japanese autocracies, which transformed backward agrarian societies into producers of steel, railroads, chemicals, and engineering products through the determined mobilization of industrial capital and the strict reg-

[2] Barrington Moore, Jr., *Social Origins of Dictatorship and Democracy* (Boston: Beacon, 1966). A. F. K. Organski, *The Stages of Political Development* (New York: Alfred A. Knopf, 1965), esp. pp. 122-58.

imentation of popular social and political demands.[3] But the developmental challenge confronting contemporary South American governments is *not* the transformation of pre-industrial, agrarian economies. The initial impulse toward industrialization had already been underway for several decades by the time these governments emerged on the scene. If anything, moreover, the politics of this initial phase of industrial transformation seemed closer to the British and French experiences than to those of Japan or Germany. Much of Chile's and Uruguay's industrialization had occurred under relatively institutionalized constitutional systems which, after World War II, extended political access to successively broader segments of the population. Even in Argentina and Brazil, where constitutionalism was not well entrenched, many viewed the "populist" politics of the 1940's and 1950's as evidence of a trend toward middle-class domination and increasingly open, if not institutionalized, patterns of political participation.

Only the most optimistic and naive observers, to be sure, assumed that these trends would necessarily culminate in stable mass democracies. Even in Chile and Uruguay, the obstacles to such developments were obvious to anyone who cared to peer beneath the surface: industrialization extended, or even exacerbated, the class tensions already present in the pre-industrial society; and twentieth-century mass communications generated expectations which continuously challenged the productive and distributive capacities of South American economies. Still, despite these problems, these industrializing societies did seem marked by increasing political participation and competition, a process which in turn seemed to increase the costs and reduce the probabilities of authoritarian developmental options. Why, then, were the contemporary governments of Brazil, Argentina, Chile, and Uruguay—governments so apparently committed to development—willing to pay these costs? And what have been the effects?

A number of authors—among them, Fernando Henrique Cardoso, Enzo Faletto, Philippe Schmitter, and Albert Hirschman—have suggested or implied that some important answers

---

[3] Alexander Gerschenkron, *Economic Backwardness in Historical Perspective* (Cambridge, Mass.: Harvard University Press, 1962).

may be found in the political and economic problems of capital accumulation encountered in the process of delayed, dependent industrialization.[4] In this chapter, I will explore some of the empirical and theoretical foundations of an important synthesis and extension of these arguments: Guillermo O'Donnell's thesis that these regimes are linked to an "advanced" phase of import-substituting industrialization (ISI) in which opportunities for small-scale investment have been "exhausted" and further expansion is perceived to depend on large-scale, usually foreign, investment in producers' goods industries. When superimposed upon the nationalist, populist, and participatory tendencies of earlier, "easier" phases of ISI, efforts to promote this new type of investment exacerbate conflicts which cannot be contained by popularly elected governments or competitive regimes. Increased requirements for long-term predictability and stability, pressures for fiscal austerity and labor discipline: all imply policy initiatives and structural changes which threaten the interests of the domestic bourgeoisie, white-collar consumers, and blue-collar workers, which had formed the bases of "national-populist" coalitions. B-A regimes, O'Donnell argues, emerge from the socioeconomic crises generated by this stalemate, seeking to resolve by force the contradictions that could not be settled through bargaining and negotiation. Far from being traditional and conservative, these regimes are in some respects dynamic and forward-looking, in the sense that their raison d'être involves a fundamental restructuring of the industrial economy and of its relation to other domestic economic sectors and to the international economic order.[5]

My purpose is to examine this argument by concentrating on

[4] Fernando Henrique Cardoso and Enzo Faletto, *Dependencia y desarrollo en América Latina* (Mexico, D.F.: Siglo Veintiuno Editores, 1970); Albert O. Hirschman, "The Political Economy of Import-Substituting Industrialization in Latin America," in Albert O. Hirschman, *Bias for Hope* (New Haven: Yale University Press, 1971), pp. 85-123; Philippe C. Schmitter, "Paths to Political Development in Latin America," in Douglas A. Chalmers, ed., *Changing Latin America* (New York: Academy of Political Science, 1972), pp. 83-108.

[5] O'Donnell deals most directly with the evolution and character of B-A regimes in "Reflexiones sobre las tendencias generales de cambio en el Estado burocrático-autoritario," Centro de Estudios de Estado y Sociedad (Buenos Aires, Argentina, 1975). See also, "Corporatism and the Question of the State," in James M. Malloy, ed., *Authoritarianism and Corporatism in Latin America* (Pittsburgh: University of Pittsburgh Press, 1977), pp. 47-89, and *Modernization*.

some limited, though critical, components of a much more elaborate chain of political-economic reasoning. I shall not, for example, deal directly with the complex historical arguments which trace the ISI of the first half of this century to earlier patterns of neo-colonial dependency, as well as to concurrent international constraints. A particularly important offshoot of this analysis, treated here largely as an assumption, is that this historical context gave rise to a technologically imitative, politically debile, domestic industrial bourgeoisie, which is currently unable to lead the "necessary" transition into producers' goods industries or to the export of manufactured products. Similarly, some of the ideological, psychological, and political-institutional factors which enrich and complete sophisticated neo-Marxist analyses of bureaucratic-authoritarianism will be noted where relevant, but a full treatment of these matters must also be left to another time and place.[6] This chapter will instead assess the explanatory contributions which are provided by a description and analysis of the contemporary socioeconomic dilemmas faced by B-A regimes. More specifically, the chapter is divided into three parts, each of which addresses a major issue deriving from the general proposition that B-A rule is "associated" with, and a necessary condition of, the transition from "easy" ISI phases to more difficult forms of industrial development.

Part I. What is the character of the four military governments that emerged in the South American cone during the 1960's and 1970's? This first section reviews, in relatively concrete and processual terms, the principal economic policies and political changes occurring under these governments.

Part II. Can the crises which led to the formation of these governments be traced systematically backward to a specifiable threshold where light-industrial investment ceases to be a viable

[6] For excellent attempts to build such factors into an explanatory framework, see: Alfred Stepan, "The New Professionalism of Internal Warfare and Military Role Expansion," in Alfred Stepan, ed., *Authoritarian Brazil, Origins, Policies, and Future* (New Haven and London: Yale University Press, 1973), pp. 47-69; and David Collier, the first and last chapters in this book. I have also tried to deal with such factors in "Corporatism, Clientelism, and Partisan Conflict," in Malloy, ed., *Authoritarianism and Corporatism*, pp. 109-49; *Transitions to Stable Authoritarian-Corporate Regimes: The Chilean Case?* (Sage Comparative Politics Series, Series 01-060, Vol. 5, 1976); and "Authoritarianism and Industrial Change in Mexico, Argentina, and Brazil," in José Luis Reyna and Richard Weinert, eds., *Authoritarianism in Mexico* (Philadelphia: Institute for the Study of Human Issues, 1977).

basis for overall economic expansion? Here, although the South American cases continue to be the central pivots of analysis, data pertaining to Mexico will be introduced to provide additional comparative perspective.

Part III. What sorts of economic changes followed the emergence of these governments, and to what extent can they be attributed to the policies of the governments themselves, rather than to changing international conditions or to "natural" upswings of the business cycle? Two types of change will be given special attention at this juncture: the acceleration of growth in producers' goods industries (an indication of what O'Donnell calls the "deepening" of industrialization); and the growth of industrial *exports*, a phenomenon which has been linked by other writers to right-wing authoritarian regimes.

These efforts, admittedly, retrace many of the steps already taken by O'Donnell, Cardoso, and others, whose general analysis derives primarily from an examination of countries in the South American cone. Their arguments, however, crystallized in the late 1960's and early 1970's, at a time when B-A rule in Brazil and Argentina was still at an early phase, and before authoritarian regimes had appeared at all in Uruguay and Chile.[7] Moreover, many aspects of their still evolving analysis remain ambiguous, and therefore subject to different interpretations and misinterpretations. The question asked and the cases examined here thus remain crucial links in the evolution of theoretical models with potentially more general applicability. To the extent that the answers to the questions just posed suggest common patterns, we can have greater confidence that these and other writers have launched us in useful theoretical and empirical directions.

PART I. AN OVERVIEW OF B-A RULE

The B-A Regimes

Let us begin by focusing on the South American B-A governments themselves. How did their economic policies, bases of

[7] Fernando Henrique Cardoso and Enzo Faletto, *Dependencia y Desarrollo en América Latina* (Mexico: Siglo XXI, 1970); Helio Jaguaribe, *Political Development: A General Theory and a Latin American Case Study* (New York, Evanston, San Francisco, London: Harper & Row Publishers, 1973); Rodolfo Stavenhagen, "The Future of Latin America: Between Underdevelopment and Revolution," *Latin American Perspectives*, Vol. 1, No. 1 (Spring 1974), pp. 124-49.

support, and methods of social control evolve after coming to power? The first part of this section presents relatively concrete thumbnail sketches of each government, taking up the account against the backdrop of the crises of political threats, inflation, foreign exchange shortages, and recession, which, in each case, accompanied the seizure of power. The second reviews some of the institutional and structural traits most commonly associated with B-A rule, as well as some of the important differences among the four specific cases.

Brazil. The central theme that dominates much of the historical analysis of this case—the most enduring and "successful" of the new B-A regimes—is the tentativeness and uncertainty with which the new military government groped toward the political-economic formula for which it is now so famous.[8] Many of the participants in the 1964 coup were, it is true, committed to an indefinite period of rule, implicitly rejecting the "moderating" role previously played by the military. But the precise contours of the new regime evolved gradually and have changed constantly ever since—the result of a succession of ad hoc experimental choices by the "architects" of the new order. From the vantage point of the mid-1970's, these choices seem to cluster into several phases, each of which represents important changes in the economic policies and structural characteristics of the regime itself.

The initial phase (1964-1967) was characterized by an apparent interaction between a strict stabilization program, designed primarily to control inflation, and a series of decisions which extended and elaborated authoritarian controls. Almost immediately, the technocrats of the new Castelo Branco administration froze wages, slashed government expenditures, and restricted the flow of credit to the private sector. Simultaneously, the government cracked down on organized labor and the supporters of the deposed Goulart regime, banning strikes and arresting or exiling officials of the previous administration. Continuing discontent with the stabilization program prompted successively

[8] See especially the articles in Alfred Stepan, ed., *Authoritarian Brazil, Origins, Policies, and Future* (New Haven and London: Yale University Press, 1973). For a useful review of Brazilian economic policy and performance, see Wilson Suzigan et al. *Crescimento Industrial no Brasil, Incentivos e Desempenho Recente* (Rio de Janeiro: IPEA/INPES, 1974). Also, Ronald M. Schneider, *The Political System of Brazil, Emergence of a "Modernizing" Authoritarian Regime, 1964-1970* (New York: Columbia University Press, 1971).

wider crackdowns, directed at broader, less obviously "subversive" elements of the Brazilian polity. An important turning point occurred after the October 1965 gubernatorial elections, in which associates of former president Juscelino Kubitschek won victories in Minas Gerais and Guanabara, two of the largest Brazilian states. Under "hard-line" military pressure, the government responded with the Second Institutional Act, which abolished existing parties, established the system of indirect presidential elections, and extended the president's authority to dismiss elected officials and suspend political rights. This decree etched rather clearly the main political-institutional outlines of the new political order. Although the Castelo Branco administration was relatively restrained in the exercise of its power, allowing considerable latitude for public debate in the press, it did act by the end of its term to suppress most major political leaders from every part of the ideological spectrum. Brazil thus seemed launched on its authoritarian trajectory.[9]

The economic aspects of the Brazilian "miracle," however, took shape more slowly. Although Castelo's defenders credit his administration with reducing inflationary expectations and instituting important changes in the fiscal and financial systems, the economic policies of this first period were not notably successful, even on their own terms. Austerity measures had produced a precipitous (and perhaps unnecessary) decline in working-class living standards, with only a moderate reduction in the rate of inflation itself. Although external public aid did flow into Brazil during this period, private investors and lenders were slow to respond to the liberal incentives offered by the Castelo government, and the recession which had gripped the industrial southeast showed few signs of abating. It was not until the second phase of the Brazilian "revolution," associated with the ascendancy of Delfim Neto as Finance Minister (1967-1974), that the Brazilian economy began to show dramatic signs of recovery.[10]

Delfim's approach was somewhat less orthodox than his predecessors, although hardly more favorable to the lower-class targets of the regime. The overall strategy of economic recovery

[9] Thomas E. Skidmore, "Politics and Economic Policy Making in Authoritarian Brazil, 1937-71," in Stepan, ed., *Authoritarian Brazil*, pp. 3-47.

[10] Albert Fishlow, "Some Reflections on Post-1964 Brazilian Economic Policy," in Stepan, ed., *Authoritarian Brazil*, pp. 69-119.

continued, as under Castelo, to be centered primarily on the strengthening of upper middle-class demand for consumer durables, and on the attraction of direct investment, import credits, and portfolio loans from abroad. However, Delfim abandoned the earlier commitment to achieving absolute price stability in favor of predictable annual price increases of about 20 percent. Credit flows to the private sector were liberalized, and exchange and minimum wage rates were "indexed" in ways designed to depoliticize these explosive issues and to hold down labor costs.[11] At the same time, Delfim accelerated earlier efforts to stimulate and diversify exports through subsidies and trade liberalization. And, by about 1970, the government's policy also turned more directly to a stimulation of producers' goods industries, after it became clear that the domestic demand for such products as steel and petrochemicals were far outdistancing previous estimates and targeted production goals. Mixed public and private commissions charged with overseeing investment in these areas were reorganized and strengthened, and approval was granted to a variety of large-scale projects that had previously been allowed to languish on the drawing board.[12]

These policies, it should be noted, coincided with extremely favorable international conditions—a major expansion of world trade and a virtual explosion of Eurodollar funds available for investment in third-world countries. It is impossible, therefore, to determine with certainty just how much of the ensuing economic recovery was, in fact, actually attributable to the Delfim strategy. Nevertheless, the apparent impact of his ministry was a rapid and sustained burst of economic expansion. In the seven years of Delfim's ascendancy, the Brazilian economy grew at an annual rate of approximately 10 percent, led first by a sharp recovery of consumer durables industries and then, from about 1970, by a rapid expansion of the capital goods sector as well.[13]

Although Delfim was appointed by a president, Costa e Silva, who had come to office promising political liberalization, this second phase of B-A rule was also marked primarily by a severe hardening and extension of the repressive apparatus. An outburst of wildcat strikes, scattered terrorism, and assorted acts of peaceful protest furnished the pretext for hard-line military factions to take the offensive. In December 1968, the Costa admin-

[11] *Ibid.* [12] Suzigan et al., *Crescimento Industrial*, pp. 50-73.
[13] *Ibid.*, pp. 111-49.

istration suspended Congress and issued the famous Fifth Institutional Act, which granted the president unrestricted powers
to protect "national security." The ensuing wave of repression—arrests, dismissals, police surveillance, and strict censorship—continued unabated during the first three years of the
Medici administration (1969-1974), which became particularly
noted for its use of torture in dealing with actual or suspected
opponents. In 1971, with the underground thoroughly de-
molished and the moderates intimidated, the Congress was
reinstated and the situation gradually "normalized." Until at
least 1974, however, the Brazilian security police remained the
most powerful arm of the government, monitoring every major
institution of civil society and stifling virtually all serious public
criticism.

A third aspect of the 1967-1974 period, finally, was the crystal-
lization of the alliance system which has been emphasized by
O'Donnell and Cardoso as a characteristic feature of "mature"
bureaucratic-authoritarian rule.[14] At the apex of the government structure, this system rested on the complementary
interests of civilian technocrats (such as Delfim) and hard-line
officers, interested in "development" and "national security" respectively. At a more fundamental level of analysis, one finds the
evolution of a close working relationship between government
officials, foreign managers and investors, and certain national
firms benefiting from state subsidies and joint stock arrangements—in short, the ruling "trio" constituted by the state,
foreign capitalists, and an "associated" domestic bourgeoisie.

With the 1974 accession of Ernesto Geisel to the presidency,
however, Brazil appeared to be embarked on still a third
political-economic phase, which involved potentially important
modifications in the economic policies and the sociopolitical
foundations of the regime. On the "political" level, Geisel promised a "decompression"—a reduction of press censorship, a relaxation of police controls, and the restoration of a limited degree of competition between the "official" ARENA and MDB
parties. Through 1976, these policies removed at least some of
the harshest aspects of the previous repression. However, hard-
line opposition and the government's vacillation prevented this

[14] O'Donnell, "Reflexiones"; Fernando Henrique Cardoso, "Associated-
Dependent Development: Theoretical and Practical Implications," in Stepan,
ed., *Authoritarian Brazil*, pp. 142-79.

process from going as far as some had hoped. Although critics of the regime were allowed greater latitude, intermittent arrests and censorship continued to generate an atmosphere of political insecurity. A politically embarrassing victory by the opposition MDB party in the 1974 congressional elections prompted the government to forbid public debate in the municipal elections of 1976. And there were no signs that military officials were prepared to abandon their control over presidential elections, to relax their control over union activities, or to renounce the special powers granted by the institutional acts of the preceding administrations.[15]

Within this somewhat more relaxed, but still authoritarian framework, there was also considerable uncertainty and debate about the economic and social directions which Brazil would take in the second half of the 1970's. By 1974-1975, the fuel crisis, the increased volume and prices of other imports, and the mounting weight of external indebtedness had slowed the country's overall economic expansion and produced substantial increases in the domestic inflation. In the context of these difficulties, a number of the policies initiated during the Delfim phase were questioned or altered. Advocates of liberalized trade and investment policies were, for example, placed on the defensive by supporters of a new, more intensive round of import substitution, designed to reduce Brazil's growing foreign debt. Some government officials also pressed for revised income policies which would strengthen the purchasing power of blue-collar workers in the more modernized sectors of the economy. And, despite a continuing rhetoric about the virtues of a free-enterprise economy, state enterprises assumed a commanding position within most of the important industrial branches, provoking strong protests from both the foreign and domestic private sectors and threatening the equilibrium of the ruling "trio" itself.

By 1977, therefore, virtually every aspect of Brazil's political economy—its institutional structures, policies, and even its supporting class coalitions—had been subjected to critical scrutiny and debate. Few *abrupt* changes, to be sure, seemed imminent,

[15] Since this paper was drafted, the Geisel administration engaged in a new crackdown, temporarily suspending the Congress and revising the electoral laws in ways that eliminate any possibility of MDB victories in state, local, or congressional elections.

but the overall direction of the system's future evolution seemed less clear than at any time since the 1964 coup itself.

Argentina. The Onganía government (1966-1970), like that in Brazil, seized power with vague commitments to purge the politically divided Argentine society of its "populist demagoguery," to end inflation and harness the productive potential widely felt to exist within the Argentine economy. The new authorities immediately announced that, in the interests of the revolution, elections would be postponed and parties banned indefinitely; this in turn was quickly followed by the banning of strikes, the intervention of key unions, and a harsh purge of dissidents within the universities. Also, within weeks of the coup, Alvaro Alsogoray, long an Argentine symbol of international economic orthodoxy, was appointed Ambassador to the United States, as a signal of the new government's commitment to impose a stabilization program and to attract new inflows of foreign capital.

With the appointment of Krieger Vasena as Minister of Economy in January, 1967, this general strategy was defined even more specifically. The government imposed a long-term wage freeze, lowered import duties, increased taxes and reduced the fiscal deficit, and decreed a "once-and-for-all" 40 percent devaluation of the peso. Although the immediate purpose was to contain inflation, these measures were also explicitly designed to lay the groundwork for the realization of three larger developmental goals: (1) the expansion and diversification of exports; (2) development of the economic infrastructure (particularly in railroad, electricity and port facilities, where the government promised to rationalize and streamline public enterprises); and (3) the promotion of massive private-sector investment in heavy industry, primarily with the aid of multinational capital.[16]

Although the Onganía government eventually collapsed in 1970, the broad outlines of its authoritarian experiment obviously paralleled the Brazilian experience. Nevertheless, several differences between the two cases are relevant to our discussion. First, Onganía's stabilization program did not, like Castelo Branco's, include a sharp reduction in monetary liquidity or credit to the private sector. Partially because of this choice and partially as a result of the timing of the international economic

[16] For major economic policy statements, see Onganía's address to the nation, *Review of the River Plate* (August 12, 1967), p. 215; Krieger Vasena, *Review of the River Plate* (October 11, 1967), pp. 19-20.

boom of the late 1960's, the new Argentine government did not have to wait as long as the Brazilians for an overall economic recovery. By the end of 1967, about the same time that the Brazilian economic miracle was appearing on the horizon, Argentine inflation rates had dropped substantially and foreign investment was returning in increasing amounts. These developments, coupled with substantial government investment in construction and a partial recovery of agricultural exports, initiated a steady process of economic expansion that lasted through 1970.

Moreover, the Argentine government accomplished these objectives with a lighter touch than the Brazilians. As in Brazil, workers in traditional light industries and small-scale domestic entrepreneurs suffered considerably from the stabilization program—commercial business failures doubled between 1966 and 1970, for example, in spite of the general prosperity.[17] Nevertheless, overall working-class living standards did not drop as precipitously as they had under Castelo Branco, or as they would subsequently in Uruguay and Chile; and torture and mass arrests did not figure prominently in Onganía's attempt to demobilize and control the society.[18]

Another possible difference between Brazil and Argentina is the relative emphasis which the latter placed on "deepening," although here the evidence is less clear. In fact, both the Argentines and the Brazilians frequently chose to supply capital and equipment needs through imports, rather than through the encouragement of local production, relying on export promotion and external credits to furnish the necessary foreign exchange. Impressionistic observation suggests, however, that local capital goods industries may have been given somewhat greater encouragement in Argentina. The concept of deepening seems to have appeared more frequently in the rhetoric of Argentine officials, and government regulations offered tax incentives to firms purchasing Argentine equipment.[19] The Argentines,

---

[17] Data from *Review of the River Plate* (April 30, 1973), p. 604.

[18] See Richard D. Mallon, in collaboration with Juan V. Sourrouille, *Economic Policy-Making in a Conflict Society: The Argentine Case* (Cambridge, Mass.: Harvard University Press, 1975), p. 30; United Nations, *Economic Survey for Latin America*, 1969, p. 109; Guillermo O'Donnell, "Estado y alianzas en la Argentina, 1956-1976" (Centro de Estudios de Estado y Sociedad, Buenos Aires, Argentina, October 1976), Grafico No. III, Series Mensuales de Salarios Industriales Seleccionados, 1956-1976.

[19] *Review of the River Plate* (July 22, 1967), p. 63.

moreover, appeared somewhat more successful in resisting the pressures toward capital and equipment imports: in Brazil, for example, domestically produced machine tools dropped from 64 percent of total consumption to only 33 percent between 1966 and 1970; in Argentina, the corresponding figures were 79 percent and 55 percent.[20] The Argentine government, finally, appeared to make more of an effort to control export earnings and to divert foreign exchange receipts into domestic investment. The massive devaluation decree mentioned above, for example, was accompanied by a large wind-fall tax—a measure which prompted considerable opposition from agricultural exporters.[21]

The factors which seem to have weighed most heavily in the collapse of the Onganía government were political and social rather than strictly economic in character. Most frequently cited are: (a) the divisions within the Argentine military itself; (b) the relative strength of the social forces negatively affected by the Onganía policies: notably, the agricultural elites, domestic entrepreneurs, and the unions; and (c) the absence in the mid-1960's of threatening, "anti-capitalist" mass movements that might have neutralized opposition from the first two sources. O'Donnell attaches particular importance to the opposition of the domestic entrepreneurs and nationalist military factions, which complained throughout the Onganía period of the penetration by multinational firms. Fear of the Peronist unions, he suggests, did not deter this opposition; for, despite the hostility with which the Argentine elites viewed these unions, the latter neither claimed to be nor were perceived as severe threats to the established social order.[22]

In this context, the famous Cordobazo of June 1969 dealt the *coup de grace* to a government which, though strong and successful on the surface, was in fact already suffering from considerable internal strain. Within a few weeks of the confrontation between workers, students, and police, Krieger Vasena resigned; about a year later, Onganía himself was ousted from the presidency by military officers who were unwilling to pay the political price of the president's development strategy. Although military

[20] *Review of the River Plate* (October 31, 1972), p. 656.

[21] See Mallon et al., *Economic Policy-Making in a Conflict Society*, p. 32; O'Donnell, "Estado y alianzas en la Argentina," pp. 26-27.

[22] O'Donnell, "Reflexiones," pp. 7-10.

presidents continued in office for the next three years, these events effectively brought Argentina's first bureaucratic-authoritarian experiment to an end. Post-Onganía governments abandoned Krieger's strict wage policies, adopted a somewhat harder (if still flexible) line toward foreign capital, and relaxed control over the unions. In the wave of strikes, guerrilla activities, and inflationary pressures which followed, the Lanusse administration in 1972-1973 eventually acquiesced to the transfer of power to the Peronist movement itself.

Chile. Whereas the Onganía government seized power in response to a relatively mild threat, the 1973 crisis which precipitated B-A rule in Chile involved an unprecedented challenge to that country's dominant elites. The escalating domestic class conflict, the foreign pressures on the Allende government, and the divisions within the Popular Unity coalition itself—all contributed to an extraordinary degree of social polarization and economic chaos that left a major imprint on the subsequent course of Chilean politics. On the one hand, the widespread middle-class fear of the revolutionary forces unleashed under the Allende government did much to consolidate the political power of the new military regime. Through 1976, there were virtually no significant signs of internal military division, and only feeble protests from white-collar and domestic entrepreneurial sectors who suffered considerably from the new government's severe anti-inflationary policies. At the same time, the military's determination to root out the deeply entrenched bases of Chile's powerful left-wing parties led it to create mechanisms of coercion which surpassed even those of Brazil during the late 1960's and early 1970's. Together with Uruguay and post-1976 Argentina, which also faced well-organized "threats from below," Chile's military government has undoubtedly been one of the most repressive of the South American B-A regimes.[23]

As in the other B-A cases, the Chilean junta called upon several internationally respected technocrats (for example, Jorge

[23] See Kaufman, *Transitions to Stable Authoritarian-Corporate Regimes*; also, Michael H. Fleet, "Chile's Democratic Road to Socialism," *Western Political Quarterly*, Vol. 26, No. 4, December 1973, pp. 766-86; Stanley Plastrik, "A First Word on the Chilean Tragedy," *Dissent*, Vol. 21, No. 1 (Winter 1974), pp. 7-11; Paul M. Sweezy, "Chile, The Question of Powers," *Monthly Review*, Vol. 25, No. 7 (December 1973); Paul Sigmund, "Seeing Allende through the Myths," *World View*, Vol. 17, No. 4 (April 1974), pp. 16-21.

Cauas) to frame policies that would reduce inflation and purge
the economic system of fundamental "irrationalities" that had
been allowed to accumulate under previous civilian administrations. The extent to which the Chileans embraced the tenets of
conservative economic orthodoxy was, however, also unusual,
even for B-A regimes. Even the Castelo Branco administration,
for example, resisted full application of the "shock treatment"
then being advocated by IMF spokesmen. The Chileans, however, imported virtually without reservation the strict monetarist
and laissez-faire doctrines inspired by Milton Friedman, apparently convinced that exceptional measures were essential to control the desperate inflationary and balance of payments crises
and to restore the shattered confidence of international lenders
and investors. More Catholic than the Pope, the junta totally
dismantled the import, price, and distribution controls installed
under previous administrations; froze wages; and severely restricted credit. Also dismantled was much of the "state enterprise" sector. Between 1973 and 1977, over three hundred firms
nationalized by Allende were returned to their former owners;
another two hundred state enterprises, many of which had
originated in the public sector, were sold into private hands.[24]
The junta's determination to attract foreign capital, finally, was
reflected by its refusal to adhere to Andean Pact restrictions on
multinationals and, in 1976, by Chile's withdrawal from the
Andean Pact itself.

The government's long-term strategy of recovery centered
primarily on the expansion and diversification of exports—a
strategy more suited than deepening to the relatively small size
of the Chilean economy. To promote copper sales, the junta
negotiated a settlement with the expropriated American mining
companies, in exchange for promises of marketing assistance
and of new investment in copper-refining industries. Commitment to the promotion of non-traditional exports was reflected
by, among other things, the formation of a new agency,
PROCHILE, charged with developing foreign markets for Chilean wines, fruits, shoes, textiles, leather products, and paper. It
should be noted that these latter efforts were also clothed in a
rhetoric of militancy which characterized so many other aspects
of the junta's behavior. Export diversification was portrayed as a

---

[24] CEPAL, Comisión Económica para América Latina, *Chile, Separata del Estudio Económico de América Latina, 1976* (E/CEPAL/1026/Add. 1), p. 305.

fundamental departure from Chile's long-standing dependence on industrial protectionism and mineral exports, a "hard, difficult" task which "require(d) talent, imagination, and perseverance." This was not, warned one official, a road for the "soft and inefficient" but for "dedicated men and women" willing to "prepare without truce, without rest, for a long, intense struggle for the conquest of markets beyond the sea. Victory will wed Chile's sovereignty to its progress."[25]

For the first three or four years of military rule, the impact of these policies seemed at best ineffective and at worst counterproductive. Despite the shock treatment applied to the Chilean economy, inflation came down only slowly, continuing at an annual average rate of about 175 percent through 1976. At the same time, a large number of Chilean firms were pushed into bankruptcy by credit restrictions and drastically liberalized import policies; and, as Figure 3 indicates, the flow of direct foreign investment remained at insignificant levels. In 1975, these policies combined with a sharp downturn in the world economy to produce one of the worst recessions in Chilean history, with a decline of almost 13 percent in the GDP. Despite a modest GDP increase of 3.5 percent in 1976, the per capita product of that year was only slightly higher than that reached in 1963. Unemployment in the post-1973 period was conservatively estimated at 15 percent; and, notwithstanding bonuses and family allowances designed to mitigate the effect of the stabilization program, Chilean wages had dropped to levels unknown in recent times.[26]

On the other hand, there were some scattered signs of improvement in the Chilean economy, and by 1977 these began to provide some basis for official optimism. Sales of both manufactured and traditional exports increased after the coup; and although European creditors refused in 1975 to refinance Chile's large external debt, private American banks and the World Bank began in the mid-1970's to provide a substantial inflow of financial aid and credit. By 1977, Chile had a balance of pay-

[25] See "Las Exportaciones: Visión al Día," and statement by Jorge Fontaine, Executive Secretary of PROCHILE; *El Mercurio*, Domingo 22 de Febrero de 1976, p. 25.

[26] GDP and inflation data from CEPAL, "Chile," *Separata del Estudio Económico de América Latina, 1976* (E/CEPAL/1026/Add. 1), pp. 299 and 301; on wages, see Ricardo Lagos and Oscar A. Rufatt, "Military Government and Real Wages in Chile," *Latin American Research Review*, Vol. x, No. 2 (Summer 1975), pp. 139-47.

ments surplus; its inflation rate had come down to about 60 percent; and its economy continued the modest recovery begun in 1976. The implications of these short-term developments remain unclear. They obviously do not provide sufficient evidence for government claims that the economy was headed for a "take-off" in the 1980's. They may, however, indicate a degree of "normalization," and the onset of a less chaotic and difficult period of economic activity.

Uruguay. The Uruguayan regime seized power more incrementally than the others with the present form of military rule evolving in stages out of the security operations conducted against the Tupamaros in the late 1960's. As the military pursued its operation, it gradually expanded its control over successively wider areas of government and society, pressing civilian authorities toward harsher, more repressive actions. In January 1973 the universities were intervened; in March 1973 a new military National Security Council was established to coordinate government policy; in June, at the military's insistence, a presidential decree closed the Congress and imposed press censorship. And, by the end of the year, harsh new labor legislation had disciplined the once powerful and independent union movement. With these measures, the state came under the domination of a somewhat uneasy alliance of high military officers and civilian agrarian interests, represented until 1976 by President Bordaberry.[27]

From a comparative perspective, one of the most significant aspects of the new, highly repressive Uruguayan government was that it was initially less capable of arriving at a clearly defined strategy of economic stabilization and recovery. Within the military, there were sharp divisions between hard-line nationalists, such as Gregorio Alvarez, and more internationally-oriented generals represented by Esteban Cristi. Moreover, Bordaberry's civilian administration was formed primarily by rancher-politicians; conservative technocrats, as a group, played no significant role. In fact, there were few such technocrats to be found among the small firms which comprised the bulk of Uruguay's industrial sector or within a university system which, even by Latin American standards, remained dominated by the "traditional" professions. In this context, the new government spent much of its first eighteen months attempting

[27] See successive issues of *Latin America* (January through July 1973).

to "eliminate corruption," the least common denominator among the disparate civil-military factions. Indeed, for over a year, these authorities could not agree on a permanent Minister of Economy, and the position was filled on an acting basis by a series of individuals.

The appointment of Vegh Villegas in September 1974, however, changed this picture significantly, signalling the ascendancy of the "internationalist" military faction and bringing Uruguayan policy more into line with that of other B-A regimes. The investment law was changed, for example, to guarantee prospective foreign investors the right to repatriate all earnings and officially committing the Central Bank to supply the necessary foreign exchange funds. Other policies ran along similarly orthodox lines, although with some differences in emphasis and tactics. Vegh's stabilization plan, for example, included a price as well as a wage freeze—a deviation from the even harsher shock treatment imposed by the Chileans. Similarly, a large (35 percent) interest-free cash deposit requirement partially offset liberalized import policies. Relevant governmental agencies were encouraged to assist exporters in developing more aggressive sales policies; but although manufacturing exports received considerable attention, the primary emphasis was on agrarian products—a reflection of the weight of the traditional rural interests in the Uruguayan government.[28]

These policy initiatives, it should be noted, did not go unchallenged. Unlike the Chileans, for example, Vegh was not able to follow through on a commitment to reduce fiscal deficits by turning inefficient public enterprises over to the private sector—a move apparently deterred by the anticipated opposition of public employees and their sympathizers within the military establishment. By mid-1975, only the municipal bus service had been detached from state control. Vegh's internationalist orientation remained under pressure as well. In 1975, for example, the joint chiefs-of-staff circulated a memorandum objecting to the "undue" influence that the IMF had acquired in economic policy making, a move which forced Vegh to threaten resignation. Finally, the 1976 ouster of President Bordaberry was additional evidence of internal division, even though, in this instance, economic policy issues played a smaller role. Despite these signs of strain, however, the major outlines of the Vegh strategy re-

[28] *Review of the River Plate* (May 30, 1975), p. 753.

mained in force throughout the mid-1970's, with few indications that they were about to be discarded. Although internal divisions were perhaps closer to the surface than in other instances of B-A rule, the "technocratic" orientation of the government appeared for the time being to be secure.

Let us, finally, review briefly Uruguay's overall economic performance between 1973 and 1976. As in the Chilean case, the record is quite mixed—although Uruguay's rulers appeared somewhat more successful than Chile's in moving quickly toward some of their principal objectives. In each of the four years between 1973 and 1976, the Uruguayan economy registered positive rates of growth, spurred primarily by a substantial increase in the volume of both agrarian and manufacturing exports. This was the first time in over two decades that Uruguay had experienced four consecutive years of economic expansion. As in most of the other cases, however (Onganía's Argentina is a partial exception), the living standards of the majority of the population deteriorated—real wages and salaries declined, for example, by 6 percent in 1976. Moreover, Uruguay's average annual growth rate of 2.2 percent during the years of military rule was still, by comparative standards, quite low—well below the rates of expansion experienced under the Onganía government in Argentina, or in Brazil since 1967. A glance at the record on inflation and foreign investment presents the same mixed picture. After a 1974 surge in the price level, the rate of inflation diminished substantially. The 40 percent inflation experienced in 1976, however, indicated that price stability was very far from being an accomplished fact. Similarly, although Uruguay's modest recovery was aided by a substantial inflow of non-compensatory foreign loans and credits (rising from a low of only five million dollars in 1973 to 130 million in 1975), the balance of payments situation remained precarious and, as in Chile, efforts to attract direct foreign investment failed almost totally. "Private capital," as one journalist put it, "is suspicious and undoubtedly Uruguay first has to prove not only that foreign capital would not run the risk of nationalization but also that it can operate freely and at a profit—that means in a stable economy with a stable currency."[29]

[29] *Ibid.*, p. 753; Data in the preceding paragraph is from Comisión Económica para América Latina, "Uruguay," *Separata del Estudio Económico de América Latina, 1976* (E/CEPAL/1026/Add. 2).

On the whole, we may conclude that—while the general economic record may well have proved encouraging to Uruguay's political authorities—the overall recovery was, like Chile's, partial and fragile at best. Even with the recovery, Uruguay remained a sluggish, low-growth economy. And with inflation and balance of payments difficulties only barely under control, even the modest gains registered between 1973 and 1976 remained vulnerable to rapid and devastating reversals.[30]

B-A Regimes Compared

For the purposes of the comparative analysis which follows, I have applied the "bureaucratic-authoritarian" label to the regimes described above and have assigned precise dates to their emergence and demise. Although this analytical abstraction may prove useful, however, it quite obviously simplifies a reality which is far more fluid and complex. Undoubtedly, the B-A military coups did bring about dramatic changes in the political structures of each country—in the scope of political participation, in the types of interests represented in the political process, and in the way such influence was exerted. Clearly, however, the new government did not entirely terminate the ongoing debates over economic policy, or the conflicts of interests which underlay this process. Indeed, the new "rules of the game" designed to contain and restructure these debates were themselves continuously tested and, at times, revised.

Above all, the preceding thumbnail sketches should make us extremely wary of assumptions that the policies or structural characteristics of any one case can necessarily be generalized to other countries. In fact, certain crucial aspects of public policy varied widely across cases and over time. In Brazil, for example, the state significantly expanded its entrepreneurial role; in Chile, the junta dismantled much of the large state apparatus that had been expanding steadily since the 1940's. All four governments paid some attention to long-term developmental goals, such as export diversification or investment in producers' goods industries. Understandably, however, economic stabilization received the highest initial priority; and, through 1976, the governments of Chile and Uruguay continued to wrestle primarily with this sort of problem. Finally, it should be noted that

---

[30] *Latin America* (August 15, 1975), p. 249.

there was substantial cross-national and over-time variation in the *kinds* of developmental projects emphasized by each regime. In Argentina, the Onganía government seemed to stress deepening objectives rather soon after the 1966 coup. On the other hand, the Brazilian capital goods industry was not seriously promoted until the 1970's, well after the initiation of higher priority efforts to stimulate the existing consumer durables sector and to diversify exports. In the smaller countries, Chile and Uruguay, deepening was hardly a realistic objective at all. There, export promotion seemed more the exclusive order of the day—again, however, with differing emphases on the relative importance of "non-traditional" and "traditional" products.

No less important were the differences in the class content of these regimes. Although each vigorously sought direct foreign investment, only two regimes (Argentina and Brazil) met with substantial positive responses. Only the Brazilians managed to consolidate a "ruling trio" of state officials, foreign capitalists, and "associated" domestic entrepreneurs; and this coalition lasted in unambiguous form for only a limited period of time. Agricultural elites strongly supported the government in Uruguay, and were virtually excluded from power in Onganía's Argentina. In every case, organized labor, white-collar workers, and domestic entrepreneurs suffered considerably. However, even the fortunes of these sectors varied somewhat: workers did not do so badly under Onganía, and may even have made some gains in Brazil during the 1970's. The economic losses of such groups, moreover, seemed to derive more directly from government-sponsored stabilization programs (as under Castelo Branco, and in Chile and Uruguay) than from the structural changes produced by the incorporation of multinationals into the ruling coalition.

It goes without saying, finally, that these four regimes differed markedly in terms of their overall political stability and economic success.

What, then, is the base of comparability among the four cases? Do they possess enough common characteristics to warrant placing them in a more general "bureaucratic-authoritarian" category? Despite their differences, each of the governments described above seems to have combined (in varying degrees, to be sure) at least three important features. Viewed in conjunction, these features in turn seem to offer a framework for generalization that does not do excessive violence to the contextual realities of the individual cases.

1. *A sharp restriction of "public contestation."*[31] Each government changed the prevailing rules of the game in ways that were quite clearly *authoritarian*. Government officials did not tolerate serious public challenge of their incumbency or basic policies; electoral competition and civil liberties were severely curtailed.

This is an obvious feature of B-A rule, but one which is nonetheless important for distinguishing our cases from others. Even with Geisel's decompression policies, for example, Brazilian politics of the mid-1970's differed substantially from the more open politics of the pre-1964 era. Top-level generals and their civilian allies continued to control the office of the presidency, which remained invulnerable to direct electoral challenge. Public critics of the regime were carefully isolated from potential mass bases of support in the universities and unions. Dissenters, though freer than in the late 1960's, were still intimidated by arbitrary arrests and continuous surveillance. And if the relatively relaxed Brazilian rule of the mid-1970's can still be considered authoritarian, the label applies a fortiori to the other cases.[32]

2. *The use of the state apparatus to depoliticize organized labor.* Despite the variation in the bases of their class support, each government focused on organized labor as a primary target of repression, employing various mixtures of police surveillance, arrests, and cooptive "corporatist" labor laws to penetrate and control the union movement. In each case, strikes were strictly prohibited and the unions purged of all leaders viewed as threatening by ruling officials.

In conjunction with more generalized restrictions on public contestation, this systematic use of *public* power should be understood as a defining characteristic of B-A rule. The absence of this feature, even in the general context of political authoritar-

[31] Robert A. Dahl, *Polyarchy, Participation and Opposition* (New Haven and London: Yale University Press, 1971), pp. 20-21.

[32] Mexico, by this criterion, can also arguably be considered authoritarian, especially if we focus on the absence of genuinely competitive electoral politics. On the other hand, despite episodic instances of repression and states-of-siege, both Venezuela and Colombia probably cannot be usefully placed within this category. Governments in both countries tolerated open and vigorous competition for important public offices.

ianism, would signify another type of regime. The traditional dictatorships mentioned in the introduction, for example, penetrated less directly and extensively into lower-class life, relying primarily on private mechanisms of social control. Moreover, members of the oligarchy and the business community, as well as workers, were frequently the targets of state power—the victims of systematic extortion, terror, and expropriation.

It is sometimes more difficult, unfortunately, to use this characteristic as a means of distinguishing B-A rule from so-called "inclusionary" regimes which employ similar means of public control for allegedly different purposes. Despite its reputation for populism, for example, Vargas' Estado Novo (1937-1945) displayed many important parallels with post-1964 Brazil. The former, to be sure, drew on nationalist and populist symbols employed by Vargas in the early 1930's, and it continued to take credit for the social welfare systems launched under earlier Vargas administrations. This provided a base of legitimacy which differed significantly from the more explicitly "exclusionary" governments of the 1960's and 1970's. Yet, as Thomas Skidmore notes, the Estado Novo itself *was* formed essentially in reaction to earlier popular mobilization and in defense of propertied classes. As in the post-1964 era, the Ministry of Labor employed corporatist legislation to purge and control existing unions and to discourage the formation of new ones. The now familiar techniques of surveillance and even torture were employed in the earlier era as well.[33] In the same sense, the Peronist regime of the 1950's, Mexico since the 1940's, and Peru since the mid-1970's bear an important resemblance to contemporary B-A regimes in their efforts to depoliticize and demobilize organized labor. This characteristic is thus not as unique or as closely tied to advanced modernization as is sometimes implied.

On the other hand, our contemporary B-A regimes *are* clearly different from authoritarian episodes most commonly cited as archetypical examples of inclusionary populist rule. Perón, until the late 1940's, actively bid for spontaneous labor support. The Argentine Ministry of Labor openly threw its weight on the side of striking workers; encouraged the formation of new syndi-

---

[33] Skidmore, "Politics and Economic Policy Making in Authoritarian Brazil, 1937-71," esp. pp. 39-43. Skidmore suggests that although "both clamped a lid on popular participation, . . . the Estado Novo was quicker and more complete in its repression than the post-1964 regimes" (p. 39).

cates; and delegated to syndical leaders considerable control of an expanded welfare system. Until Velasco's ouster, the labor policies of Peru's military government were also easily distinguishable from its South American counterparts. Strikes increased in the years following the 1968 military coup, and the better-organized unions acquired substantial new benefits for their members.[34] The Velasco government did not, like Perón, welcome union militancy, and indeed established corporatist controls designed to defuse it. However, in marked contrast to our cases, it also tolerated the continuing leadership of its APRA rivals on the coastal sugar plantations and in other major unions where the APRA had already acquired considerable strength. Professional associations continued to be strongly influenced by Acción Popular, as well as APRA. And in the mines, the Communist Party was allowed to control a large portion of the workers' movement.[35]

3. *A "technocratic" policy style.* Despite differences in specific objectives, each government also shared a common style, derived primarily from a self-image as pragmatic defenders and rationalizers of "capitalist" modes of economic modernization. It is probably not necessary for there to be a large "critical mass" of technocratic roles in order for a regime to adopt this style; nor is it likely that occupants of such roles will necessarily support right-wing regimes. What *does* seem an important aspect of this style is that individuals experienced in the management of complex organizations—technocrats—occupy strategic positions in the economic policy process. From their vantage points in the ministries of economy or finance, men such as Krieger Vasena, Delfim Neto, Jorge Cauas, and Vegh Villegas were more than simply the principal architects of economic policy: they were intellectual brokers between their governments and international capital, and symbols of the government's determination to rationalize its rule primarily in terms of economic objectives.

Viewed more broadly, the approach of such men and the regimes which brought them to power can be understood in terms

[34] See Richard Webb, "Government Policy and the Distribution of Income in Peru, 1963-1973," in Abraham F. Lowenthal, ed., *The Peruvian Experiment, Continuity and Change under Military Rule* (Princeton: Princeton University Press, 1975), pp. 79-128.

[35] I am indebted to Alfred Stepan for clarifying this point. Personal communication, February 1977.

quite distinct from the religious, inward-looking, anti-capitalist
and traditionalistic themes which prevailed in Spain and Portugal until the 1960's. Instead, cooperation with international
business, a fuller integration into the world economy, and a
strictly secular willingness to adopt the prevailing tenets of
international economic orthodoxy, all formed a different, but no
less ideologically bounded, set of intellectual parameters within
which the technocrats could then "pragmatically" pursue the requirements of stabilization and expansion. Their style did not
necessarily preclude experimentation, debate, or even some ges-
tures toward national independence and social welfare. Stabilization and growth, however, were the paramount considerations, ones that were to be elevated above any others and worth
virtually any social or political cost. The "technically rational"
pursuit of these twin objectives, rather than the inherent desira-
bility of authoritarian political structures or some other social
goals, in turn constituted the primary bases of efforts to legitimate and justify B-A rule.

II. The Origins of B-A Regimes:
Developmental Setting

Guillermo O'Donnell has discussed the emergence of these
labor-repressive, authoritarian coalitions in terms of several
interdependent levels of explanation. In the most direct sense,
B-A regimes can be understood as elite "problem-solving" responses to sociopolitical crises: particularly, a sharp economic
deterioration marked by inflation and recession, coupled with
the perception of a revolutionary "threat" from below. Figures 1
through 4 document at least one aspect of this crisis, displaying a
rather striking pattern of regularity from one country to the
next. In each case, B-A coups occurred in the context of accelerating prices and falling economic growth rates. In each
country where the relevant data are available (Argentina, Brazil,
and Chile), the figures also show a decline in the inflow of direct,
foreign investment. Not included in the figures, but equally important as components of the crises, were the political challenges
that accompanied these economic trends: the fears unleashed by
the Allende and Goulart governments in Chile and Brazil; the
severely corrosive challenges of the Uruguayan Tupamaros;
and the milder, but still significant threats posed by the electoral
gains of the Peronists in Argentina.

Another aspect of O'Donnell's analysis is also supported by the preceding discussion: the repressiveness of the governments that emerged in these situations can be linked directly to the severity of the crisis itself. The mildest version of B-A rule examined above emerged in Onganía's Argentina, which faced a relatively moderate Peronist challenge and comparatively mild inflationary pressures; the harshest forms were in Chile and Uruguay, where the capitalist system quite literally appeared on the verge of disintegration. From a strictly "technical" economic point of view, as Albert Fishlow notes in the Brazilian case,[36] the rigid orthodoxy and repression with which such regimes confronted these problems may have been unnecessarily harsh or even counter-productive. From the immediate perspective of the besieged initiators of B-A rule, however, the combination of economic crisis and political threat seemed to leave little room for choice.

At a more "basic" level of analysis, O'Donnell, Fernando Henrique Cardoso, and others have suggested that these crises and B-A choices can both be located within a much broader socio-economic "problem space" which typically emerged at the point where investment in light industries (textiles is the principal example to be used below) declined as the principal engine of manufacturing expansion.[37] The end of this initial phase of industrialization was arguably associated with changes in the class and industrial structures and with new cleavages and issues, all of which diminished elite opportunities to accommodate "populist" political and economic claims on the system. O'Donnell argues that, for domestic military actors and technocrats, as well as for the international bourgeoisie, the "costs of toleration" increased at this point, and broad incentives were created for the maintenance or establishment of the "exclusionary" practices and policies eventually brought together by B-A regimes.[38]

In this section, the focus will be on some of the principal characteristics of this still vaguely defined new "problem space" as it emerged in the four South American cases and in Mexico—a country which reached a comparable phase of industrialization at about the same point in time. The links between populism and the initial phase of industrialization will be reviewed first—

---

[36] Fishlow, "Some Reflections on Post-1964 Brazilian Economic Policy."

[37] O'Donnell, *Modernization*, pp. 53-78; 132-48.

[38] O'Donnell, *Modernization*, p. 90.

FIGURE 1: ARGENTINA

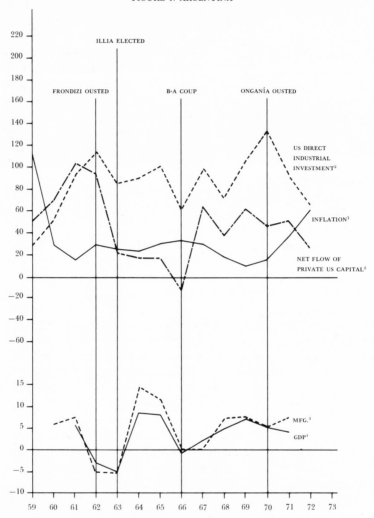

NOTES FOR FIGURES 1-4

[1] *Inflation figures*: Raymond F. Mikesell, "Inflation in Latin America," in Charles T. Nisbet, ed., *Latin America, Problems in Economic Development* (New York and London: Free Press and Collier-MacMillan, 1969), p. 146; U.N. Economic Commission for Latin America, *Economic Survey of Latin America*, successive years.

[2] *U.S. Direct Industrial Investment; Net Flow of U.S. Private Capital*: U.S. Department of Commerce, *Survey of Current Business*, various years.

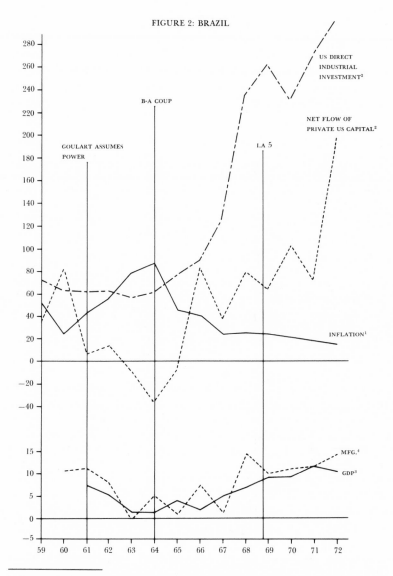

FIGURE 2: BRAZIL

[3] *Annual GDP*: U.N. Economic Commission for Latin America, *Economic Survey of Latin America*, 1964, pp. 62-72 and successive years.
[4] *Annual Mfg.*: U.N. Economic Commission for Latin America, *Economic Survey of Latin America*, various years.

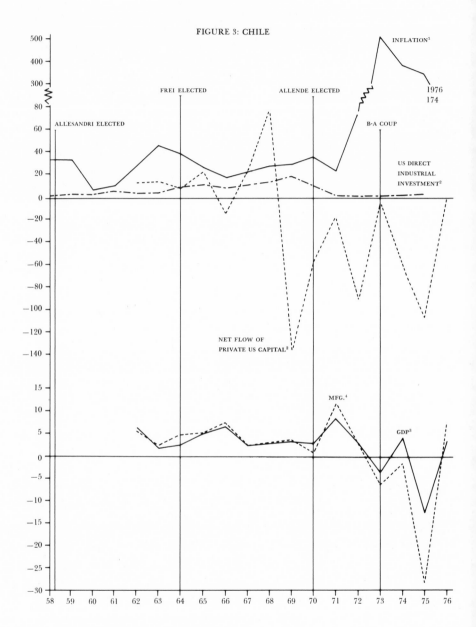

FIGURE 3: CHILE

FIGURE 4: URUGUAY

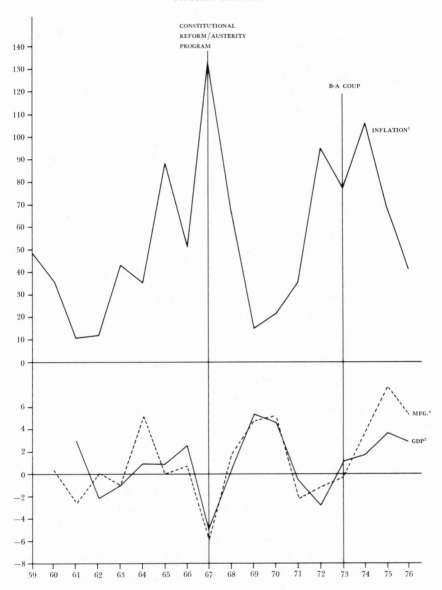

essentially as a means of setting the stage for the subsequent discussion. The second part will discuss some of the typical conflicts connected with new options which seemed to be placed on the "development agenda" at the end of this initial phase. In the last part, I will survey some of the principal variations in the way these problems were dealt with within the five "advanced" industrial countries prior to the advent of B-A rule itself.

The specific emergence and character of this generic form of rule, it should be noted, cannot be directly explained solely in terms of this broad analysis. A more fully elaborated predictive model would need to build in many additional "intervening variables"—not only the timing and character of the "triggering crisis," which after all was possible within a variety of developmental settings, but also such factors as the characteristics and perceptions of military and political leaders, variations in the balances among contending interests, and the way these interests were defined in concrete terms.[39] Nevertheless, it makes sense to consider these as *intervening* variables only if we can define with some clarity the new parameters and constraints allegedly arising from the changing industrial and class structure. Is it possible to identify common structural patterns underlying the political-economic variation among the South American countries and Mexico? Does the interaction between policy, political structure, and economic performance occur within a set of predictable limits that imply an increase in the "cost of toleration"? There is no utility in attaching theoretical primacy to any particular patterns of "delayed" or "dependent" socio-industrial change unless these questions can be answered affirmatively.

The Initial Industrial Phases and Populism

As a point of departure, let us assume that, despite vast differences in size and resources, these five countries were broadly comparable in the character and timing of their early phases of industrialization. First, common external stimuli seemed to weigh heavily in each case—prompting existing manufacturing firms, import merchants, and segments of the local export oligarchy to expand existing plants and to establish many new

---

[39] See David Collier's discussion of these factors, Chapter 9 in this book. For another highly important perspective: Alfred Stepan, *The State and Society: Peru in Comparative Perspective* (Princeton: Princeton University Press, 1978). Also, Kaufman, *Transitions to Stable Authoritarian-Corporate Regimes: The Chilean Case?*

small firms, all producing primarily for protected domestic markets.[40] The catalytic role played by the 1930's depression in this process is well-known. The drastic contraction in industrial imports, together with emergency pump-priming measures taken by local governments, created important new opportunities for local producers (both domestic and foreign) to enlarge productive capacity through the purchase of underutilized or obsolete equipment in the advanced countries. World War II indirectly stimulated an extension of this process. After 1945, pent-up domestic demand and accumulated foreign exchange reserves provided additional opportunities and incentives for increased manufacturing investment.

A second shared feature of this initial phase was the important role played by light industrial branches, such as textiles, in the overall expansion of the manufacturing sector. Manufacturing was not, to be sure, limited to "final touch" consumer industries. Most of our countries during the 1930's and 1940's had also begun to produce simple machinery, equipment, and supplies; and in at least one case (Brazil), large-scale public investment in the steel industry also played an important role. Nevertheless, in most of the largest and most rapidly growing industrial branches, barriers to entry were low, and there were substantial opportunities for small-scale private firms, requiring relatively limited, incremental inputs of capital and technology. In Brazil, perhaps the most industrially integrated of the South American countries, textiles alone accounted for over 20 percent of the value added in manufacturing during the 1940's, and remained until the end of that decade the largest single industrial branch.[41] A similar pattern has been widely documented for each of the other countries.[42]

---

[40] See Albert O. Hirschman, "The Political-Economy of Import Substituting Industrialization," in Charles T. Nisbet, ed., *Latin America: Problems in Economic Development* (New York: The Free Press; London: Collier-MacMillan, Limited, 1969), pp. 237-67; Celso Furtado, *Economic Development of Latin America* (Cambridge: Cambridge University Press, 1970).

[41] Werner Baer, *Industrialization and Economic Development in Brazil* (Homewood, Illinois: Richard D. Irwin, Inc., 1965), p. 76.

[42] Among the various works consulted on each country, see:

Brazil: Joel Bergsman, *Brazil, Industrialization and Trade Policies* (London, New York, Toronto: Oxford University Press, 1970); Celso Furtado, *Diagnosis of the Brazilian Crisis* (Berkeley and Los Angeles: University of California Press, 1965)

Mexico: Timothy King, *Mexico, Industrialization and Trade Policies since 1940*

In each of the five countries, finally, these initial phases of industrialization seemed to terminate within the same decade. By the late 1940's, Argentina, Brazil, and Chile had reached the point where local producers could supply most of the existing demand for light industrial products; Uruguay and Mexico arrived at this point during the mid-1950's.[43] The import-coefficient data gathered by Ayza et al.[44] suggest that, for general purposes, 1950 is a useful cut-off date. By that time, each of the five countries were producing approximately 90 percent of their textile consumption—the first of the Latin American countries to have done so.[45] Again, it should be noted, this point was reached in the context of quite similar international market conditions. Protectionist barriers narrowed U.S.-European markets for Uruguayan and Argentine cattle and wheat during the late 1940's; and revenues from the "traditional" exports of Chile, Brazil, and Mexico began a sharp decline in the aftermath of the Korean war. These difficulties, coupled with the rapid exhaustion of wartime foreign exchange reserves, magnified the importance of international lending institutions and private creditors in dealing with persistent balance of payments difficulties. The other important component of the new international

(London, New York, Toronto: Oxford University Press, 1970); Sanford A. Mosk, *Industrial Revolution in Mexico* (Berkeley and Los Angeles: University of California Press, 1950); Clark W. Reynolds, *The Mexican Economy, Twentieth Century Structure and Growth* (New Haven and London: Yale University Press, 1970)

Argentina: Mario S. Brodersohn, ed., *Estrategias de industrialización para la Argentina* (Buenos Aires: Editorial del Instituto, 1970); Carlos F. Díaz Alejandro, *Essays on the Economic History of the Argentine Republic* (New Haven and London: Yale University Press, 1970)

Chile: P. T. Ellsworth, Chile, *An Economy in Transition* (New York: The MacMillan Company, 1945); *La Economía de Chile en el Período 1950-1963* (Instituto de Economía, Universidad de Chile, 1963); David Felix, "Chile," in A. Pepelasis et al., eds., *Economic Development, Analysis and Case Studies* (New York: Harper and Row, 1961); Markos Mamalakis and Clark Winton Reynolds, *Essays on the Chilean Economy* (Homewood, Illinois: Richard D. Irwin, Inc., 1965).

Uruguay: Israel Wonsewer et al., *Aspectos de la industrialización en el Uruguay* (Montevideo: Publicaciones de la Universidad, 1959).

[43] See, *intra alia*, works cited above.

[44] Juan Ayza, Gerard Fichet, and Norberto González, *América Latina: Integración económica y sustitución de importaciones* (CEPAL, Fondo de Cultura, Mexico, D.F., 1976).

[45] In 1950, by contrast, Colombia and Peru were supplying about 20 percent of their textile consumption through imports; Bolivia and Ecuador, close to 40 percent; in Venezuela, the figure was over 70 percent.

environment was, of course, the competitive growth of multi-national oligopolies—manufacturers of both consumer durables and producers' goods—which sought to defend or enlarge international markets through direct investment.

These changes in domestic investment opportunities and world marketing patterns comprise the economic dimensions of the common problem space faced by the advanced industrial countries in Latin America. It should, of course, already be evident that the decline of light industrial investment opportunities was only one of these dimensions, and that it by no means dealt a fatal blow to prospects for further economic expansion. The end of this industrial phase did, however, seem to call for policies that could adjust to new domestic and international exigencies—the acceleration of investment in more complex industrial branches of the local economy and/or new trade policies which might deal more directly with postwar external bottlenecks. Before we turn to a fuller discussion of these new developmental choices, however, it is necessary to review a second sociopolitical component of this new problem space—specifically, the populist pressures and policies which had overlapped with the initial phases of industrial change and, in varying degrees, spilled over into the new one.

"Populism," broadly understood, was rooted in the discontent of three separate, often antagonistic, social groupings. The oldest and politically most important of these were white-collar employees—the clerks, professionals, administrators, and service workers who emerged originally as spin-offs of the export sector. The groups within this category pressed primarily for increased access to the political system, using the state to guarantee consumption and mobility opportunities that would secure their status vis-à-vis the lower classes. Blue-collar workers in the mines, railroads, ports, and the factories constituted the second grouping—interested principally in securing union recognition and collective protection in matters of job and social security, wages, and working conditions.[46] After 1929, finally, fractions of the local entrepreneurial classes began, with much ambivalence, to identify with populist movements emphasizing protectionism and import-substitution. From about the time of World War I,

[46] For an excellent discussion of the social bases of the populist movements, see Frederick S. Weaver, *The Industrialization of South America* (New York: Urizon Press, forthcoming).

politicians appealing to various combinations of these interests began to challenge the political dominance (although not the economic role) of the agro-export elites, uniting their diverse followings around vague anti-oligarchical and nationalist appeals and general promises of social reform. At certain points in their careers, leaders such as Alessandri, Irogoyen, Battle, Cárdenas, Vargas, and Aguirre Cerda, all figured prominently in such populist episodes.

In the absence of an aggressive bourgeois leadership, these movements concentrated on reforming the mechanisms of distribution, rather than on altering the structures of production. Indeed, prior to 1929, white-collar workers and industrialists themselves identified their welfare primarily with the continued expansion of the export-economy. With the exception of Mexico, moreover, there was never a serious challenge to the property of traditional elites or to their control of the agrarian and export sectors—a fact which allowed these elites to tolerate, if not welcome, the occasional political victories of populist coalitions. The great depression, however, not only intensified the pressures for distributive reforms, but for the first time contributed to a widespread disillusionment with the export model, linking questions of distribution to the patterns of industrialization described above. Faced with the threat of economic collapse, "conservative" and "progressive" governments alike engaged in inflationary fiscal and credit practices, with the expectation that local producers and consumers both shared an interest in the maintenance of domestic purchasing power. Protectionist barriers were erected around the light industrial branches, while the import of heavy industrial equipment and supplies was encouraged. Trade and price policies (again with the exception of Mexico) tended also to place a heavy burden on the producers of exportable agricultural products, as political authorities attempted to divert food products or foreign exchange to meet the immediate requirements of the local market.

In each of the countries we are examining, these pressures and policy themes formed an important component of the political context in which manufacturing growth initially gained momentum. The historic coincidence of these phenomena, a pattern consistent with O'Donnell's general analysis, in turn sets the stage for the subsequent dilemmas which contributed to the rise of B-A regimes. At this point, however, it is necessary to introduce an important caveat: although populist pressures and import substitution coincided during the 1930's and 1940's, they were not as causally interdependent as O'Donnell and other writers have implied. Both processes owed as much to common pre-industrial political and economic structures as they did to each other; and the looseness of the direct "functional fit" between them allowed industrialization to proceed initially under a wide variety of concrete sociopolitical circumstances. Although it is beyond the scope of this chapter to pursue these arguments in detail, a brief elaboration of these points is necessary if we are to understand fully how individual countries coped with the conflicts arising at the end of the initial phases of industrialization.

To turn first to the sources of populism, it should already be reasonably clear that the impulse for these pressures came initially from the urban centers and/or extractive enclaves connected with the export trade. Industrialization, to be sure, undoubtedly contributed to an *expansion* of the popular sector, especially to its blue-collar components. Nevertheless, even the workers' movements were shaped significantly by pre-industrial patterns of integration into the world economy: Argentine packing house and port workers; Chilean nitrate and copper miners; Mexican railway and petroleum workers, for example, all figured prominently in the populist pressures emerging within their respective countries.

More than industrialization itself, moreover, the form of pre-industrial dependency also helps to explain the varying political *outcomes* of these populist pressures.[47] For example, Julio Cotler traces the strongly rural-revolutionary character of Mexican populism to the predominance of foreign agrarian and mining enclaves in the nineteenth-century Mexican economy. The explosive pressures against these enclaves in turn contributed in the 1930's to the early containment of populism within the framework of authoritarian institutions.[48] Similarly, Vargas' successful corporatist preemption of working-class pressures in the industrializing Brazilian southeast can be understood only in

[47] Pre-industrial political institutions are also quite obviously crucial to the analysis. Many of the essential features of Chile and Uruguay's institutionalized constitutional orders, for example, were in place by the early 1900's.

[48] Julio Cotler, "State and Regime: Comparative Notes on the Southern Cone and the Enclave Societies," Chapter 6 in this book. Cotler here is following the lead of Cardoso and Faletto, *Dependencia y Desarrollo*.

the context of the large, depressed, "patriarchical" sugar economies of the northeastern states. Finally, it is certainly no accident that urban populist pressures were strongest and most enduring in Argentina, Uruguay, and Chile, where domestic control of relatively prosperous and commercialized nineteenth-century agrarian sectors generated the most uniformly modernized pre-industrial societies.[49] In short, despite comparable levels and patterns of industrialization, populism operated within these countries with different degrees of strength and success, in the context of both open and closed political regimes.

Conversely, and even more important for our purposes, industrialization during the 1930's and 1940's did not seem to depend closely on governments which tolerated or actively encouraged the organization and political participation of the popular sectors. Indeed, overtly "nationalist-populist" coalitions rose to power relatively infrequently during this period—the Cárdenas regime of the 1930's, and the Popular Front and Peronist governments of the 1940's are among the few that come to mind. Such regimes, it should be emphasized, provided at least one viable framework for the growth of the manufacturing sector. The industrialization records of the Chilean Popular Front or of the 1940's Peronist administration were, for example, no worse than that of their more conservative predecessors, even though Perón's policy toward the export sector is generally viewed as unnecessarily harsh and counter-productive. Although national entrepreneurs sometimes supported such arrangements or profited from them, however, they did not require them. The post-depression industrialization processes of Argentina and Chile began, after all, under the aegis of regimes strongly influenced by the agro-export oligarchies themselves.[50]

[49] Foreign control of the large Chilean copper enclave sets this country apart from Argentina and Uruguay, helping particularly to explain the explicitly Marxist orientations of Chile's workers' movement. Despite these "enclave" features, however, a relatively prosperous and commercialized nineteenth century agricultural base, coupled with a domestically-controlled "small-mining" sector, supported quite high levels of pre-industrial modernization.

[50] In the case of Argentina, Díaz-Alejandro notes that the stages of industrial growth "cut across political regimes," with the initial phase (1925/29-1948/50) initiated by conservative governments and carried forward by the Peronist regime. *Essays on the Economic History of the Argentine Republic*, p. 229. In Chile, industrial production grew by an average rate of 5.6 percent under Alessandri (1934-1939), and 4.7 percent under the Popular Front (1940-1942). Ellsworth, *Chile: An Economy in Transition*, p. 162.

And in post-Cárdenas Mexico and the Brazilian Estado Novo, manufacturing expanded under governments which, like contemporary B-A regimes, placed strict restrictions on the political activities of the popular sectors.

The distinctive feature of this early phase of industrialization, the quality which most differentiates it from subsequent phases, was that it was a relatively "spontaneous" process. Given other historical and international circumstances, it did not require the hegemony of any particular class coalition, or any specific set of political-institutional arrangements.

The "other circumstances" which most plausibly explain industrialization in these countries were export economies which, for a variety of reasons (a large number of backward linkages, domestic control of key economic sectors, etc.), had by the 1930's stimulated the emergence of comparatively modernized preindustrial societies.[51] Despite important differences among them, each country had by the 1930's developed relatively extensive domestic markets, entrepreneurial skills, and some local industry; and, in this context, governments, domestic entrepreneurs, and some fractions of the export oligarchy could respond relatively rapidly to the opportunities provided by depression and war. For reasons already suggested, it was not particularly costly for governments—whatever their overall political orientations—to engage in ad hoc pump-priming and protectionist measures. Given these incentives, private entrepreneurs could quickly move into established markets, with limited investments that were quickly amortized and not highly vulnerable to changing political conditions. Industrialization of this sort could thus proceed under regimes which were open or closed, popularly-based or repressive, stable or relatively unstable. As the initial industrialization phase ended, however, the political parameters of continuing industrial expansion appeared to narrow. In the 1950's and 1960's, variations in the structure of the state began to make more of an economic difference—particularly the capacity of the state to insulate economic decision-making from the populist pressures described above.

---

[51] See William P. Glade, *The Latin American Economies* (New York: American Book, 1969). My interpretation here is at variance with Andre Gunder Frank, who stresses *isolation* from the advanced industrial countries as a source of industrialization. See Frank, *Lumpenbourgeoisie: Lumpendevelopment, Dependence, Class, and Politics in Latin America* (New York: Monthly Review Press, 1972).

The End of the Light Industrial Phase:
Alternate Development Policies

We can now turn directly to a discussion of developmental options and conflicts facing the industrially advanced Latin American countries in the postwar era. The list of purely economic "bottlenecks" deriving from the earlier phase is, of course, quite well known. With some variations, this list has usually included: a high-cost industrial structure, unable to compete effectively in world markets; an undercapitalized or inefficient agro-export sector; and inadequate mechanisms for mobilizing public and private resources. It is also generally agreed that these, in turn, were underlying sources of recurrent foreign exchange scarcities, shortages of necessary equipment imports, inflationary pressures, idle industrial capacity, unemployment and underemployment.

The immediate crises which triggered B-A coups can be traced to these bottlenecks. The connections, however, are complex and indirect; for such crises were neither the unique products of this phase of industrialization nor did they follow inevitably in its wake. Indeed, Mexico and Brazil in the 1950's survived the decline of "easy" ISI opportunities relatively uneventfully, without serious problems of "stagflation" or political polarization. These phenomena were, on the other hand, familiar features of the Chilean and Argentine landscapes before as well as after the postwar era. The significance of the 1950's transition point was not so much that it brought about inherently unmanageable economic or political difficulties, but that it marked the end of a period in which these difficulties could be dealt with (or by-passed) through investment and marketing patterns that did not seriously exacerbate class or sectoral antagonisms. The problems of postwar eras were *socio*economic, rather than purely economic in character.

The multi-dimensionality of these dilemmas is recognized rather clearly in O'Donnell's discussion of deepening, if not perhaps in his earlier formulation of the connection between ISI and bureaucratic-authoritarian rule. The initial work[52] seems to attach primacy to the saturation of domestic markets—the

---

[52] O'Donnell, *Modernization*. In this book as well, however, O'Donnell does suggest the argument he develops more fully in "Reflexiones," see esp. pp. 60-70.

"exhaustion" of ISI possibilities and a consequent emergence of "mass praetorianism" and B-A coups. His subsequent work[53] gives more emphasis to a complex, escalating conflict between advocates of deepening—a vertical integration of the industrial economy—and the social forces that had gained strength in earlier decades. For military and technocratic elites, he suggests, the need for deepening seemed to flow logically from chronic shortages of imported producers' goods and from increasing opportunities to attract direct foreign investment in these areas. This objective, however, implied "orthodox" policies and structural changes which threatened vested populist interests; and this spiraling clash of interests, in turn, increased the "costs of toleration" for elites interested in promoting development within a capitalist framework. Figure 5 diagrams these themes.

However, though O'Donnell's elaboration of the sociopolitical dilemmas of "deepening" improves significantly on simpler, purely "economistic" explanations of B-A rule, his argument is still cast too narrowly. A broader, more complex, but potentially more useful extension of the argument can be obtained by considering the coalitional implications of a number of other postwar developmental strategies as well. These strategies, which are summarized in Figure 6 (as well as Figure 5), are reviewed schematically below. Each of these was, like deepening, also pursued in at least some of the industrially advanced Latin American countries, and each also implied potentially significant conflicts with at least some populist interests. Let us, therefore, briefly examine some of the most typical cleavage patterns connected concretely with these options.

1. *Deepening.* I will hereafter use this concept to refer primarily to large-scale investment in such "producers' goods" branches as petrochemicals and steel, as well as in heavy machinery and equipment. These branches—particularly the first two—were most emphasized by B-A regimes and some of their predecessors, and their expansion seemed to generate the most observable controversy within the industrial sector. In Argentina, Brazil, and Mexico, proposed or actual multinational investment in these branches during the 1950's and 1960's attracted the most direct opposition from smaller, local producers in the same industrial branches and from nationalist politicians,

[53] O'Donnell, "Reflexiones."

FIGURE 5

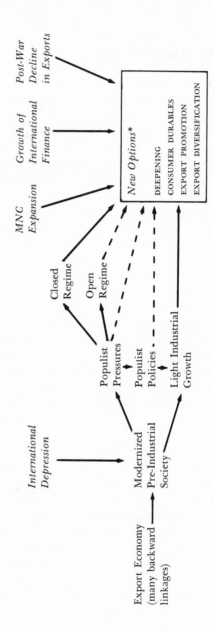

* Market expansion options not included.

▲ represents compatible, "flow" relationships

◀- - - indicates contradictory relationships

intellectuals, and military officers who feared a loss of control over strategic areas of the industrial economy. The creation or expansion of state-owned enterprises, on the other hand, encountered opposition from another source: downstream producers who generally preferred to purchase cheaper, more reliable, imports. Less directly, the expansion of dynamic producers' goods sectors was also a challenge to the relative political and economic influence of workers and entrepreneurs in the more "traditional" industrial branches. Perhaps most important, finally, were the broad defensive struggles generated by the stabilization plans which both governmental authorities and international business perceived to be necessary conditions of this sort of investment.

The very uncertainty generated by such pressures were, O'Donnell argues, at variance with the interests of the large-scale investors themselves; for such actors placed a special emphasis on the stability and predictability of the "rules of the game"—on the capacity to make long-term projections about price and exchange rates, import policies, domestic marketing conditions, relations with other domestic buyers and with industrial unions.[54] Both before and after the institution of B-A rule, uncertainty about such issues caused the delay or abandonment of several major investment projects planned by governmental authorities and multinational companies.[55]

2. *Consumer durables investment: strengthening middle- and upper-class markets.* The automotive industry was the most typical beneficiary of this strategic option. During the 1950's, this branch expanded dramatically in each of the "big three" countries (Argentina, Brazil, and Mexico); more recently, it was a central component of growth patterns in post-1964 Brazil.

Multinational producers in these areas have typically assumed a considerable amount of the investment and marketing initiative; and in a protected consumer market, they may also have had a somewhat greater tolerance for price and cost uncertain-

[54] *Ibid.*, pp. 11-21.

[55] Conflicts over such issues were regularly reported in such journals as *The Economic Unit Intelligence Report, Review of the River Plate*, and *Visão*. On the Argentine steel and petrochemical industries, see, for example, *Review of the River Plate*, Nov. 22, 1967, p. 249; On Brazilian steel and petrochemicals, see *Visão*: October 12, 1967, pp. 26-30; November 9, 1967, p. 29; Nov. 21, 1967, pp. 77-86. *Economic Unit Intelligence Report*, No. 1, 1972, p. 14.

Figure 6

Overall Strategy and Characteristic Policies	Strongly Favored Interests		Swing Interests		Strongly Threatened Interests
Deepening Stabilization Devaluation	MNC's—producers' goods	External lenders	Export elites	Competing local producers	
	Upper middle-class consumers	Skilled workers	MNC's—consumer durables		Workers and management of traditional industries
Consumer-Durables Promotion Stabilization—needed to obtain import credits	MNC's—consumer durables	External lenders	Export elites	Local component suppliers	Lower-income consumers White-collar consumers
	Upper middle-class consumers	Skilled workers			
Primary Products Export Promotion Devaluation Stabilization	Export elites	External lenders	MNC's Upper-middle class consumers		White-collar consumers Urban labor Local firms

Ind. Export Promotion				
Devaluation Stabilization Export Subsidies	Producers of exportable mfg. products-MNC and domestic	Export elites External lenders	Underemployed and unorganized workers	Local producers' goods firms	White-collar consumers Domestically-oriented MNC's and traditional firms Organized workers

Domestic Market Expansion			
Tax reform Land reform	Unorganized workers Consumer-goods firms	Most MNC's External lenders	White-collar consumers Organized workers Export elites

ties, particularly in the larger countries.[56] Nevertheless, automotive expansion in the 1950's and 1960's produced cleavages and difficulties which required the mediation of governmental authorities. The most common conflict was over the supply of components. The automotive companies themselves generally preferred imported to locally produced components, and multinational suppliers to domestic ones. Domestic suppliers and their nationalist political allies have pressed in the opposite direction, with a good deal of success but with a probable cost in terms of productivity and prices.[57] Encouragement of the upper-middle class market has, of course, also had a widely noted impact on income distribution and employment patterns—particularly in the case of post-1964 Brazil, where the government purposively relied on regressive incomes policies to stimulate the recovery and expansion of the consumer-durables branches. The relatively large import requirements of these branches, finally, have magnified the importance of international creditors for the domestic economy. Perhaps even more than direct investors themselves, these creditors have in turn placed a special emphasis on the "respectability" and creditworthiness of the local governments.

3. *Primary product exports.* With the decline of light-manufacturing opportunities and the persistence of chronic foreign exchange shortages, there have also been strong postwar pressures to replace "inward-looking" patterns of industrial growth with a more favorable treatment of the primary product export sector. This strategy, in combination with others, was attempted in Argentina during the 1950's and after 1976, in Brazil during the late 1940's, and in contemporary Chile and Uruguay. Its premise, derived from classical economic theory, was not an unreasonable one: the long-term interests of exporters, domestic manufacturers, and consumers were complementary, rather than conflicting. Emphasis on the comparative international advantage of traditional exports, it was argued, would maximize the capacity to import producers' goods that could not be manufactured as efficiently within the local econ-

---

[56] Felix, "Technological Dualism in Late Industrializers."

[57] Jack Baranson, *Automotive Industries in Developing Countries* (Baltimore: The Johns Hopkins Press, 1969). See also, address by Douglas B. Kitterman, President of Ford Motor Argentina, S.A., *Review of the River Plate*, September 22, 1966, p. 481.

omy, and relieve the external bottlenecks that beset the domestic industrial sector.

This strategy was sounder than some of its ECLA critics have suggested, and might well have produced a more dynamic process of industrial expansion if it had been pursued consistently over the past forty years.[58] Yet advocates of primary product exports have tended to understate the difficulties posed by wide fluctuations in commodity prices, as well as by U.S. and European trade barriers. Even leaving these objections aside, moreover, there was in the postwar era little chance of coordinating industrialization and export promotion without generating strong political antagonisms. The depression, as we have seen, had shattered faith in export models and, during the 1940's, this was reinforced by the ECLA arguments about a secular decline in the terms-of-trade for primary products. By the 1950's, attempts to reemphasize traditional exports involved a number of measures—devaluation, stabilization, and simplification of exchange-rate structures—which reversed deeply entrenched governmental practices and implied major short-term transfers of income away from urban consumer and industrial interests. In the politically open, competitive systems of the 1950's, therefore, export promotion efforts (particularly devaluation decisions) were quickly nullified by urban pressures for compensating wage and price increases.

4. *Industrial export promotion.* During the late 1960's, this strategy had attracted increasing attention as a means of reducing external vulnerability and of expanding growth opportunities for the industrial sector. Concrete experience with industrial export promotion is still relatively new, and its political implications, unclear. Of the various options considered here, however, this probably involves the widest number of potential coalitions and cleavages, since so much would depend on the types of products exported and whether they are sold in world or regional markets.

Conceivably, for example, a new, economically viable base for much of the "popular sector" could be generated by an export drive which concentrated on the "traditional" manufacturing

[58] See Nathaniel H. Leff, "Export Stagnation and Autarkic Development in Brazil," in Charles T. Nisbet, ed., *Latin America: Problems in Economic Development* (New York: The Free Press; London: Collier-MacMillan, Ltd., 1969); Díaz-Alejandro, *The Economic History of the Argentine Republic*, pp. 254-76.

branches—textiles, leather products, and other simple consumer goods which require relatively low capital and technological inputs. The labor-intensive character of these industries provides the Latin American countries with competitive advantages in international markets and speaks to continuing problems of unemployment and underemployment at home. Indeed, it has been suggested that countries such as Argentina and Brazil might well have avoided many subsequent political-economic difficulties if, after World War II, they had engaged in concerted drives to continue wartime textile exports through vigorous diplomatic and promotional initiatives.[59] Despite unfavorable American trade policies, such efforts might have worked. However, it should be noted that in at least one instance (Brazil) textile producers did initiate proposals of this sort during the 1940's, only to have them rejected by political authorites attaching a higher priority to meeting the needs of the domestic market.[60]

By the 1970's, moreover, a "neo-populist" export coalition appeared even less likely. Three decades had passed since wartime markets were lost, and high-cost "marginal" firms had proliferated behind protectionist barriers. Moreover, the picture was vastly complicated by the international differentiation and specialization of MNC subsidiaries which transfer products across national boundaries. Export-bound MNC investment, David Felix has suggested, may be especially sensitive to political uncertainties—particularly when the investment involves large capital outlays which might eventually become hostage to the vagaries of price and exchange fluctuations.[61] More generally still, manufacturing exports of any sort arguably require policies which threaten a variety of domestic populist interests: devaluation and subsidy burdens on urban consumers; requirements of low labor costs and union discipline; liberalization of import

[59] This point has been suggested in private conversation by James Kurth, Swarthmore College (Fall 1976). See also the comments on this issue by Albert O. Hirschman, "The Political-Economy of Import Substituting Industrialization in Latin America," esp. pp. 259-65.

[60] Stanley J. Stein, *The Brazilian Cotton Manufacture; Textile Enterprise in an Underdeveloped Area, 1850-1950* (Cambridge, Mass.: Harvard University Press, 1957).

[61] Felix, "Technological Dualism in Late Industrializers"; Albert Hirschman makes the more general argument in "The Political-Economy of Import Substituting Industrialization."

policies; and stable expectations about price and exchange levels—in short, many of the requisites of predictability and stability that O'Donnell suggested were necessary for deepening.

5. *Income redistribution and domestic market expansion.* In the 1960's, some economists and reformist politicians argued that redistributive policies which enlarged the domestic market would provide a new impetus to manufacturing growth, primarily in non-durable consumer goods and in some low-price consumer durables sectors. This strategy was one component of the general policies of several otherwise quite different administrations: those of Frei and Allende in Chile, and of Campora-Perón in Argentina. Typically, however, the option encountered particularly serious political and economic constraints. It implied, for one thing, tax and land reforms which antagonized not only traditional elites, but much of the urban middle class. Moreover, it made unrealistic assumptions about the investment capabilities of the domestic bourgeoisie and/or the state itself. Other important limitations of this strategy will be dealt with at somewhat greater length below.

What were the political implications of these five development strategies? Viewed from one perspective, the schematic list presented above suggests some degree of flexibility for postwar decision makers. Some options, to be sure, were mutually exclusive—for example, consumer-durables promotion (2), and income redistribution (5). But the others could be linked in a fairly broad variety of interdependent combinations that invited support from many different quarters. Some of the strongest conflicts associated with these options, moreover, were over "short-term" measures that, after a few years, could arguably have produced an "expanding pie" situation from which many social sectors could benefit. None of the strategies "required," in any strict, direct sense, the highly repressive B-A regimes which eventually appeared in South America.

Nevertheless, as I have already suggested in the preceding section, economic decision makers *were* operating within a set of constraints which differed significantly from those in the earlier phases of industrial change. As previously noted, these earlier phases could occur under non-hegemonic conditions—without serious confrontations between contending social forces and even under fairly extensive conditions of political uncertainty. "Populist" reforms, accommodating some of the contending

white- and blue-collar claims, were feasible, though not necessary, concomitants of this process. Each of the postwar strategies, on the other hand, involved policies which (whatever their
potential long-term benefits) posed major, concrete threats to
the immediate interests of at least some segments of the old
populist coalitions. This was, it should be noted, true even of the
income redistribution options (no. 5), since white-collar and
many unionized blue-collar workers, as well as traditional elites,
could be required to bear much of the burden of the accompanying tax and land reforms. A fortiori, the argument applied
to the other postwar options as well. Governments attempting
such strategies were, therefore, continuously threatened with
serious erosion of popular support—a threat which substantially
reduced their room for maneuver within the framework of an
open, participatory political framework.

The problem of controlling inflationary pressures—what Albert Hirschman once called a form of peaceful civil war—[62]was
both a symptom and cause of these changing circumstances. No
popularly elected government (and only a few authoritarian regimes) could impose the sacrifices necessary to contain these
pressures.[63] During the initial industrialization phases, however,
rapidly rising prices did not seem to deter, and may well have
aided, the process of industrial expansion. Either way, during
the 1930's and 1940's industrial growth proceeded in an inflationary context in Argentina, Chile, Brazil, and Mexico. By
the 1950's, however, predictable price levels (and therefore
some policy resistance to populist demands) were widely understood to be preconditions of new forms of expansion, either into
"heavier" industrial branches, or into new markets. The only
apparent exception to this was Brazil during the 1950's—where,
in spite of price instability, market size and tight control over the
labor force encouraged continuing industrial growth. In the
other, more open South American countries, however, inflation
and industrial expansion seemed to fluctuate in opposite directions—almost immediately in the case of Uruguay and Chile,

[62] Albert O. Hirschman, *Journeys Toward Progress* (New York: The Twentieth
Century Fund, 1963), p. 221.
[63] See Thomas E. Skidmore, "The Politics of Economic Stabilization in Postwar
Latin America," in James Malloy, ed., *Authoritarianism and Corporatism in Latin
America* (Pittsburgh: University of Pittsburgh Press, 1977), pp. 149-91.

and after about a one-year lag in Argentina (see Figures 1, 3, and 4).

Beyond the specific problem of price stabilization, moreover, it seems reasonable to say that four of the five strategies listed above were predominately "conservative" in character. International business elites, the export oligarchy, or the upper middle class received most of the immediate benefits of the first four options. Workers in "traditional" industries, the urban and rural poor, or urban consumers generally, all bore most of the immediate burdens and the most serious long-term risks. One can, to be sure, conceive of moderate as well as extreme versions of each strategy—versions that would soften "short-term" costs and insure a relatively equitable distribution of "long-term" gains. In the real political world, however (especially one so uncertain and conflictual), the pursuit of short-term interests was neither unusual nor irrational. Governments seeking to implement these options were thus likely to attract their most vigorous support from the more conservative social sectors and to penalize the most vulnerable ones.

Finally, income redistribution and market expansion, the remaining "neo-populist" option, was probably the least viable postwar choice, for a combination of economic and political reasons. Much of the support for this strategy had, for one thing, to be mobilized from among the politically weak, socially heterogeneous mass of the urban and rural poor. The only immediate beneficiaries among the more "established" social sectors were producers of traditional finished goods, as well as a few multinationals able to adjust their production to meet the needs of a low-income mass market. As previously noted, on the other hand, considerable opposition was to be expected from the most politically powerful elements of domestic society, often including white-collar and some union groups at the core of the old populist movements.

In addition, the acquisition of imported equipment and supplies posed especially serious problems for market-expansion strategies—more even than consumer-durables promotion, which also relied heavily on such imports. Both types of strategy were sooner or later likely to run into balance-of-payments difficulties. Market expansion options, however, were likely to encounter the most serious problems in overcoming this obstacle.

One reason was that the traditional export sector, rather than the poor, was more likely to be a target of governments engaged in progressive redistributions of income. Moreover, international credit institutions—which sometimes relieved balance-of-payments pressures on governments favoring high-income consumers—were far less likely to do so in the case of market-expanding regimes. The political uncertainties associated with land and tax reforms, with unionization and popular mobilization, and with the opposition of conservative domestic opponents—all made such regimes poor credit risks, even for relatively moderate sectors of the international business community inclined to be sympathetic to reformist efforts. In short, market-expanding options were among those most in need of sustained external support and least likely to receive it.

Three governments—those of Frei and Allende in Chile, and of Campora-Perón in Argentina—were previously mentioned as ones which attempted to incorporate market-expansion options into their overall programs. Of these, only Frei's comparatively moderate version was able to juggle these conflicting pressures for even a short period of time. Between 1965 and 1967, income and land redistribution, rising copper revenues, massive Alliance for Progress aid, and some direct foreign investment, all combined to stimulate a three-year period of industrial expansion. By 1968, however, prices resumed their upward spiral and the economy slowed again. Stung by new taxes and inflation, many of Frei's middle-class supporters moved toward the right-wing Nationalist Party. This defection was not offset by gains among low-income sectors, which also began to lose ground to inflation after the middle of Frei's term. Foreign manufacturing investment also dropped off sharply after 1968, apparently in response to the growing domestic conflict and the forthcoming 1970 presidential elections. In 1970, Radomiro Tomic, the candidate of a battered Christian Democratic coalition, ran a poor third to both Allende and Jorge Alessandri, the right-wing candidate; and what had seemed a promising beginning in 1964 thus ended in disappointment and defeat. The successes of the victorious Allende government and of the Campora-Perón regime in Argentina were even briefer, and their crashes more disastrous. In the absence of external aid and direct investment, brief spurts of industrial expansion ground to a halt, once existing plant capacity had been fully utilized. The concomitant and reinforcing processes of political polarization and domestic inflation eventually triggered B-A coups.

THE NEW PHASES OF INDUSTRIALIZATION AND THE INCREASING ROLE OF THE STATE

Let us consider the argument about these changing constraints from a more aggregated national perspective. The preceding discussion and the comparisons below indicate considerable plausibility for the following propositions: (1) in each country, the end of the initial phase of light industrialization (circa 1950-1955) marked a threshold point at which the trade-offs between populist pressures and industrial expansion became more immediate and severe; and (2) the stronger these pressures in a given time or country, the more severe the economic difficulties. A corollary proposition also seems to make sense: (3) that the new phases of industrial expansion depended substantially on the capacity of political elites to implement conservative economic strategies and/or to devise state structures which could insulate them from the pressures of competitive politics. This insulation did not, as we shall see, have to take extreme B-A forms except in situations of extraordinary crisis and threat. Nor were either extreme or moderate forms of political insulation *sufficient* conditions of expansion in the advanced industrial setting. Much continued to depend on the vagaries of international conditions and on "autonomous" domestic economic forces. Nevertheless, the main feature of the new industrial phase seemed to be that the state—particularly a conservative and restrictive one—seemed to play a more crucial role in mediating the relationship between domestic politics and economic conditions.

Table 1 presents a cross-sectional snapshot of some political and economic patterns consistent with these arguments. The lefthand columns of the table deal with countries which, by the early 1950's, were still in a relatively early phase of industrial modernization. In contrast to the Southern Cone countries and Mexico, locally based firms in this group of countries had not yet been able totally to meet the domestic demand for textiles or other light industrial products. Comparisons within this "less-advanced" group of countries generally support arguments relating to the "spontaneity" of the initial industrialization phase;

TABLE 1
Politics and Economic Performance, by Levels of Industrial Development

	Pre-threshold countries*						Post-threshold countries**			
Regime/ policy type[1]	Annual GDP Growth (1945-1960)[1]	Average	Annual Industrial Growth (1955-1960)[2]	Average	Annual Inflation (1950-1958)[3]	Average	Countries	Annual GDP Growth (1945-1960)[4]	Annual Industrial Growth (1955-1960)[2]	Annual Inflation (1950-1958)[3]
Civilian/ Conventional										
Ecuador	6.1		5.6		2		Mexico	6.2	8.1	8
Civil/Mil./ Conventional		5.4		5.6		6.4	Brazil	5.7	10.3	17
Colombia	4.2		6.1		9					
Peru	4.3		6.1		8					
Military/ Conventional										
Nicaragua	6.8		3.9		8					
El Salvador	5.8		6.6		5					

Incremental alternation of conventional and reform					
Honduras	4.1	4.7	5.7		3
Costa Rica	6.8		7.7		3
Radical alternation of conventional/reform					
Venezuela	8.3	4.6	7.7	17.0	1
Guatemala	3.3		6.2		2
Bolivia	1.1		-4.3		76
Argentina	2.1	3.7			22
Chile	3.3	3.2			38
Uruguay	2.1	1.0			10

Sources:

[1] Charles W. Anderson, *Politics and Economic Change in Latin America* (Princeton, New Jersey: D. Van Nostrand Company, Inc., 1967), pp. 314-15.

[2] United Nations, *Economic Survey for Latin America, 1965*, p. 308.

[3] Raymond F. Mikesell, "Inflation in Latin America," in Charles T. Nisbet, ed., *Latin America, Problems in Economic Development* (New York: The Free Press; London: Collier-MacMillan Limited, 1969), p. 145.

[4] United Nations, *The Economic Development of Latin America in The Post-War Period, 1964*, pp. 87, 95, 103, 115.

* Less than 90 percent of textile demand supplied by local producers-circa 1950.

** Over 90 percent of textile demand supplied by local producers-circa 1950.

for, if we accept the validity of Charles Anderson's regime and policy classifications,[64] then "politics" seem to have made little substantial overall difference in overall economic performance. "Reform" experiences in Costa Rica, Honduras, and Venezuela did not prevent these countries from achieving growth rates comparable to societies subjected more consistently to "conventional" policies. Rates of inflation in the "reformist" countries were in general even lower than those of the more "conservative" ones. Only in Bolivia and Guatemala—nations then in the process of revolutionary and counterrevolutionary upheaval—are there indications of exceptionally severe economic difficulties.

Against this comparative backdrop, the contrasts found among the more "advanced" countries on the right-hand side of the table seem striking. They suggest that, at high levels of industrial modernization, political structures and policies do weigh heavily in economic outcomes. In Mexico and Brazil, which entered the 1950's with relatively high degrees of state control over populist pressures, GDP and manufacturing continued to grow at very high rates throughout the 1950's. In Argentina, Chile, and Uruguay—countries where populist pressures were extremely strong—growth rates were among the lowest in the continent, comparable only to Bolivia and Guatemala among the less modernized countries.

A closer look at pre-B-A "performance profiles" of these five countries suggests a similar conclusion. In each, the avoidance of economic "stagflation" crises seemed to be associated with some combination of policy and institutional characteristics later brought together by B-A regimes: restrictions on public contestation; control over labor organizations; and the adoption and maintenance of internationally oriented, technocratic revisions of earlier populist policies.

Mexico (high growth, low inflation: no crisis). "Revolutionary" Mexico was the only one of the five industrially advanced countries to enter the 1950's with populist pressures more or less fully under control. Although the government vigorously pro-

---

[64] Charles W. Anderson, *Politics and Economic Change in Latin America, The Governing of New Nations* (Princeton, Toronto, London, Melbourne: D. Van Nostrand Company, Inc., 1967), p. 314. Anderson does find differences in more disaggregated aspects of performance: tax structure, infrastructure, social services, government investment, etc. See pp. 310-63.

moted commercial agriculture during the early industrialization phase, "typical" populist policy orientations otherwise prevailed until the mid-1950's: the protection of small producers, the facilitation of capital-goods imports, and inflationary fiscal and monetary policies. Nevertheless, the official PRI dominated the electoral arena; organized labor was tightly controlled; and, in general, political authorities were in a good position to resist domestic opposition to the kinds of conservative options listed above.

Various combinations of these strategies were, in fact, implemented between the end of the light industrialization phase and the mid-1970's. In 1954 Mexico was the only one of the five countries to respond successfully to severe balance of payments and inflationary pressures with devaluation and austerity measures designed to reinvigorate agricultural exports and control prices. Despite opposition from nationalist sectors of the PRI and domestic producers represented by CNIT, the Mexican government also opened the door wide to foreign investors at about this time. As Table 2 indicates, subsidiaries flooded into Mexico in far greater volume than in any of the other three countries, producing both consumer durables for a middle-class market and, to a lesser extent, producers' goods. It should be noted, finally, that Mexico began to export industrial goods much earlier than the other countries. By 1960, manufactured products (mostly transshipped from the U.S. border platform) constituted almost one-quarter of all Mexican export sales, as opposed to only 4 percent and 2 percent for Argentina and Brazil respectively.[65] High rates of industrial expansion continued, with some cyclical variations, throughout the 1950's and 1960's, until 1975 in a context of comparatively little inflation.

Mexico's proximity to the U.S. market, the tourist trade, and, more recently, her substantial oil reserves explain some, but not all, of this relative economic success. As I have argued in more detail elsewhere,[66] comparisons with the similarly well-situated, but politically distinct economies of Argentina and Brazil indi-

[65] Calculated from the *United Nations Handbook of International Trade Statistics*, various years.

[66] Robert R. Kaufman, "Authoritarianism and Industrial Change in Mexico, Argentina, and Brazil," in José Luis Reyna and Richard S. Weinert, eds., *The State and Society in Mexico* (Philadelphia: Institute for the Study of Social and Humanitarian Issues, 1977).

Robert R. Kaufman

TABLE 2
Number of U.S. and European MNC Subsidiaries Established

	Argentina	Brazil	Mexico	Chile
1948	4	6	4	0
1949	2	4	1	1
1950	3	5	5	1
1951	1	14	5	0
1952	4	15	12	1
1953	2	8	11	0
1954	7	14	6	1
1955	7	13	14	0
1956	11	18	7	0
1957	7	23	25	1
1958	13	17	22	2
1959	18	16	27	3
1960	13	11	15	3
1961	22	9	29	2
1962	20	14	14	7
1963	8	7	17	2
1964	13	4	25	6
1965	9	20	30	2
1966	7	21	34	4
1967	18	17	29	6
Total	189	256	332	42

Source: Harvard Business School Multinational Enterprises Project, directed by Raymond Vernon. Data reorganized and supplied by Lars H. Thunell, Center for International Affairs, Harvard University.

cate that the political factors sketched above played an important role. The institutionalization of authoritarian controls during the 1930's and 1940's subsequently permitted Mexican authorities to implement a series of incremental, orthodox policy changes adjusting to the end of the light-industrial phase. The capacity to preempt the crises so often linked to the end of this phase allowed the Mexican system to continue through the 1950's and 1960's without traumatic political transitions or substantial increases in the level of repression.[67]

[67] Conversely, it should be noted, the serious economic difficulties of the mid-1970's seemed directly associated with the resurgence of populist pressures under the "reformist" Echeverria administration.

Brazil (high growth, moderate inflation: delayed crisis). Brazil entered the 1950's with a political structure that shared as many similarities with Mexico as with her more open, populist neighbors to the south. The legacy of the Estado Novo was a strong central state which continued to exert a stern domination over organized labor and which assumed a tutelary role vis-à-vis a relatively weak local bourgeoisie. However, the competitiveness of the Brazilian electoral system from 1945 to 1964 provided greater leverage for populist social forces than existed in Mexico, and this imposed important constraints on some aspects of Brazilian policy making. This combination of factors does much to explain the "mixed" characteristics of Brazilian economic performance until 1964: vigorous industrial expansion throughout the 1950's in a moderately inflationary context, followed "belatedly" by a severe economic crisis and political polarization, and then by the imposition of B-A rule.

Consumer-durables promotion and, secondarily, deepening were apparently the main motors of Brazilian growth during this period. Despite their nationalist rhetoric and unorthodox fiscal policies, both the Vargas and Kubitschek administrations pursued these objectives with considerable determination. Mixed public-private commissions were established to coordinate investment in several consumer durables and producers' goods branches. With high-level political support, these commissions were able to cut through nationalist opposition and to strike relatively durable long-term bargains with foreign companies. Throughout most of the Vargas administration, and again during the Kubitschek period, the Ministry of Labor continued to discourage an independent labor movement. Strikes were held to a minimum and wages were allowed to lag behind productivity. This combination of political features, as well as Brazil's large market size, attracted foreign subsidiaries into the country throughout the 1950's, making for a relatively smooth transition from light to heavy industrial investment. In neighboring Argentina—a country with comparable market attractions but a far less hospitable political climate—the flow of foreign investment was far more uneven, with the major surge coming only around 1960 under Frondizi (see Table 2). Although Argentina did in the 1950's experience considerable growth in the production of automotives, machinery, and chemicals, Brazil's growth rates in these areas were substantially higher.[68]

Many of the constraints in this initial success story seemed to flow directly or indirectly from Brazil's relatively open electoral process. Brazilian authorities, unlike the Mexicans, continued many of the expansionist fiscal policies characteristic of the 1930's and 1940's, and they were unable or unwilling to reverse trade policies which favored urban consumers at the expense of exporters. Eventually, moreover, electoral competition had "corrosive" influences at more fundamental levels, allowing populist politicians to challenge the state's control over organized labor and bringing Goulart into the presidency in 1961. The cumulative effect of these factors were surging inflation; a decline in the confidence of direct investors and external creditors; recession, and increasing challenges from below.[69]

Argentina, Chile, Uruguay (low growth, high inflation: prolonged stalemates and severe crises). Though very different in size and economic potential, these countries resembled each other in the relative strength of their populist social forces and in the severity of the economic difficulties they faced since the onset of the 1950's. Argentina entered this period with Perón's populist authoritarian regime attempting to reverse direction: stabilization, crackdowns on organized labor, and efforts to attract foreign investment were the principal policy lines between 1951 and 1955. These policies enjoyed some short-term success; but they also reduced Perón's support among workers without fully allaying the suspicions of international business, the export oligarchy, or conservative military officers. The regime thus disintegrated in 1955; and throughout the next decade it was followed by a succession of politically weak military and civilian governments, no one of which was able to contain the praetorian antagonisms among Peronist national-populist currents, international investors, agrarian exporters, and conflicting military factions. Chile and Uruguay inherited more institutionalized, highly competi-

[68] Between 1950 and 1960, Brazilian petrochemical production increased by almost 600 percent, whereas in Argentina, the increase was 88 percent. Between 1955 and 1960, Brazilian production of metal machinery tripled and automotive output increased seven-fold. In Argentina, the respective increases were 76 percent and 120 percent. Calculated from ECLA data gathered by Guillermo O'Donnell.

[69] See Skidmore, *Politics in Brazil, 1930-1964.*

tive systems from past decades—systems which in many ways exposed decision makers even more to populist pressures.

It is significant that even within these open systems, economic performance seemed to correlate inversely with the ebb and flow of these pressures. Until the 1970's, Chile's most serious postwar difficulties occurred during the "Peronist-style" regime of Carlos Ibáñez (1952-1958), when soaring inflation and widespread rioting in Santiago forced the imposition of a state of seige and an abrupt turn of the government toward the right.[70] Economic performance improved under Alessandri and Frei (1958-1970)—a recovery facilitated after the mid-1960's by rising copper revenues. Yet domestic prices tended to turn upward, and manufacturing slumped around presidential election time, as each of the governing coalitions faced increasing internal strain and external opposition (see Figure 3). The worst economic periods in Argentina came during 1958-1959, when Frondizi was courting the electoral support of the Peronist movement; and in 1962-1963, just after he was overthrown. The best years were during the more orthodox phases of the first Peronist government and its immediate predecessor; and during 1960-1961, when Frondizi turned his back on the Peronists, froze wages, and opened the door wide to foreign capital.[71] Even in Uruguay, virtually stagnant since the mid-1950's, a brief economic recovery correlated with the abolition of the collegial executive and the imposition of an emergency austerity program (see Figures 1 and 4).

Perhaps even more important than these short-term fluctuations was the contrast between the overall performance of these polities and that of the more closed, restrictive Mexican and Brazilian systems. Argentina—the most comparable country in terms of size and economic potential—did move beyond the light industrial phase during the 1950's, with spurts of consumer durables investment and with some growth in the producers' goods branches. As previously noted, however, movements in these directions were far more uneven and erratic than in Brazil and Mexico. The major acceleration in heavy investments came

[70] Hirschman, *Journeys Toward Progress*, pp. 210-20.
[71] Mallon et al. *Economic Policy-Making in a Conflict Society*, GNP growth was extraordinarily high during 1964 and 1965; but this was largely an artifact of recovery from the extraordinarily bad recession of 1962-1963.

only in the early 1960's, more than a decade after the decline of textiles and other light industrial branches.

Uruguay, lacking either market size or political advantages, remained almost totally "stuck" at the end of the initial phase. Indeed, the averaged figures in Table 1 tend to disguise this fact, and to mask the changing trade-offs between open politics and industrial expansion. Between 1950 and 1955, the manufacturing sector (led as elsewhere by textiles and food processing) grew quite vigorously, at an annual rate of almost 7 percent. After 1955, the Uruguayan economy stagnated, with the industrial sector growing at an average annual rate of only 1 percent during the next ten years. Price levels, which had been quite stable during the early 1950's, also began to fluctuate widely after 1958, with inflation reaching a peak of 136 percent in 1967.

Economic performance in Chile seems to fall somewhere between Uruguay and Argentina—a function again of natural resources and market size. As noted, overall Chilean economic growth picked up during the 1960's; and, during the same decade, Chile began to assemble automobiles and to attract some new investment in various branches of the chemical industry. As in the other two open systems, however, Chilean politicians were not able to arrive at a political-economic formula which allowed for sustained economic expansion. Indeed, a good deal of Chilean political history during the postwar era was interpreted by current military rulers as a succession of unsuccessful "experiments" in finding such a formula. The unreconstructed populism of Ibáñez was abandoned in the late 1950's, even by political leaders and intellectuals who had originally supported it. Alessandri's moderately conservative approach lacked sufficient electoral support. Frei's moderate reformist formula, characterized in part by the market-expansion strategy, failed for reasons already alluded to above, debilitating the political center and contributing to Allende's election. In other words, by Allende's time, if not before, most of the "tools" available for dealing with political-economic immobilism within an open constitutional context were perceived as "exhausted." Rightly or wrongly, the repressive authoritarian rule which replaced Allende appeared to be the only remaining "rational" choice.

There is, of course, much to quarrel with in this self-justifying logic, not only as it applied to Chile but to other B-A governments as well. Political factors, for one thing, explained only part of the economic successes or failures described above. Much of this economic performance was conditioned by domestic and international factors over which no set of political leaders could exert control. It is far from clear, moreover, that the emergent B-A governments can improve substantially on the performance of their predecessors. Nevertheless, even for military officers and technocrats who were not tied directly to contending class interests, political-economic patterns within the five countries seemed to support the view that the costs of tolerating populist pressures had increased—a perspective which undoubtedly grew and hardened among multinational business executives and domestic elites in the course of the 1950's and 1960's. It is in some respects immaterial to debate whether these views were accurate assessments of causal realities, misperceptions of accidental correlations, or self-fulfilling prophecies: by the 1960's they were sufficiently rooted in an experiential base to become part of the "givens" of the social and political scene. It is not surprising, therefore, that where populism had already been fully or partially suppressed, there were strong disincentives for relaxing political controls. And where populist social forces had grown strong, the experience of stalemate and crisis produced powerful incentives for the establishment of regimes which might root these forces out of the body politic.

One is tempted to conclude this section with a final proposition which, in effect, turns a central argument of the "conventional" development literature on its head.[72] The most repressive B-A regimes seem most likely to emerge in countries where competitive systems had become strongly entrenched early in the process of industrialization. It was, after all, in Uruguay and Chile (countries which had the earliest and most institutionalized competitive systems), where the threats, crises, and the resulting B-A regimes were the most severe. Mexico and, in hindsight, Brazil seem mild in contrast. The experience of Argentina in the 1960's, however, does not fit this pattern quite so well. Given the historic strength of populist social forces in that country, we might have expected greater polarization and a far more severe version of B-A rule from 1966 to 1970. That Onganía's quite moderate regime emerged instead is a reminder

[72] Cf. Dahl, *Polyarchy*; Richard A. Pride, *Origins of Democracy: A Cross-National Study of Mobilization, Party Systems, and Democratic Stability*, Sage Professional Papers in Comparative Politics (Beverly Hills: Sage Publications, 1970).

that the course of things is not so neatly determined. The success, stability, and repressiveness of B-A regimes will be shaped in part by situational factors and choices which are not necessarily derived directly from broad economic or political institutional patterns. Nevertheless, it does seem plausible in general that, within the developmental context sketched above, social contradictions are likely to cumulate most intensely within competitive systems—and the more profound the contradictions, the harsher the authoritarian responses. The sequence of events following the collapse of the Onganía regime is germane to this larger point: the resurgence of populist pressures and the ensuing collapse of the Argentine economy eventually evoked a new round of far harsher B-A rule which brought that country back "into line" with the other, once open, countries of the Southern Cone.[73]

III. The Economic Consequences of B-A Regimes: An Analysis of the "Success Stories"

To what extent have B-A regimes managed to resolve the contradictions in which they were born? The collapse of the Onganía government in Argentina, as well as the continuing economic problems in Chile and Uruguay, certainly indicate that political repression is no guarantee of economic success. On the other hand, it has been argued that, given favorable political and economic conditions, B-A rule may be instrumental for converting vicious developmental circles into "virtuous" ones. Two major developmental projects—arguably the newest and most fundamental of the options discussed above—have been emphasized in this connection. O'Donnell, as noted, stresses the potential role of B-A regimes in cutting through the conflicts associated with deepening.[74] Felix, on the other hand, has argued that the drive toward manufacturing exports has "invariably occurred under the aegis of tough, right-wing authoritarian regimes, anti-egalitarian and fervently committed to the pro-

---

[73] This argument has been sketched in more detail in Kaufman, "Authoritarianism and Industrial Change in Mexico, Argentina, and Brazil" and "Notes on the Definition, Genesis and Consolidation of Bureaucratic-Authoritarian Regimes," unpublished manuscript, March 12, 1975.

[74] O'Donnell, "Reflexiones."

motion of foreign and domestic investment, with extra induce-ments for export-bound investment." The politics of these regimes, he suggests, "are an integral part of the economics of such a model. . . ."[75]

Brazil is suggested by both writers as one of the principal "success stories," while the briefer spurt of expansion in Onganía's Argentina can be considered a possible indication of a similar, although aborted, tendency. Each regime included deepening and export diversification among its objectives, and each showed some evidence of movement in those directions. Although market size, multinational initiatives, and world market conditions undoubtedly account for some of this movement, it is possible that these regimes' assurances of predictability and stability were necessary conditions of both projects.

A closer look at both cases, however, raises some doubts about this proposition. Each government, as well as those of Uruguay and Chile, was gripped by many of the same tensions and policy uncertainties which beset their predecessors, and neither moved with single-minded determination toward any one, overriding developmental objective. At least until the late 1960's, moreover, much of the Brazilian "miracle" was attributable to greater utilization of existing consumer durables capacity. And both countries, as I have already suggested, benefited enormously from the international prosperity of the Vietnam era. Are we, then, actually dealing with governments partially responsible for unleashing major new developmental impulses? How much of the change which did occur can actually be attributed to the policies and structures of these governments, and how much would have happened anyway as the result of autonomous external marketing and investment forces?

Although no definitive answer to these questions can be provided here, a beginning can be made by examining the changes in deepening and manufacturing exports which accompanied the rise and fall of these regimes. Did these processes actually accelerate under B-A rule? Did they decelerate in Argentina between 1970 and 1975, after the collapse of the Onganía government? Affirmative responses would provide support for the assertion that authoritarian politics are "integral parts" of these

[75] Felix, "Technological Dualism in Late Industrializers," p. 226.

particular economic models. They would also add credence to the more general arguments connecting B-A rule with the broader problems of "advanced industrialization" in Latin America.

Deepening under Brazilian and Argentine B-A Rule

If a reasonably large domestic economy is a precondition of deepening, then Brazil and Argentina were the only advanced South American countries where this option was a genuine possibility. The parameters of size placed this objective beyond the reach of governments in Uruguay and Chile, although B-A officials in the last country occasionally echoed the rhetoric of their larger neighbors. On the other hand, Brazil and Argentina *were* large countries, with reasonable aspirations to regional hegemony. B-A authorities in these nations, like some of their predecessors, thus considered the development of a producers' goods industry an essential, realistic feature of these larger national aspirations. Whether one judges the reality to have matched their rhetoric depends largely on the perspective adopted. Compared to earlier administrations, some progress in this direction was registered under these governments. At the same time, this progress did not seem sufficient to meet the needs of a rapidly growing economy. Each of these perspectives is considered in detail below.

First, Argentine and Brazilian B-A rule coincided with a resumption and acceleration of the trends toward large-scale industrialization which had started in the 1950's, but were choked off during the crises of the early 1960's. This can be seen most clearly in the case of foreign investment, which, together with the state itself, was the most important source of heavy industrial capital and technology. At least three data sources show the same pattern of upward movement in foreign investment within a few years of the B-A coups: the Harvard Business School survey of new foreign subsidiaries; O'Donnell's compilation of the dollar value of all foreign capital inflows; and my own compilation of the dollar value of U.S. investment in industrial plant and equipment.[76] In Brazil, the last-mentioned type of investment

[76] Harvard Business School Multinational Enterprises Project, directed by Raymond Vernon. These data have been reorganized and supplied by Lars H. Thunell, Center for International Affairs, Harvard University. O'Donnell, "Re-

literally took off after 1967-1968, surpassing levels witnessed under Kubitschek and far outdistancing Argentina after the collapse of the Onganía government in 1970.

Production data from both countries show a similar pattern of recovery and acceleration, concentrated primarily in the producers' goods sector. After lagging behind other industrial branches throughout much of the 1960's, the Brazilian capital goods industry replaced consumer durables as the major source of industrial growth during the early 1970's. From 1969 to 1972 (the most repressive phase of Brazilian B-A rule) the capital goods sector expanded at an annual rate (19.3 percent) which was almost double the yearly ten percent increases in industry as a whole.[77] From about 1967 through 1970, the Argentine chemical, basic metals, and machine industries averaged growth rates of 10 percent or more—up from the rates of 6 to 7 percent achieved during the first half of the 1960's, and substantially higher than the overall increases in manufacturing production.[78]

The deepening thesis is also supported by comparisons between the industrial booms of the late 1960's and those occurring under Kubitschek and Frondizi. Although each spurt of industrialization involved producers' goods as well as consumer durables, the bulk of the case study literature seems to point strongly to the fact that, by the late 1960's, the emphasis had shifted toward the more "basic" industrial branches.[79]

Some brief references to summary data will suffice to illustrate this point. Between 1955 and 1960, automotives accounted for almost 17 percent of all gross fixed investment in Brazilian manufacturing, a figure only slightly lower than chemicals, basic metals, and machinery combined (18 percent). By 1970, on the other hand, the combined share of the last three branches had grown to over 30 percent of gross fixed investment, while that of automotives had declined to approximately 12 percent.[80]

The Harvard Business School data on Argentina, though incomplete, suggests a similar picture. Between 1959 and 1961,

---

flexiones"; Kaufman data, from U.S. Department of Commerce, *Survey of Current Business*, various years.

[77] Suzigan et al., *Crescimento Industrial no Brasil*, p. 117.

[78] Calculated from ECLA data, furnished by Guillermo O'Donnell.

[79] See Note 41.

[80] Calculated from data in Suzigan et al, *Crescimento Industrial no Brasil*, p. 121.

over one-quarter (26 percent) of new foreign subsidiaries were in the automotive branches alone, while 21 percent were devoted to chemical production. Between 1966-1967, the automotive share had declined to only 8 percent, while chemicals had grown to 28 percent. Data on U.S. investment are unavailable for the years 1968-1970. However, the information on the twenty-three European subsidiaries established in those years indicate an even more substantial shift. Almost half (48 percent) of these subsidiaries were in chemicals alone, while only one was in automotives.[81] In short, the new industrialization spurt in both countries was not merely an acceleration of earlier trends but also to some degree a more qualitative change in their character and direction.

The evidence about vertical integration of the industrial structure, however, must also be viewed from still another angle, which suggests the need for careful qualification of the deepening thesis. Although producers' goods investment increased substantially over past levels, growth in this area nevertheless appeared to lag behind overall domestic requirements. Brazilian import coefficients rose sharply in virtually every major producers' goods branch in the years following the B-A coups, and Argentina followed a comparable, although somewhat less pronounced pattern.[82] In both countries, moreover, current accounts deficits also rose sharply, reaching levels of approximately 500 million dollars by 1970-1971. This was roughly equivalent to the deficits incurred in each country in the late 1950's and early 1960's. In Brazil, imports of machinery, petroleum derivatives, and fertilizers doubled between 1968 and 1973;[83] and by 1972, well before the fuel crisis hit the third world, the Brazilian current accounts deficit had grown to 1.4 billion dollars.[84]

[81] Harvard Business School Multinational Enterprise Project, directed by Raymond Vernon. Proportions of U.S. and European investment in automotives and chemicals had been roughly similar in earlier years.

[82] Ayza et al., *América Latina: Integración económica y sustitución de importaciones*; Wilson Suzigan et al., *Crescimento industrial no Brasil* (Rio de Janeiro: IPEA/INPES, 1974), p. 140; José Serra, Chapter 4 in this volume.

[83] Data presented by Fernando Henrique Cardoso, "Estatização e autoritarismo esclarecido: Tendencias e limites," unpublished paper, São Paulo, 1975, p. 3.

[84] Current accounts data from ECLA, *Economic Survey for Latin America*, 1973, pp. 20-21.

Short- and medium-term credits and external portfolio loans were the primary mechanisms for covering these deficits and financing growing import requirements. Between the late 1950's and 1971, external financing had doubled its share of all foreign capital inflows, while that of direct investment declined at about the same rate.[85] Despite gigantic current accounts deficits, this credit flow made possible rather large balance of payments surpluses throughout the late 1960's and early 1970's—the result at least in part of the confidence which the new regime inspired among international creditors. What should be emphasized, however, was that it was the availability of import credits, as much as the expanding industrial capacity, which functioned as a mainstay of the economic boom. By 1976 Brazil's external debt was estimated at almost 30 billion dollars, one of the highest in the world.[86]

A good deal of caution, to be sure, must be exercised in making inferences from such information. For example, the rises in import-coefficients noted above are in part the products of recovery from the drastic import restrictions imposed by both Argentina and Brazil in the wake of previous balance of payments crises in the early 1960's. To an extent, therefore, these increases reflect a return to more "natural" levels of import flows consistent with the overall needs of a growing economy. It should be emphasized, moreover, that by the late 1960's or early 1970's both the Argentine and Brazilian governments *did* institute measures designed to protect the local producers' goods sector from external competition. And the capacity of these industries *did* as we have seen, increase. Therefore, despite evidence of growing external difficulties—which after all were at least partially the result of exogenous factors such as the oil crisis—it may well be argued that Brazil's "net" capacity to cope with such problems had increased.

Finally, it should be noted that O'Donnell did not suggest that B-A deepening policies would in fact resolve problems of indebtedness and dependency, but rather that such difficulties would be transposed into a new structural setting.

Nevertheless, the concept of deepening should not obscure the fact that the commitment of B-A governments to the de-

[85] Calculated from Central Bank data, as reported in the *Economic Unit Intelligence Report–Brazil*, May, 1961 and subsequent years.

[86] *New York Times*, March 28, 1977, p. 43.

velopment of a vertically integrated industrial sector was at most partial—often set aside in favor of other, more "conventional" objectives, such as facilitating the importation of supplies necessary for the expansion of existing public and private enterprises. It should also be clear that the heavy industrial expansion which occurred in Argentina and Brazil did not, in any absolute sense, imply dramatic "breakthroughs" in reducing the vulnerability of these countries to the external economic environment.

The Promotion of Industrial Exports

Whatever the commitment of B-A rulers to the expansion of a producers' goods base, their primary objective was not a self-contained industrial economy but a more open one, in which the financing of ongoing import requirements would be met by greater flexibility and diversity on the export side. Export promotion and diversification did not, as we have already seen, prevent mounting trade deficits or increasingly burdensome levels of external debt. More than deepening, however, this objective was probably the newest, most general, aspect of B-A developmental strategies. The aim was not a more autarkic industrial structure, but a more internationally competitive one which would reduce its external vulnerabilities and assure its capital and equipment needs as much through greater export capabilities as through increased domestic capacity. Albert Fishlow, David Felix, and others have already identified this as one of the central features of the Brazilian model.[87] It obviously made even greater sense in countries with small domestic markets, such as Uruguay and Chile. And, as noted in the first section, each of the B-A regimes with which we are dealing seemed to pursue this objective through a variety of policy instruments—devaluation, subsidies and rebates for exported products, the establishment of new bureaucratic agencies or the reorganization of existing ones, designed to assist exporters in opening new markets.

The data presented in Table 3 suggest that a major spurt in industrial exports was in fact associated with the advent of B-A governments. During the second half of the 1960's, manufactur-

[87] Felix, "Technological Dualism in Late Industrializers"; Albert Fishlow, "Foreign Trade Regimes and Economic Development, Brazil." Prepared as a background paper for April 8, 1975 meeting of the Survey Discussion Group on International Aspects of Brazil's Development, Council on Foreign Relations.

ing exports in Argentina and Brazil increased substantially over earlier levels, as a proportion of total exports from each country, and as a proportion of all Latin American industrial exports. Although Brazil is the country in which this phenomenon has been most commonly identified with B-A rule, it is noteworthy that export diversification was even more spectacular in Onganía's Argentina. In the first half of the 1960's, Argentine manufacturing exports grew hardly at all; by 1970, they increased by almost 170 percent over 1965 levels. Authoritarian Mexico seemed to follow a similar pattern. Although growth rates in Mexican industrial exports lagged behind the two South American countries, Mexican exports were already highly diversified by the beginning of the 1960's and became even more so in the course of that decade.

A similar kind of acceleration also appeared to follow the B-A coups in Chile and Uruguay. Industrial exports from Chile increased by an annual average of almost 111 percent in the three years following the coup; and the share of industrial products in Chile's total export sales rose from 6.1 percent in 1971 to 15.8 percent by 1976 (see Table 4). In Uruguay, manufacturing exports increased by almost 50 percent in 1974, after having increased by an annual average of 15.0 percent in the period from 1969 to 1973. Data on Uruguayan manufacturing exports are incomplete after 1974, but the available evidence suggests that this trend continued. The share of livestock—Uruguay's "traditional" export product—declined from over three quarters of all exports in 1973 to less than one-half in 1976. Although agricultural products continued to comprise the bulk of new export sales, the value of processed foods, manufactured leather goods, and textile exports had grown by 1976 to a value of about 93 million dollars, about 17 percent of all Uruguayan exports in 1976.[88] These three-year export spurts do not, of course, necessarily signify a long-term trend; it is far from clear that either Chile or Uruguay will be able to sustain the export momentum evident in the mid-1970's. Nevertheless, the available data on the two smaller B-A countries are at least not inconsistent with hypotheses linking export diversification to B-A rule.

[88] Data from Comisión Económica para América Latina, *Uruguay*, Separata del Estudio Económico de América Latina, 1976 (E/CEPAL/1026/Add. 2), pp. 830-33.

TABLE 3

Manufacturing Exports in Argentina, Brazil, and Mexico

	Annual Percent Change in Mfg. Exports (1960-1965)	Annual Percent Change in Mfg. Exports (1966-1970)	Mfg. as % of all Exports (1965)	Mfg. as % of Exports (1972)
Argentina	10.0	169.0	6.0	23.0
Brazil	68.0	80.0	8.0	20.0
Mexico	31.7	50.3	21.0	41.0
Rest of Latin America	74.0	66.0		

Source: Calculated from data in: Comisión Económica para América Latina, *Las exportaciones de manufacturas en América Latina: Informaciones estadísticas y algunas consideraciones generales* (Santiago de Chile: E/CEPAL/L. 128: 22 de Enero de 1976), pp. 69, 71, 73, 75, 79.

TABLE 4

Manufacturing Exports in Chile and Uruguay

	Annual Percent Change in Mfg. Exports[a] (1969-1973)	Percent Change in Mfg. Exports[b]			Mfg. as a Percent of All Exports[b]		
		1974	1975	1976	1971	1973	1976
Chile	14.0	225.3	85.8	21.7	6.1	3.6	15.8
Uruguay	15.0	47.0	*	*	*	*	*
All other LA countries except Argentina, Brazil, Mexico	27.0	36.0	*	*	*	*	*

* Data not available.

[a] *Source:* Calculated from data in: Comisión Económica para América Latina, *Las exportaciones de manufacturas en América Latina: Informaciones estadísticas y algunas consideraciones generales* (Santiago de Chile: E/CEPAL/L.128: 22 de Enero de 1976), pp. 69, 71, 73, 75, 79.

[b] *Source*: Data on Chile from Comisión Económica para América Latina, *Chile*, Separata del Estudio Económica de América Latina, 1976 E/CEPAL/ 1026/Add.1), p. 334.

A disaggregation of the manufacturing export data, finally, suggests some interesting avenues for further exploration of this link. In the smaller countries, as might be expected, the bulk of the new exports were generated by light industries, or by the processing of relatively abundant natural resources. In Uruguay, textiles and leather products alone accounted for 86 percent of the manufacturing export growth in 1973-1974; in Chile, almost 80 percent came from paper products derived from southern forest lands. Both types of products presumably offered a comparative advantage, as a result of either low labor or raw material costs.[89]

Such "traditional" industries also played significant roles in the larger countries. Processed foods, for example, were particularly important in Argentina; textiles, leather goods, and furniture, in Brazil. All together, "traditional" manufacturing sectors accounted for approximately 50 percent of the growth in the industrial exports of these two countries during the late 1960's. It is also noteworthy, however, that more complex industrial products also loomed large in these countries' export booms. "Metal-mechanics"—a category which includes automotive equipment and other types of machinery—accounted for approximately 30 percent of the growth in Argentina and over 40 percent in Brazil.[90] Mallon, examining the Argentine case, suggests that this growth may derive from the advantage in labor skills and technological resources that the larger countries possess within Latin American markets.[91] A complementary explanation, however, might focus more directly on the increasing division of labor within the production systems of MNCs. A high proportion of the automotive trade within Latin America, for example, involves the transshipment of components among subsidiaries. It is also possible that Argentina and Brazil were becoming incorporated into the MNC practice of "hiving off" the labor-intensive portions of their production process to third-world countries and of reexporting the product back to the United States or Europe.

[89] Source: Comisión Económica para América Latina, *Las exportaciones de manufacturas en América Latina: Informaciones estadísticas y algunas consideraciones generales* (Santiago de Chile: E/CEPAL/L.128: 22 de Enero de 1976), pp. 73 and 79.

[90] *Ibid.*, pp. 69 and 71.

[91] Mallon et al., *Decision Making in a Conflict Society*, pp. 82-85.

As noted in the preceding section, all of this suggests rather more complex possibilities for intra-industrial alliance and conflict than is implied by the deepening thesis. The latter suggests that B-A governments have sought primarily to resolve the conflicts between foreign-dominated basic industries and weaker, domestic bourgeoisie in the traditional branches. The export model implies cleavages which cut across this line, dividing the internationally oriented companies in both heavy and light industry from firms geared more extensively to the domestic market. Whereas deepening implies a commitment to a more diversified and self-contained industrial base, moreover, the export model tends toward a more specialized, internationally competitive industrial structure—a "streamlining" process which threatens producers in many different branches. There were, in fact, debates between advocates of deepening and export diversification in both Argentina and Brazil; and these may intensify in the wake of the current external difficulties faced by each country.[92]

A good deal of further research will be necessary to understand just what this implies for both the origins and consequences of B-A governments. None of the discussion above, however, provides a priori grounds for rejecting the proposition that authoritarianism may facilitate export diversification. In export drives, as in deepening, divisions between strong foreign firms and weaker domestic ones are likely to loom large; political and policy predictability may be even more important; and the demand for union discipline and low labor costs even more pressing. In any event, in the cases we have examined, the international opening of previously closed and protected industrial economies seems to have "correlated" with the institution of more closed and repressive political orders.

Are these "correlations" sufficient to warrant a more general conclusion—that B-A governments were associated with "major" economic changes? Again, the limits of the changes in both deepening and export diversification must be underlined, even in the most successful cases of B-A rule. Both types of change were accompanied by more conventional policies and economic processes—reliance on external loans, consumer durables ex-

[92] E.g., *Review of the River Plate*, September 21, 1968, pp. 417-25.

pansion, etc. And neither implied qualitative reductions in external dependency.

Within this framework of continuing dependency, however, the advent of B-A rule seemed to coincide with important economic turning points in Brazil and Argentina, if not also in Uruguay and Chile. The newest and most general of these, as I have suggested, was the move toward export diversification—a process which was also at least potentially within the reach of B-A governments in small countries as well as large. An acceleration of heavy industrial growth also occurred within the larger countries, even if this did not carry with it some of the more dramatic connotations of deepening. To these changes, we might add a mention of several others which, although not dealt with above, are relevant to the general argument: the growth of agro-businesses in Brazil, for example, or the expansion and concentration of industrial banking in Argentina and Brazil.

Whether these changes, viewed singly or in combination, are characterized as "fundamental" or insignificant will depend as much upon the theoretical purposes of the observer as upon empirical analysis alone. They are clearly no more revolutionary in character than those which had occurred in earlier decades— the shift away from export-led growth during the depression era, or the decline in light-industrialization opportunities in the 1950's. Yet these earlier dates seem useful in the designation of important turning points in Latin American political-economic history. The combination of economic changes in Brazil during the late 1960's and 1970's may well be comparable to these earlier turning points. Argentina under Onganía appeared to move in similar directions.

Deepening and Industrial Exports in the
Absence of B-A Rule: Argentina, 1970-1976

In Argentina, from 1970 to 1976, a succession of military and Peronist administrations attempted to redress some of the social and political imbalances which had accumulated under Onganía, without necessarily abandoning his major objectives regarding industrial exports and producers' goods development. For our purposes, the efforts of these administrations came at a particularly useful time and place, because they offer a unique opportunity for distinguishing the B-A impact on the economy from that of other factors which presumably contributed to the changes described above. On the one hand, we can compare performance under these post-B-A administrations with that under Onganía himself—two sets of regimes operating within identical national parameters. At the same time, since the reopening of the Argentine polity overlapped with one of the most repressive phases of Brazilian authoritarianism, a cross-national comparison allows us to "hold constant" some of the international forces operating simultaneously on each country.

Despite the publicity attached to guerrilla activities and to the final catastrophic year of Isabela Perón, Argentine politics in the early 1970's appeared to contain some promise. The Levingston and Lanusse administrations adopted more relaxed policies toward labor and more favorable ones toward the domestic bourgeoisie. Yet both they and their Peronist successors continued to display a strong rhetorical commitment to industrial exports; and each sought a reduced, but still important and profitable, role for foreign capital. The principal theme of this era was one of class conciliation rather than conflict—a theme expressed most explicitly by the Peronist social pact of 1973, which was based on the assumption that mutual restraint by workers and capitalists would lead to an expanding sum situation in which all sides would gain.[93] On the whole, moreover, the Argentine economy seemed to do relatively well until about 1974. In spite of increasing inflation and strikes, GDP expanded at an average rate of 4.4 percent during those years, while the manufacturing sector grew at a rate of about seven percent annually.[94]

I do not, of course, wish to understate the difficulties which accompanied this process all along—nor, still less, the virtual sociopolitical disintegration into which Argentina had fallen by 1975-76. The point is that Onganía was not replaced by chaotic demagoguery or unreconstructed national-populism, but by a series of military and civilian administrations which, on the surface, seemed to be struggling toward a reasonable alternative to the B-A model.

In this context, the previous tendencies toward deepening

[93] See Robert L. Ayres, "The 'Social Pact' as Anti-Inflationary Policy: The Argentine Experience since 1973," *World Politics*, Vol. 28, July 1976, No. 4, pp. 473-502.

[94] Calculated from *Economic Survey for Latin America*, various years.

seem to have been interrupted with striking abruptness. Disaggregated growth figures for various manufacturing branches, presented in Table 5, indicate how sensitive these sectors were to the changes occurring in the Argentine political arena. Only the machinery branch continued to perform well in the 1970's. Chemicals and basic metals, the leading branches in the late 1960's, lagged well behind the manufacturing sector as a whole in the 1970-1973 period, the very years in which the Brazilian capital goods industry was averaging growth rates of almost 20 percent! While foreign investment to Brazil continued to accelerate rapidly after 1970, it tailed off sharply in Argentina (see Figures 1 and 2 and Table 2).

The pages of the *Review of the River Plate*, an internationally oriented Argentine business magazine, provide a useful insight into the way investors themselves interpreted this decline. The comments of business leaders, editorials, and articles—all chronicled a growing "loss of confidence," connected to the relaxation of political controls established under Onganía. At the beginning of 1970, a *River Plate* editorial complained of "a mood of disillusionment afflicting many people in the business world" and lamented the passing of the "high hopes that had prevailed in the early months of 1969."[95] By the following year, well before the polarization of the mid-1970's, E. M. Morgan, president of the American Chamber of Commerce, noted that: "changes in the rules of the game took place in several areas relating to foreign investment. Again, the result is known: there has been a sharp reduction in the amount of foreign investment entering the country."[96] The issues were drawn even more clearly in the speech of a British financier, reprinted in the journal in mid-1972. It is worth quoting at some length:[97]

"Not long ago, the City would not consider Brazil, but now they continually talk about the economic boom in that country. It is being acclaimed as the Latin American country of the future. . . . But the question, which has never been satisfactorily answered is, will the economic success continue when Brazil's technocratic government relaxes its very tight control over the

[95] *Review of the River Plate*, January 10, 1970, p. 16.

[96] E. M. Morgan, speech to the American Chamber of Commerce, *Review of the River Plate*, July 13, 1971, p. 38.

[97] Earl Cowley, Speech to the British House of Lords, *Review of the River Plate*, February 29, 1972, p. 250.

TABLE 5
Growth in Producers' Goods Industries in Argentina

	1967	*1968*	*1969*	*1970*	*1971*	*1972*	*1973*
Chemicals	−1.7	23.2	10.9	13.3	7.8	3.7	2.5
Metals, excl. machinery	0.7	25.6	16.6	11.3			
Basic metals				14.4	10.1	5.5	0.4
Metal machinery and equipment				4.5	9.6	15.1	14.1
Paper and cellulose				8.5	4.7	−0.7	−1.1
Manufacturing sector	0.0	7.9	7.3	6.0	7.1	7.2	6.8

Source: *U.N. Economic Survey for Latin America*, various years.

country and allows the whole population to take part in the running of the State.

"On the other hand, not long ago Argentina was considered by the City to be a country for sound investment, but now it is being held up as an example of a country suffering from economic and political upheavals. At the moment Argentina is suffering from an adverse balance of payments, inflation of 50 percent, a former dictator living in Madrid doing his best to wreck any political solution, and a president desperately trying to find an answer to what seems to be insoluble."

It exceeds my purpose to trace in detail the way such perceptions interacted with government policy to produce the eventual political-economic collapse of the mid-1970's. The preceding discussion should, however, suffice to underline the importance which large-scale investors attached to the predictability of domestic politics. It also indicates a relatively low level of tolerance for the uncertainties associated with Argentine attempts to negotiate a more integrated and consensual political system. The comparisons of this Argentine period with the Onganía and Brazilian governments, on the other hand, seem to warrant the inference that these B-A governments had made the difference in providing what large-scale investors viewed as an appropriate investment climate. In the absence of strong, right-wing authoritarian controls (but well before either Perón or the guerrillas had become credible threats), not even Onganía's relatively "respectable" military successors could provide such assurances. And, in the absence of such assurances, neither the size of the Argentine market, nor the profits to be made within a generally expanding economy, nor the dynamics of multinational competition, were sufficient to prevent a decline in the rates of foreign investment or heavy industrial production.

In contrast to the basic industrial branches of the economy, manufacturing exports did not show such extreme sensitivity to the vicissitudes of domestic politics. On the contrary, the trend toward export diversification accelerated even more rapidly during the early 1970's than it had in the mid-1960's—a reflection among other things of expanding opportunities offered by the Latin American common market and the international price inflation of 1973-1974. As Albert Hirschman has pointed out with respect to Colombia,[98] therefore, B-A governments did not seem essential to a successful export diversification drive. Much of this expansion might have happened anyway, even without the harsh imposition of authoritarian controls.

Nevertheless, a closer look at post-1970 Argentina suggests that B-A rule contributed partially to this process, at least within the cases we are examining. Although political and business leaders continued after 1970 to express a general satisfaction with Argentine export performance, familiar complaints about currency overvaluation and labor unrest began to appear in the Argentine press about this time. A long strike in the Acindar steel plant, for example, was reported to have resulted in a one-third decline in the volume of rolled steel exports during 1970.[99] Moreover, in 1971-1972, while Argentina was still under military rule, the expansion of manufactured exports lagged well behind Brazil and Mexico, each of which doubled their sales during the same years.

Table 6 presents a still broader comparative picture of export performance for the years 1969-1975, and indicates clearly that the Argentine drive was not as impressive as it appeared at first glance. Although all three countries began the decade with ap-

[98] Albert O. Hirschman, "The Turn to Authoritarianism in Latin America and the Search for its Economic Determinants," this volume.

[99] *Review of the River Plate*, November 11, 1970, p. 806. Also, subsequent issues: October 13, 1970, p. 577; March 31, 1971, p. 545; April 30, 1971, p. 607; May 21, 1971, p. 726; August 10, 1971, pp. 211-12; February 20, 1973, pp. 224; September 30, 1974, p. 473; October 31, 1974, p. 619.

TABLE 6
Value of Manufacturing Exports
(millions of current dollars)

	1969	1970	1971	1972	1973	1974	1975
Argentina	387	420	442	588	978	1400	1000
Brazil	426	580	729	1055	1672	2534	2900
Mexico	368	444	510	731	1200	1620	n.a.

Source: Calculated from data in Comisión Económica para América Latina, *Las exportaciones de manufacturas en América Latina: Informaciones estadísticas y algunas consideraciones generales* (Santiago de Chile: E/CEPAL/L.128: 22 de Enero de 1976), p. 63.

proximately equal export sales, by 1974 Argentina had fallen well behind. Brazil's manufacturing export sales in 1974 (2.5 billion dollars) were almost 70 percent higher than Argentina's. Between 1970 and 1974, Argentine exports to the competitive European and American markets grew at an average rate of 30 percent, as compared with 49 percent for Mexico and 40 percent for Brazil. These figures, it should be noted, do not incorporate the results of the disastrous political and economic downturn of 1975. If that year is taken into account, the differences are even more dramatic. Argentine industrial exports dropped during that year in absolute terms, while Brazil's continued to grow to a level of almost three times that of her South American competitor. Argentina's annual 19 percent growth rate for the entire 1970-1975 period was only one-half that achieved by authoritarian Brazil.

These comparisons should not, to be sure, obscure the fact that we are dealing with differences in rates of *expansion*—which even in Argentina were considerable. The widening gap in exports which followed the relaxation of authoritarian controls in Argentina, however, does contribute an additional piece of evidence that there was a systematic connection between such economic changes and B-A rule.

IV. SUMMARY AND CONCLUSIONS

This study derives from a general interest in the political implications of what has sometimes been called "delayed, dependent development." This rather awkward label (which I have tried to use sparingly in the body of this paper) refers most broadly to the processes of modernization experienced in the twentieth century by highly stratified societies which had previously specialized in the export of primary products and which remained linked in many ways to a world economy already dominated by advanced industrial powers. In many of the Latin American countries, particularly those which began to industrialize in the 1920's and 1930's, these historical-international conditions seem to have issued in the following interrelated structural patterns; (1) an initial spread of "light industries," producing for a protected home market; (2) a politically weak domestic bourgeoisie, which unlike their nineteenth-century counterparts, were not impelled to lead the search for new markets or technologies; (3) the emergence of "populist" distributive and political pressures relatively early in this process of industrialization; and (4) the reliance on imported technology and capital goods, financed through external credits or commodity exports. My focus here has been on the transitional problems of countries which have achieved relatively high levels of industrialization within this context. Following O'Donnell, I have examined the proposition that these transitional problems provide a useful "first-order" explanation of the contemporary movement toward B-A regimes and, therefore, a good point-of-departure for a comparative analysis of their similarities and differences.

A strong presumption in favor of this proposition was, of course, created by the sudden, nearly concurrent "eruption" of right-wing authoritarianism in Argentina, Brazil, Chile, and Uruguay—now among the most advanced of the Latin American countries, and the first to have initiated the process of industrial modernization. Who would have believed at the start of the 1960's that these otherwise dissimilar countries, with such diverse experiences with constitutionalism, militarism, and levels of political institutionalization, would have "converged" so dramatically during the next decade? These earlier experiences were, to be sure, far from irrelevant to an understanding of the contemporary authoritarian orders, particularly to variations in their stability and economic success. Still, there seems to be a strong preliminary case for examining the impact of these variables within the framework of the socioeconomic characteristics which the South American countries shared in common. This is one important reason why such wide, and favorable, attention has been given to O'Donnell's "daring hypotheses," as well as to the general approach from which they are derived.[100] The primary significance of O'Donnell's work is that it was one of the first attempts to explain in systematic, theoretical terms an apparent connection between B-A rule and advanced Latin American industrialization. It is all the more compelling because so much of it was elaborated in advance of the 1973 coups in Chile and Uruguay, and before the reemergence of B-A rule in Argentina in 1976.

Ironically, however, the dramatic way in which the recent events in South America seem to have "confirmed" these arguments is also a good reason for looking at them more critically. In what is, after all, a rather faddish field of study, theoretically plausible propositions, thus reinforced, have a way of catching on too quickly, with the careful qualifications that originally buttressed the argument gradually being lost from view. There are grounds for concern, for example, that the concept of bureaucratic-authoritarianism may itself break loose from its historical and empirical moorings, and be applied indiscriminately to an unacceptably broad range of cases. Provisional hypotheses can also prematurely become part of the "givens" of analysis, passing beyond the realm of sustained critical attention. On the other hand, as the inevitable discrepancies between theory and reality are "rediscovered" and noted, there is the alternative danger of intellectual disillusionment and of premature rejection of the entire line of analysis.

These concerns underlay the research strategy reflected in the preceding pages. My intent was to remain relatively close to the data, constructing a synthesis that provided some comparative perspective for those who wish to undertake more detailed South American case studies and, at the same time, a firmer empirical anchor for those who wish to extend the general line of analysis beyond the South American cone. Thus, specific B-A governments in Argentina, Brazil, Chile, and Uruguay formed the pivots of the discussion. Around these, I then attempted a relatively concrete mapping of the economic and political changes which preceded and followed B-A coups. In keeping with the holistic assumptions of the general theoretical approach

---

[100] See Hirschman, "The Turn to Authoritarianism in Latin America and the Search for its Economic Determinants," this volume.

to the topic,[101] I have tried to embed this "before-and-after" analysis in the organic complexities of the individual cases. There was, in other words, no "mechanistic" expectation that "economic" factors would, in all circumstances, produce the same political "results," or, worse still, that the countries examined would be found to have marched in lockstep toward some predetermined bureaucratic-authoritarian outcome. It was assumed, however, that the validity of the overall argument did rest on the capacity to identify at least some common patterns of change: it was expected that the reciprocal interactions between "politics" and "economics" would vary within predictable limits and that this variation, in turn, would contribute systematically to an understanding of why B-A rule emerged when and where it did.

Like virtually any analysis of a complex phenomenon, the "findings" presented here are subject to different interpretations. In some instances, I have noted the points where the stubborn idiosyncrasies of the individual countries seem to strain against the boundaries of the general argument; the reader may well find others. It is clear, in any event, that several specific propositions found in the writing on B-A rule do not seem supported by comparative analysis. Among the criticisms already suggested above are the following:

1. A large, "critical mass" of technocrats did not appear necessary for the formation of B-A regimes. The Uruguayan government, shaky though it was in the development of its economic policy, managed to acquire a "technocratic orientation" without a large mass of domestic technocrats to draw upon.

2. There did not seem to be a uniform relation between regime types and phases of industrialization, with populist regimes occurring in the initial phases and B-A rule later on. Populist *pressures* generally overlapped with the early phases of industrialization, and were extremely important to an understanding of authoritarian tendencies in the more advanced phases. These pressures, however, occurred within many different kinds of political order, including some that were highly repressive.

3. B-A regimes did not in general come to power in order to

[101] Raymond D. Duvall, "Dependence and Dependencia Theory: Notes toward Precision of Concept and Argument," prepared for inclusion in special edition of *International Organization* 32, No. 1 (Winter 1978), edited by James A. Caporaso.

pursue the objective of deepening. In fact, there was often little consensus within these regimes about any specific developmental strategy, with short-term commitments to stabilization usually the overriding initial concern. Moreover, the most severe repression usually seemed more directly linked to stabilization objectives than to long-term antagonisms generated by changes in the industrial structure.

4. The formation and short-term survival of B-A regimes did not depend on the initiative or support of foreign direct investors—the MNCs. To be sure, B-A officials actively sought such support and shaped the regime in ways designed to attract it. There is some evidence, moreover, that international lending institutions—private banks, the IMF, etc.—provided funding, as well as ideological encouragement, for the "orthodox" economic approaches of these regimes. But the "dual alliance" between MNCs and B-A officials was fully consumated only in Brazil and Argentina.

Even if we discard these specific propositions, however, many of the themes which lie at the core of O'Donnell's analysis seem to hold up reasonably well. Our study indicates, at least in a preliminary way, that important new social problems, developmental bottlenecks, and policy issues did seem connected to higher levels of industrialization, creating "problem spaces" in the advanced Latin American countries which were "significantly different from those that existed prior to their horizontal industrial expansion *and* from those existing at lower levels of modernization in other South American countries."[102] More than in the past, new spurts of industrial growth seemed to depend on coordinated policy initiatives which emphasized stabilization, the confidence of the international industrial and financial bourgeoisie, and the cooperation of the more "internationalized" segments of the local export and manufacturing oligarchies. This, in turn, seemed to imply a funnel-like narrowing of the coalitional choices and institutional alternatives available to political and economic elites: on the one hand, an apparent decline in the viability of liberal and/or "weak" state structures which tolerated political pluralism and broad electoral competition; on the other, an increasing requirement for a "strong" state, less penetrated by the conflicting forces of civil society—particularly, its populist components.

[102] O'Donnell, *Modernization*, p. 78.

A relatively convincing case for this argument can be constructed from the broad pattern of evidence presented above. Even before the advent of B-A rule, there was in the advanced countries a consistent difference in the economic performance of the more open and restrictive political regimes—a circumstance which seemed less pronounced in these countries prior to the 1950's, and in the less industrialized Latin American countries during the postwar era. Moreover, although overall economic "success" by no means followed each B-A coup, the inauguration of these governments did seem to be associated with several important new economic "projects"—most uniformly, the attempt to open the industrial economy and to expand and diversify exports. It must be emphasized again, however, that variations in economic performance are also attributable in part to a variety of "non-political" factors: country size, autonomous market forces, natural resources, geographic advantage, etc. There is probably no definitive way to disentangle such factors from more politically oriented explanations. Nevertheless, one helpful contribution could undoubtedly come from more detailed historical case studies, which traced longitudinal fluctuations in industrial growth, on the one hand, and changes in policy, regime, and inflationary pressures, on the other. If the general argument is correct, then such factors might be expected to become more closely correlated over time. More in-depth studies of the less industrialized Latin American states are also essential for purposes of cross-sectional comparisons.

A second caveat is also relevant at this point: even if it can be demonstrated conclusively that the range of political choice has declined with advanced industrialization, there is no indication that nakedly repressive B-A regimes are the only, or even the most viable, alternatives to open, broadly competitive systems. Cardoso's distinction between "the state" and "regimes" can be useful here. He applies the first term to the broad network of roles and processes which define the connection between "public" and "private" spheres of power, while the latter refers more narrowly to the specific institutions and procedures which govern the way in which public office is seized and held.[103] By impli-

---

[103] Fernando Henrique Cardoso, "On the Characterization of Authoritarian Regimes in Latin America," this volume. In some respects, Cardoso's distinction parallels the one drawn by David Easton between "political systems" and "regimes." *A Systems Analysis of Political Life* (New York, London, Sydney: John Wiley and Sons, Inc., 1965), esp. pp. 190-212.

cation, he suggests that the alliances, reward structures, economic policies, and patterns of political influence typical of B-A regimes can be maintained through different, possibly more benign, institutional means of control. Much of the material presented above implies the utility of some such conceptual distinction, even though Cardoso's was not employed explicitly in the present analysis. In Mexico, for example, public authorities contained populist pressures primarily through the manipulation of legitimating myths and "corporatist" structures, maintaining some civil liberties and at least some of the symbolic apparatus of liberal democracy. The experience of Brazil in the 1950's, as well perhaps as Colombia and Peru in the 1960's and 1970's, also suggest that "strong" state structures may for a time insulate themselves from the contending forces of civil society without having to rely on direct military rule, the coercion of blue-collar workers, the manipulation of middle-class fears, and questionable claims of "economic rationality."

A crucial question suggested by such arrangements concerns the conditions in which they are feasible alternatives to B-A rule. Can the authoritarian government of Mexico continue to draw effectively on the symbolic resources and institutions derived from the revolution? Do the "roads not taken" early in the industrialization of Argentina, Chile, and Uruguay now preclude the evolution of less coercive, yet viable regimes? Such issues are of significance not only for the countries treated here, but also for other Latin American and "third world" nations just beginning the process of industrialization. Systematic answers, if they can be found at all, will flow not only from a knowledge of socioeconomic structure, but also from an assessment of the changing opportunities provided by political institutions and traditions, prevailing ideologies, and the choices and perceptions of individual political leaders.

In this connection, this study may shed some light on another important feature of the O'Donnell argument: the role of sociopolitical crisis situations in stimulating the formation of B-A regimes. It is, of course, conceivable that such regimes might simply *evolve*—as traditional or populist authoritarian rulers attempt to preempt revolutionary threats or to embark on new economic projects. Perón in the 1950's and Peru in the 1970's seemed, for example, to be moving in this direction. Still, the South American political orders we have examined seem distinctive in the extent of their explicitly anti-labor, anti-populist orientations, and in their reliance on "technocratic rationality" as a basis of legitimation. Even within the restricted "problem spaces" of the advanced industrial countries, such orientations seem comprehensible only as responses to rather severe economic and political breakdowns. Since a great many Latin American societies have always been vulnerable to such breakdowns, however, it seems necessary to specify a bit more just how an analysis of such "triggering crises" might be more usefully incorporated into the broader discussion of industrial change presented above. Two propositions are suggested by the preceding analysis.

First, as I have already indicated, the probability of crisis, and therefore of B-A regimes, may be predictable in terms of the kinds of institutional "choices" and coalitional alignments which develop during the early phases of "delayed" industrialization. Although the bottlenecks associated with the end of "easy" ISI opportunities did not automatically produce political and economic breakdowns, the countries with histories of politically open and/or competitive politics seemed particularly vulnerable as they approached high levels of industrial modernization.

A second hypothesis relates, not to the timing and probabilities of crisis, but to the way in which changes in the developmental setting can shape elite responses to such occurrences. The economic shocks suffered by most Latin American countries during the 1920's and 1930's were at least as severe as the contemporary ones. In some instances, moreover (for example, Chile after World War I and again in the late 1930's), these episodes also involved a substantial, highly threatening activation of urban workers. Repression and exclusion was most certainly *one* response to such challenges. But at least some of the time, elites did acquiesce to symbolic and material concessions designed to broaden the base and expand the legitimacy of the political system. In the advanced industrial states of contemporary South America, on the other hand, "exclusionary" responses seem more and more to predominate. In part, this is due to the fact that the threats from below now involve a greater proportion of such societies. In part, it can also be traced to the changing investment and marketing opportunities detailed above—changes which seemed to raise the economic price of social concessions and which, in crisis situations, appeared to make repression, rather than reform, the most viable alternative to revolution.

Whether this was, in fact, a valid perception remains unclear. The Argentine experience between 1966 and 1976 suggests that perhaps it was. On the other hand, in other instances, it is arguable that, even in extreme crisis situations, B-A regimes were not "objectively" necessary.[104] In Brazil, for example, the conservative military and civilian officials who formed this type of regime exaggerated the real strength of the leftist forces operating under the deposed Goulart administration. One wonders what might have happened if these elites had simply waited for such forces to exhaust themselves and for Goulart to be opposed and then replaced through "normal" constitutional mechanisms. As the international economy expanded in the late 1960's, it is not inconceivable that political stabilization and economic recovery could have occurred under far less restrictive political conditions.

It is hardly surprising, however, that the military and technocratic architects of B-A rule typically chose to act rather than to wait, seizing power with a determination to eradicate the sources of the storm. In a polarizing situation, it was far from irrational for them to isolate labor, and to search among the remaining international and domestic social forces for allies which would support stabilization efforts and viable developmental "projects." It is impossible, and in many respects irrelevant, to determine if efforts to promote exports, consumer durables, or producers' goods were causes or consequences of the desire to win the support of international capital. And it is not necessary to prove that these objectives were already on the drawing board when B-A officials seized power in order to appreciate the centrality which they had for the process of authoritarian rule. In the developmental context described above, such objectives were plausible, and international support, essential. There was thus a

[104] I have profited considerably on this point from conversations with James Kurth, who has suggested that the capitalist systems of Southern Europe could have survived the crises following World War I without authoritarian seizures of power. "Political Parallelisms in Southern Europe since 1815," delivered at the Conference on Southern Europe, Columbia University, New York, March 21-23, 1977. There are, of course, important differences between the Latin American and Southern European cases. In the latter, a large class of peasant landowners provided a nucleus of potential support for conservative, but non-fascist regimes. Nevertheless, the analogies are worth exploring.

logic in the way these pieces seemed to fit together in the search for an acceptable political-economic formula. We should not, to be sure, be deceived by the rhetoric that frequently followed from this search: that the economic objectives selected for emphasis were essential for the fulfillment of the "national destiny," and that these could be achieved only in the context of long-term authoritarian rule. On the other hand, to discard the core of economic realities and hard sociopolitical interests which underlay this rhetoric would be to ignore an essential basis for understanding the way these regimes were formed and the manner in which they operated.

CHAPTER 6

STATE AND REGIME: COMPARATIVE NOTES ON THE SOUTHERN CONE AND THE "ENCLAVE" SOCIETIES

*Julio Cotler**

The emergence of political regimes characterized as bureaucratic-authoritarian by some—and as fascist by others—in the more "developed" countries of Latin America has once again posed in stark terms the problem of the region's political alternatives in its process of socioeconomic transformation. The discussion tends to focus on extreme positions. On the one hand, many analysts argue that systematic repression of the popular sector by the state is a necessary condition for maintaining dependent capitalism. On the other hand, other analysts focus on the social, economic, and political factors that contribute to the survival of liberal-democratic systems in these societies.

In his contribution to this book, Cardoso's analysis of these advanced countries suggests, in contrast to both these positions, that there is no necessary correlation between the class character of the state and the political regime. The same underlying "pact of domination" may be implemented through distinct political regimes, as in the contrast between present-day Argentina, Mexico, and Venezuela. But it is clear that, while there is no necessary causal relation between state and regime in these countries, this relationship is not a random one either. It is shaped by the distinctive historical evolution of the articulation of the interests of different classes in each society and by the attempts of different classes to generalize their own interests to the broader society.

These analyses of the relation between the character of the state and the emergence of bureaucratic-authoritarian political regimes in the industrially advanced countries of Latin America are sometimes applied to those Latin American societies that have not reached this "stage of development"—in the expectation that they eventually will. This extension of the argument

* I would like to thank David Collier for his substantive suggestions and editorial assistance in preparing this chapter.

corresponds to Marx's idea that the experience of the more advanced countries suggests the future of those that are less advanced. Thus, the tragic historical experience of the "classic" cases of the Southern Cone may foretell the destiny that awaits the other Latin American countries.

Yet the temptation to deduce the future of Latin America from the history of the Southern Cone brings with it the risk of failing to consider crucial differences in the type of dependent development that the other countries of the region have experienced—differences that have led to distinctive patterns of political change. Thus, one could say, as the Peruvian song affirms, "*toda repetición es una ofensa y toda supresión es un olvido*" (every repetition is an offense and every suppression is forgetting).

A useful starting point for analyzing the distinct patterns of development outside the Southern Cone is found in the work of Cardoso and Faletto.[1] They argue that one of the decisive factors in the political formation of Latin American societies was the role which the national bourgeoisies and foreign capital played as the region assumed its role as part of the "periphery" in the international capitalist system. They identify two basic variants in this role. In Argentina, Chile, Brazil, and Uruguay, the national bourgeoisie played a leading political role in the process of national integration and in the process through which the economy and society became integrated in a subordinate manner into the international system. In many other countries, by contrast, the role played by foreign capital, primarily through investment in export "enclaves" and in direct association with the pre-capitalist latifundia, blocked national integration. The most extreme examples of this pattern are the "banana republics" of Central America, but the pattern also occurred, without reaching these extremes, in the central Andean countries, in Venezuela, and in Mexico.

The goal of this chapter is to explore further the political implications of this distinction as a starting point for assessing the relevance of analyses of bureaucratic-authoritarianism in the

[1] Fernando Henrique Cardoso and Enzo Faletto, *Dependencia y desarrollo en América Latina* (Mexico City: Siglo Veintiuno Editores, 1969). Also published as *Dependency and Development in Latin America* (Berkeley and Los Angeles: University of California Press, 1978).

advanced countries for these other Latin American societies that have followed the enclave pattern of development.

"NATIONALLY" CONTROLLED ECONOMIES

In the case of the "nationally" controlled economies referred to above, the export oligarchy, because it directly organized and controlled production, was capable of establishing its relative hegemony over the remaining segments of the dominant class and over the popular sector. This hegemony formed the basis for constructing a national state which became a central point of reference in developing a national identity and, in turn, in reinforcing this hegemony.

Though this export oligarchy was in a sense shaped by its role as an intermediary for foreign capital, its role as the organizer and director of both economic production and political life gave it a significant degree of autonomy in relation to international capital. This was reflected in its capacity to retain a significant proportion of its earnings, thereby broadening the scope of capitalist economic activity and definitively subordinating the pre-capitalist sector, with which it found itself closely linked.

This situation made it possible for the bourgeois fraction of the dominant class to expand the domestic market and to develop "spontaneously" an initial process of import-substituting industrialization, basically of wage goods. In contrast to what occurred in the most advanced capitalist economies of Europe and America, this industrialization did not involve the vertical integration of the economy, which would have linked the production of capital goods—the crucial dynamic force in modern economies—with the production of consumer goods.

However, the increasing predominance in these countries of the capitalist mode of production and the growth of import substitution led to increasing social differentiation. This in turn led, toward the end of the last century, to a series of attacks on the oligarchic political structure, as the popular sector and the middle class struggled to broaden their political and social rights. The oligarchic state found it necessary to respond segmentally to these demands and to implement measures which benefited the *urban* sectors of these classes. The different "radical" governments of the Southern Cone thus promoted public spending, which enlarged the distribution of social resources to the middle classes and later to the workers. This, in turn, gave further impetus to the urban demands and to the industrial development to which we have referred. The incorporation of these social sectors into the political process broadened the support coalition of the state, increasing its autonomy in relation to the traditional dominant classes. Thus, the Southern Cone countries appeared to repeat the Western European and North American experience.

In all of these countries, the crisis of the 1930's, which brought widespread unemployment and a decline of real wages, produced an intensification of the popular and middle sector conflicts as these groups sought at least to regain their former levels of well being, and led to a long period of crisis in the system of oligarchic domination. Within this context, the bourgeoisie and the state faced a two-fold problem: the need to reactivate capital accumulation and to control popular political participation (which was neither politically centralized nor embodied in an autonomous movement). The alternative adopted was that of applying a Keynesian policy *avant la lettre*. In this way, through different types of policies, these countries entered even more fully into the process of import-substituting industrialization, promoted in part by the state apparatus.

In Chile, the social conflicts that emerged, starting at the beginning of the century, were expressed in substantial measure through institutional channels, thus establishing the legitimacy of parliamentary representation and of the relative subordination of the army to the civil power of the state. The state evolved slowly away from its oligarchic form, becoming increasingly more representative of a broader range of political interests. As a result of the political crisis which developed during the 1930's, this political pattern became consolidated, due largely to the formation of Frente Popular. In this way, there occurred simultaneously in Chile a significant degree of political democratization of the state (but one in which the peasants did not participate), the emergence of a state role in directly supporting the industrialization of the country through favoring capital accumulation within the urban fraction of the bourgeoisie at the expense of the agrarian sector, and a policy of distribution to the urban middle sectors of the cities. Chile thus followed the typical pattern of populism.

In Argentina and Uruguay, the crisis of the 1930's resulted in the erosion of the political democratization that had already occurred in these countries. Dictatorships were established which, though they prevented a return to popular political activity, advanced industrial development and increased industrial employment. The economic and political strength of the bourgeoisie, combined with the relatively weak political articulation of the popular sectors, led to this result, thereby interrupting the "democratic" pattern of political development which these countries had exhibited.

In Brazil, the export crisis brought the political downfall of the landowners and the emergence of the army as an agent of state cohesion. This first type of "military state" supported the development of the industrial sector and promoted political control over the popular urban masses, while denying political participation to the peasant masses, who were still dominated by the pre-capitalist landowners. Subsequently, the period of the Second World War brought increases in the prices and volume of exports, constraints on industrial imports, and a wage freeze "in order to further the efforts of the allies." These developments led to greatly increased capital accumulation in the industrial sector and to the numerical growth of the middle classes and urban workers. Yet these groups continued to have a restricted political and economic role in the society.

The reinitiation of class conflict led to the elimination of this contradiction and to the emergence of a political configuration that resulted in the total displacement of the oligarchic-imperialist coalition. It also led to the modification of the character of the state, which came to be a representative of the "national" interests embodied in a national bourgeoisie in association with the middle and working classes. The triumph of this national coalition resulted in what Perón—or later, in Peru, the propagandists of the "Peruvian Revolution"—would have called a "second independence," which resulted in the formation of the populist state—yet without making any attempt to attack the existing agrarian structure.

Whereas in Uruguay and Chile populism developed through the route of liberal-democratic representation, in Brazil and Argentina the state organized the popular classes in a corporative fashion, subordinating them to government control and thus to the interests of national capitalist development.

Despite the differences among the political regimes in these countries, the class character of the populist state was relatively similar. It simultaneously promoted a policy of capitalist accumulation in industry—including the public sector—and of distribution to the popular and middle strata of the cities, based on resources extracted from the agricultural and mineral export sectors. In this way, the state assumed the role of sponsor and arbitrator of a new pact of domination.

There were, however, problems inherent in the pattern of growth that occurred during the populist period. Import substitution required increased importation of intermediate and capital goods which, coinciding as it did with the lack of dynamism in the export sector, led to a growing loss of international reserves and a substantial increase in the external debt. The high level of tariff protection which had been extended to national industries, the oligopolic nature of international commerce, and the protectionist tariffs of the advanced capitalist countries meant that these Latin American societies could not resolve this "bottleneck" through the export of manufactured goods. In addition, the regressive pattern of income distribution may have restricted the size of the domestic market, with the result that industrialization responded to the demands of the sectors of the population with higher income levels.

The results of these contradictions are well known: problems with balance of payments and balance of trade, fiscal deficits, printing of unbacked currency, and, finally, runaway inflation which devastated these countries during the decades of the 1950's and 1960's. In one sense, as Hirschman has put it, this inflation served as an alternative to civil war, making it easier to maintain the balance among the social classes. Yet the class conflict which developed around the issue of inflation ultimately unmasked the basic character of the "pact of domination," making the harmonization of the different class interests surrounding the state increasingly more difficult. In Chile and Uruguay, where the political organizations of different social classes confronted one another within the parliament, the state was able to channel the conflicts inside the existing institutional structure. In Argentina and Brazil, on the other hand, the formal representative organizations of the popular sector were subordinated to the state. This contributed to a different type of popular sector mobilization, to the growing autonomy of this sector from the state, and finally, to a confrontation with the state and with its policy of class conciliation. Thus in Argentina, the political "exclusion" of these classes was on the "agenda" of the state beginning in the middle of the 1950's, and in Brazil since the end of that same decade, when the populist state began to disintegrate.

Yet, in all of these cases, the political parties of the popular sector were in fact incorporated into the system of legitimation that supported the basic class orientation of the state, and they did not attempt to present an anti-capitalist political alternative. These parties, which had by then significantly increased their political strength, sought to perpetuate the existing situation. There thus emerged a situation which, in Gramscian terms, involved a hegemonic impasse. This impasse was ended when the bourgeoisie, with the open support of foreign governments and foreign capital—that in the meantime had come to control important areas of industry, commerce, and finance—mobilized middle-class support and resolved the crisis through a military coup.

It is at this outer "limit" of this pattern of development that the differences among distinct types of capitalist development become clear, as in the contrast between the states of the European capitalist "core" and these Latin American "late" developers. In these latter cases, this political mobilization of the "dangerous classes" exposed the class character of the state, forcing it to reveal its coercive nature and its inability to absorb popular pressures in the European or North American fashion by successfully incorporating them within the larger class orientation of the state. Instead, the dominant class defeated the popular forces with the support of the middle classes, effectively incorporating the middle classes in a project of national capitalist expansion. The political mobilization of the popular classes in the more advanced Latin American countries thus led to an organic crisis of the system of domination which forced the state to abandon its ambiguous role as an arbitrator of class conflict and to reveal its coercive and dependent nature.

The armed forces eliminated the representative institutions over which the dominant class had lost control. They simultaneously expanded the sphere of military influence to the point of "militarizing" the state apparatus so as to be able to participate actively in the social struggle and defeat their class enemy—the popular sector. The militarization of the state involved eliminating protections of civil liberties which had been developed after long and difficult social struggles, permitting the military state to carry out a warlike operation which, for its systematic brutality, stands out as a signal event in the history of the region. The militarization of the state was also intended to insure the subordination of the popular classes once they had been defeated in this social struggle. This was done in order to create the conditions for reconstituting and expanding the dependent-capitalist mode of production. In this new context, the military saw the protection of this form of capitalism as essential to the national security interests of the military as an institution.

This abbreviated and simplified version of the development of the advanced Latin American countries has obviously left out many important details. It is intended only to provide a point of comparison with those countries which did not follow this "classic" pattern of the Southern Cone countries.

THE "ENCLAVE" SOCIETIES

The societies which were incorporated into the periphery of the international economic system through the direct involvement of foreign capital in the production of primary products for export experienced a distinct pattern of evolution which we will now examine. In these cases foreign capital penetrated—literally—a pre-capitalist economic and social structure without significantly altering this structure. Indeed, foreign capital aligned itself with the more conspicuous representatives of the pre-capitalist mode of production: the large landowners and the commercial bourgeoisie. Thus emerged the "feudal-imperialist" alliance whose appearance was noted by various writers of that era.

This led Haya de la Torre to observe, paraphrasing Lenin, that while imperialism constitutes the final phase of capitalism in the advanced countries, it corresponds to the first phase of capitalism in late-developing countries. It was this symbiosis that led various analysts during the first decades of the century to characterize these as "dual" societies, involving a "modern," capitalist sector oriented around foreign enterprise and a "traditional," pre-capitalist sector controlled by the landowners and the national commercial class.

Enclave capitalism was linked to the pre-capitalist economic structures through various means. The pre-capitalist sector provided the enclaves with workers whose wages were lower in relation to those of the metropolis, in part because their alternative sources of employment were quite restricted, due to the maintenance of a pre-industrial structure. Another factor that contributed to the low cost of maintaining the labor force was the fact that the workers received part of their wages in food. In many instances the enclaves maintained their own farms, where, on the basis of pre-capitalist modes of production, they produced food which was later sold through the local marketing system. In this manner, the enclaves not only extracted surplus value from the work of their employees, which was returned to the foreign countries from which the capital for the enclaves had originally come, but also benefited indirectly from the participation of their workers in these pre-capitalist modes of production.

Since the purpose of the enclaves was to extract primary products which were inexpensive in relation to those which could otherwise be obtained in the home market of the metropole, they did not encourage the industrial development of the enclave country, organizing it instead as a monocultural producer of primary products. Thus, not only were the plantations and the mines in the hands of foreign capital, but also the entire system of transportation, both internal and international, which was designed and constructed in their interests; the financial institutions, through which the funds required by their national and international operations were transferred; and the marketing not only of exports, but also of imports—in which the enclaves became involved on both a wholesale and retail basis. Thus, the enclave came to be linked to many different facets of economic and social life and also came to be closely tied to the local commercial bourgeoisie, as well as to the traditional landowners.

Under these conditions, the character of the dominant sectors of national society came to be shaped by the presence of the enclaves. They became a clientele class in relation to these enterprises—and to the governments of the respective countries of origin of the foreign enterprises. They sought to obtain favors from these external actors in order to link themselves to the activities which derived from the enclaves.

The state, which was in the hands of different fractions of the landowning class which competed with each other for favors from the enclaves, served the dominant economic interests in this situation. Within the complex historical evolution of these countries, there were certainly some important class conflicts *within* the dominant class. Yet, for present purposes, it is sufficient to note that the dominant tendency was toward the complete subordination of the local landowners to the interests of foreign companies and governments.

The ideological justification for this total subordination of the local landowners and their political representatives to the enclaves derived from the idea that these "countries" could not rely on their own resources for their development. Since the enclaves created resources for the capitalization of the landowners and merchants, the state—by supporting the enclaves—was helping to create opportunities for national development which had previously not existed. There appeared to be no realistic alternative other than that of meeting all of the conditions required by foreign capital and of maintaining the system of pre-capitalist exploitation that made it possible for the exports to have a comparative advantage in international markets. Only in this manner would foreign capital and the accompanying technology enter into these countries, thereby making it possible to achieve political stability and economic development.

Though this argument was endlessly repeated in all cases, it did not prevent the leading intellectuals of the dominant class from perceiving that this situation placed the country in a quasi-colonial situation. Yet their "realism" led them to perceive that there was no alternative other than the political anarchy and wars among local caudillos that they had experienced prior to capitalist penetration.

In this way, in contrast to what happened in the Southern Cone, the "national dominant" class had only a very narrow margin of economic and political autonomy in relation to foreign capital and foreign governments. This derived from their inability to accumulate capital, except in a very limited fashion and in activities which were intimately linked and subordinated to the enclaves. The extension and deepening of the domestic market was also extremely limited, even at the simplest level of import-substitution. For all of these reasons, the pre-capitalist manorial structure of the society in which the greater part of the population found themselves was thus perpetuated in these semi-colonial societies.

Under these conditions, the politically dominant class, which was the direct representative of the combined interests of foreign capital and their "junior partners," the landowners and merchants, failed to establish hegemony and to create a national identity. It was impossible for the dominant classes to create an identification on the part of the exploited masses with national political institutions and to obtain their loyalty, particularly in the countries in which these masses were Indians.

Likewise, the nature of the social structure made it impossible to construct a national state of the type that had emerged in the Southern Cone. By supporting the perpetuation of the traditional local power structure, foreign capital severely limited the formation of an economic, social, cultural, and political "internal market" that could help to homogenize political and social life.

Yet this same oligarchic-imperialist political order created in turn its own contradictions. On the one hand, the capitalist nature of the enclave led to a process of dislocation of the working population from their traditional means of production to the plantations and the mines and, therefore, from their traditional form of social and cultural relations. Likewise, capitalist development led to the elimination of some traditional sectors of power, as well as of segments of the middle class composed of small and medium landowners, merchants, and artisans.

On the other hand, the demand for food created by the proletarianization of the enclave laborers led the landowners to demand a higher level of rent from their dependent laborers. It also led them to control more carefully the channels for marketing agricultural products in order to maximize their control of the newly expanded market, thereby preventing the peasants from selling directly to this new market.

This recomposition of the class structure led to widespread protest movements in which workers, peasants, and members of the middle classes joined together and identified as their common enemy the coalition that had formed around foreign capital. Moreover, in those countries in which the mass of the population differed ethnically and racially from this dominant coalition, the protests took on clear indigenous, messianic, and nativist connotations.

In the countries organized around enclaves, this popular mobilization brought together the peasantry, the nascent proletariat, and the middle classes in political movements which were simultaneously anti-oligarchic and anti-imperialist. That is to say, these movements were prepared to destroy, by means of the direct intervention of the masses, both the bases of pre-capitalist power and those of foreign capital. This implied such actions as eliminating the manorial hacienda, nationalizing foreign enterprises, and promoting a process of political and social democratization which would provide the basis for the formation of a national state and a national society. These movements were thus revolutionary in nature and had a nationalist and popular orientation. These national-populist, or national revolutionary movements adopted positions that coincide with those of socialism. Because these movements aimed at the elimination not only of the pre-capitalist bases of domination but also of foreign capital, which constitutes the core of capitalism in these societies, they in effect assumed an anti-capitalist posture.

It is thus no coincidence that Mexico, Guatemala, Panama, Peru, and Bolivia have experienced national populist movements. Nor is it coincidence that Mexico and Peru have produced the most ideologically pure versions of this type of political movement and that the political writings of Haya de la Torre and Mariátegui are still enormously important for understanding these societies.

ENCLAVE SOCIETIES AND POLITICAL IDEOLOGY: HAYA AND MARIÁTEGUI

At an early point in the development of the national popular mobilization in Peru during the 1920's, Haya de la Torre, in a book which is classic in the political literature of Latin America, proclaimed the need to create a popular and national political movement, based on workers and peasants and led by the middle class.[2] This movement would destroy "feudalism" and eliminate the dominance of foreign capital by means of the formation of an anti-imperialist state, similar to that which was emerging from the Mexican revolution. This state, directed by the middle class, would create a state capitalist sector which would dominate the economy and also promote the development of the bourgeoisie. However, it would also control this bourgeoisie in order to maintain its national and nationalistic character.

[2] Victor Raúl Haya de la Torre, *El antiimperialismo y el Apra* (Lima: Editorial Amanta, 1972), fourth edition.

Yet, at the same time, the state would protect the interests of the peasants and of the workers, thus transforming itself into a political structure through which the middle class would hold power and seek to represent other social classes, simultaneously controlling them and organizing them through corporative mechanisms.

Nevertheless, according to Haya's argument, because of the poverty and weakness of the Latin American societies—which were the consequence of colonial exploitation, first by Spain and later by England and the United States—these Latin American countries would have to find a way to obtain capital and technology from the imperialist countries on terms consistent with "national interests." Only a state based upon national-popular support could bargain effectively with imperialist capital. Only in this way could the interests of the nation and those of foreign capital be harmonized. The country would thereby achieve economic growth and the foreign capitalists could acquire the primary products needed for their industrial development.

Mariátegui, writing from a socialist position, agreed with Haya on the need to form a broad multi-class coalition.[3] But, unlike Haya, Mariátegui maintained that only through the achievement of socialism could the bourgeois-democratic reforms which Peru and Latin America required be carried out successfully. Only in this way could the nationalization of the society through a popularly based mass movement effectively be achieved.

Mariátegui based his analysis on the premise that the nature of foreign domination derived from the intimate link between capitalist-imperialism and local "feudalism." Hence, the elimination of one of these elements necessarily implied the elimination of the other. In addition, the imperialist character of capitalist domination made autonomous capitalist development impossible in these countries. Moreover, though the middle classes had a somewhat marginal political position, they in fact shared with the landowners and foreign capital a strong opposition to the emergence of any effective form of popular demand-making. This was due in part to the pronounced ethnic and social differ-

---

[3] José Carlos Mariátegui, *7 ensayos de interpretación de la realidad peruana* (Lima: Editorial Amanta, 1965), sixth edition. Published in English as *Seven Interpretive Essays on Peruvian Reality* (Austin: University of Texas Press, 1971). See also his *Ideología y política* (Lima: Editorial Amanta, 1972), sixth edition.

ences between them and the popular masses. He thus concluded, in an argument that has been borne out by history, that the development of capitalism in fact involved the development of semi-colonial domination of Peru and of Indoamerica.

There is no better means of confirming this analysis of Mariátegui, and of refuting the national-populist analysis of Haya de la Torre, than to examine the actual historical experience of Mexico and Peru.

MEXICO

The liberal revolution that occurred in Mexico in the mid-nineteenth century brought the seizing of church land and the selling of this land, which led to the emergence of a new process of formation of haciendas. Due to the emergence of the United States as a major capitalist power, these haciendas were soon linked to the capitalist development of that country, at the same time that the haciendas maintained intact, and in many cases reinforced, pre-capitalist forms of social relations.

At the end of the century, United States capital effectively penetrated Mexican society, forming powerful mining and agricultural enclaves that had close ties with Mexican landowners and merchants. The massive dislocation produced by the enclaves encouraged the development of an incipient internal market and with it a few industrial centers which, for the reasons discussed above, were soon blocked in their development.

These disruptive processes which reshaped Mexican society produced a powerful political movement which included the nascent bourgeoisie, the middle class, industrial workers, and peasants—both those who were deprived of their land by the haciendas and those who had been subjected to new and more intense exploitative practices which bordered on slavery. These groups all sought through this movement to improve their position within the social order.

Through the direct action of the peasant masses, the Mexican revolution eradicated the existing hacienda system and the North American enclaves. Yet the "anti-imperialist" state, representing the interests of the "national classes," quickly found that it had to establish mechanisms of class conciliation in order to achieve control of the new political situation. That is, the ruling middle classes needed to "interrupt" the revolutionary process and to institutionalize the participation of different sectors—especially of the popular classes. Plutarco Elias Calles, at the end of the 1920's, thus created the corporative foundation of the Mexican state by establishing a party organization which brought together the different sectors of the society through a type of functional representation and which served as an intermediary between these sectors and the state apparatus. The party sought to define the permissible limits of the political activity of each of these sectors in a way that was consistent with the overall interests of the state and of the nation, which were in turn defined by the middle classes. This arrangement permitted the development of state capitalism and, under its tutelage, the development of the national bourgeoisie—which nevertheless was institutionally encapsulated and deprived of a capacity for autonomous political expression.

Having succeeded in interrupting the revolutionary process and establishing these corporative structures, the Mexican state initiated the process of consolidating Mexican capitalism and of "investment bargaining" with foreign capital during the crucial period of the Second World War. Starting at that point, a favorable investment "climate" for foreign capital was created, with the corresponding opportunities for unrestricted exchange of currency and repatriation of profits, on the understanding that this would facilitate the industrial development of the country. Thus emerged the "constructive anti-imperialism" to which Haya de la Torre had alluded in his political plan for Peru. In Mexico this came to be referred to as *"desarrollo estabilizador"* (stabilizing development).

The effective control over the popular sector, together with the retention of pre-capitalist forms of production (with the exception of the conditions of near-slavery, which had been eliminated) and state subsidies, facilitated high rates of earnings for the foreign capitalists, who reinvested part of this profit within Mexico. The role of foreign capital was thus extended beyond the enclave, thereby contributing to industrial development *within* the country. This development in turn encouraged the emergence of a national bourgeoisie which was subordinated both to the state and to the foreign enterprises. Along with foreign and local private capital, the state sector of the economy also assumed an important role, with the goal of subsidizing and, at the same time, "counterbalancing" private capital. But, as in the Southern Cone cases, the industrialization process primarily involved finished consumer goods. As a result, Mexico came to be caught in an increasingly unfavorable pattern of profit repatriation by foreign investors, heavy dependence on imports of capital and intermediate goods, and external indebtedness, with a concomitant pattern of regressive income distribution.

Nevertheless, the country experienced an unparalleled economic expansion, involving nearly thirty years of sustained growth. Yet, because of the dependent-capitalist character of this development, Mexico has in fact not solved the economic and social problems posed by the Mexican Revolution. One thus observes a growing relative emiseration of broad sectors of the popular classes who are concentrated in the major cities and who constitute a "marginal" population or, to put it in classic terms, a structurally unemployed population. Mariátegui's prediction about the fate that awaited Mexico as a result of selecting a neo-capitalist development strategy has been confirmed.

The effective corporative control which the state exercises through the PRI over the popular masses is based on its ability to establish clientelistic political ties through political and union "caciques." Due to the rapid economic expansion, both the state and the bourgeoisie were able to partially incorporate the popular classes in a "segmentary" manner, while the state-party-union apparatus sought to maintain control over the population, thereby inhibiting all possibility of autonomous development.

On the basis of these political instruments, the state and its party have created an image of great effectiveness, of a capacity to neutralize opposition, which has in turn increased their capacity for political control of the population. Likewise, the state has identified itself closely with the symbols of nationalism, effectively mobilizing its resources to reinforce this identification of the state with the nation. Under these conditions, anyone who attacks the state or its party can be accused of "anti-national" behavior and of being in league with the oligarchic and foreign interests which the revolution originally opposed.

Nonetheless, the popular classes have overcome the control imposed upon them by the state at various times since the 1940's, demonstrating that mere rhetoric does not compensate for the severe class limitations of this "revolutionary-nationalism." These outbreaks, which threatened to undermine the institutional political order, were systematically and violently repressed. At the same time, there was an intensification of the distributive, cooptive use of patronage politics and a tightening of corporatist controls, with the result that this protest has been neutralized. The pendulum-like alternation between "stabilizing" and "nationalist" governments in Mexico, to which frequent reference is made in the literature, occurs precisely in response to these episodes of popular mobilization.

The intensification of these pressures during the past decade that led to the explosion of 1968 provided a clear warning that the political regime had to adopt a nationalist position, revitalizing its reformist ideology and policies. The diversification achieved through thirty years of capitalism and the policy of "*desarrollo compartido*" ("shared development"), which would come to be the substitute formula for "*desarrollo estabilizador*" ("stabilizing development"), finally provoked a crisis in the existing system of revolutionary nationalism.

Initially, beginning in 1970, the executive sought to democratize the political regime, dismantling the key mechanisms which had previously made possible the functioning of a system which had been carefully controlled from the pinnacle of the state apparatus. The opposition of the state-party organization and of the bourgeoisie—both "national" and foreign—quickly made it clear that this effort was destined to failure. What remained was the rhetoric and the policies typical of populism.

Regarding the rhetoric, the government once again engaged in nationalistic discourse which was cast in the new mold of Third Worldism and which sought to strengthen its identification with the "people," attacking imperialism and the "rich." Regarding economic policy, public spending dedicated to aiding segments of the lower middle and popular sectors was expanded considerably, at the same time that public resources were also used to expand state capitalism, with the goal of ultimately "nationalizing" the economy. In the meantime, the government continued the firmly established practice of subsidizing the national and foreign bourgeoisie.

These policies and the ongoing inflation and stagnation in the United States led to a crisis in the contradiction between accumulation and distribution. After more than thirty years of stability, Mexico began to suffer from the economic problem of other Latin American countries: balance of payments difficulties, fiscal deficits, and inflation, which, along with the nationalist rhetoric, led to a sharp reduction in foreign investment. All of this led to a profound crisis, so profound that at the end of 1976 Mexico faced the unprecedented situation of experiencing a spectacular run on bank deposits, an explicit threat of a coup, and a currency devaluation of nearly 100 percent.

Today, the situation is totally different from that of the 1940's. A powerful national bourgeoisie, which is intimately linked to foreign investment and which has emerged within the protective framework of revolutionary nationalism, plays a political role that involves increasing degrees of autonomy from the state. Public capital investment overlaps with private investment—national and foreign—to such an extent that it can ignore the nationalist and reformist rhetoric.

At the same time, however, workers in the most dynamic sectors of production, who belong to labor organizations that are linked to the vertical structure of the PRI, are increasing their demands to maintain or improve their level of income. This pressure from the workers forces the coopted labor leaders to present these demands to the state, thereby legitimating the crucial role that these leaders play within the system of domination. However, these demands conflict with the interests of the national and foreign bourgeoisie, which seeks to establish a program of economic "stabilization," with the goal of improving its economic position at the expense of worker income.

This heightening of the contradictions within the system may surpass the ability of the PRI and of the government to balance and arbitrate the conflicting interests of capital and labor. Thus, the state is today tending to lose its capacity for disciplining and controlling these sectors of society which are emerging as increasingly autonomous from the state. Given these conditions, it might seem that Mexico is gradually evolving toward a bureaucratic-authoritarian regime through coming to resemble the regimes of this type in South America. However, it has not had to move toward this type of system by means of a "national security" regime based on a military dictatorship, given that it can still rely on the PRI.

Yet, under these new conditions, a contradiction has emerged which will be difficult to resolve and which could push Mexico in this direction. The hegemony of the state in relation to different social classes is based on the legacy of the revolution and on the role it is believed to play in defense of "national" and "popular" interests. The widespread economic and political repression required by a stabilization policy will undermine the support coalition of the state, provoking a cleavage between state and society, with the consequent dismantling of the political apparatus created in the aftermath of the Mexican Revolution. The political precariousness of class domination would then be fully evident, necessitating the total reorganization of the regime, with all the critical consequences that this would entail.

PERU

Toward the end of the nineteenth century, Peru continued to be ruled by *gamonales* and *caudillos* who were linked to the divergent interests of different regional landowning and commercial groups, which in turn dominated the Indian population. In this sense, the social and political system was of a colonial character. No sector of the dominant class was capable of forming a national state and providing a national identity for Peruvian society.

Moreover, the country had become seriously "decapitalized," despite having enjoyed forty years of relatively high revenue that derived from the guano exports. This decapitalization was due, fundamentally, to the fact that these revenues led primarily to the enrichment of the commercial bourgeoisie, which found no better opportunity for investment than to devote its capital to the import trade and to make loans to the government, which was in a permanent state of indebtedness. Public revenues, in turn, were used to subdue the rebellions of the caudillos and their followers, who were eager to capture control of the lucrative revenue from guano. There was thus a failure to transform the productive and social structure of the country. Later, in the 1870's, the government incurred an exorbitant debt to construct railroads, in the hope that this would increase the opportunities for primary product exports and for the territorial integration of the country. The failure of this project, the decline in the production of guano, and the European financial crisis led the country to bankruptcy. This cycle of disaster was completed by the defeat of Peru by Chile in the War of the Pacific (1879-1883).

At the end of the century a new cycle of development of an increasingly capitalist character was reinitiated, but this quickly came to be dominated by foreign capital, in part because of the absence of local capital. Foreign capital began to dominate the most important areas of production, entering into agriculture, mining, transportation, banking, and international commerce and creating a typical export enclave economy. The enclaves, in turn, established links with the large landowners and local bourgeoisie, with the goal of maximizing their earnings and benefiting from the political connections provided by this group.

Although during the first two decades of this century a permanent situation of tension existed between the foreign enclaves and some of the affected sectors of the national dominant class, by 1920 this situation had been resolved in favor of a pattern of development heavily dependent on foreign capital. By then the government began to represent directly the interests of foreign capital, subordinating the large landowners and local merchants to these interests. In this role, the government enjoyed the economic and political support of the enclave enterprises within the country and of the United States government. One of the manifestations of this support was the growing flow of loans which the state received in order to supplement the modernization process which foreign capital was carrying out and to promote the territorial and national integration of the country.

In the context of these changes, there occurred an important reorganization of the Peruvian class structure which had a major impact on Peru's future development. In the north, the sugar enclaves undermined the old landowning aristocracy, absorbed many small- and medium-sized landholdings, converted many tenant farmers and members of Indian communities into a rural proletariat, and partially displaced the commercial bourgeoisie and the artisan class. In the central highlands, in the area of the mining enclave, a high degree of concentration of production was achieved through buying out hundreds of medium-sized landowners. Large farms were also established to provide pasture land for the production of wool, following the pattern of the southern part of the country.

At the same time, however, the landowners who were not displaced by the enclave expansion were now in a better position to sell agricultural goods produced by the peasants on their haciendas and by the Indian communities, given the increased demand for food stimulated by the development of the enclaves and by the resulting dislocation of the workers from their means of production. In this way, as was noted above, the enclaves were able to reduce their costs of production considerably.

All this gave rise to a protest movement which was led by Mariátegui and Haya de la Torre. The economic crisis of 1930 unleashed the popular forces that had been created, leading to the formation of the first mass-based political parties to have a national and popular orientation and a strong indigenous component. These parties sought to alter the social bases and fundamental policies of the state. But like Mexico, and in contrast to the Southern Cone, the limited political-economic autonomy of the local owners and of the state with respect to foreign capital impeded them from absorbing and channeling these popular aspirations. Moreover, the possibility that the Indians might participate as citizens in the political life of the country was unacceptable to the *gente decente* (decent people), providing additional reasons for blocking any major opening of the political system. Under these conditions there occurred a violent confrontation among the principal classes of society. This confrontation occurred between the army (since the previously dominant coalition was unable to control the political situation) and the Apra party, which came to play the role of representing the popular sector. The result was the total defeat of Apra and the suppression of this party for over a decade.

In 1945, due to a change in the political atmosphere which occurred as a result of the military defeat of Germany and renewed popular mobilization, the country experienced a short period of democracy which interrupted the fifteen years of persecution which the Apra party and popular organizations had suffered. The popular masses once again demanded their social and political rights which, as in 1930, the dominant class was unable to grant. Hence, this short democratic period came to a close with a new military coup in 1948.

Starting in 1950, as a result of a major transformation in the international system, a new cycle of foreign investment began in Peru. This involved both investment in natural resources and in industrial development. To this was added the expansion of public spending programs which were destined for urban centers in an effort to neutralize the political demands of the popular sector. This led to an accentuation of rural-urban differences and contributed to increasing cityward migration, which produced fundamental changes in Peru's class structure. These developments were of course consistent with Haya's prediction of the 1920's that the expansion of foreign investment would bring an end to "feudalism" and would thus promote the modernization of the country.

In 1956, the export sector of the bourgeoisie—in order to achieve direct representation of its interests within the state—opposed the "reelection" of President Odría, who had come to power in the 1948 coup. At this point, in order to legitimate its rule through "democratic" channels, it had to give Apra an opportunity to share power. The export elite established an informal alliance with Apra which formed the coalitional basis for the presidency of Manuel Prado, starting in 1956. This alliance brought an end to the period of repression of Apra and gave Apra an opportunity to initiate from within the government incremental measures that satisfied short-term needs of the urban popular sector. This incremental, non-radical approach avoided a sharp shift in policy that elites feared might contribute to the development of "international communism"—or that might lead to a return to the earlier repression of Apra.

Apra's alliance with the elite, which was sharply criticized by the new middle class and popular sector groups that had emerged in the context of the ongoing urbanization and social change, created a political vacuum which these groups were eager to fill. Once again, the national-populist slogans of the 1930's came to be a central part of the political rhetoric of the country. "Structural changes" would be carried out which would create a true national society and would make it independent of "external" domination.

At the same time, there emerged in Peru a wave of peasant movements which continued into the 1960's. The goal of these movements included regaining peasant land that had been taken over by haciendas and eliminating pre-capitalist forms of control of agricultural labor—which by this time were clearly an anachronism. The labor movement was gradually achieving an autonomous position that was independent of the control of Apra. Likewise, within the church and the army, which had been pillars of the oligarchic system, there emerged a new development ideology which emphasized the urgency of carrying out fundamental structural changes in Peru as a means of avoiding social conflicts that might ultimately tear apart the national society.

Thus, by the beginning of the 1960's, there was virtually unanimous agreement that the country needed to carry out structural reforms of a national-popular character. In 1963, after a brief experiment with the first institutional military government of the armed forces to appear in Latin America—which had come to power in 1962 in order to block the election of Haya to the presidency—Fernando Belaúnde Terry came to power with the support of the new reformist parties that had emerged in the 1950's, as well as of the church and the armed forces.

At this juncture, it appeared that a meaningful reform program would finally be carried out in Peru. Yet two crucial factors blocked this reform. First, although the latifundista sector of the dominant coalition had lost much of its political strength, it continued to have a disproportionate political importance due to the exclusion of illiterates—i.e., the Indian peasants in the areas of the latifundia—from the rights of citizenship and voting and to the resulting over-representation of the latifundistas in the national legislature. In this context, Apra entered into a conservative alliance with the political movement led by General Odría, the same general who had ruthlessly persecuted the party after the military coup of 1948. This alliance blocked all reformist measures proposed in the legislative chambers in the very midst of the political upheaval of the 1960's—which included peasant land seizures in the highlands and the massive formation of new squatter settlements, the growing autonomy of labor organizations from Apra control, growing student militancy, and finally, in 1965, a guerrilla movement which, in the eyes of military observers, threatened to undermine the social order. The contradiction between this state of political upheaval and the failure of reform definitively convinced the military leaders that the "representative democratic" system was incapable of meeting the fundamental needs of the country.

During the Belaúnde period, both the governing coalition and the opposition, led by Apra, had been supporting a pattern of public spending oriented around extending political patronage to different parts of the popular sector as a substitute for social reforms. This substantial (and inadequately financed) increase in public spending coincided with the granting of important tax exemptions for industrial development. However, beginning in 1965, the export boom which had supported this public spending was interrupted and exports began to decline. An economic crisis was thus added to the political problems which had been building up. In addition, there was a series of public scandals involving high officials in the government and their families. In this situation, it became necessary to devalue the currency and to implement a package of stabilization policies that was supposed to have been accompanied by massive new foreign investment in mining that would supposedly help to alleviate the economic problems of the country.

It was in this context that yet another scandal, involving the dubious negotiations between the Peruvian government and the International Petroleum Company—a subsidiary of Standard Oil and a symbol of foreign domination—completely destroyed the legitimacy of the government. This finally brought to the fore the interventionist tendency that had been developing in the army and led to the military coup of October 3, 1968 and the inauguration of the "Peruvian revolution."

The lack of political articulation of society and the high degree of organizational development of the army allowed the revolutionary government of the armed forces to emerge with considerable autonomy with respect to all of the different sectors and classes of Peruvian society, allowing the military to attempt a fundamental transformation of the society according to its own design for building a nation-state. From its inception, this government thus developed a broad program of basic reforms, achieving in a few short years the elimination of the hacienda system—one of the most important pre-capitalist components of society, the elimination of the export oligarchy, and the nationalization of the majority of the agro-mining enclaves, which led to a major growth in the public sector.

But because the government was attempting to carry out a program, the responsibility for which resided in the armed forces, all of these measures were carried out in a narrowly administrative and technocratic manner which sought to preclude any role for political mobilization. Precisely because of the technocratic character of the reforms and of the attempt to impose corporatist controls, the popular movement that had been growing during the 1960's could not be contained within the framework of the governmental directives, making the attempts to organize society according to the mold of the military state ineffective. Even the cooptation of a large number of intellectuals and professionals who had been disillusioned by the politics of the 1960's and the widespread use of Third World nationalist and anti-capitalist rhetoric by the government did not solve this problem.

Since the state was unable to organize the population in a corporatist fashion, it sought to break the autonomy of the popular organizations by incorporating them in its own labor organization. This attempt was tenaciously resisted by the existing labor groups. The final result was the political defeat of the government in its attempt to control popular participation as a component of the military's effort to transform society.

The industrial bourgeoisie, though it enjoyed numerous benefits and the direct support of the state in capital formation, was likewise reluctant to follow the state's directives, which sharply restricted its autonomy and the political expression of its interests, making it difficult for it to defend itself against unfavorable government policies.

These two areas of policy failure—involving workers and the bourgeoisie—illustrate clearly the more generic dilemma of the military government in dealing with the whole spectrum of domestic class and sectoral interests. Though it sought to provide benefits for a broad range of groups and to link them to the state in a corporative strategy of class conciliation, its efforts were, for different reasons, rejected by virtually all social classes.

The military government ultimately encountered failure in the international sphere as well. In spite of the nationalistic and "Third World" rhetoric of the government, foreign capital was in fact compensated—indeed, in excess—for the expropriations which the government undertook. This occurred in important measure as a result of mediation by the United States government, which sought to prevent the "Cubanization" or "Chileanization" of Peru. The concern with preventing this outcome also led the United States to support the military government in its effort to get major new foreign loans in order to finance its program of economic development, which in turn led to a substantial increase in the level of imports. In addition, beginning in 1974, the military government initiated massive purchases of armaments in response to the perception of the imminent danger of a war with Chile following the rise to power of the Pinochet government.

With the onset of the world recession of the early 1970's, exports fell in volume and in price and the growing external debt soon began to account for around 45 percent of the total value of exports. By 1975, the fiscal deficit and the acute balance of payments problems threatened Peru's international monetary standing.

By the middle of 1975, the armed forces had to reorient economic policy, gradually moving toward a stabilization policy which, in turn, was met with a decisive popular mobilization, thus hastening the emergence of a sharp cleavage between the state and society.

The intensification of the economic crisis in 1977 compelled the government to negotiate a program of stabilization policies with the International Monetary Fund as a precondition for renegotiating Peru's debts with the private international banking community. As was to be expected, the IMF demanded faithful compliance with its classic doctrine, which was resisted by the government, due to the social and political consequences that would result. However, the government soon had to yield. Yet even this arrangement did not please the bourgeoisie, who demanded the elimination of the state sector of the economy and the definitive opening of the economy to the "free" movement of capital, especially foreign capital.

The national general strike of July 19, 1977, which represents a milestone in Peruvian history; the acts of repression against the labor movement that followed this strike; and two subsequent general strikes in 1977-1978 which were led by the labor movement and supported by a broad spectrum of different class groups, strikingly revealed the isolation of the military-state from society. It was under these conditions that the military junta called for a Constitutional Assembly for 1978 and offered to carry out the "transfer" of the government, but not power, to civilians in 1980, possibly setting the stage for the final military extrication from power.

With this call for civilian participation, the old political parties reemerged and, along with them, new parties of the revolutionary left that demanded the political democratization of the country and a package of redistributive economic policies.

Thus, the political situation, as of early 1978, involved a blatant contradiction between the attempt to adopt IMF-type stabilization policies and the demands of the organized popular sectors. There exists a range of possible outcomes, within which the odds are very much in favor of the establishment of a new military dictatorship which will "put things in order" before the popular demands lead to an open political confrontation with the state and the bourgeoisie.

These events have only intensified internal tension within the army, since the original goal of the military government was to achieve national unification—as the slogan put it—through an alliance of "the people and the armed forces." The application of the economic policies required by the IMF represents the final dashing of the hopes which led the military into its "revolutionary" phase. To dismiss everything which was attempted and was achieved involves not only completely discarding the possibility of national integration, but also isolating the military from society—and this at the centennial of the War of the Pacific.

CONCLUSION

What implications can be drawn from this analysis? The basic comparison on which this chapter has focused involves a set of consistent differences between the countries of the Southern Cone plus Brazil, on the one hand, and Mexico and Peru, on the other. Taking as a starting point the contrast between those countries in which the period of export growth that began in the last century was to a significant degree "nationally controlled," as opposed to being centered around foreign-dominated enclaves, we identified a series of contrasts in the impact of export growth, the nature of the system of domination that supported this growth, and the types of populist movements that subsequently emerged in these countries.

However, the analysis of the most recent turn of events in Peru and Mexico raises serious questions regarding whether these two sets of countries are in fact still following different developmental trajectories. In the mid-1970's, both Peru and Mexico not only experienced a sharp turn to the right in economic policy, but appeared to be moving toward a pattern of blatant repression that may become increasingly similar to that experienced in the Southern Cone. It was suggested above that the special feature of the Mexican system that has made it so distinctive—the role of the PRI in both implementing and legitimating the system of domination—may increasingly be undermined. Likewise, the energetic efforts of the Peruvian military government to achieve national integration and a conciliation of class interests have backfired and have produced one of the most stark disjunctures between the state and society ever experienced in that country. In both cases, these events seem to point to the possibility of an important degree of convergence with the countries of the south.

It is beyond the scope of this chapter to provide a definitive answer as to whether this convergence will occur. Instead, we may conclude simply by proposing an agenda of research priorities suggested by the possibility of this convergence. A central point of the analysis of the earlier historical period in these two sets of countries was that the nature of the populist experience was quite different. In the enclave countries, the issues of national integration faced by populist leaders were in many ways far more profound, involving both the problem of dealing with proportionally much larger pre-capitalist sectors of the economy and dealing with a far greater degree of ethnic and cultural diversity that derived from the presence of large indigenous populations. The symbolic resources and patterns of mobilization that emerged in these contexts therefore appear in important ways to be distinct.

It was stressed at several points above that as these systems of domination are always centrally concerned with the problem of protecting capital accumulation, and that their ability to do this without the use of naked repression depends on the skills and resources that they can bring to the task of balancing the pressures for accumulation and the pressures for redistribution. Ultimately, one must seek to discover whether these skills and resources are, in any fundamental way, really different in Peru and Mexico, in contrast to the countries of the South. This will require both extensive further research on the past experience of these countries with populism and also an ongoing "monitoring" of their future political evolution.

PART THREE

Future Evolution of Authoritarianism
and Directions for New Research

CHAPTER 7

TENSIONS IN THE BUREAUCRATIC-AUTHORITARIAN STATE AND THE QUESTION OF DEMOCRACY

Guillermo O'Donnell*

Reality is compelling. In 1974 I wrote an essay in which I focused on the experience of the bureaucratic-authoritarian states that existed at the time—and was convinced of the imminent reappearance in Argentina of this type of state.[1] In that essay I discussed the conditions that contribute to the emergence of bureaucratic-authoritarian (BA) states, but my interests had already shifted toward the study of the dynamic generated by the internal tensions of BA and by the impacts of this type of state on society. Now, at the end of 1978, with Brazil making cautious yet significant advances toward political democracy, with Chile and Uruguay subjected to systems of domination that seemingly face no serious challenge, and with Argentina in the throes of the first stage of the implantation of BA, I would like to reconsider the interrelationship between the internal tensions of BA and its impact on society.

In contrast to my earlier essay, I will examine here only the first stage in the evolution of the BA state and, within it, the effects of factors which have previously been insufficiently analyzed: i.e., strictly political factors and, in particular, the problem of democracy. On a superficial level, the fact that the possibility of a return to democracy has been raised might at first appear to be attributable to a "false consciousness" on the part of the leaders of BA or to external pressures. At a more fundamental level, however, I will argue that profound and abiding issues are involved regarding the nature of this state. I will maintain

* To the memory of Kalman Silvert, whom I admired.

[1] Initially presented to the "Conference on History and Social Science," Universidad de Campinas, Brazil, 1975 and published as "Reflexiones sobre las tendencias generales de cambio en el Estado burocrático-autoritario" (Documento CEDES/G.E. CLACSO/No. 1, Centro de Estudios de Estado y Sociedad, Buenos Aires, 1975). This was published in English as "Reflections on the Patterns of Change in the Bureaucratic-Authoritarian State," *Latin American Research Review* Vol. 13, No. 1 (Winter 1978), pp. 3-38.

that the fact that the issue of democracy has arisen at all (regardless of whether it is qualified as "organic" democracy, "responsible" democracy, or even "authoritarian" democracy) is an indication of fundamental tensions within the core of this system of domination, as well as with the social sectors which BA excludes.

This topic is important because focusing on the superficial features of the BA state can lead to erroneous conclusions. The institutions of BA often appear as a monolithic and imposing force whose rhetoric celebrates the superior rationality which must be imposed upon the nation in order to save it from its deepest crisis. These institutions also give the appearance of change and adaptation on the basis of the "impartial" and "technical" evaluation of the progress that is being made in the imposing task of saving the nation. Yet behind this facade, the BA state is subject to tensions—contradictions, dilemmas, and perils[2]—which reflect the extraordinary difficulties of consolidating a system of domination that can conceal neither the fact that it is founded on coercion nor the fact that its most crucial supporters represent a spectrum of society far more narrow than the entire nation which BA claims to be serving. Its domination is particularly severe because, by the nature of its founding, this state entails an anticipated rejection of the basis for its own legitimation. BA arises from an overwhelming political defeat of the popular sector and its allies, which was imposed at the extremely high cost of making it impossible for BA to legitimate itself. Indeed, this high cost suggests how much was at stake in the conflicts that preceded the implantation of BA. It is from this perspective that one must consider a topic which might seem as surrealistic as that of democracy. Before addressing this theme, however, we must consider some more general questions.

CONCERNING THE STATE

The state is fundamentally a social relationship of domination or, more precisely, one aspect—as such, comprehensible only analytically—of the social relations of domination.[3] The state

---

[2] A similar argument is presented by Philippe C. Schmitter, "Liberation by *Golpe*: Retrospective Thoughts on the Demise of Authoritarian Rule in Portugal," *Armed Forces and Society*, Vol. 2, No. 1 (November 1975), pp. 5-33.

[3] This discussion represents a revision of the conception of the state which was

supports and organizes these relations of domination through institutions that usually enjoy a monopoly of the means of coercion within a defined territory and that generally are viewed as having a legitimate right to guarantee the system of social domination. As such, the state should be understood from and within civil society, though in its objective, institutional form it appears to be, and proclaims itself to stand, above society.

What interests us here is a type of capitalist state. As such, it maintains and structures class domination, in the sense that this domination is rooted principally in a class structure that in turn has its foundation in the operation and reproduction of capitalist relations of production. These relations of production are the "heart of civil society," within which we view the state as the strictly political aspect of the social relations of domination. From this perspective the state is, first and foremost, a relation of domination that articulates in unequal fashion the components of civil society, supporting and organizing the existing system of social domination. What makes this support effective are certain objective manifestations of the state—its institutions and the law. Yet the true meaning and consequences of these can be understood only in terms of their being the objective manifestations of certain aspects of the system of domination in society.

I wish to stress two interrelated themes regarding the state—first, its analytic reality as the political aspect of certain social relations of domination, and, second, its concrete objectification as a set of institutions and legal norms. By keeping in mind the interrelation between these two faces of the state—analytic and concrete—one can see the falsity of the claim by the state's institutions to embody a rationality that is distinct from and superior to that of civil society, as well as the corresponding falsity of denying the state's fundamental role in articulating civil society in an unequal (or more precisely, contradictory) fashion.

Further, the apparent separation of the institutions of the state from civil society fosters the emergence of diverse linkages or "mediations" between the opacity and fractionalization of that which is "private"—i.e., civil society—on the one hand, and the

---

implicit in my essay "Reflections." I now view this earlier conception as excessively focused on the institutional features of the state. Unfortunately, I can only briefly introduce here the most indispensable elements of this revised conceptualization. For a more complete discussion, see my "Apuntes para una teoría del Estado" (Documento CEDES/G.E. CLACSO/No. 9, Centro de Estudios de Estado y Sociedad, Buenos Aires, 1977).

"public" and universalistic role (for the population within its borders) in which the state institutions usually present themselves to ordinary consciousness. I do not have space to develop here the reasoning that underlies this conclusion, but the state is usually also the organizational focus of consensus within society, from which it derives the basis for its own legitimation. In order to achieve consensus, these institutions must appear as *the* state, as agents of a general interest of a community—the nation—that transcends the reproduction of daily life in civil society. The reification of the state in its institutional objectifications obscures its underlying role as guarantor of domination within society; yet—inasmuch as it implies that state and society appear to be separate—it tends to generate various mediations between them through which consensus tends to be created. The state ultimately is based on coercion, but it usually is also based on consensus, which both encompasses and conceals coercion.

The principal mediation alluded to above is the nation. I mean by nation the collective identities that define a "we" that consists, on the one hand, of a network of solidarities superimposed upon the diversity and antagonisms of civil society and, on the other hand, of the recognition of a collectivity distinct from the "they" that constitutes other nations. The nation is expressed through a dense symbolism epitomized by the flag and national anthem, as well as by an official history that mythologizes a shared, cohesive past and extols a collective "we" which should prevail over the cleavages (not only those between social classes) of civil society.

There are two other fundamental political mediations. One is citizenship, in the double sense of: 1. Abstract equality which—basically by means of universal suffrage and the corresponding regime of political democracy—is the foundation of the claim that the power exercised through the institutions of the state by the occupants of governmental roles is based on the consent of the citizens; and 2. the right to have recourse to juridically regulated protection against arbitrary acts on the part of state institutions. The second mediation is the *pueblo* or *lo popular*.[4] This mediation is based on a "we" that derives neither from the idea of shared citizenship, which involves abstractly equal rights, nor

---

[4] Translator's note: These two terms are not translated because the most nearly equivalent terms in English, "people" and "popular," have different meanings. The meaning intended by O'Donnell is indicated in the text above.

from the idea of nation, which involves concrete rights which apply equally to all those who belong to the nation without respect to their position within society. *Pueblo* and *lo popular* involve a "we" that is a carrier of demands for substantive justice which form the basis for the obligations of the state toward the less favored segments of the population.

Normally, in a capitalist state the subject of the state is the citizen, who has the right, which is not systematically denied, to lodge claims of substantive justice before the appropriate state institutions. Of course, this right is actually limited by the systematic inequalities that arise from the underlying class structure of society and from other forms of social inequality. Nonetheless, this right is partially real, and the belief in its existence is normally an important element of consensus, which entails challenging neither the domination which is exercised in society nor the role of the state as the agent or representative of the general interest of the nation.

The efficacy of this idea of the nation, along with that of citizenship and *lo popular*, allows the state institutions to appear as agents which achieve and protect a general interest—that is, the general interest of a "we" that stands above the factionalism and antagonisms of civil society. Moreover, the effective functioning—as an institutional reality and in terms of subjective acceptance on the part of a large portion of relevant social actors—of the ideas of citizenship and *lo popular* usually provides a consensual basis for the exercise of power, and ultimately of coercion, by the state institutions. They do this because the basis of state power must appear to reside outside the state itself. The state can only be legitimated by appearing to reside in external referents whose general interest the state institutions are supposed to serve. These external referents are normally the nation, jointly with citizenship and *pueblo*, which represent the intersection of an abstractly equal "we" (i.e., citizenship) and a "we" which is concretely unequal (involving the tutelage of the less favored portion of society, i.e., the *pueblo*). From these referents there usually emerge collective identities that stand above the class cleavages that can potentially arise from civil society. Because the state appears separated from society and objectified in its institutions, these institutions cannot by themselves legitimate the power they exercise except by means of the collective referents whose general interests they claim to serve. Each of those collective referents mediates the relation between the state and society, transforming its underlying reality; hence their role in achieving consensus and, correspondingly, in legitimating the power exercised by the state institutions.

On the other hand, these mediations are the means through which the social subject, as a member of society, rises above his private life. Identifying himself in the symbols of the nation, exercising the rights of citizenship, and eventually making demands for substantive justice as part of the *pueblo*, the social subject transcends his daily life and recognizes himself as part of a "we" which is, from another perspective, the referent evoked by the state institutions. Hence, these institutions do not usually appear as the organizers and guarantors of social domination, but rather as agents of the general interests expressed through those mediations. This fact tends to result in a consensus which expresses the belief that what the state institutions do and do not do—even though systematically biased by the underlying system of social domination—is the consequence of the rights derived from being a citizen, as well as a member of the nation and *lo popular*. This tension between the underlying reality of the state as guarantor and organizer of social domination, on the one hand, and as agent of a general interest which, though partialized and limited, is not fictitious, on the other, is characteristic of any state. This tension is the key to the theoretical analysis of the state. We cannot attempt such an analysis here. Yet by examining certain characteristics of the BA state we will be able to see, in a context in which the above-mentioned mediations are largely missing, their crucial importance in facilitating what is fundamental for any system of social and political domination: to mask the reality of domination and to appear to be the expression of a general, encompassing interest.

Before turning to the main topic of this chapter, I must present other observations indispensable for understanding both the situation prior to the installation of BA and its subsequent impact once installed.

1. In Latin America the formation of the nation was accomplished much more through the mediation of *lo popular* than through that of citizenship. Whether or not it occurred through so-called "populisms," the political activation of the previously marginal popular sectors occurred through political relationships in which they were treated much more as a *pueblo*, as a carrier of demands for substantive justice, than as citizens.

2. This same process of constituting the nation involved the postulation of a "we" that defined itself as an adversary of an "anti-national" social order whose most conspicuous components involved the role of transnational capital in the exportation of primary products and the dominant national classes that were more intimately tied to transnational capital.

3. This process contributed to the downfall of the system of oligarchic domination and its replacement by a system of bourgeois domination supported by the expansion of the institutional system of the state which opened the way for the supremacy of transnational capital in the urban productive structure.

4. In the periods preceding the installation of BA, the great advance in the transnationalization of the productive structure led to a fundamental alteration in the nature of civil society in relation to the territorial scope of the authority exercised by the state. That is, many of the principal centers of economic decision making in society, the final destination and criteria for the distribution of the capital generated in the local market, and many aspects of the social relations (not only economic ones) extended beyond the state's capacity for control within the scope of its territorial authority. This "denationalization" was added onto that which had occurred earlier in connection with the exportation of primary products, and now came to affect the most dynamic components of the urban productive and class structure.[5] Other factors that came into play prior to the implantation of the BA state, such as the different levels of "threat," the interaction between the pattern of economic growth that followed the transnationalization of the urban productive structure and the growing popular political activation, and the severity of the crisis that preceded it, have already been treated elsewhere.[6]

We can now delineate the most important features of the BA state as a starting point for analyzing the contradictory dynamic that is set in motion by its implantation.

THE BUREAUCRATIC-AUTHORITARIAN STATE

BA is a type of authoritarian state whose principal characteristics are:

[5] The most enlightening contribution on this and related topics continues to be that of Fernando Henrique Cardoso and Enzo Faletto in *Dependencia y desarrollo en América Latina* (Mexico City: Siglo Veintiuno Editores, 1969).

[6] Here again, see "Reflections" and the references cited in that article.

1. It is, first and foremost, guarantor and organizer of the domination exercised through a class structure subordinated to the upper fractions of a highly oligopolized and transnationalized bourgeoisie. In other words, the principal social base of the BA state is this upper bourgeoisie.

2. In institutional terms, it is comprised of organizations in which specialists in coercion have decisive weight, as well as those whose aim it is to achieve "normalization" of the economy.[7] The special role played by these two groups represents the institutional expression of the identification, by its own actors, of the two great tasks that the BA state is committed to accomplish: the restoration of "order" in society by means of the political deactivation of the popular sector, on the one hand, and the normalization of the economy, on the other.

3. It is a system of political exclusion of a previously activated popular sector which is subjected to strict controls in an effort to eliminate its earlier active role in the national political arena. This political exclusion is achieved by destroying or capturing the resources (especially those embodied in class organizations and political movements) which supported this activation. In addition, this exclusion is guided by a determination to impose a particular type of "order" on society and guarantee its future viability. This order is seen as a necessary condition for the consolidation of the social domination that BA guarantees and, after achieving the normalization of the economy, for reinitiating a highly transnationalized pattern of economic growth characterized by a skewed distribution of resources.

4. This exclusion involves the suppression of citizenship, in the twofold sense defined above. In particular, this suppression includes the liquidation of the institutions of political democracy. It also involves a denial of *lo popular*: it prohibits (enforcing the prohibition with coercion) any appeals to the population as *pueblo* and, of course, as class. The suppression of the institutional roles and channels of access to the government characteristic of political democracy is in large measure oriented toward eliminating roles and organizations (political parties

[7] I use this phrase to refer to the tasks undertaken by the civilian technocrats in charge of the economic apparatus of BA, whose aim is to stabilize certain crucial variables (such as the rate of inflation and the balance of payments) in a manner that will gain the confidence of major capitalist interests—above all, in the first stage of BA, of transnational finance capital.

among them) that have served as a channel for appeals for substantive justice that are considered incompatible with the restoration of order and with the normalization of the economy. In addition, BA appears as if placed before a sick nation—as expressed in the rhetoric that derived from the severity of the crisis that preceded its implantation—whose general interest must be invoked; yet, because of the depth of the crisis, BA cannot claim to be the representative of that sick nation, which is seen as contaminated by innumerable internal enemies. Thus, BA is based on the suppression of two fundamental mediations—citizenship and *lo popular*. In an ambiguous way it may evoke the other mediation—the nation—but only as a "project" (and not as an actual reality) which it proposes to carry out through drastic surgical measures.

5. BA is also a system of economic exclusion of the popular sector, inasmuch as it promotes a pattern of capital accumulation which is highly skewed toward benefiting the large oligopolistic units of private capital and some state institutions. The preexisting inequities in the distribution of societal resources are thus sharply increased.

6. It corresponds to, and promotes, an increasing transnationalization of the productive structure, resulting in a further denationalization of society in terms of the degree to which it is in fact contained within the scope of the territorial authority which the state claims to exercise.

7. Through its institutions it endeavors to "depoliticize" social issues by dealing with them in terms of the supposedly neutral and objective criteria of technical rationality. This depoliticization complements the prohibition against invoking issues of substantive justice as they relate to *lo popular* (and, of course, class), which allegedly introduces "irrationalities" and "premature" demands that interfere with the restoration of order and the normalization of the economy.

8. In the first stage that we are considering here, the political regime of the BA state—which, while not formalized, is clearly identifiable—involves closing the democratic channels of access to the government. More generally, it involves closing the channels of access for the representation of popular and class interests. Such access is limited to those who stand at the apex of large organizations (both public and private), especially the armed forces and large oligopolistic enterprises.

The characteristics that I have just enumerated permit us to distinguish the BA state from other authoritarian states and to identify shared traits among various cases of BA. These traits in turn interact with other features of BA that differ from case to case. These similarities and differences represent the terrain in which we will place ourselves starting in the next section, which explores some of the basic tensions of BA.

AMBIGUITIES IN THE SYSTEM OF DOMINATION

What goes on behind the imposing façade of power of the BA state? In what way is the imposing rhetoric of its institutions, directed at an ailing nation which the state is determined to save even against its will, a sign of uncertainties and weaknesses inherent in this state? I hope that the discussion of the state presented above will aid us in exploring a reality that is more complex than is suggested by these appearances.

Fundamentally, BA is a type of state which encompasses sharply contradictory tendencies. On the one hand, BA involves the further denationalization of civil society noted above that occurs first as a consequence of the urgent search for the transnational capital which is a requisite for the normalization of the economy, and later due to the necessity of maintaining a "favorable investment climate" in order to sustain the inflow of such capital. At the same time, BA entails a drastic contraction of the nation, the suppression of citizenship, and the prohibition of appeals to the *pueblo* and to social class as a basis for making demands for substantive justice. This contraction derives from the defeat of the popular sector and its allies; from the reaction triggered by the threat that the political activation of this sector seemed to pose for the survival of the basic parameters of capitalist society; and, once BA is implanted, from the aim of imposing a particular social "order" based on the political and economic exclusion of the popular sector.

Such exclusion appears as a necessary condition for healing the body of the nation, an organism with infected parts upon which, for its own good, it is necessary to perform the surgery of excluding the popular sector and its allies. This exclusion involves redefining the scope of the nation, to which neither the agents that promoted this illness nor the parts that have become infected can belong. They are the enemy within the body of the nation,[8] the "not-we" of the new nation that is to be constructed by the institutions of BA. When the leaders of these institutions speak of the nation, the referent has been restricted, by the very logic of their discourse, to a far less comprehensive "we" than in the past; only those can belong who fit into their design—socially harmonious and technocratic—of the future nation.

On the other hand, like all states, BA claims to be a national state. Lacking the referent of the nation as a universally comprehensive idea that encompasses the entire population, the rhetoric of the institutions of BA must "statize" the meaning of the nation—at the same time that, in relation to the normalization of the economy, the same rhetoric defends an intense privatization. Such statizing of the idea of the nation implies that its general interest be identified with the success of the state institutions in their quest to establish a particular order in society and to normalize the economy. As a result, the state institutions no longer appear to play the role through which they usually legitimate themselves, that of serving an interest superior and external to themselves—i.e., the interests of the nation as a community that encompasses the totality of, or at least most of, the population. On the contrary, when the state institutions attempt to redefine the nation in terms of exclusion and of national infirmity, the power they exercise no longer has an external basis of legitimation and cannot but appear as its own foundation. In other words, domination becomes naked and dilutes its consensual mediations; it manifests itself in the form of overt physical and economic coercion. In addition, the suppression of citizenship, together with the prohibition against invoking *lo popular*, not merely dilutes but radically eliminates other legitimating mediations between the state and society.

Why are these costs incurred, which ultimately involve the prior renunciation not only of the basis of legitimation of the state, but also of the possibility that the system of domination that BA supports and organizes could ever achieve hegemony? To answer this question we must understand that the implantation of BA is the result of a frightened reaction to what is perceived as a grave threat to the survival of the basic capitalist parameters of society. The overarching network of solidarities of

[8] This organic image is, of course, reinforced by the doctrines of "national security."

the nation has been shattered by a multitude of conflicts. Acute antagonisms have appeared in civil society, involving the emergence of "sectoral egotism" and of the threatening symbolism of class identifications. As a result, the leaders of the BA are not, nor can they see themselves as, the representatives either of this embattled nation or of the antagonisms of civil society. By contrast, their mission is to transform society profoundly in such a way that, in some distant future, the "we" of the nation will be sustained by a utopia of social integration. I have already suggested that the often repeated organic image of the infirm body, which still does not realize that radical surgery is in its own best interest, is also the radical denial of the role of the state as representative of the nation (and society). In turn, the suppression of *lo popular* and of citizenship, along with the elimination of the institutions of political democracy, are the tourniquet that impedes the spread of the poison and gives time for healing. As a result, BA cannot help but abandon the usual referents of legitimation and presents itself instead as the basis of its own power. It thus abandons the mediations which partially, yet effectively, transform the private life of civil society into the shared existence of collective identities through which social actors recognize themselves as members of the nation, as citizens, eventually as part of the *pueblo*, and as being included in a state to which they normally grant the right to rule and coerce.

The institutions of the BA state attempt to fill the void thus created through an intensive use of the martial and patriotic symbols of the nation. But these symbols must be anchored in some of the aforementioned referents if they are not to be merely grandiloquent rhetoric. The BA leaders attempt to recreate mediations with society by inviting "participation"; but the state's denial of its own role as representative of the nation and the elimination of the ideas of *pueblo* and citizenship mean that such participation can only involve a passively approving observation of the tasks that the state institutions undertake.

Under these conditions, the best that can be hoped for is a "tacit consensus," i.e., depoliticization, apathy, and a retreat into a completely privatized daily existence. And fear. Fear on the part of the losers and the opponents of BA, which results from BA's conspicuous capacity for coercion. And fear on the part of the winners, who face the specter of a return to the situation that preceded the implantation of BA. There is also the fear, on the part of those who carry out the physical coercion, of any "political solution" that could possibly lead to such a return; this last fear at times appears to drive them down a path of coercion that knows no limits.

Tacit consensus is a foundation too tenuous to sustain the state. Fear, together with the upper bourgeoisie and the "modern" sectors of the middle class more closely tied to it, are the major social supports of the BA state. But fear hardly serves as an adequate mediation between the state and society. Moreover, the fear on the part of the winners tends to diminish with the passage of time (in spite of efforts to refresh their memory) and with an awareness of the costs imposed on many of them by the continuation of BA.

In reality, the surgery that the higher institutions of the BA state attempt to perform upon the nation inflicts heavy costs on many of those who supported the implantation of BA. The imposition of "order" of course severely punishes the political and class organizations that served as channels for the political activation of the popular sector. The economic exclusion of this sector and the prohibition against raising issues of substantive justice around the symbols of *pueblo* and class make it clear that whatever the BA state may proclaim the nation to be, it does not include the popular sector. Those who were until recently an active political presence are ostracized from their own nation through their political and economic exclusion. On the other hand, the attempts to normalize the economy through a close alliance with the upper bourgeoisie (in the first stage of BA, above all with transnational and domestic finance capital) inflict serious hardships on a good portion of the middle sectors and the weakest (and more indisputably national) fractions of the bourgeoisie. As a result, a rapid contraction of the alliance that supported its implantation takes place in the initial period of BA. The supporters who withdraw from the alliance enter into the "tacit consensus" and engage in a disillusioned defense of their specific interests in the interstices of state institutions. Depending on the lesser or greater degree of previous threat, those who withdraw their support because of the policies of economic normalization may or may not, respectively, combine with the excluded sectors and participate, as in Argentina in 1969, in a decisive challenge to the BA state.[9] In cases of a high level of previous threat in which they do not withdraw, these sectors reinforce the silence and opacity of civil society.

The withdrawal of these initial supporters underscores the fact that the principal (and at that moment virtually the only) base of social support of BA is the upper bourgeoisie—i.e., the upper fractions of the local bourgeoisie and of transnational capitalism. But this is—ostensibly—the principal economic beneficiary of the new situation and the most transnationalized and, therefore, the least national component of society. In light of the economic and political exclusion of the popular sector, the economic hardships suffered by an important portion of the original alliance, the contraction of the nation, and the suppression of the mediations of citizenship and *pueblo*, the BA state remains—and overtly appears to be—sustained basically by the oligopolistic and transnationalized fractions of the bourgeoisie, along with—in its own institutional system—the armed forces and the technocrats who attempt the normalization of the economy. These oligopolistic and transnationalized fractions of the bourgeoisie serve poorly as a legitimating referent for the state because they are the antithesis of *lo popular* and of the symbolism of the nation defined as a "we" that stands in contrast to the "they" of other nations. On the other hand, the local bourgeoisie hardly provides an adequate legitimating referent for the state either. Though the BA economic policies have variegated impacts on different economic activities, they further weaken the already weak local bourgeoisie, placing part of it among those who are part of the "tacit consensus" and hardly leaving this class in an appropriate position to fill the role of a dominant class whose interests can plausibly be argued by the state institutions to be coequal with the general interests of the nation.

Thus, BA is the negation of the usual legitimating mediations of the state—the nation contracts, *pueblo* and citizenship are suppressed, and the state cannot sustain itself through the hegemonic potential of an unquestionably *national* dominant class. As a consequence, the ultimate basis of the state—coercion—is starkly revealed. In addition, it is evident that BA be-

---

[9] This and other arguments to which I will refer in the following pages have been presented in greater detail in "Reflections."

stows immense advantages on the most oligopolistic and least national fractions of the bourgeoisie. The effort to saturate the mass media with symbols of the nation therefore fails because it falls into the abyss created by the further denationalization of civil society and the contraction of the nation.

In the face of these dilemmas, one escape might lie in the possibility that the state can convert itself, not only in its discourse but in the reality of its activities, into the institutional center of a national development project which could be invoked as representing the paramount general interest. That is to say, the state institutions themselves would become the economic and social center of such a project, emerging as the leaders of "development" and taking the place of the absent bourgeois leadership. This approach would lead toward state capitalism. Yet this alternative conflicts with the high degree of transnationalization of the productive structure and with the crucial role that private capital, especially the upper bourgeoisie, must play if BA is to endure. It generates ambiguities and tensions, both within BA and with its principal social base, which we will consider below.

On another level, the institutional system of BA reflects the priorities that its own actors set for themselves. The institutions specialized in the use of coercion occupy the apex of this system by virtue of having themselves ended the crisis that preceded BA and because they remain in charge of imposing order and, no less important, of guaranteeing the future effectiveness of this order. At the same time, the task of normalizing the economy is assigned to civilian technocrats closely identified with the upper bourgeoisie and with transnational financial institutions. The technocrats believe in the rationality of economic orthodoxy, know how to apply it, and are trusted by the local and transnational elements of the upper bourgeoisie. The policies and institutions of the first phase of BA are organized around these two concerns. The two great tasks of imposing order (with its organizational agent, the armed forces) and of normalizing the economy (with its social base in the upper bourgeoisie, and its agents in the technocrats who direct it) are institutionally inserted into the BA state. As a result, BA cannot but appear as the transparent conjunction of coercion and economic domination.

These priorities reflect something fundamental which has already been mentioned, but which I hope we may now understand better. The implantation of BA is an attempt to salvage a society whose continuity as a capitalist system was perceived as threatened. This goal can only be achieved, given the magnitude of this threat, by, on the one hand, severely imposing "order," and, on the other, by carefully obeying the rules of orthodoxy upon which the support of transnational capital and of the most dynamic and economically powerful fractions of these societies is contingent. These measures, together with the suppression of mediations and the resulting exposure of the underlying system of domination, are the immense homage which is rendered to the reproduction of society *qua* capitalist. In the face of the alternative posed by the depth of the crisis that preceded BA and the accompanying threat, the state is first and foremost a capitalist state, rather than a national, a popular, or a citizens' state. Yet the implementation of these measures entails the immense risk of implanting a state that is incapable of converting itself into the foundation of its own legitimacy. The state must rely instead on tacit consensus, coercion, fear, and the support of the least national fractions of its society.

There cannot be consensus unless the connection between coercion and economic domination is veiled. Yet the opposite occurs in BA. Moreover, in BA the proximity of coercion and economic domination juxtaposes two social actors—the armed forces and the upper bourgeoisie—who usually are separated, on a political level, by the mediations mentioned above and, on the institutional level of the state, by other institutions of civilian bureaucracy and democratic representation. That is to say, the social basis of BA in the upper bourgeoisie, their ostensible support for BA, and their "bridgehead" in the institutional system of the state in the form of the economic technocrats intersect directly and visibly with the armed forces. The upper bourgeoisie and the technocrats have a strongly transnational orientation, both in their beliefs and in their economic behavior. For them, the political boundaries of the nation are basically a useless constraint on the movement of the factors of production, on the free circulation of capital, and on considerations of efficiency at the transnational level. They also interfere with the efforts to reintegrate these economies into the world market in the aftermath of the pre-BA crisis. All of these aims clash with what is perceived by these actors as the narrowness of the nation and of "nationalism." On the other hand, these actors are the most fully and dynamically capitalistic members of these societies. Hence, they are unabashedly motivated by profit, the driving force behind an accumulation of capital which is sanctioned by an ideology which claims that the maximization of profit will, in the long run, contribute to the general welfare.

But a great problem within BA is that the other central actor in its institutional system—the armed forces—tends to be the most nationalistic and least capitalistic of the state institutions. With their sense of mission, the martial values with which they socialize their members, and their doctrines of national security which presuppose the existence of a nation characterized by a high degree of homogeneity in the orientations and actions of all civilians, the armed forces are the state institution most predisposed to define the nation as that which is *not* foreign, and to define appropriate behavior as that which is inspired by an introverted and exclusivist vision of the nation. In addition, the profit motive appears to them to be of secondary importance, at most, and sordid in comparison with the larger concerns and ideals that derive from their own orientations. Profit may be necessary, but in any case it should not become "excessive" or work against the mission of homogenizing the totality of the nation.[10]

How is it possible that social actors with such different orientations and values can join together as the principal actors within the institutions of BA? The answer is that with the legitimating mediations suppressed—and, of course, pending always the problem of maintaining the deactivation of the popular sector and the prohibition against evoking *pueblo* and class—economic domination and coercion tend to become transparently close and mutually supportive. Particularly after many of the original

[10] After closely examining the orientations of the armed forces in the countries in which BA has emerged, I am convinced that this is a valid generalization. However, this generalization does not preclude the possibility that in some cases the upper echelon of the armed forces might be controlled by groups more favorably disposed toward the orientations of the upper bourgeoisie. This greater affinity would doubtless mitigate the problems which I analyze below—but it does not eliminate them, since it seems to mean that the control over the armed forces exercised by this military leadership will be more precarious. The most important case of such congruence between the attitudes of high level military leaders and the upper bourgeoisie and the officials in the economic team of the BA state is that of Castelo Branco and his group in Brazil, from 1964 to 1967. Another case is that of the Lanusse presidency in Argentina, from 1971 to 1973. However, in this case it was not the consolidation of BA that was being attempted, but rather the negotiation of the conditions for its liquidation.

supporters of BA withdraw to "tacit consensus" (in addition to the initial exclusion of the popular sector), the upper bourgeoisie needs coercion as a guarantee of present and future social "order," without which it could neither reinitiate accumulation for its own principal benefit nor place its confidence in the future of the economy.[11] On the other hand, without this support and the resulting confidence, a BA state whose alliances have narrowed to such an extent could not even attempt economic normalization and would soon crumble.

In the BA state, economic domination and coercion, along with their social carriers, are mutually indispensable. But this mutual indispensability does not prevent the alliance forged in this way from being marked, on both sides, by numerous tensions. Nor does it prevent the emergence of a desire to reconstitute a system of domination which would again separate these two components by interposing the lacking mediations. This point, fundamental for understanding the dynamic of BA, will receive our attention in the following sections.

Tensions in the Alliance

The mutual indispensability of the upper bourgeoisie and the armed forces is the key to discovering the dissonances and tensions that arise between them. The goal of constructing a more homogeneous nation is inconsistent both with the denationalization of civil society promoted by the most transnationalized actors within society and with their orientation toward a pattern of capital accumulation which cannot remain confined within the local market, either in terms of its principal criteria for decision-making or in terms of the main beneficiaries of that accumulation. The overt alliance of the pinnacle of the state apparatus with the least national elements in the nation occurs in conjunction with the exclusion of the popular sector and with the withdrawal of support by important—and unequivocally national—portions of the middle sectors and the bourgeoisie that actively supported the implantation of BA.

How can the tensions be resolved that arise among the armed

[11] These points, including that regarding the importance of the guarantee that both order and the rationality of the management of the economy (from the perspective of the upper bourgeoisie) will be maintained in the future, are dealt with in my "Reflections."

forces' conception of the nation, the transnational orientation of their principal allies in the BA state, and the national character not only of the popular sector but also of the original allies who have subsequently suffered from the impact of the normalization policies? One possibility would be the enlargement of the state apparatus that might greatly expand its direct economic role, including its role in economic production. Supposedly, this state role would provide a counterweight to the expansion of large-scale private capital (especially transnational capital) and would permit the state apparatus to ally itself with the local bourgeoisie—admittedly weak, but which could, presumably, recover its dynamism under the tutelage of the state apparatus. This approach would involve a nationally oriented pattern of development in which the principal economic actor would be a productive state apparatus serving as a vanguard for the local bourgeoisie. Yet, at least in the initial stage of the BA state, this approach is most unlikely to meet with success. In the period of normalization, economic orthodoxy must be observed carefully, above all when the pre-BA crisis has been particularly acute. One of the practices that is prohibited in this context is the continuation of "state interventionism," especially in productive or commercial activities. One of the tenets of orthodoxy, on the contrary, is to reduce the fiscal deficit drastically, to return potentially profitable activities to the private sector, and to eliminate subsidies to consumers and inefficient producers (including state enterprises). These policies are explicitly referred to in the agreements on the basis of which transnational financing is acquired, involving not only the International Monetary Fund but other lenders as well. Moreover, they are proclaimed as a central article in the professions of orthodox faith on the part of the BA technocrats. Deviating from these and related criteria would undermine the internal and international confidence without which normalization would be impossible. Hence, a shift toward state capitalism is blocked in the initial period of BA.[12]

[12] Nonetheless, the relative importance of the state apparatus continues to be substantially greater than the orthodox technocrats would like, and the state's capacity for control increases greatly. The increasing state role in part involves the hypertrophic growth of the institutions most directly linked to coercion and of the rest of the institutional mechanisms designed to guarantee the exclusion of the popular sector. It also involves a major expansion of the state institutions responsible for the normalization policies. These expanded institutions are gen-

The fact that this alternative is precluded is a source of acute concern within the core of the armed forces, many of whose members express their dislike of the emphasis on transnationalizing the economy that the alliance with the upper bourgeoisie entails. To other members of the armed forces—above all those who hold high positions within the government—it is clear that, "for the moment," the viability of BA and the hopes for restoring national cohesion depend on economic orthodoxy and a close alliance with the upper bourgeoisie. Yet the ambivalence that underlies the acceptance of this formula is a sword of Damocles which hangs over the consolidation of bourgeois domination.

The period from 1967 to 1970 in Argentina is an instance of normalization policy under BA in which these tensions manifested themselves most strongly, introducing a major element of uncertainty in a context in which these policies had, in fact, met with an important degree of success. Already by the end of 1967, as an alternative to the policies then being pursued, other proposals were being considered in which the state would take a more active role, encourage the development of certain fractions of the local bourgeoisie, impose significant restrictions on transnational capital, and reincorporate previously domesticated and "de-Peronized" labor unions into the political arena. This alternative had important support in the armed forces, and this support generated within the upper bourgeoisie a grave concern that the armed forces might adopt this path. The bourgeoisie saw in this alternative precisely the consequences which later ensued: the end of all attempts to normalize the economy, a

---

erally superimposed on the more traditional state agencies. At the same time, the attempts to make the enterprises which remain in the state's control more efficient have an interesting medium-run consequence: the "administrative rationalization" which is carried out in these enterprises, the elimination of subsidies from the central treasury, and the major increase in their relative prices (which typically had been held down as a means of appealing to the popular sector during the period which precedes BA) help these enterprises to become important centers of capital accumulation. This tendency converts them into a seed of state capitalism (which did not exist in the previous period and is a paradoxical result of the orthodox approach which sought to reduce their role), and later allows a major "statization" to be sustained. The clearest example of this is Brazil, but the results of the economic policy in Argentina between 1967-1970 were similar. In Chile, in spite of the orgy of "privatizations," this same phenomenon may be occurring in an important sector of state enterprises.

rapid flight of capital, and a renewal of the crisis that the implantation of BA had tried to end. Two factors appear particularly important in determining the speed with which this nationalist and statist path—along with the accompanying reorientation of political alliances, including the search for some support from the popular sector—emerges as an alternative. One of them involves the different levels of threat that precede each BA.[13] The second involves the issue of how quickly and decisively the initial economic policies of the BA state meet with success. The greater the degree to which this occurs, the sooner the nationalist and statist alternative is likely to be posed and the stronger its impact on the armed forces.[14] In Argentina, the level of economic crisis and threat was lower than in other cases of BA, and the stabilization program which began in March 1967 had already achieved some significant success by 1968-1969.[15] It was therefore tempting to discontinue orthodox policies and return to the earlier policies involving state support for weaker, national fractions of the bourgeoisie and a moderate redistribution of income for the benefit of the popular sector. These options only appeared reasonable if one ignored the true parameters of the situation, yet this fact did not prevent a realignment of political forces in a direction that inevitably shook the recently renewed confidence of the upper bourgeoisie. This group, in turn, in addition to warning ominously against this unexpected revival of statist and nationalist tendencies under BA, tried to encourage the replacement of the leaders of the government, including President Onganía, by military groups more attuned to their orientations and interests. Thus, the political concerns of the upper bourgeoisie further eroded the internal cohesion of BA and, along with the great social explosions of 1969-1970, hastened its demise.[16]

[13] I have dealt with this topic in "Reflections," which, in the interest of brevity, I shall again only cite.

[14] For a similar argument from a more general point of view, see Alfred Stepan, *The State and Society: Peru in Comparative Perspective* (Princeton: Princeton University Press, 1978).

[15] In particular, the rate of inflation was low, the fiscal deficit had been reduced substantially, the balance of payments deficit had been alleviated, and the economy had achieved a respectable rate of growth.

[16] A detailed analysis of these processes will be provided in my forthcoming book about the bureaucratic-authoritarian experience of Argentina from 1966 to 1973.

In contrast, post-1973 Chile and post-1976 Argentina show that if the pre-BA crisis is significantly more intense and the level of threat—as well as the corresponding fear of winners and losers—is higher, it makes reducing the rate of inflation to minimally acceptable levels more difficult, permits the speculative activities typical of the previous period to continue, diminishes the capacity of the state to invest, and likewise prolongs and deepens the recession provoked by the normalization policies. As a result, orthodox economic policies must be followed closely, in spite of the fact that in significant measure it is these policies that bring on such consequences. This necessity, in turn, means that in spite of innumerable expressions of disagreement, the nationalist and statist alternative delineated above does not really appear possible. As a result, more time is available for the application of orthodox policies and for continuing, in an overt and almost exclusive form, the alliance with the upper bourgeoisie.

Stated briefly, the lower the level of prior crisis and threat, the greater the probability of rapidly achieving normalization and restoring economic growth. But, on the other hand, success in restoring growth will increase the temptation, even within the armed forces, to abandon orthodox economic measures at a point which is "premature" from the perspective of the upper bourgeoisie and of the technocrats who control the economic apparatus of BA. Thus, with a lower level of prior crisis and threat, the confidence of the bourgeoisie is more rapidly and easily achieved, but at the same time this confidence remains subject to a greater degree of uncertainty. Inversely, the higher the level of prior crisis and threat, the less the probability of achieving success (even from the point of view of the leaders of BA and their allies) in the normalization of the economy, but, for this very reason, the greater is the certainty on the part of the upper bourgeoisie that orthodox economic policies will be maintained.

The perpetuation (alleviated in some respects but aggravated in others) of the economic crisis that precedes BA is the best guarantee that its ties with the upper bourgeoisie will be maintained in spite of the tensions discussed above. But this ongoing crisis means, among other things, that high rates of inflation will continue and that, owing to the absence of economic growth and to the drastic reduction in popular consumption prescribed by economic orthodoxy, there exists substantial unused installed capacity for production. As a result, the upper bourgeoisie accumulates capital much more through financial speculation, in which it has numerous advantages over other sectors, than through the production and investment which are supposed to provide the basis for renewed economic growth. This speculation in turn serves to further accentuate the economic crisis. In the cases of Chile and Uruguay, this situation has been prolonged in a pathetic fashion for a number of years after BA was implanted, and no serious challenge to the continuation of orthodox economic policies has occurred. This outcome, perverse even for the leaders and supporters of BA, can be understood from the perspective presented in this chapter. The case of contemporary Argentina, after more than two years of a BA implanted in reaction to a crisis and threat much more profound than those of 1966, has so far exhibited these same characteristics.[17]

The case of Brazil is the only one that, after four years of orthodoxy, experienced, starting in 1968, an important resurgence of economic growth that included a vigorous expansion of the state role in economic production and a return to assisting some of the fractions of the local bourgeoisie, yet without undermining the original alliance with the upper bourgeoisie.[18] This shift coincided with the period of greatest repression. It served to demonstrate what the Argentine BA, and particularly

[17] This consideration would have to be incorporated in the concept of "deepening" that I presented in "Reflections," along with the arguments regarding this concept that have been made by other authors in this volume. As long as a situation such as that described above persists, deepening is clearly impossible, primarily because of the continuation of this speculative behavior on the part of the principal economic actors and because of the existence of an important degree of unused installed capacity. But to the extent that these conditions persist, the orientation of economic policies (which principally focus on the primary sector, and to the extent that they deal with industry are opposed to any effort to carry out the type of import substitution implied by deepening) is much more the result of a crisis which leaves little latitude for divergence from economic orthodoxy. But this pattern will not necessarily be followed in the long run, at least in the cases where economic growth is not excessively limited by a small internal market.

[18] This last point represents a crucial contrast with the Argentine case, where a more state oriented and nationalistic pattern of economic policy was adopted toward the end of 1970, at a point when BA was falling apart and the upper bourgeoisie had lost all confidence in the future prospects for stability.

the "Cordobazo" of 1969, could not: that the state continued to be, despite the tensions internal to the alliance and to the armed forces, a power capable of applying the necessary coercion to crush the reemergence of movements that attempted to invoke the excluded sectors as *pueblo* or as class. This renewal of BA's coercive guarantee confirmed the confidence of the upper bourgeoisie and was accompanied by changes in economic policy and by the great wave of investments of transnational capital that launched the "Brazilian miracle." At this point it became possible to pursue simultaneously two goals in a way that had been impossible at the onset of BA: the combination of rapid advances in the transnationalization of the productive structure through the increasingly important role played by transnational financial and industrial capital, on the one hand, and the expansion of the productive activities of the state, on the other. Yet each of these processes imposes limits on the other. The movement toward transnationalization is limited by an expansion of state activities that in the last few years has generated an outcry against the "statization" of the Brazilian economy. On the other hand, such statization could not go further than partial incursions into the areas of capital accumulation that the upper bourgeoisie—transnational and domestic—claims as its own, without undermining the hard-earned climate of "business confidence" and precipitating a crisis whose potential severity frightens all parties involved. Both sides see the precipice that defines the limit of their sometimes noisy debates. As a result, in the midst of such debates, the upper bourgeoisie takes care to reiterate its support of a state whose expansion it wishes to limit, but not to prevent. At the same time, the Brazilian authorities are careful to reiterate that they accept and understand the rules of a game based on maintaining the confidence of the upper bourgeoisie. Meanwhile, the celebration of the Brazilian "miracle," with its evocation of "national grandeur" and of the triumphal fulfillment by the BA state of its goals, has unquestionably facilitated the perpetuation of this system of domination. Yet, as the elections of recent years, among other things, have shown, not even this combination of economic success and political propaganda was sufficient to achieve a more or less solid consensus. Likewise, the evocation of this "miracle" as a legitimation of the state and of the increasingly notorious social costs that it imposes is further undermined because it is impossible to sustain the "miracle" year after year. The risk faced by the allies of the Brazilian BA is not only that of intolerable transgressions of the rules of the game that is the basis for the alliance with the upper bourgeoisie; the risk also involves the very real possibility of an active reemergence of genuine opposition.

Brazilian BA is unique in relation to the others because it has lasted so long and because of the greater degree to which it has been successful in its own terms. Yet, as noted above, it has not been able to escape the dilemmas and fears shared by the other BA's: being a type of political domination which is not veiled by a network of mediations and which is, therefore, permanently haunted by the specter of an explosive negation. Taking this dilemma as a starting point, we may now draw together what has been said in this and previous sections and discuss of some fundamental and crucial issues involved in the underlying political *problématique* of BA.

The Nostalgia for Mediations or the Question of Democracy[19]

The observations of the preceding section suggest that BA is a suboptimal form of bourgeois domination. BA is comprehensible as an alternative only in the face of the abyss of the threat—both in the past and potentially in the future—of the elimination of the capitalist parameters of society. I have presented the reasons for this conclusion, but it is appropriate to summarize here the principal ones: (1) BA reduces or suppresses mediations on the basis of which consensus is normally established; (2) it reveals starkly what is the underlying, but not normally the exclusive, reality of the state—i.e., coercion; (3) it likewise reveals the fact that the upper bourgeoisie is the principal—and, in the initial period of economic normalization, virtually the only—social base of this state; (4) as a result of the historical context in which these societies have evolved, this portion of the bourgeoisie is likewise conspicuously the least national element within these societies; and (5) organizations specialized in coercion acquire enormous importance within the institutional system of the state, while the values and behavior of these organizations are

[19] No discussion of this theme is complete that does not mention the fundamental contributions of Fernando Henrique Cardoso. See especially his *Autoritarismo e Democratização* (Rio de Janeiro: Paz e Terra, 1975).

not consonant with those of the principal social base of that state—i.e., the upper bourgeoisie.

The suboptimal character of this type of political domination manifests itself in the fragilities that derive from the shrinking of the legitimating referent of the nation, the suppression of the mediations of citizenship and *lo popular*, the political and economic exclusion of the popular sector, and the fear of the reactions that may be growing beneath the silent surface of society as a result of the heavy costs that derive from the imposition of order and normalization. On the other hand, these fragilities are also reflected in the departure of an important portion of the middle sectors and of the weakest and most clearly national fractions of the bourgeoisie from the supporting alliance of BA, with its twofold consequence: first, their departure makes it impossible to achieve the support which the state seeks; and, second, it encourages the efforts of those actors, who are divided into a myriad of different groups, to make discrete demands on the state institutions in an effort to minimize the costs that economic normalization imposes on them. Another factor that contributes to the fragility of BA and further increases the problems of legitimation is the notorious support for this state by the upper bourgeoisie and its conspicuous presence in the economic apparatus of BA. Still another element in this fragility results from the interaction between the large role of the upper bourgeoisie in the state apparatus and the defensive movements of the weaker fractions of the bourgeoisie. These fractions find that the principal economic policy makers are deaf to their demands, but that other institutions of the state are attentive to their complaints—above all, the armed forces, precisely because of the dissonances noted above with the prevailing social basis and economic orientations of BA.

Though the BA state is thus characterized by numerous fragilities, it presents itself, in its majestic and martial discourse, as a monolithic power guided by a superior rationality that is constructing its own greatness, which will in turn make possible the future epiphany of a cohesive nation. But what has been said up to this point allows us to understand why, at the same time, the institutions of BA are so vulnerable to the internal erosion that results from the efforts of the dominant classes (involving offensive tactics in the case of the upper bourgeoisie and defensive tactics in the case of other bourgeois factions and middle sectors) to satisfy their demands upon the state. The suppression of institutionalized public demand-making through which interests can be aired and whose presentation must be justified with plausible references to a general, national interest, converts these efforts into an extremely fragmented and narrowly based assault on the state. This assault leads to a continuous effort by some technocrats and members of the armed forces to coordinate the institutional system of the state and to create new entities empowered with decision-making capacity which is removed from the agencies that have become too colonized to perform these tasks. It is also the reason for the failure of this task of Sisyphus—which involves climbing the mountain of the social basis of a state without mediations. As a result, the very same state that appears before the excluded sectors as a monolithic wall is, for its allies, highly porous. But, on the other hand, to complete this sketch of the complexity of the situation, the apex of the BA hierarchy continues to be occupied by the armed forces which, in manifold ways, express their dissonances with the alliance which sustains that very same state.

The silence of those who are excluded, the covert defensive efforts on the part of the sectors that have ceased to be supporters of BA, and the fractionalization of the upper bourgeoisie as it seeks to optimize discrete gains, generate a very special situation: that of a state that, from the apex of its institutions, loudly proclaims the importance of the tasks it is performing and announces a future of greatness, and yet does not receive in return even the echo of its voice. This discourse is lost in the silence of the excluded and coerced sectors, and in the surreptitious tactics employed to penetrate the institutions of BA by those who originally supported its implantation. That such discourse is merely a monologue suggests to the rulers the depth of the mystery regarding what is in fact occurring behind the silence of civil society. This mystery adds to the difficulty of imposing limits on the bourgeoisie's access to the state apparatus and of allowing latitude for decision making and implementation through which the state apparatus may increase its autonomy in dealing with its own allies. The opaque assaults of these allies, which are not mediated through formal channels that would oblige them to present their demands in terms of broader, general interests, corrode the continually proclaimed unity, efficiency, and technical rationality of the state, as well as the vigilant attention to the supreme national interests, with reference to which the apex of the state's apparatus continues to celebrate its own performance.

But the principal mystery is the silence of those who have been excluded. The implantation of BA is a terrible defeat for the popular sector. If any doubt remains about this, it is quickly dispelled by the policies designed to establish order and achieve economic normalization. In addition, the suppression of mediations adds to the silence and opacity of civil society, leaving the state without the legitimating referents of nation, *pueblo* and citizenship. Nevertheless, this domination, like all others, seeks to legitimate itself through means other than the weak—and inevitably short-term—support provided by fear and by the prospect of eventual economic "miracles."

Yet how can the mediations be created that would resolve "the difficulties that derive from the solitude of power"?[20] One solution would be, of course, to re-invent the Mexican political system with its dominant party, the PRI, which provides these mediations and at the same time efficiently helps to prevent popular challenges. However, the PRI can be only a nostalgic aspiration because its origin is precisely the opposite from what occurred in cases with which we are concerned here: a popular revolution, rather than the reaction of the terrified bourgeoisie which implanted the BA states. Another possibility would be that of a corporative structuring of society. But for corporatism to truly take the place of the missing mediations, it would have to incorporate in a subordinate fashion the entire society rather than simply restricting itself to being a form of state control of workers. Yet this outcome is precisely what the upper bourgeoisie cannot accept. With good reason, they have no objection to the re-imposition of harsh controls over the popular sector, but why should the upper bourgeoisie, an indispensable supporter of BA, have to be incorporated into a state that subordinates it? For this reason corporatist ideology, in spite of its important influence on many of the actors in BA, represents a Utopia that is as archaic as it is unachievable. Corporatism can serve—in the form of tight control over unions—to consolidate a class victory,

[20] Phrase used by the President of Argentina, Lt. General Videla, as quoted in *Cronista Comercial* April 27, 1977, p. 1.

but not as a means of replacing the mediations between state and society that BA has suppressed.[21]

If some version of the PRI is not possible, if corporatism cannot replace the mediations which are lacking, and if the state's resonant exhortations for "participation" bounce off of the silence of society, then the only thing that remains is the aspiration for the very thing that BA has radically denied: democracy. The use of this term on the part of those at the apex of state institutions and on the part of the upper bourgeoisie would be inexplicable if we did not recognize that such use reflects the fundamental problem of a state without mediations and, hence, of a system of naked domination. If political democracy were to be restored, at the very least the mediation of citizenship would reappear. As a result, there would once again be a possibility that many members of the society could be treated as, and would also see themselves as, participants in a form of abstract, but not insignificant equality—in addition to the implication of the restoration of some basic legal guarantees to the individual. In this way, the basis of state power could be attributed to this source exterior to the state—a condition which is not sufficient, but yet is necessary, for its legitimation. The restoration of political democracy would also permit the resolution of another problem that arises from the lack of mediations and from the militarization of the state: that of presidential succession. From the perspective of the upper bourgeoisie, solving this problem would have the advantage of reducing the institutional weight of the armed forces, of allowing it to cushion its ties with the armed forces through civilian groups which would have policy-making capabilities regarding non-economic issues, of giving greater access to government to civilians whose orientations are more consonant with those of the upper bourgeoisie, and—ultimately—of reducing the visibility of the coercion through which the state supports its economic domination.[22]

[21] I have dealt with this topic in my article "Sobre el 'corporativismo' y la cuestión del Estado" (Documento CEDES/G.E. CLACSO No. 2, Centro de Estudios de Estado y Sociedad, Buenos Aires, 1976). This was also published in English in James M. Malloy, ed., *Authoritarianism and Corporatism in Latin America* (Pittsburgh: University of Pittsburgh Press, 1977).

[22] The concern with these goals is another of the reasons why the Mexican political system and the PRI represent such an attractive (if unattainable)

But what kind of democracy? It would have to be one that achieves the miracle of being all of this and that at the same time maintains the exclusion of the popular sector. In particular, it would have to be one that sustains the suppression of invocations in terms of *pueblo* and class. Such suppression presupposes that strict controls of the organizations and political movements of the popular sector are maintained, as well as controls over the forms of permissible discourse and rhetoric on the part of those who occupy the institutional positions which democracy would reopen. The search for this philosopher's stone is expressed in the various qualifying adjectives that customarily accompany the term "democracy."

Though the alternative of democracy might initially seem implausible, it is useful to consider several questions that may make the absence of democracy seem even more implausible in the medium run. How long can a kind of domination endure which is based in such a thin consensus and which is so overt—and particularly so overtly coercive? How long can a state apparatus sustain itself in the face of the silence and opacity of civil society? How many Franco's Spains and Salazar's Portugals can there possibly be? How can the leaders of this state help but search for solutions that would permit the system of domination that BA represents, and the social domination which it supports and organizes, to believe that it can be extended into the distant future, and to establish hegemony? These questions point to the weaknesses of a state which proclaims itself to be, and in fact is widely perceived as being, an imposing power. The terror of this state in the face of the silence and the void of civil society, its aborted attempts at introducing corporatism, and its nostalgia for democracy are oblique yet crucial expressions of the difficulties faced by a form of power that lacks both mediations and legitimacy.

But, how to democratize? It seems clear to the rulers that any move in this direction can open a Pandora's box of popular political reactivation, along with invocations in terms of *pueblo* and eventually of class, which could lead to a renewal of the crisis that preceded BA. And for the dominant alliance this outcome would be much worse than the continuance of a form

model—since they provide all of these advantages without even raising, in connection with presidential succession, the uncertainties of a genuinely competitive election.

of domination without mediations and legitimacy, in spite of the tensions and frailties discussed above. Moreover, if BA originally emerged in response to threatening political activation, and if the silence that is imposed on society does not hide the heavy costs of the economic normalization and the imposition of order, is it not reasonable to fear that this threat would reappear in an even more severe form as soon as the dike of exclusion that has been constructed is even partially opened? Because of this fear, the aspiration to restore at least some of the mediations of citizenship and democracy is simultaneously the hope and the dread of this system of domination.

The philosopher's stone would be a form of democracy which is carefully limited, in the sense that invocations in terms of *pueblo* or class are prohibited, but which at the same time is not such a farce that it cannot provide the mediations and, ultimately, a legitimacy that could transform itself into hegemony. The question of how this form of democracy will be achieved poses an enigma that severely tests the ingenuity of the "social engineers" who offer their expertise to accomplish a task which amounts to squaring the circle. Yet the goal which the most enlightened actors in this system of domination seek to achieve is clearly this type of democracy. In cases of a high level of prior threat and crisis, as in Chile, a democratic alternative was not proposed from within the state apparatus and was introduced instead by members of the initial BA alliance who subsequently withdrew their support: the church and the Christian Democrats. In the case of a low degree of prior threat, as in Argentina in 1966, the issue of democracy was posed almost at the beginning as a goal toward which BA should progress as an alternative to the corporatist leanings of the governing military group. In Argentina in 1976, as a result both of the "lesson" derived from this earlier experience and of the underlying tensions that are the concern of this chapter, the goal of restoring democracy has been mentioned from the start, although the obstacles that must be overcome in order to achieve this goal appear today to be far more difficult than they did in 1966. In Uruguay, the topic continues to be raised, accompanied by the curious contortions intended to preserve an image of civilian government in the form of a figurehead president completely subordinated to the armed forces. In Brazil, there was an attempt during the Castelo Branco period to retain some of the institutions of political democracy. The authoritarian dynamic of the situation took things in a different direction than that foreseen in this initial period, but some elements nonetheless remained: the parliament, the two official parties, and periodic elections for non-executive positions. However, the experience with elections has made quite evident the potentially disruptive dynamic that is set into motion when the alternative of democracy is raised, regardless of how surrealistic this alternative may appear to be when it is done by, and during the period of, a BA state.

The nakedness of BA domination and of the alliance that supports it, as well as the highly visible character of its negative social consequences, generate the great issues raised by those who oppose BA: human rights, economic nationalism, and demands for substantive justice. The great dread of a system of domination which is simultaneously so imposing and so insecure is the fear that the opponents—who, despite their silence, quite clearly exist—will galvanize themselves around these issues into one great explosion that will destroy not only BA but also the system of social domination that it has helped to impose. The "Cordobazo" and the events that followed it are the symbol of this possibility, and not just in Argentina. The unsuccessful attempts to reestablish a cohesive and harmoniously integrated nation, the prolongation of the ominous silence of civil society, and the notoriety of the domination which BA supports, are the basis of the insecurity of this system of domination—which tends to make it more dangerous and more coercive. This coercion further biases the institutional system of BA toward a larger role for the armed forces, and further deepens the silence of society, which is exactly the opposite of what should happen if some legitimacy is to be achieved. Nevertheless, democracy continues to be mentioned, at times being eclipsed, but then reemerging in the official rhetoric or as the proposal of one or another of the groups that struggle for power in the BA state.

The issue of democracy is important not only because it contains the Achilles heel of this system of domination, but also because it contains a dynamic that can be the unifying element in the long-term effort to establish a society that is more nearly in accord with certain fundamental values. The issue of democracy is not equivalent to the other—already mentioned—great issues which BA raises as a result of its policies and their impacts. The proposal for a limited form of democracy, without *pueblo* and ultimately without nation, is not the gracious concession of a triumphant power, but the expression of its intrinsic weakness. The ambivalence with which democracy is mentioned both from the institutional apex of the BA state and by its principal allies, and the evident fear of transgressing limits beyond which it would be too risky to go in a process of democratization, does not generate its own contrasting negation as do the other unequivocal policies and impacts of BA. The antithesis of the distorted and limited democracy proposed by the BA's institutions does not have to be the political and social authoritarianism which is, precisely, the true and evident reality of this state. As a result, the issue of democracy, even the mere mention of the term, remains suspended in political discourse, and thus liable to be expropriated by giving the term meanings that supersede the limitations and qualifications with which the only public voices to be heard in the initial period of BA try to control it.

The possibility of democracy may simply represent an invitation to opportunism for those who wish to use it just to enter into a pre-determined game. This possibility may also invite the imbecility of rejecting democracy out of hand because it is initiated from above and because there is such a careful effort to impose limits upon it. But what it can also be, if indeed the powers-that-be are not the only ones who have learned something from the tragedy of the Southern Cone, is the discovery of a purpose and style of politics that would not be limited to a careful calculation of the limits up to which it can be expanded at each point in time. It would be, more fundamentally, a struggle for the appropriation and redefinition of the meaning of democracy, oriented toward impregnating itself with the meanings carried by those who are excluded by the BA state and constituting, together with them, the basis for an alternative system of domination.

There are circumstances in which the discussion of certain topics can seem to be useless nostalgia. But the fact that certain words, such as democracy, are employed at all cannot simply be attributed to idiosyncrasies, to tactics of accommodation with the international situation, or to false consciousness. The evident contradiction between the mere mention of democracy and the reality of daily life is much more than this. This contradiction is a key to understanding the weaknesses and profound tensions of the present system of domination. It is also an indication of the immense importance of what remains implicit behind the superficial appearance of these societies—the importance of those who are excluded and forced into silence, who, on the one hand, are the focus of any hopes for achieving legitimacy and yet, on the other hand, are a Pandora's box that must not be tampered with. This implicit presence of those who are excluded and silent is the source of the dynamic and tensions of BA to no less a degree than that which occurs in the grand scenarios of this type of state.

Later on, after the first period of BA—that of the implantation—on which this chapter has focused, the dikes of exclusion begin to crack, the effects of fear begin to be diluted, and some of the voices which had been silenced are heard once again. More or less obliquely, but with a meaning that no one can fail to understand, they begin to resound, not only throughout the society, but also within the state apparatus itself. These changes do not just involve the end of the silence imposed on those who were defeated, nor the thousand ways of demonstrating that the "tacit consensus" in fact represents a suppressed opposition. Nor is it merely a vain search for mediations on the part of those at the apex of the institutions of BA who know, on the one hand, that without them they cannot continue to be dominant and, on the other, that by attempting to restore the mediations they may also revive the old ghosts which, with the implantation of BA, they attempted at such high risk and such a high cost to destroy. At such a point, the fissures which from the very moment of implantation of BA are opened by the absence of mediations pose a great opportunity. The response to this opportunity—in terms of the scope of the potential democratization that it involves—in large measure will depend on those who in the phase of the implantation of BA were so radically excluded. But for a whole series of reasons, this still unmapped future lies beyond the scope of the present analysis.

CHAPTER 8

INDUSTRIAL CHANGE AND POLITICAL CHANGE:
A EUROPEAN PERSPECTIVE

James R. Kurth

I. INDUSTRIAL EXPLANATIONS OF POLITICAL OUTCOMES:
A EUROPEAN TEST OF LATIN AMERICAN THEORIES

The study of Latin American politics in the last decade has placed great emphasis on the connections between the process of industrialization and the process of political change. Particular attention has been given to two different aspects of the industrialization process and to their consequences for politics. First, attention has focused on the *timing* of industrialization in Latin American countries in relation to the industrialization of other nations. Latin America is an area of delayed development, industrializing after most of Europe and after the United States, and some analysts have seen this economic condition as linked, if indirectly, to certain political phenomena, such as bureaucratic-authoritarianism. Second, attention has also focused on the *phases* of industrialization, i.e., the successive phases of production of non-durable consumer goods, intermediate and capital goods, and consumer durables. Latin America is an area in which several countries have recently made the transition from the consumer-goods phase to that of capital goods or from the capital-goods phase to that of consumer durables, and here too some analysts have identified linkages to important political outcomes, including bureaucratic-authoritarianism.

The other essays in this book have examined critically models and hypotheses relating the timing of industrialization and the phases of industrialization to political outcomes in Latin America. But the validity and vitality of these models can also be tested by applying them to other regions of the world. And in many ways the region which can provide the most interesting and useful test and comparison is Europe. It was in regard to Europe, and to differences between the countries within it, that one of the first theories of the timing of industrialization was developed by Alexander Gerschenkron. This theory was later amended and extended into Latin America by Albert Hirschman and Philippe Schmitter.[1] As we shall see, the delayed development of parts of Europe, especially Southern or Latin Europe, has much in common with the delayed development of Latin America. In addition, most of the countries of Europe have already passed through each of the phases of industrialization that Latin Americanists have analyzed. Europe thus provides a rich array of historical experience with which to test and perhaps refine hypotheses about the connections between industrial change and political change, including Guillermo O'Donnell's model of bureaucratic-authoritarianism.

This chapter is an attempt to apply, to "try out," these hypotheses about industrialization and politics in the European setting. It first considers the question of the political consequences of differences in the timing of industrialization and, in particular, examines the ideas of Gerschenkron. We conclude that, by itself, the variable of industrial timing yields explanations which are rather amorphous and indirect. The discussion then turns to the question of the political consequences of the phases of industrialization and, in particular, extends some of the ideas of O'Donnell into the European arena. It will be argued that the variable of industrial phasing is indeed useful and illuminating in constructing explanations of European political history. And since the consumer-goods phase and the capital-goods phase each had a different political impact in later industrializers than in earlier ones, the combination of the variables of timing and phasing is especially useful. The chapter concludes with a section which draws some explicit comparisons between political developments in Europe and in Latin America.

The focus, then, will be on industrial explanations of political outcomes. The industrial factor, of course, is not the only one which has contributed to the shaping of the outcomes we will

[1] Alexander Gerschenkron, *Economic Backwardness in Historical Perspective* (Cambridge: Harvard University Press, 1962); Albert O. Hirschman, "The Political Economy of Import-Substituting Industrialization in Latin America," *The Quarterly Journal of Economics* 82, No. 1 (February 1968), pp. 2-32, reprinted in his *A Bias for Hope: Essays on Development in Latin America* (New Haven: Yale University Press, 1971); Philippe C. Schmitter, "Paths to Political Development in Latin America," in Douglas A. Chalmers, ed., *Changing Latin America: New Interpretations of its Politics and Sociology* (New York: The Academy of Political Science, Columbia University, 1972), pp. 83-105.

discuss. The rise of the liberal state in the nineteenth century, the establishment of authoritarian regimes in much of Europe in the 1920's and 1930's, and the stability of democratic systems for thirty years after World War II—these momentous occurrences were the product of many factors, and historians have developed a rich array of complex and competing interpretations of them. We make no claims that the industrial factor alone can provide a full explanation and understanding of these outcomes. In particular, our investigation will at times also emphasize the crucial importance of pre-industrial political institutions and of choices made by political actors, i.e., of political background variables and of political intervening variables. The industrial factor, however, does have a consistency over time and a commonality across many countries that permits it to assume among explanatory variables an especially prominent place.

II. The Timing of Industrialization in Europe and Latin America

Early Industrializers and Late Industrializers

Students of European economic history have long debated about differences between countries that industrialized early (beginning with Britain and then France) and countries that industrialized later (such as Germany and Italy). One of the most important analyses of the timing of industrialization is that of Alexander Gerschenkron. Gerschenkron ranked the major countries of Europe along a continuum defined in terms of their economic backwardness as of the mid-nineteenth century. The most advanced country was England, followed by France, Germany, Austria, Italy, and Russia, in that order. Gerschenkron then argued:

"The main proposition we can then make with regard to countries so ranked is that, the more delayed the industrial development of a country, the more explosive was the great spurt of its industrialization, if and when it came. Moreover, the higher degree of backwardness was associated with a stronger tendency toward larger scale of plant and enterprise and greater readiness to enter into monopolistic compacts of various degrees of intensity. Finally, the more backward a country, the more likely its industrialization was to proceed under some organized direction; depending on the degree of backwardness, the seat of such direction could be found in investment banks, in investment banks acting under the aegis of the state, or in bureaucratic controls. So viewed, the industrial history of Europe appears not as a series of mere repetitions of the 'first' industrialization but as an orderly system of graduated deviations from that industrialization."

At a later point, he added some other propositions, among them: "The more backward a country's economy, the greater was the stress upon producers' goods as against consumers' goods. . . . [and] the heavier was the pressure upon the levels of consumption of the population."[2]

For analysts of Latin American development, Gerschenkron's analysis of Italy is especially interesting. He argued that in general Italy fitted his pattern of delayed development, including monopolistic compacts among industrial producers, organized direction by investment banks, and substantial government assistance with subsidies and tariffs. But Gerschenkron also found that Italy departed from the pattern in that "the great spurt" was less vigorous, the role of consumer goods (especially textiles) was more pronounced, and the tariff protection was more retarding in its effects, than in the other late industrializers.

Late Industrializers and Late-Late Industrializers

These Italian variations on the late industrializer theme suggested that there has been another pattern of delayed development. And in fact, in his well-known article on import-substitution industrialization, Albert Hirschman considered another group of countries, which he designated the "late-late industrializers," in particular the countries of Latin America. Hirschman argued that few of Gerschenkron's propositions about the late industrializers actually fit the late-late industrializers:

". . . almost the opposite can be said to hold for our late late comers. Their industrialization started with relatively small plants administering 'last touches' to a host of imported products, concentrated on consumer rather than producer goods, and often was specifically designed to improve the levels of con-

---

[2] Gerschenkron, *op. cit.*, pp. 44, 354.

sumption of populations who were suddenly cut off, as a result of war or balance of payments crises, from imported consumer goods to which they have become accustomed. . . . As a result, late late industrialization shows little of the inspiring, if convulsive elan that was characteristic of the late industrializers such as Germany, Russia, and Japan."[3]

In brief, Hirschman's late-late industrializers seem to be distinguished from Gerschenkron's late industrializers in much the same way as Gerschenkron's Italy was distinguished from his other late industrializers. Italy and a fortiori the other countries of Latin Europe, Spain and Portugal, seem to fit the late-late pattern characteristic of Latin America. We should not forget, however, that in both the late and the late-late industrializers, there have been monopolistic compacts among industrial producers, organized direction by investment banks, and substantial government assistance with subsidies and tariffs.

Can we explain different patterns of political change in terms of these three patterns of early, late, and late-late industrialization? Gerschenkron himself argued that the various economic features which he identified in the late industrializers led them to establish or to reinforce authoritarian governments, in order to mobilize capital and to repress wages and consumption, although he was somewhat vague about the process by which this political change came about. It is true that in both the late industrializers (Germany and Austria) and the late-late industrializers (Italy, Spain, Portugal, and much of Latin America), as compared to the early ones (Britain and France), the industrial cartels and investment banks formed centers of economic power which were few in number, large in size, and coordinated in their operations. It could be argued that this concentration of economic interests and coordination of economic operations enabled industrial and financial elites to establish authoritarian governments against the opposition of liberals and labor, once they developed a strong incentive to do so. But the explanatory connections are rather imprecise, and in any event authoritarian governments already existed in Germany and Austria and had for many years when these two countries undertook industrialization.

A political difference can also be drawn between the early and

---

[3] Hirschman, *A Bias for Hope*, p. 95.

the late industrializers, on the one hand, and the late-late industrializers, on the other. As Hirschman observes, in contrast with the industrial elites in the early and the late industrializers, those in the late-late industrializers lacked prestige and elan; they were not so much a "conquering bourgeoisie" as a collaborating one.[4] The British and French industrialists first produced consumer goods for foreign markets (textiles), then capital goods for foreign markets (rails, locomotives, merchant vessels, and machinery), and finally capital goods for national defense (naval vessels). The German industrialists did the same, with much more emphasis on the second and the third categories. In these three countries, the vital role of the industrialists in foreign exchange and national defense gave them high prestige. And the pioneer achievement of the British and "the great spurt" of the French and Germans gave them great elan. But for many years the industrialists of Latin Europe and Latin America mainly produced consumer goods in a protected market. And they were not so much involved in "a great spurt" as in the adding of "last touches." Lacking a distinctive industrial vocation, identity, and ideology, the industrial elites of the Latin world were more willing than their British, French, and German counterparts to follow the political lead of the agricultural elites and to merge the economic interests and political parties of the two. The result in Latin Europe in the late nineteenth century was a withering away of political parties and party competition which had been based upon conflicts between the urban and the agrarian sectors. Instead, there emerged a system of patron-client politics, based on factions orchestrated by a strong leader through the use of patronage and benefits, a phenomenon known as *trasformismo* in Italy and *el turno* in Spain.[5] And when radical movements or economic turmoil threatened the industrial and agricultural elites of Europe in the 1920's, those in Latin Europe

---

[4] The concept of the conquering bourgeoisie was developed in Charles Morazé, *The Triumph of the Middle Classes* (Garden City, N.Y.: Anchor Books, 1968) (first published in France under the title of *Les Bourgeois Conquerants*).

[5] On Italian politics during this period, see Arthur James Whyte, *The Evolution of Modern Italy* (New York: W. W. Norton, 1965); and Dennis Mack Smith, *Italy: A Modern History*, revised edition (Ann Arbor: University of Michigan Press, 1969). On Spanish politics, see Gerald Brenan, *The Spanish Labyrinth: An Account of the Social and Political Background of the Civil War* (Cambridge: Cambridge University Press, 1950); and Joan Connelly Ullman, *The Tragic Week: A Study of Anticlericalism in Spain, 1875-1912* (Cambridge: Harvard University Press, 1968).

could more easily and readily come to agreement upon the establishment of a "corporatist" or authoritarian regime, as with Mussolini in Italy in 1922, Primo de Rivera in Spain in 1923, and Salazar in Portugal in 1928.[6] In contrast, some important industrial elites in Germany and Austria (in particular those in the chemical, electrical, and textile industries) during the 1920's opposed the establishment of an authoritarian government and were driven to support this only by the impact of the Great Depression in the early 1930's.[7]

As the era of a country's industrialization—its "great spurt" if it had one—receded into the past, the political differences between early, late, and late-late industrializers began to diminish. It would be difficult to trace the differences in the politics of Britain, France, and West Germany after World War II to the differences between early and late industrialization. However, some features of the still later industrializers continued to have a political impact in the thirty years after World War II. As Gerschenkron observed, the later industrializers have been especially reliant upon state participation in their industrialization process. And, as others have observed, the still later industrializers have been especially reliant upon multinational manufacturing corporations in theirs. It happened that the era of late-late industrialization largely corresponded with the era of massive foreign investment—what Raymond Vernon has analyzed as the foreign investment phase of the product cycle—[8] for large American corporations, especially automobile corporations. Of the three sources of entrepreneurs and capital—private domestic corporations, state corporations, and multinational corporations—the late-late industrializers have depended heavily upon the second and third. Thus Italy's figure for the proportion of state industrial enterprise to total industrial enterprise has been among the highest in non-Communist Europe. Still later industrializers, such as Spain, Portugal, Brazil, and

[6] Corporatism in Latin Europe is discussed by Philippe C. Schmitter, "Still the Century of Corporatism?" *The Review of Politics* 36, No. 1 (January 1974), pp. 85-121.

[7] The shift of these industrial elites in Weimar Germany is extensively discussed by David Abraham, *Inter-Class Conflict and the Formation of Ruling Class Consensus in Late Weimar Germany* (doctoral dissertation submitted to the Department of History, University of Chicago, December 1977).

[8] Raymond Vernon, *Sovereignty at Bay: The Multinational Spread of U.S. Enterprises* (New York: Basic Book, 1971).

Argentina, have had comparable high proportions for state industry and higher ones than Italy for multinational industry.

The combination of a large state industrial sector and a long patrimonial political practice, both characteristic of Latin Europe,[9] delivered enormous resources for patronage into the hands of a dominant party (the Christian Democrats in Italy) or an authoritarian government (that of Franco in Spain or Salazar in Portugal). This made it easier for the government to perpetuate itself (and to deny resources to an opposition). Thus, the rule of the Italian Christian Democrats and the Spanish and Portuguese corporatist-authoritarians was more enduring than it otherwise would have been. Conversely, the presence of a large multinational industrial sector puts some limit upon patrimonial practices (since the multinational enterprise has the ultimate recourse of going elsewhere). The arrival of multinational corporations on a large scale in Spain and Portugal in the late 1960's and early 1970's may have helped to bring about at last the end of their particular authoritarian regimes.

The timing of industrialization, then, can yield some propositions about political outcomes in Europe. In general, however, the connections are rather vague and indirect. More substantial connections between industrialization and politics can be discerned if, while keeping timing in mind as a background variable, we shift our focus to the phases of industrialization.

III. PHASES OF INDUSTRIALIZATION IN EUROPE AND LATIN AMERICA

Analysts of Latin American economies have frequently focused on different phases of industrialization. A common formulation has been to distinguish three phases, involving the

[9] On patrimonialism in Latin Europe and in Latin America, see Richard M. Morse, "The Heritage of Latin America," in Louis Hartz, ed., *The Founding of New Societies* (New York: Harcourt, Brace and World, 1964), p. 157; and Howard J. Wiarda, "Toward a Framework for the Study of Political Change in the Iberic-Latin Tradition: The Corporative Model," *World Politics* 25, No. 2 (January 1973), pp. 206-35. On patrimonialism in general, see Max Weber, *The Theory of Social and Economic Organization*, edited by Talcott Parsons (New York: The Free Press, 1964), especially pp. 341-58; Reinhard Bendix, *Max Weber: An Intellectual Portrait* (Garden City, N.Y.: Anchor Books, 1962), especially pp. 329-84; and Guenther Roth, "Personal Rulership, Patrimonialism, and Empire-Building in the New States," *World Politics* 20, No. 2 (January 1968), pp. 194-206.

production of non-durable consumer goods, intermediate and capital goods, and consumer durables. Similarly, analysts of Latin American politics have frequently identified different periods in a country's political development. Here, it has been common to distinguish between periods of traditional authoritarian or oligarchic rule, populism or national populism, and bureaucratic-authoritarian regimes. It was natural, therefore, that some Latin Americanists might seek to find connections between industrial phases and political regimes. In particular, as other essays in this book attest, it has been argued that there are important interconnections between the consumer-goods phase of industrialization and the shift from traditional authoritarian or oligarchic rule to populist politics, and between the capital-goods phase (or the combination of the capital-goods phase and the consumer-durables phase) and the collapse of populist politics and the establishment of a bureaucratic-authoritarian regime.

As we shall see, European industrial development has been characterized by phases similar to those of consumer goods, capital goods, and consumer durables. And European political development over the last one hundred fifty years can also be divided into a number of periods, which are, however, somewhat different from those in Latin America. In particular, there have been three great political transitions in a number of European countries: the shift from absolutist monarchies (traditional authoritarianism) to the liberal state and parliamentary systems in the nineteenth century; the breakdown of parliamentary systems and the establishment of new authoritarian regimes in much of Europe in the 1920's and 1930's; and the establishment of stable democracies after World War II. Although the causes of these three great political transitions have obviously been many and complex, it might be useful to examine the possible role among them of successive phases of industrialization. As we shall see, the strength of the connection between political change and industrial phases has varied considerably over time and between countries.

The Establishment of the Liberal State

In 1815, on the morrow of the Napoleonic Wars and under the aegis of the Restoration, the political system of most countries in Europe was absolutist monarchy. The major exceptions were Britain and the Netherlands (then including Belgium); these maritime nations on the opposite sides of the North Sea had long been the leading commercial powers of Europe and, relatedly, had long been political systems in which the dominant power rested with a parliament composed of landed aristocrats and urban patricians and in which there was substantial freedom of the press and freedom of religion: what would come to be called constitutional monarchy and civil liberties.[10]

In 1875, three generations later, and a few years after the Franco-Prussian War, the picture was rather different. The political system of constitutional monarchy, including a strong parliament and substantial civil liberties, had spread outward from its North Sea redoubt, north to Denmark (then including Iceland) and Sweden (then including Norway), south to Portugal, Spain, Italy, and even Greece, and east (although here the parliament was clearly subordinated to the monarch and his ministers) to Germany and Austria-Hungary. France had become a parliamentary republic, as had Switzerland. And this particular distribution of political systems, with the addition of expansions in the suffrage, was to continue in its essentials down until World War I.

What accounts for this spread of the system of constitutional monarchy, strong parliaments, and civil liberties, i.e., "the liberal state," from 1815 to 1875 and for the variations from one country to another in the strength of liberal institutions and in the timing of their establishment?

Part of the answer is provided by looking at the *pre-industrial* economic and political structure. Some analysts have focused on the power of the landed aristocracy and the continuity of the traditional monarchy as the major explanatory variables. Liberal institutions were strongest in those countries where, at one time or another before the beginning of the nineteenth century, the old landed aristocracy had been defeated in civil war and diminished in political power and, relatedly, where the old absolutist dynasty had been displaced (as in Britain in the Civil War

[10] In 1815 the restored Bourbon monarchy in France was also supposed to govern by a charter. But the actual results fell short of a constitutional monarchy with substantial civil liberties. For an overview of Europe during the French Revolution and the Restoration, see E. J. Hobsbawm, *The Age of Revolution: Europe 1789-1848* (London: Weidenfeld and Nicolson, 1962).

of the 1640's and in the Glorious Revolution of 1689, in France in the Revolution of 1789, and in Belgium—then the Austrian Netherlands—in the associated Revolution of 1789).[11] Liberal institutions were less strong in those countries where only half of this process had occurred, where the Napoleonic Wars had displaced, if only temporarily, the old absolutist dynasty but had not significantly diminished the old landed aristocracy (as in Italy, Spain, and Portugal and as in the new states of Latin America). (The significant exception in Latin America was Brazil, where the Portuguese monarchy exiled itself during the Napoleonic Wars and where the dynasty continued to rule even after Brazil became independent of Portugal.) In these countries, the displacement of the old legitimate monarchy made for an absence of "institutionalized" political authority and led to a long period of military coups, popular insurrections, and civil wars. In Latin Europe, this era of "praetorianism" lasted a half-century, from the 1820's to the 1870's.[12] And even after the 1870's, the continuing power of the old landed aristocracy inhibited the fullest development of liberal institutions. Finally, liberal institutions were weakest in those countries which happened to be both the great powers of the East and the lands of "the second serfdom," where the Napoleonic Wars had neither diminished the old landed aristocracy nor displaced the old legitimate monarchy (Prussia, Austria, and Russia). In these countries, the alliance between throne and manor had not only been unbroken but indeed was strengthened after 1815 by the mutual interest of aristocracy and monarchy in preventing anything like a new French Revolution. Agrarian class power joined with dynastic political institutionalization prevented both liberalism and praetorianism.

However, this explanation based upon pre-industrial factors does not tell us much about differences in timing in the establishment of liberal institutions. To explain these variations over time, it is useful to look at another factor, the process of industrialization in its first phase, that of production of non-durable consumer goods.

[11] This is one aspect of the comprehensive analysis by Barrington Moore, Jr., in his *Social Origins of Dictatorship and Democracy: Lord and Peasant in the Making of the Modern World* (Boston: Beacon Press, 1966).

[12] The concept of "praetorianism" is from Samuel P. Huntington, *Political Order in Changing Societies* (New Haven: Yale University Press, 1968).

The Consumer-Goods Phase and Liberal Politics

The process of industrialization in almost all countries has begun with the creation of industries producing simple consumer goods, in particular textiles, shoes, and household utensils. Of these, the textile industry has been by far the largest and most important, so much so that it normally has assumed something of a hegemonic role among industries in this phase.

The creation of the industries producing consumer goods has required the mobilization of relatively modest amounts of capital, modest, that is, in relation to the amount of capital already available in the country as a result of pre-industrial enterprises and also modest in relation to the amount of capital that has been needed for the creation of later industries, such as steel, railroads, chemicals, and automobiles. Consequently, the consumer-goods industries of Europe (and also of the United States and the most advanced countries of Latin America) were created for the most part by family firms, and the industries grew through the reinvestment of their earnings. In contrast with later industries, the capital accumulation for consumer-goods industrialization could be accomplished largely without dependence upon financing from banks, the state, or foreign investors.[13]

The lack of dependence upon the state is probably most important. The capital accumulation for consumer-goods industrialization could be accomplished largely without state intervention, except for the elimination of barriers to a free market within the national boundaries (e.g., internal tariffs) and for the erection of external tariffs on occasion for the protection of the "infant industry." Indeed, the consumer-goods manufacturers

---

[13] Hobsbawm, *op. cit.*, Chapter 2; also the country studies in Carlo M. Cipolla, ed., *The Emergence of Industrial Societies* (London: Collins, Fortana Books, 1973). Statistics on the growth of the textile industry in European countries can be found in B. R. Mitchell, *European Historical Statistics, 1750-1970* (New York: Columbia University Press, 1976), pp. 427-36; and in Cipolla, *op. cit.*, pp. 780-88. Less detailed statistics, but for both Europe and Latin America, are given in W. S. Woytinsky and E. S. Woytinsky, *World Population and Production: Trends and Outlook* (New York: The Twentieth Century Fund, 1953). Two useful overall accounts of European industrialization, from contrasting perspectives, are David S. Landes, *The Unbound Prometheus: Technological Change and Industrial Development in Western Europe from 1750 to the Present* (Cambridge: Cambridge University Press, 1969); and Tom Kemp, *Industrialization in Nineteenth Century Europe* (London: Longman, 1969).

in Europe in the first half of the nineteenth century were opposed to many of the traditional activities of the state. These manufacturers did not want the dynastic-authoritarian state of the past, and they did not need the technocratic-authoritarian state of the future. They did not want the internal tariffs, the consumer taxes, and the tedious regulations of the absolutist monarchies, which prevented the manufacturers from selling their goods in a nationwide market. And they did not want the local guild monopolies and local welfare systems, which also prevented them from drawing their labor from a nationwide market.[14] To systematically eliminate these impediments, however, they needed institutionalized representation at the national center of power; to achieve this institutionalized representation, they needed "the supremacy of parliament," ideally within "the liberal state." But the consumer-goods manufacturers also did not need the assistance of the state to mobilize large amounts of investment capital; nor did they yet need its assistance to demobilize large numbers of socialist workers, services that would later be performed by such diverse authoritarian governments as those of Napoleon III in France, Bismarck in Germany, Mussolini in Italy, Primo de Rivera and Franco in Spain, and Salazar in Portugal.

The liberal state, with parliamentary supremacy and with property suffrage, appeared to solve the problems of the consumer-goods industries. The liberal state abolished traditional barriers to trade, parliamentary supremacy meant that they would be represented at the center of national power, and property suffrage meant that only they and the traditional elites would be so represented.[15] As such, there appears to have been, in the familiar phrase of Max Weber (and of Goethe before him), an "elective affinity" between the consumer-goods industries and such a regime. The political theory of the manufacturers was summed up by Thomas Macaulay in 1830:

"Our rulers will best promote the improvement of the nation by confining themselves strictly to their legitimate duties, by

[14] Frederick B. Artz, *Reaction and Revolution, 1814-1832* (New York: Harper and Row, 1963), Chapter IV; William L. Langer, *Political and Social Upheaval, 1832-1852* (New York: Harper and Row, 1969), Chapters I-III; Karl Polanyi, *The Great Transformation: The Political and Economic Origins of Our Time* (Boston: Beacon Press, 1957), Part II; Hobsbawm, *op. cit.*, Chapter 2.

[15] Langer, *op. cit.*, Chapters III-IV, VI; Hobsbawm, *op. cit.*, Chapter 6.

leaving capital to find its most lucrative course, commodities
their fair price, industry and intelligence their natural reward,
idleness and folly their natural punishment, by maintaining
peace, by defending property, by diminishing the price of law,
and by observing strict economy in every department of the
state. Let the government do this, the people will do the rest."[16]

This liberal tendency of the consumer-goods industries did
not result in a liberal state in all parts of Europe, however. Other
factors were also at work, making for considerable variations
from one country to another. We can distinguish three broad
patterns of liberal politics in Europe. We shall call them the
Western, the Eastern, and the Southern (or Latin).

The Western Pattern. The connection between consumer-goods
industrialization and liberal institutions seems most obvious in
the first industrializer, Britain, which in the early nineteenth
century was simultaneously "the workshop of the world," "the
mother of parliaments," and the center of "Manchester Liberalism."[17] Of course, as we have noted, Britain even before industrialization was well known as one of the freest of political
societies. Other social groups, such as an independent rural gen-
try, dissenting Protestants, and substantial merchants and
bankers had their own reasons for supporting limits on the
power of the state. But it was the manufacturers who had the
most consistent and comprehensive liberal vision and program.[18]

The consumer-goods industries also had a major political impact in the second wave of industrializers, that is, France, Belgium, and Switzerland, each of which experienced rapid growth
in these industries in the 1820's. These countries lacked one or
more of the pre-industrial social groups which supported various aspects of liberal politics in Britain, and in them the liberal
movement was even more dependent upon the new manufacturers than in the British case. The manufacturers were a major

---

[16] Quoted in Artz, *op. cit.*, pp. 85-86.

[17] E. J. Hobsbawm, *Industry and Empire: The Making of Modern Society, Vol. II,
1759 to the Present Day* (New York: Pantheon, 1968), Chapters 3-4; Langer, *op.
cit.*, Chapters II-III.

[18] On the dynamism of "the Liberal Creed" in Britain, see Polanyi, *op. cit.*,
Chapter 12. Also Charles P. Kindleberger, "The Rise of Free Trade in Western
Europe, 1820-1875," in his *Economic Response: Comparative Studies in Trade, Fi-
nance, and Growth* (Cambridge: Harvard University Press, 1978), pp. 39-65.

force in the Revolutions of 1830 in each of the three countries (as they were in the related conflict over the Great Reform Bill in Britain in 1830-1832), and they were a major force in the establishment and support of the succeeding liberal regimes: the Orleanist Monarchy in France (the "Bourgeois Monarchy" or *monarchie censitaire*), the new and similar monarchy in now independent Belgium, and the new regimes in the most industrialized cantons of Switzerland. In itself, the displacement of the Bourbon monarchy in France and the Dutch monarchy in Belgium might well have led to mere political praetorianism. One of the factors that appears to have contributed to a degree of political stability in France and Belgium after the genteel revolutions of 1830 was the emergence of a new coherent and confident social class, composed of manufacturers and financiers.[19]

We have already noted that in Britain, France, and Belgium prior to industrialization the old absolutist monarchy had been displaced and the landed aristocracy had been diminished in power. This meant that the consumer-goods industries could grow up in a relatively open political space, at least compared to the countries to the East and to the South, and that it was easier for the industries to achieve their political aims.

In addition, these industries and especially the textile industries in the early industrializers were relatively competitive in the international market. This was most obviously true of Britain, but even France, Belgium, and Switzerland were successful in selected international textile markets. This meant that, for textile manufacturers in these countries, there was no conflict between the economic and the political parts of liberalism, between free trade and civil liberties. Again, this made it easier for the textile industry to develop a coherent vision and then to develop, in Gramsci's sense, an ideological hegemony.

The Eastern Pattern. The political impact of the consumer-goods industries was very different in the next or third wave of industrializers, Prussia and Austria, which experienced rapid growth in these industries only in the 1840's-1850's. Here, as we have noted, the Napoleonic Wars had displaced neither the old

[19] Industrialization in France, Belgium, and Switzerland is discussed by Alan S. Milward and S. B. Saul, *The Economic Development of Continental Europe, 1780-1870* (Totowa, New Jersey: Rowman and Littlefield, 1973), Chapters 4-5, 7. Politics in these countries is discussed by Langer, *op. cit.*, Chapters III-IV, and Artz, *op. cit.*, Chapters VIII, IX.

landed aristocracy nor its ally, the absolutist monarchy. Accordingly, the consumer-goods industries grew up in a relatively
closed political space, cramped and contained by a well-
entrenched agrarian upper class and the political institutions left
by the reactionary "Metternich System."[20]

One consequence was that consumer-goods industrialization
in the East (1840's-1850's) was somewhat delayed in relation to
when it might otherwise have occurred and to when it occurred
in the West (1820's-1830's, even earlier in Britain). Yet certain
social groups in the East, in particular students, professors, and
lawyers, imported liberal ideas from the West during the
Napoleonic Wars and the Restoration. The result was that a gap
opened up between liberalism and industrialization. In the East
in the 1810's-1830's, liberalism was a movement without much
of a social base, what William Langer has called "the liberalism
of the intellectuals" rather than the liberalism of the manufacturers.[21] At this point liberalism outpaced industrialization.

A second, later consequence was that when consumer-goods
industrialization did occur, the manufacturers were not strong
enough relative to the agrarian upper classes to impose their
political vision on the rest of society. The 1840's to the 1860's
were the high point of liberal movements in the history of the
Hohenzollern and Habsburg monarchies, yet these movements
never achieved the power they had in the West. At this point the
gap between liberalism and industrialization continued but was
reversed: industrialization outpaced liberalization.

Indeed, from the 1820's to the 1860's, the political economies
of Britain and Prussia were almost mirror-images of each other.
British textiles were competitive in the international market,
while British grain was not. Conversely, Prussian grain was
competitive in the international market, while Prussian textiles
were not. Thus British textile manufacturers favored both free
trade and liberal institutions, British grain producers favored
neither, Prussian textile manufacturers favored liberal institutions but not free trade, and Prussian grain producers favored
free trade but not liberal institutions. The fact that British textile

---

[20] Industrialization in Prussia and Austria is discussed by Knut Borchandt,
"The Industrial Revolution in Germany 1700-1914" and N. T. Gross, "The Industrial Revolution in the Habsburg Monarchy, 1750-1914," both in Cipolla, *op.
cit.*, pp. 76-156, 228-76; and Milward and Saul, *op. cit.*, Chapter 6.

[21] Langer, *op. cit.*, Chapter IV.

manufacturers could impose free trade upon British grain producers (the abolition of the Corn Laws in 1846) reinforced the
social power of political liberals. Conversely, the fact that Junker
grain exporters could impose free trade upon Prussian textile
manufacturers (the low-tariff policy of the Zollverein) reinforced the social power of political conservatives. In Britain,
economic liberalism worked to reinforce political liberalism; in
Prussia, economic liberalism worked to undermine political
liberalism.

The Southern Pattern. From the perspective of the analyst of
Latin American politics, the most interesting pattern is the
Southern. The political impact of the consumer-goods industries was very different again in the next or fourth wave of industrializers, in Italy, Spain, and Portugal. Here, consumer-
goods industrialization was delayed for a generation after that of
Germany and Austria, two generations after that of France, Belgium, and Switzerland, and more than three generations after
that of Britain. The countries of Latin Europe are thus the first
severe case of delayed or dependent industrialization.[22]

But like the East, the South also imported liberal ideas from
the West during the Napoleonic Wars and the Restoration. Indeed, the first use of the term "Liberal" for a political group was
in Spain in 1810, in the Constituent *Cortes* at Cadiz. Unlike the
East, however, the social base of liberalism in the South also included military officers and bureaucratic officials, primarily because the old legitimate monarchies at the apex of the military
and bureaucratic organizations had been displaced. With such a
social base, Southern liberalism was stronger than Eastern
liberalism, whose social base was confined to intellectuals, but
weaker than Western liberalism, whose social base included
manufacturers. Southern liberalism, as we have described it,
thus seems to have been common not only to Latin Europe but
to Latin America at the time. And in both Latin Europe and
Latin America, liberalization outpaced industrialization for half
a century after the end of the Napoleonic Wars. However, the
absence of a new cohesive industrial class, of the old cohesive agrarian class, and of the old legitimate monarchy combined in

---

[22] Industrialization in Italy and Spain is discussed by Luciano Catagna, "The
Industrial Revolution in Italy 1830-1914" and Jordi Nadal, "The Failure of the
Industrial Revolution in Spain 1830-1914," both in Cipolla, *op. cit.*, pp. 279-325,
532-620.

such a way that for Latin Europe and much of Latin America this half-century was a period in which no social group could exercise political authority, a period of praetorianism.

When consumer-goods industrialization did occur, the manufacturers could grow up to a rough coequality with the agrarian upper classes. And this eventually issued in political stability and a special kind of liberal state. By the mid-1870's, each of the three countries of Latin Europe had entered into an era of relative political calm that was to last in its essentials almost until the eve of World War I. The military coups, popular revolutions, and civil wars of the earlier phase were left behind, and political change took place within a political system whose formal features were constitutional monarchy, parliamentary majorities, frequent elections, and civil liberties. In actual practice, however, these systems were rather more complex.

Italian politics from 1876 to 1914 has been called the era of *trasformismo*, a period in which strong and supple prime ministers, and on occasion the king himself, "transformed" opposition deputies into government supporters, with the ample but subtle use of political patronage, government contracts, and personal rewards. The result was the obliteration of differences between the Right and the Left, the two parties which were the heir to the liberals of the *Risorgimento*, and the institutionalization of a political process devoid of political issues, an early case of "the end of ideology."[23] A similar process characterized the politics of Spain and Portugal. In Spain, under the Restoration Settlement of 1875, the leaders of the Conservative and Liberal parties reached an agreement on *el turno*, "whereby two political parties automatically rotated in power through the mechanism of contrived elections."[24] This agreement was coupled with the practice of making offers to flexible deputies from smaller, more radical, parties, which was known as "the policy of attraction." In Portugal, by the late 1870's, a similar arrangement between the Regenerator and Progressive parties was fairly well institutionalized and became known as "rotativism." In both Spain and Portugal, as in Italy, the king on occasion played a central and sometimes authoritarian role in the game. The results were similar to those of *trasformismo* in Italy.

What were the conditions that brought about the *trasformismo*

---

[23] Whyte, *op. cit.*; Smith, *op. cit.*   [24] Ullman, *op. cit.*, p. 10.

systems of Latin Europe and their rough stability in the last quarter of the nineteenth century? First, the old liberal program had been largely fulfilled, and the political class had become largely homogeneous. With the confiscation and redistribution of church and communal lands, there was a merging of the interests of the old landlords and the military officers and bureaucratic officials, now new landlords. Further, the new manufacturers who were growing up in these countries had a positive interest in more political stability, so they could better carry out their business. They were also brought into the emerging *trasformismo* systems by tariffs on *both* industrial products and agricultural ones, a marriage of cloth and wheat comparable to the "marriage of iron and rye" of this same period in Bismarck's Germany. Finally, the radical (socialist, anarchist, syndicalist) challengers to the existing systems were largely excluded by suffrage restrictions on industrial workers.

In certain other countries, political systems similar to the *trasformismo* one seem to have issued from similar economic conditions. Some descriptions of the Orleanist Monarchy in France sound rather like our description of the *trasformismo* systems in Latin Europe.[25] And in regard to its level of economic development, in particular its degree of industrialization, France in the 1830's-1840's was similar to Italy and Spain in the 1870's-1890's. In Brazil, a similar political system was the Old Republic from 1894 to 1930; the similar industrial period was the 1890's-1910's.

The Establishment of New Authoritarian Regimes

In 1914, on the eve of World War I, most of the countries of Europe were governed through liberal institutions, including strong parliaments, contested elections, and substantial civil liberties. The exceptions were Germany and Austria-Hungary, where the parliaments remained unable to control the monarch and his ministers but where contested elections and civil liberties nevertheless were present, and of course Russia, where there were virtually no liberal institutions at all. And in 1919, after the defeat of the Central Powers, the fall of their dynasties, and the creation in Eastern Europe of what might be called the second wave of new states (the first had been those in Latin America a

[25] For example, Langer, *op. cit.*, Chapter III.

hundred years before), the triumph of liberal institutions in Europe proper (i.e., without Russia) appeared virtually complete. Yet by 1939, the eve of World War II, almost all of the countries of Central, Eastern, and Southern Europe were ruled by authoritarian regimes. The realm of the liberal state had shrunk to roughly what it had been a century before (i.e., Britain, France, the Low Countries, and Switzerland—the area of our Western pattern of consumer-goods industrialization), plus the Northern or Scandinavian countries. How and why did this massive political change to authoritarianism come about?

The great recessional of the liberal state began in Italy with the coming to power of Mussolini and the Fascists in 1922. Authoritarian regimes were established soon thereafter in the other countries of Latin Europe, in Spain in 1923, and in Portugal in 1926. It appeared that the distinctiveness of the Southern pattern was continuing but in a new form.

At roughly the same time, however, authoritarian regimes were established in several states on the Eastern frontiers of Europe, and the advent of the Great Depression produced new pressures toward authoritarianism. In 1930 the Brüning government in Germany began to rule by decree, because it could not construct a majority in the Reichstag. The resulting system was curiously like the old German Second Empire, that is, an ineffective parliament but contested elections and civil liberties. But in 1933 Hitler and the Nazis came to power and imposed a totalitarian state. Similarly, in 1933 the Dollfuss government in Austria dismissed parliament, suspended elections, and prohibited assemblies, in part to contain the Austrian Nazis. The Nazis assassinated Dollfuss in 1934, but the Schuschnigg government established a "corporative" state, whose actual practices were rather like those of the Habsburg monarchy twenty years before. This corporative experiment was brought to an end when Nazi Germany annexed Austria in 1938. With the Nazis, German and Austrian, the distinctiveness of the Eastern pattern also was continued, and in a particularly perverse form.

What accounts for this spread of authoritarian regimes after 1922? Why did some countries succumb to authoritarian rule early, others later, and others not at all?

At first glance, the impact of three great international events, World War I, the Russian Revolution and "the great fear" it produced in Europe, and finally the Great Depression, might seem to be a sufficient explanation. Yet there are problems with such an interpretation. The first or 1920's wave of authoritarian regimes came only a number of years after the threat from radical forces had peaked and receded. In addition, the War and the Revolution do not explain why Germany and Austria did not turn to authoritarian regimes in the 1920's, even though both were defeated in the War and though Bavaria (and Hungary) had been ruled briefly by Communist regimes in 1919. The Great Depression can explain why Germany and Austria *did* turn to authoritarianism in the 1930's. But it cannot explain why the countries of Western and Northern Europe never succumbed to authoritarian regimes at all (unless and until they were imposed by the Nazi occupations of 1940).

Earlier, in analyzing the shift from the absolutist monarchy to the liberal state, we focused on the political role of the consumer-goods industries, especially the textile industry. In analyzing the shift from the liberal state to the authoritarian regime, there may be some value in focusing on the political role of the capital-goods industries, especially the steel industry. As the other essays in this book demonstrate, the role of capital-goods industries in the turn toward authoritarian regimes is a central concern in the study of Latin American politics. Accordingly, we will examine the role of these industries in European political development.

Several European countries undertook their capital-goods phase of industrialization during the nineteenth century. But in nineteenth-century Europe, unlike in twentieth-century Latin America, capital-goods industrialization was overwhelmingly dominated by steel industrialization and the building of railroads.[26] Accordingly, we will discuss the steel industry at some length and will consider both its creation phase and its saturation phase. It will be argued that, in Europe, the greatest consequences of the steel industry for authoritarianism came, not in the creation phase of the industry, as might be expected from the Latin American case, but in the saturation phase.

The Capital-Goods Phase and Authoritarian Politics

The Creation Phase of the Steel Industry. The creation of a country's iron and steel industry and its crucial consumer in the nineteenth century, the railroads, required the mobilization of

[26] A useful overall account of the growth and impact of the European iron and steel industries and railroads is Hobsbawm's *The Age of Capital, 1848-1875* (New York: Charles Scribner's Sons, 1975).

far larger amounts of capital than that required in the creation of the consumer-goods industries. One is reminded of O'Donnell's argument that in Latin America the end of the consumer-goods phase of industrialization and the transition to the capital-goods phase are associated with severe balance-of-payments problems and the need to mobilize large amounts of capital, which may encourage economic and technocratic elites to adopt the solution of the bureaucratic-authoritarian regime, as in Brazil in 1964 and in Argentina in 1966.[27] But, as we shall see below, in Europe the actual evidence for the causal connection between the creation phase of the steel industry and authoritarian politics is rather mixed.

How were the large amounts of capital for steel and railroads mobilized in Europe? The ways varied from one country to another, but several European nations were able to draw on means and sources which would be unavailable to Latin American countries when they began to mobilize capital for their own capital-goods industries.

In Britain, the first industrializer, the capital mobilization for this phase occurred without any dramatic change in financial institutions or in state intervention. Indeed, the capital mobilization for the British iron and steel industry and for the British railroads was achieved about as easily and as incrementally as was that for the British consumer-goods industries. But in Britain the ease of capital mobilization for this new phase was itself partly a consequence of the prior overwhelming success of British textiles in foreign markets, which generated large profits and large amounts of capital for new enterprises. At the time of the rapid growth in iron, steel, and railroads in Britain in the 1840's-1860's, 50-70 percent of British textile production each year was exported, and 40-50 percent of British export earnings came from these textile exports.[28]

In France, the pattern of capital mobilization for the iron and steel industry and for the railroads was somewhat different. After a slow growth of the iron industry and of railroads before 1848, France experienced rapid growth in these sectors in the 1850's and 1860's. It is an oft-told tale that this rapid growth required new financial institutions, such as investment banks (e.g.,

---

[27] Guillermo A. O'Donnell, *Modernization and Bureaucratic-Authoritarianism: Studies in South American Politics* (Berkeley: Institute of International Studies, University of California, Berkeley, Politics of Modernization Series No. 9, 1973).

[28] Hobsbawm, *Industry and Empire*, Chapters 6-7.

the Crédit Mobilier of the Periere brothers); in turn, these new investment banks, it is said, needed the support of a strong state (e.g., the Second Empire of Napoleon III, 1852-1870) to break the power of the traditional banks.[29] Indeed, it can be argued that the French Second Empire was the first case of a tech-nocratic-authoritarian regime engaged in an industrial *projet*. It did assist in the "deepening" of French industrialization, and it did so under an ideology of "developmentalism," i.e., Saint-Simonism or positivism (whose motto, "Order and Progress," took on a special meaning for Brazilians, then and now).

By the end of the 1860's, however, many French iron and steel industrialists believed that the government of Napoleon III had ceased to support industrial growth but rather now suppressed it. Like Louis Philippe before him, Louis Napoleon first achieved power through an alliance with industrialists against bankers and then maintained power by an alliance with bankers against industrialists. Accordingly, many industrialists were looking about for some alternative political formula on the eve of the Franco-Prussian War.[30]

The Third Republic, which replaced the Second Empire after its defeat in that war in 1870, was not an authoritarian regime. Yet in the 1880's it organized and supported, through the Freycinet Plan, another major expansion of the French steel industry and the French railroads.[31] This casts doubts on the argument that steel and railroad industrialization in France was associated with the establishment of an authoritarian regime. On the other hand, just as in Britain in the first half of the nineteenth century, so too in France in the 1880's, the export of textiles in part provided the capital to finance the expansion in steel and railroads. At the time, 30-40 percent of French export earnings came from textile exports.[32] In Britain, the financing of the expansion had been eased by British domination of the

[29] See, for example, Gerschenkron, *op. cit.*; Rondo E. Cameron, *France and the Economic Development of Europe, 1800-1914, Conquests of Peace and Seeds of War* (Princeton: Princeton University Press, 1961), Chapter IV; Guy P. Palmade, *French Capitalism in the Nineteenth Century*, translated by Graeme M. Holmes (Newton Abbot, Devon: David and Charles, 1972).

[30] Sanford Elwitt, *The Making of the Third Republic: Class and Politics in France, 1868-1884* (Baton Rouge: Louisiana State University Press, 1975), Introduction and Chapter I.

[31] *Ibid.*, Chapters III-IV.

[32] William Woodruff, "The Emergence of an International Economy, 1700-1914," in Cipolla, *op. cit.*, pp. 673-74.

international markets for low-price cotton goods; in France, the financing of the expansion was eased by French domination of the international market for high quality, especially woolen and silk, goods. It was France's special vocation in the quality products of the last stage of the pre-industrial era which eased its transition through the *second* stage of the industrial revolution—and made it easier to do without the supposed capital-mobilization capabilities of an authoritarian regime.

The issues raised by the cases of Germany and Austria are somewhat different, since these countries were governed by largely authoritarian regimes from their origins until 1918. Hence, the primary question concerns the form and the degree of authoritarianism. The rapid growth of the German steel industry and railroads occurred in the 1860's-1880's. Like the French Second Empire (1852-1870), the German Second Empire (1871-1918) with its Anti-Socialist Law (1879-1890) seems to have been somewhat similar to more recent technocratic-authoritarian regimes. The authoritarianism increased after what has been called the Second Founding of the Second Empire in 1879, when steel industrialists and Junker agrarians agreed upon a mutually beneficial high-tariff policy, the famous "marriage of iron and rye." But there does not seem to be a neat relationship between the authoritarianism in Prussia in the 1860's (and in united Germany later) and the capital-mobilization needs of the German steel industry and railroads during their creation phase. Nor does the rapid growth of the new chemical and electrical industries at the end of the century seem to have resulted by itself in more authoritarianism.[33]

In Britain, France, and Germany, the iron and steel industry and the railroads developed together, as a sort of "steel-rail complex." In Italy, Spain, and Portugal, however, this nexus was severed, much as it was in Latin America. The major railroads of Latin Europe were built with rails and rolling stock imported from Britain and France and were financed with capital loaned

[33] A useful and detailed discussion of the relationships between economics and politics in Germany under Bismarck is presented by Fritz Stern, *Gold and Iron: Bismarck, Bleichröder, and the Building of the German Empire* (New York: Alfred A. Knopf, 1977); German industrialization during the late nineteenth century is also discussed by Gustav Stolper, Karl Häuser, and Knut Borchardt, *The German Economy, 1870 to the Present*, translated by Toni Stolper (New York: Harcourt, Brace, and World, 1967).

by British and French investment banks.[34] The result was rail-road expansion without steel industrialization. Since the capital mobilization for the railroads of Latin Europe came from foreign investors rather than from the national government, i.e., from abroad rather than from above, no dramatic reorganization of the state was necessary. It is not surprising, therefore, that the construction of the railroads of Italy, Spain, and Portugal in the mid- and late-nineteenth century could coexist with the conservation of their liberal institutions and *trasformismo* systems.

Italy did construct a substantial steel industry between 1900 and 1910, however. (Spain would not do so until after World War II.) But, as in Britain and in France in earlier times, the capital mobilization in Italy was in part derived from the export of textiles. In Italy's case, it was a relatively temporary domination of the international market for high-quality silk products. It was also another case where the transition through the *second* stage of the industrial revolution was made easier by the achievements of the last stage of the pre-industrial era. Another substantial source of foreign exchange earnings was the remittances from the large numbers of Italian emigrants in these years.[35]

Later steel industrializers such as Spain, Brazil, and Argentina lacked the capability to dominate the international market for a particular industrial product. This led them into severe balance-of-payments difficulties (even though they were exporters of agricultural products), once they tried to move from the phase of consumer-goods industrialization to the phase of capital-goods industrialization. A second reason why these later developers had unusual difficulties was that now capital-goods industrialization meant "tightly-staged" or multi-sector industrialization, including not only steel and railroads but chemicals, electricity, and shipbuilding. The conjunction of (1) the need to mobilize large amounts of capital and (2) severe balance-of-payments deficits leading to erratic devaluations and severe inflation created an influential constituency among economic, bureaucratic, and technocratic elites in support of an authoritarian regime. In contrast with a democratic system, an authoritarian re-

[34] Cameron, *op. cit.*; W. O. Henderson, *Britain and Industrial Europe: 1750-1870: Studies in British Influence on the Industrial Revolution in Western Europe*, third edition (London: Leicester University Press, 1972).

[35] Cafagna, *op. cit.*, pp. 289-90, 302-25.

gime was better able to destroy labor unions, repress wages and consumer demand, and thus squeeze capital out of the working class in order to finance the new capital-goods sectors. In Spain, however, the phase of capital-goods industrialization did not really occur until the 1950's, long after the authoritarian regime of Primo de Rivera (1923-1930) and twenty years after the military revolt of 1936 that began the Spanish Civil War and led to the installation of the Franco regime. And in Brazil and Argentina, as Albert Hirschman and Robert Kaufman argue in their chapters in this book, this connection between the formation of an austerity coalition and the advent of an authoritarian regime is in fact complex and indirect.

The Saturation Phase of the Steel Industry. The most pronounced impact of the steel industry upon political change came, not in the creation phase of the industry but in its stagnation phase, that is, after steel production reached saturation in its home market. This first occurred when the building of the home country's railroads was essentially completed, as in Britain in the 1870's and in France and Germany in the 1880's. In Britain, the railroads normally had absorbed 50-60 percent of steel production in the early 1870's.[36] The first response of the British steel industries and of the banks associated with them was simply to continue their old activity in a new place; i.e., they shifted the building and financing of railroads from Europe to the "regions of recent settlement" (e.g., the United States, Canada, Australia, and Argentina) and to the regions on the borders of Europe (e.g., Turkey and Egypt). In some of the latter regions, however, the inability of weak and corrupt governments to meet their bond payments led Britain in the 1870's and 1880's to interventions and even annexations. Thus began the first steps toward "the new imperialism." France and Germany also initiated new colonial policies in the 1880's and more active ones in the 1890's. Of course, the factors making for "the new imperialism" were many, and historians have developed a variety of explanations, such as strategic calculation, bureaucratic activities, and popular moods. The industrial and financial factor, however, seems to have been an especially consistent and common one.[37]

[36] Duncan Burn, *The Economic History of Steelmaking, 1867-1939: A Study in Competition* (Cambridge: Cambridge University Press, 1961), Chapter 11.

[37] Various aspects of imperialism are analyzed in Roger Owen and Bob Sutcliffe, eds., *Studies in the Theory of Imperialism* (London: Longman, 1972). A

Later, as railroad-building in these new regions also approached saturation, Britain and Germany turned to the building of commercial steamships and finally to the building of warships. The needs of the British and German steel industries were one factor propelling the Anglo-German naval race from 1894 to 1914, which soon took on a reciprocal dynamic of its own.[38]

The Italian steel industry was largely constructed in the decade 1900-1910. Even more than the preceding steel industries, it was dependent upon state contracts and guarantees. Almost immediately, it became a major force for a vigorous foreign policy to achieve railroad concessions in the Balkans (especially in Montenegro and Albania) and in the Ottoman Empire and a force for a major buildup of the Italian navy.[39] Indeed, in the last years before World War I, there was something of a railroad war between Italy and Austria-Hungary in the Balkans. It was this rivalry which gradually separated Italy from its cooperation with Germany and Austria-Hungary in the Triple Alliance, and

---

critique of analyses which stress the economic factors is given by D. K. Fieldhouse, *Economics and Empire* (Ithaca, New York: Cornell University Press, 1971). This period after the completion of railroad building in Western Europe has often been referred to as the Great Depression of 1873-1896. The connections between the end of railroad building and the beginning of the Great Depression are discussed in Hobsbawm, *Industry and Empire*, and W. W. Rostow, *British Economy in the 19th Century* (Cambridge: Cambridge University Press, 1948). An excellent comparative analysis of the politics of the Great Depression is Peter Alexis Gourevitch, "International Trade, Domestic Coalitions, and Liberty: Comparative Responses to the Crisis of 1873-1896," *The Journal of Inter-Disciplinary History* 8 (Autumn 1977), pp. 281-313. An earlier, classic account is Hans Rosenberg, "Political and Social Consequences of the Great Depression of 1873-1896 in Central Europe," *Economic History Review* 13 (1943), pp. 58-73.

[38] I have discussed the connection between the British and German steel industries and the Anglo-German naval race in more detail in my "The Political Consequences of the Product Cycle: Industrial History and Political Outcomes," *International Organization* 33, No. 1 (Winter 1979), pp. 1-34. The topic is also discussed in Arthur J. Marder, *The Anatomy of British Sea Power: A History of British Naval Policy in the Pre-Dreadnought Era, 1880-1905* (New York: Alfred A. Knopf, 1940), Chapter 2; V. R. Berghahn, *Germany and the Approach of War in 1914* (New York: St. Martin's Press, 1973); and, the classic analysis of German naval procurement, Eckart Kehr, *Battleship Building and Party Politics* (Chicago: University of Chicago Press, 1975). (Kehr's book was originally published in Germany in 1930.)

[39] R. A. Webster, *Industrial Imperialism in Italy, 1908-1915* (Berkeley: University of California Press, 1975).

it was this search for new colonial territories to the East which drove Italy into the war on the side of the Triple Entente of Britain, France, and Russia in 1915.

On the morrow of World War I, the steel industries of Europe were again faced with their old problem: how could they keep themselves in business, after the period of postwar reconstruction came to its inevitable end?

The British for the most part chose simply to do more of the same. They retained their overseas empire after the war, and thus they could continue to build railroads to span their colonies, steamships to service them, and warships to defend them. They thus continued their three responses to the earlier era of saturation. In addition, however, they began the transition to a new leading industrial sector. Having based much of their earlier industrialization on textiles and having had high earnings from foreign trade and investment, the British had, more than other European countries, a consumer-oriented economy and high per-capita income. Accordingly, they possessed in 1920 the second largest (after the Americans) automobile industry in the world, and this experienced a slow but steady growth during the 1920's.

The French followed the British pattern, but on a smaller scale. Before the war, their empire, their earnings from textile exports, and their earnings from foreign investment had each been second only to Britain's. After the war, they too poured the output of their steel industry into more colonial railroads, steamships, and warships and also into a small automobile industry, which nevertheless was the third largest automobile industry in the world.

The Germans, having lost the war and having remained a country without a strong consumer-goods sector, had in 1920 neither an overseas empire nor an automobile industry. For the German steel industry, consequently, there seemed to be only two feasible paths, and these were mutually reinforcing. One was renewed armaments production. The other was exports of steel products to markets in Eastern Europe and, relatedly, gaining control over the growing and competing steel industries of Austria, Czechoslovakia, and Poland. Throughout the 1920's, the steel industry supported those political parties which in turn supported rearmament, revision of the Treaty of Versailles, tariff barriers against Western Europe, German domination of

Eastern Europe, and authoritarian measures and wage repression at home. Its favorite political vehicle was the National People's Party, led by Alfred Hugenberg, which advocated the abolition of the Weimar Republic.[40] The steel industry was joined in its support by the Junker agrarians, making the National People's Party a renewal of the old marriage of iron and rye. The Junkers, imbued with military traditions and threatened by cheap grain imports from Poland, had their own reasons for rearmament, revision of Versailles, domination of Eastern Europe, authoritarianism, and wage repression.

By the 1920's, however, the German economic scene included two other large industries in the intermediate and capital-goods sector, the chemical industry and the electrical industry, and these had a very different political tendency. The German chemical industry was the most advanced chemical industry in the world and the largest one in Europe. (Its leading enterprise, I. G. Farben, was the world's largest chemical corporation and the largest corporation of any kind in Europe.)[41] This meant that the chemical industry had a strong interest in free trade or at least in conditions which encouraged exports. The same was true of the German electrical industry, which was the largest and the most advanced electrical industry in Europe. And since the largest and best markets for chemical and electrical products were other advanced industrial economies, these two industries were vitally interested in good relations with Western Europe. This led them to support those political parties which in turn supported "fulfillment" of the Versailles Treaty and concluding of the Locarno Treaty of 1925 between Germany and its Western neighbors. Conversely, they were basically indifferent about Eastern Europe in the 1920's (and there was never an "Eastern

[40] The politics of the German steel industry during the 1920's are discussed in Gerald D. Feldman, *Iron and Steel in the German Inflation, 1916-1923* (Princeton: Princeton University Press, 1977); Charles S. Maier, *Recasting Bourgeois Europe: Stabilization in France, Germany, and Italy in the Decade After World War I* (Princeton: Princeton University Press, 1975); and David Abraham, *Inter-Class Conflict and the Formation of Ruling Class Consensus in Late Weimar Germany* (doctoral dissertation submitted to the Department of History, University of Chicago, December 1977).

[41] On I. G. Farben, see Frank A. Howard, *Buna Rubber: The Birth of an Industry* (New York: D. Van Nostrand, 1947); and Joseph Borkin, *The Crime and Punishment of I. G. Farben* (New York: The Free Press, 1978), an informative and perceptive industrial history, which goes beyond the connotations of its title.

Locarno"). The favorite political vehicle of the chemical and electrical industries was the German People's Party, led by Gustav Stresemann.[42]

In addition to their interest in free trade, the chemical and electrical industries also had an interest in promoting mass consumption and therefore in supporting social welfare and democratic politics. I. G. Farben, encouraged by the widespread consensus among experts in the 1920's that world petroleum supplies would soon be exhausted, diverted most of its new capital investments into building enormous plants to produce gasoline from coal by a process known as hydrogenation.[43] It thus acquired a strong interest in the development of a large German automobile industry. Similarly, the German electrical industry, a producer of consumer durables and municipal electrical equipment, also had a strong interest in social welfare and municipal services. These features led the industries into support of parliamentary coalitions which included the Social Democratic Party. In brief, then, the Weimar Republic, with its foreign policy of "fulfillment" and its domestic policy of social welfare, was in many ways based upon a coalition of chemistry, electricity and labor in opposition to the coalition of iron and rye.[44]

The Weimar system was an unstable equilibrium, however. Its major leader, Stresemann, died in October 1929. At the same time, the New York stock market crash marked the beginning of the Great Depression. The American responses to the economic crisis had momentous consequences for Germany. The Smoot-Hawley Tariff of 1930 led to the raising of tariff barriers in other countries, dealing a serious blow to the free trade policies of the German chemical and electrical industries. In addition, the drying up of American loans to Germany broke a crucial link in the international economic chain which had contributed to German prosperity in the 1920's (American loans to Germany → German reparations to Britain and France → British and French imports from Germany). These two developments meant that the free trade option, the *Westpolitik*, of the chemical and electrical industries suddenly became far less

[42] The politics of the German chemical and electrical industries during the 1920's are discussed by Maier, *op. cit.*, and Abraham, *op. cit.*

[43] Howard, *op. cit.*; Borkin, *op. cit.*, Chapter 2.

[44] Abraham, *op. cit.*, presents a thorough and sophisticated demonstration of this argument.

viable. And they meant in turn that the coercive trade option, the *Ostpolitik*, of the steel industry suddenly became more attractive. Finally, the depression-induced sharp drop in world oil prices in 1930-1931 and the opening up of the vast East Texas oil field in 1931 meant that I. G. Farben, with its enormous investments in hydrogenation plants, was suddenly threatened by massive imports of cheap American oil, much as the Junker agrarians had suddenly been threatened by massive imports of cheap American grain sixty years before. For I. G. Farben, the only solution to the Texan problem was a German government which would be strong enough and willing enough to guarantee a market for its coal-based gasoline, by erecting tariff barriers, by granting subsidies, by buying the gasoline itself, and by legitimating the vast expenditures entailed with an ideology of economic autarky and military preparedness—i.e., the same ideology promoted by the steel industry and the grain producers.[45]

Together, these new developments in the world market propelled the chemical and electrical industries during 1932 from political opposition into political cooperation with the steel industry and the grain producers. And as the National People's Party under Hugenberg proved insufficiently popular to win the several elections of 1932, first the steel industry and then the chemical and electrical industries shifted their financial support to the National Socialist Party under Hitler.[46] This industrial support was one factor in the conjunction of circumstances which brought the Nazis to power in 1933.[47]

[45] Borkin, *op. cit.*, Chapter 3.

[46] Abraham, *op. cit.*; Borkin, *op. cit.*, Chapter 3. On the industrial role in the 1932 elections, also see Alan Bullock, *Hitler: A Study in Tyranny*, revised edition (New York: Harper and Row, 1964), Chapter 4. General accounts of the relations between industry and the Nazis are Arthur Schweitzer, *Big Business in the Third Reich* (Bloomington, Indiana: Indiana University Press, 1964); and Franz Neumann, *Behemoth: The Structure and Process of National Socialism* (New York: Oxford University Press, 1942).

[47] Major interpretations emphasizing factors other than the industrial one include Karl Dietrich Bracher, *The German Dictatorship: the Origins, Structure, and Effects of National Socialism*, translated by Jean Steinberg (New York: Praeger, 1970); Ralf Dahrendorf, *Society and Democracy in Germany* (Garden City, New York: Doubleday Anchor, 1969); and Ernst Nolte, *Three Faces of Fascism: Action Française, Italian Fascism, National Socialism*, translated by Leila Vennewitz (New York: Holt, Rinehart, and Winston, 1966).

The German experience had had an earlier and a simpler trial run in Italy. Of all the European steel industries before World War I, the Italian had been the most recent and the least competitive, the ideal-typical case of delayed and protected industrialization. Relatedly, it had been the steel industry most dependent upon armaments contracts. It was, therefore, unusually vulnerable to a period of peace, especially one in which the peace treaty, like Versailles, gave Italy no substantial territories on which new railroads could be laid. The first postwar economic depression hit Italy in 1921 especially hard. Accordingly, the steel industrialists supported popular movements demanding revision of "the mutilated peace" and the annexation of new territories. The major such movement, the Fascists, achieved power in 1922.[48] But Italy's efforts at territorial expansion would have to wait for more than a decade until the Great Depression produced a diplomatic constellation of the greater powers which was more favorable to Italian aims.

The steel industries of Germany and Italy, thus, were a factor in explaining the strength of the Nazi and Fascist parties and the timing of their coming to power. It would be satisfying, therefore, if we could convict the steel industry, or the capital-goods industries generally, in other countries of similar authoritarian or totalitarian crimes in the interwar era. But in fact there was no substantial steel industry in Spain, Portugal, and the several small countries of Eastern Europe that succumbed to authoritarian rule. (Ironically, among the small countries of Eastern Europe, the only substantial steel industry was in Czechoslovakia, which remained a stable liberal democracy from its origins in 1918 until its occupation by Germany in 1938-1939.) Indeed, most of these small countries of Eastern Europe had only begun their phase of consumer-goods industrialization during these years. The industrialization of Southeastern Europe in the 1920's-1930's in particular was rather like that of Latin Europe in the 1870's. In itself, this might have predicted new cases of *trasformismo* systems. And in fact this was the kind of system in Greece in 1926-1936 and in Romania and Hungary for most of these years. However, these political systems were easily undone by any one of a variety of threats, such as a small Communist

---

[48] Roland Sarti, *Fascism and the Industrial Leadership in Italy, 1919-1940* (Berkeley: University of California Press, 1971).

party in Greece, the Iron Guard in Romania, or German diplomatic pressure in Hungary, and they were replaced by the late 1930's with authoritarian regimes.[49]

The Establishment of Stable Democracies

At the end of World War II, the American army, in the role of a "conquering bourgeoisie," affected a liberal-democratic restoration in virtually every part of Europe that it occupied. At one level, then, there is little to explain about the reestablishment of democratic systems in Europe in 1945. The cause is obvious.

At another level, however, certain questions are raised. The stability of some of these democratic systems for thirty years after World War II contrasts greatly with their instability after World War I. This is especially and obviously the case with Germany, Austria, and Italy, but it is also true even of France.

Can this political contrast be explained in part by industrial factors? By analogy with our earlier practice, one approach would be to examine the political impact of the consumer-durables industries in Europe, especially the automobile industry. Europe did not really move into its "auto-industrial age"[50] until after World War II. In 1935, Britain had only one automobile per 20 persons, France one per 35, Germany one per 100, and Italy one per 200. (In contrast the United States in 1935 already had one automobile for every 5 persons, a figure that the European countries would not reach until the 1960's).[51]

The Consumer-Durables Phase and Democratic Politics

How were the large amounts of capital for consumer-durables industrialization mobilized in Europe after World War II? One

[49] Comparative statistics on industrialization in the countries of Southeastern Europe and Latin Europe can be found in Mitchell, *op. cit.* Eastern European politics in this period are discussed in Hans Rogger and Eugen Weber, eds., *The European Right: A Historical Profile* (Berkeley: University of California Press, 1965); and in Hugh Seton-Watson, *Eastern Europe Between the Wars, 1918-1941*, third edition, revised (New York: Harper and Row, 1967).

[50] The phrase is from Emma Rothschild, *Paradise Lost: The Decline of the Auto-Industrial Age* (New York: Random House, 1973).

[51] W. W. Rostow, *Politics and the Stages of Growth* (Cambridge: Cambridge University Press, 1971), pp. 227-29. A systematic survey of the European automobile industry before World War II, and of other industries also, is Ingvar Svennilson, *Growth and Stagnation in the European Economy* (Geneva: United Nations Economic Commission for Europe, 1954).

method, analogous to the mobilization of capital for steel and railroads in Britain, France, and Italy decades before, was through the export of manufactured products developed in an earlier stage, i.e., "export-led growth." Here, an important factor was not only the high quality of the products, but the low wages of European labor (relative to the United States) in the two decades after the end of the War. No authoritarian regime was required to repress wages in Europe. The low expectations of union membership, deriving from the privation of World War II, and the political divisions in union organization in France and Italy, deriving from the anti-communism of the Cold War, were for many years the functional equivalent of wage repression. The role performed in some Latin American countries by their own armies through authoritarian rule was performed in Europe by the ghost of the German Army and the specter of the Russian Army.

A second method, analogous to the earlier mobilization of capital for railroads in Italy, Spain, and Portugal, was through the import of foreign funds. Until the mid-1950's, this involved U.S. government aid (i.e., the Marshall Plan), and from the mid-1950's until the mid-1970's it involved massive American direct investment in the European automobile industry. Even in the late 1940's, General Motors and Ford owned a large share of the European industry, and in the 1950's the American automobile industry entered on a large scale into the foreign investment phase of its product cycle. The American automobile corporations first undertook large manufacturing investments in Britain, then West Germany, and then (Chrysler) France. Normally, when a country of more than 20 million population or so has reached a certain level of economic development (roughly $1,000 per capita GNP in 1965 dollars), it has developed a market in consumer durables which is large and prosperous enough to attract large-scale direct investment in manufacturing by the American automobile corporations. And since European labor was relatively self-restrained in its wage demands, the continued flow of American direct investment also did not require the labor-repressive policies of an authoritarian regime. Of course, labor-repressive policies and authoritarian regimes did not inhibit the flow of foreign direct investment in Europe either, as was demonstrated by multinational automobile corporations when they undertook large manufacturing investments in Spain as that country rolled over the $1,000 threshold in the late 1960's.

Although the automobile industries of Britain, West Germany, France, and finally Spain were built up in part with American direct investment, the automobile industry in Italy was built up independently of it. The dominant automobile corporation in Italy, Fiat, had long differed from other European automobile corporations in that it was a giant and profitable conglomerate which produced locomotives, aircraft, and other machinery, as well as automobiles. Other Italian automobile producers were owned or financed by the government.

In general, the capital mobilization for building up the consumer-durables industries in Europe could occur without radical intervention by the state.[52] Accordingly, the consumer-durables industrialists desired no major change in the democratic political systems as they existed in the late 1940's on the eve of this phase. However, the massive size of this sector suggests that it might have had some substantial political impact as it moved beyond capital mobilization to full production.

The basic context for European politics after World War II was formed by the widespread revulsion against Fascism, the reduction of the European states to a subordinate role in the international system, the fear of the Soviet Union, and the military dependence upon the United States. These features by themselves might have brought about stable democracies by preventing Fascist or Communist parties from developing enough strength to take power or to throw a country into political turmoil or civil war. As we shall see below, however, the features of the consumer-durables phase also worked in the same direction, supporting and reinforcing tendencies toward stable democracy.

Britain, West Germany, France, and Italy entered the

---

[52] The relationships between different industries and the state in Europe from the 1940's to the 1960's are discussed in Raymond Vernon, ed., *Big Business and the State: Changing Relations in Western Europe* (Cambridge: Harvard University Press, 1974); Andrew Shonfield, *Modern Capitalism: The Changing Balance of Public and Private Power* (New York: Oxford University Press, 1969); Sima Lieberman, *The Growth of European Mixed Economies, 1945-1970* (New York: John Wiley and Sons, 1977); and M. M. Postan, *An Economic History of Western Europe, 1945-1964* (London: Methuen, 1967). The volume edited by Vernon includes a comprehensive analysis of the automobile industry by Louis T. Wells (pp. 229-54).

consumer-durables phase, "the auto-industrial age," in the 1950's. The boom in the production of consumer durables, especially automobiles, in these countries during the 1950's and 1960's was at the core of their more general economic prosperity and growth during that time. As many political analysts have observed, this general economic prosperity and growth contributed to the legitimation of the European liberal-democratic systems, to the deradicalization of the European working class, and to the demarxification in the late 1950's of the programs of the British and West German Socialist parties, which had a large working class constituency.[53] The consumer-durables boom further contributed to the deradicalization of the European working class by inducing something of a shift from group activities in working-class organizations to individual or family activities centered on the automobile, television, etc.

Many factors worked to prevent a Fascist revival in Europe after World War II, and we have already noted the most important, the historical experience with Fascism and the new international setting of Europe. But the consumer-durables phase also contributed to the same result. The decreased radicalism of the European working class removed a major incentive for middle-class persons to join right-wing mass movements and for upper-class persons to fund them; the deradicalization of the working class made unnecessary any counter-radicalization of the middle and upper classes, whereas in the 1920's-1930's the opposite situation had existed and had contributed to the rise of Fascism in Italy and Germany and to a substantial Fascist movement in France.[54] In addition, in the 1950's-1960's the capital-goods industries could pour their products into the new consumer-durables industries, their steel into automobiles, whereas in the 1920's-1930's their options had been restricted to colonial railroads and military weapons, i.e., imperialism and militarism. The consumer-durables boom thus eliminated some of the sources of what had been the mass base and the elite base for Fascist policies at home and abroad.

The growth of the automobile industry was especially rapid and pronounced in the ex-Axis countries of Germany and Italy. Not surprisingly, the liberal policies toward business of these

[53] In Britain and West Germany, the absence of strong Communist parties also contributed to the demarxification of the Socialist parties.

[54] Nolte, *op. cit.*

countries in the 1950's and 1960's, the sort of policies natural to a confident capitalism engaged in a great boom, resembled the liberal policies toward business of the United States in the 1920's, the time of the first great boom in American automobile production.[55] Working-class parties did not participate at all in the German and Italian governments during the 1950's and early 1960's.

By the early 1970's, however, the number of automobiles in Britain, France, West Germany, and Italy had reached the level of about one car per 3 or 4 persons, something like a point of saturation. One result was to contribute to the economic recession and stagnation of 1974-1978. Of course the causes of the economic troubles of the last few years in Europe are many, but the saturation of the automobile market in Britain, France, West Germany, and Italy suggests that there is little basis for a sustained recovery unless governments engage in *strukturpolitik*, that is, the conscious creation of new leading industrial sectors and the consequent recasting of the nation's industrial structure. A holder of Raymond Vernon's product-cycle theory would predict that the Europeans would adopt as their new (or renewed) sectors those same industries which were the American new sectors a decade or a generation ago, i.e., aerospace, computers, telecommunications, and nuclear power. And this would explain the intensity of the French export drive in aerospace and the French and German export drive in nuclear power since 1975.

The relatively new automobile industries of Spain and Brazil (which now rank about eighth and ninth among the world's automobile industries), are probably of special interest to Latin Americanists. These have developed in a rather different way from those in Britain, France, West Germany, and Italy.

First, in Britain, France, and West Germany, the multinational presence in automobile production has largely been an American one (and in Italy there has been no multinational production). In Spain and Brazil, by contrast, one finds multinationals with home offices in various European countries and Japan, as well as in the U.S. For in the 1960's, corporations such as Leyland, Renault, Volkswagen, Fiat, and Toyota entered into

[55] On German and Italian policies toward business during this period, see especially Vernon, *Big Business and the State*, and Shonfield, *op. cit.*

the direct foreign investment phase of their own product cycles.

Second, Spain and Brazil have been the first societies to undertake mass production and consumption of automobiles within an authoritarian political system. But the political consequences of this coexistence of auto-industrial age with authoritarian regime have been different in the two countries.

In Spain, the multinational automobile corporations were one of the forces pushing the governments after Franco's death in 1975 toward the liberalization and even democratization of the political system. The major reason was that automobiles produced in Spain would be very competitive within the European Common Market if Spain were a member. Spain at the present time could be as cost effective in automobiles as Italy was in the early 1960's, because Spain today is roughly at the relative wage position that Italy was at then. But the Common Market would not admit Spain into membership until, in the words of a resolution passed by each of its main institutions in 1975, "freedom and democracy have been established in Spain." (Indeed, given the self-interest of French and Italian farmers, it may not admit Spain even now.) In Brazil, as we shall discuss in the next section, the background conditions have been different, and the impact of the multinational automobile corporations upon politics has been much less benign.

Summary of European Patterns

To summarize the political impact of industrial phases in Europe, it seems clear that the general tendency of the two consumer industries, non-durables and durables, has been toward a more liberal, more democratic politics. But in the consumer-non-durables phase, this tendency was often contained and limited in its political consequences by preexisting social groups and political institutions. And in the consumer-durables phase, something like the opposite obtained: there were so many other factors already working toward the establishment of stable democracies that the consumer-durables industries seem redundant, the automobile industry something like a spare tire.

Conversely, among the capital-goods industries there has sometimes been a tendency toward a more authoritarian politics. But in the creation phase of the industries, this tendency was often limited in its effect by the availability of sources of capital mobilization other than the state. And in the saturation phase, the tendency very often was deflected into colonial or military activities (a sort of exporting of authoritarianism), and these did not immediately or necessarily issue in authoritarianism at home. Or it has been deflected at times into its opposite, more liberal politics, as the capital-goods industries have seen opportunities to produce for the consumer market themselves, as did the chemical and electrical industries in Weimar Germany and as have most industries in Europe more recently.

Together, these observations show that the political impact of industrial phases in Europe, for good or for ill, has been more configurative than determinative. And this suggests that in the future, as in the past, there will be ample space for the play of political actions and political choice.

CONTRASTS BETWEEN EUROPEAN AND LATIN AMERICAN PATTERNS

The political impact of our three phases of industrialization—non-durable consumer goods, capital goods, and consumer durables—has clearly been rather different in Latin America than it was in Europe.

One factor contributing to this difference is again the pre-industrial economic structure. At one time various European countries had been competitive exporters of basic agricultural commodities; a well-known example was Prussia in the first half of the nineteenth century. But after the 1870's, the countries of the New World became the most competitive exporters of these commodities, and the European grain producers were utterly extinguished (as in Britain) or retreated from free trade into tariff protection (as in Germany, Italy, and Spain). In Latin America, this meant that agricultural exporters amassed great wealth, acquired some degree of political hegemony over their countries, and imposed free trade policies.

Deprived of infant-industry protection, the consumer-goods phase of industrialization, including textile industrialization, was delayed even more in Latin America than it had been in Latin Europe. An important exception was Brazil, which underwent textile industrialization (and also established a *trasformismo*-type political system) about the same time as Spain (the 1890's). Elsewhere in Latin America, however, industrialization did not really begin until World War I. This meant that there the growth of an industrial working class took place after Europe had experienced the political consequences of a militant working class organized from below. The political response of some Latin American elites to the conjunction of the growth of a local working class and their interpretation of the European experience was preemptive organization and cooptation of the working class from above, i.e. "populism." Populist politics were probably as well suited to the consumer-goods phase of industrialization in Latin America as liberal politics had been to the similar phase in Europe. Indeed, for a time, populist politics meant higher wages and higher welfare benefits and thus higher domestic consumption of consumer goods than would have been the case in a strictly liberal state. But these same populist measures would also make more difficult the mobilization of capital for investment in the next, or capital-goods, phase of industrialization.

When the capital-goods industries did develop in Latin America after World War II, they grew up in a context also different from that of their earlier European counterparts. For the European steel industries, the most natural market had been the railroads. But for the Latin American steel industries after World War II, this market did not exist. The railroads of Latin America and indeed of the rest of the world had already been built—and for the most part built with European steel. A second market for the European steel industries had been military weapons, especially warships. But this was again irrelevant for the steel industries of Latin America. Given the strategic hegemony of the United States in the Western Hemisphere, it would have been hard enough before World War II for Brazil or Argentina to engage in a military build-up and an aggressive foreign policy in the European style; after World War II, it was impossible.

Given the irrelevance of these two traditional markets for steel, the Latin American steel industries were especially dependent upon the third traditional market—automobiles. An expanding steel industry was facilitated by an expanding automobile industry. Thus in Latin America the steel and the automobile phases of industrialization, and more generally the capital-goods and the consumer-durables phases, have tended to converge and cluster. This has made the leap from consumer-goods industrialization to the next phase(s) a grander enterprise and a more difficult one in Latin America than in Europe. Further, given the structure of the world automobile market after

World War II, the build-up of national automobile industries in Latin America in the 1960's almost inevitably meant dependence upon multinational automobile corporations.

Whereas the steel industries in Europe had been associated at certain times with Fascist mass movements, there have been no Fascist mass movements in Latin America during its steel-industrialization phase. One reason, of course, is that Fascism had already been thoroughly discredited because of its crimes and debacle in the continent where it originated. At the time that Latin America could have "legitimately" imported Fascism from Europe (the 1920's-1930's), it was still in its phase of consumer-goods industrialization. The result was that on occasion there were political leaders and movements with a little Fascist style and content but with much more pro-labor social policies than in Europe, e.g., Vargas and Perón. Conversely, at the time that Latin America had developed to the "appropriate" level of steel industrialization (the 1960's-1970's), it was no longer legitimate to import Fascist symbols from Europe—or to develop them at home. Another reason for the absence of Fascist mass movements is that American multinational corporations may not be able to operate comfortably in the same country with them. Compared with the contemporary authoritarian governments in Latin America, an authoritarian regime based on a Fascist mass movement would be more unpredictable and more intrusive, features especially unattractive to multinational corporations which are large bureaucratic organizations seeking stability and also extensive international organizations seeking to maximize their profits through secret practices such as transfer pricing.

Multinational corporations can easily operate in countries whose authoritarian governments do without a mass movement, however. And these governments can benefit in turn from the presence of the corporations. The case of the multinational automobile corporations in Brazil is especially interesting.

Multinational automobile corporations began manufacturing operations in Brazil in the 1950's, and during the Kubitschek period the Brazilian automobile industry experienced considerable growth. However, during the period of the more populist, more radical Goulart government in the early 1960's, there was a rapid acceleration of inflation and an increase in labor unrest. During the last two years of the Goulart government, foreign investment in Brazilian manufacturing declined sharply. Among the economic, bureaucratic, and technocratic elites of Brazil, it was a plausible argument that an authoritarian regime was a necessary condition for the renewed flow of foreign investment and a fortiori for the expanding flow which was necessary to continue the advance into the new phase of industrialization. And, in fact, in the years after the military coup of 1964, American and European investment did pour into Brazil; the output of the automobile industry doubled between 1964 and 1970 and doubled again between 1970 and 1974. However, the foreign investment in the Brazilian automobile industry was somewhat anomalous. Whereas the per capita GNP in other host countries had been above $1,000 when the multinational automobile corporations made their large investments in manufacturing, the per capita GNP of Brazil in 1966 was only $340. This made for a rather thin automobile market, despite Brazil's large population. This "premature" foreign investment in the Brazilian automobile industry was clearly induced by the political stability, repression of labor unions, and low wages which were imposed by the authoritarian regime established after the military coup of 1964.

Since Brazil had and continues to have a much lower per capita GNP than other large automobile producers, it has been hypothesized that the greatly increased consumption of automobiles in Brazil required a special form of the redistribution of income, that is, redistribution to the middle class from the lower class. This has been accomplished through government measures which repressed working-class real wages, reduced welfare and public health programs, increased middle-class real salaries, and provided government credit for automobile purchases.[56] These policies necessary for a premature auto-industrial age could be imposed far more easily by an authoritarian government than by a liberal-democratic one. The calculations of the Brazilian regime were suggested in 1974 by its Finance Minister, Mario Henrique Simonsen: "A transfer of income from the richest 20 percent to the poorest 80 percent probably would increase the demand for food, but diminish the demand for au-

---

[56] Edmar L. Bacha, "Issues and Evidence of Recent Brazilian Economic Growth" (Cambridge: Harvard Institute for International Development, Development Discussion Papers, 1976).

tomobiles. The result of a sudden redistribution would be merely to generate inflation in the food-producing sector and excess capacity in the car industry."[57]

When the military sought to legitimize its rule, its principal argument was the success of Brazilian industrialization and the greatly increased consumption of consumer durables, especially automobiles. Of course, even without the multinational automobile industry, there probably would still have been a military coup in Brazil in 1964 and an authoritarian regime. But the *stability* of the authoritarian regime may have been increased by the successful growth of the automobile industry.

What, then, does our analysis of the politics of industrialization predict about the political future of Latin Europe and Latin America? One possibility is that the Latin countries will not be able to invent new industrial products but will be able to manufacture only the products previously invented by others, that they will continue to be dependent upon foreign capital and to be deeply in debt to international banks, and consequently that there will be continuing pressures for the establishment and maintenance of labor-repressive, authoritarian regimes.

But a quite different prediction could be made in light of the pattern of international industrial diffusion resulting from the product cycle and foreign investment and in light of the world markets for certain goods, in particular consumer durables. For in the early 1980's, the very economic backwardness of Spain and Brazil in the new industries of the last generation (computers, telecommunications, aerospace) could make them the most cost-effective producers in the world market in the industries that were new two generations ago (automobiles, appliances). For the United States and Western Europe in the near future, Spain and Brazil could be the best bargains in consumer durables, just as Italy and Japan were in the 1960's. The Spanish and Brazilian governments will have a natural and influential ally in the multinational corporations and international banks whose interests lie in low tariff barriers for their goods in the United States and Western Europe. And "export-led" growth in Spain and Brazil could provide, as it did in Western

[57] Quoted in Normal Gall, "The Rise of Brazil," *Commentary* 63, No. 1 (January 1977), pp. 49-50.

Europe in the 1950's-1960's, the economic basis for more liberal politics.

Which of these two predictions will be realized in the next few years? Economics will not by itself give the answer, since it gives two opposite answers; the Latin world is once again in one of those historical conjunctures when "politics takes command." And it is a time when the international economic policies of the old liberal democracies of the West can once again make a difference.

CHAPTER 9

THE BUREAUCRATIC-AUTHORITARIAN MODEL: SYNTHESIS AND PRIORITIES FOR FUTURE RESEARCH

David Collier

The goal of this book has been to advance the understanding of authoritarianism in contemporary Latin America and its relationship to problems of economic development. The authors have approached this analytic problem within the framework of what was described in Chapter 1 as the bureaucratic-authoritarian model, focusing on the generic issues and specific substantive topics that are the principal components of this model. Within this shared set of analytic concerns, they have sought to evaluate, refine, where appropriate modify or reject, and build upon the concepts and hypotheses that have been developed in conjunction with this model.

The five sets of questions posed at the end of the first chapter provide a useful basis for drawing together the arguments developed in this book. First, how have the authors used concepts such as bureaucratic-authoritarianism and populism to deal with the difficult problem of developing a meaningful "comparative" description of Latin American authoritarianism? Second, what progress has been made in explaining the emergence of contemporary authoritarianism? Third, can this explanation be refined by incorporating other Latin American countries into the model? Fourth, what insights have been gained regarding the dynamics of authoritarian rule, and in light of current patterns of change, what directions can future research on Latin American politics most usefully take? Finally, can elements of the model usefully be extended to other world regions, and can such extensions lead to improvements in the model as it applies to Latin America?

This concluding chapter seeks to synthesize some of the lines of analysis presented in the book and to suggest some priorities for future research. The discussion will focus on these five questions.

The Concept of Bureaucratic-Authoritarianism

O'Donnell's original effort to map the complex "constellation" of traits that he saw as defining characteristics of bureaucratic-authoritarianism represented a valuable attempt to find patterns within the complexities of Latin American politics. It made the contribution of explicitly calling attention to important links among the issues of regime, coalition, and policy and of bringing into sharp focus a series of arguments about the occurrence of simultaneous, interrelated changes in all three of these dimensions in the context of the recent rise of authoritarianism in Latin America. O'Donnell's formulation of this concept served as a valuable "signpost" that helped to orient later research on Latin American authoritarianism.[1]

Since the presentation of this initial formulation, a number of useful modifications of this concept have been proposed, including several in this book, leading to a striking diversity in the way in which the term bureaucratic-authoritarianism has been used. Given the complexity of the political phenomena being studied, it is hardly surprising that this would happen. Within reasonable limits, it likewise seems appropriate that individual scholars should adopt usages that best fit their own analytic concerns, provided that they clearly identify the meaning intended— which I believe is the case within each of the chapters in this volume.

However, if one considers the aggregate affect of this diversity of usage, it can pose a major problem, both for those who are "consumers" of this literature and for those who wish to build systematically upon it. I think that the tendency to introduce new ideas and new comparisons into the analysis of contemporary Latin American politics by building them into the definition of bureaucratic-authoritarianism has gone too far. As a result, a number of different definitions have been proposed. In different analyses, depending on the particular aspects of political change that the authors wish to stress, the concept of bureaucratic-authoritarianism has alternatively been used to refer to a type of political system; a type of political regime; a type of state, in the sense of the state as a set of concrete institutions; and a type of state, in the sense of the state as an analytic abstraction that consists of the political relationships that serve to maintain

[1] This expression was suggested to me by Carla Robbins.

the social relations of domination. The distinct concerns of different analysts have also led to rather different "check lists" of defining characteristics of bureaucratic-authoritarianism. Finally, there are also crucial differences regarding which cases are included within this category. For instance, some analyses, which have stressed the similarities between contemporary Mexico and other cases of bureaucratic-authoritarianism, have included Mexico; whereas other analyses have stressed instead the dissimilarities and have excluded Mexico. Post-1968 Peru has been treated in some analyses as bureaucratic-authoritarian and in other analyses as populist.

What is the most constructive way of dealing with these problems? I think that the concept of bureaucratic-authoritarianism should be retained as a "zone word," as a signpost that usefully identifies the shared subject-matter not only of analyses in this volume, but of many other studies as well. However, this concept has so many definitions and so many defining characteristics that it does not serve well as a tool for comparative analysis. It often leads to confusion rather than clarity in the effort to bring into sharp focus the similarities and differences among countries that are the most important for understanding contemporary authoritarianism.

Disaggregation

In order to bring these similarities and differences into sharper focus, it is helpful to make explicit an approach implicitly used in several chapters in this book: that of disaggregating this broad concept and focusing on the interplay among the separate issues of regime, coalition, and policy. This approach makes it easier to carry out the three basic political comparisons that are central to the analysis: the comparison *among* the political systems in the more industrially advanced nations of Latin America; the broad historical comparison contained in the hypothesis that bureaucratic-authoritarianism is, in fact, a *new* kind of authoritarianism; and the contrast between bureaucratic-authoritarianism and the systems that existed immediately prior to its emergence. The following discussion will review some of the similarities and differences that are most salient within the framework of the larger bureaucratic-authoritarian model.

The multi-faceted contrasts among contemporary Argentina, Brazil, Chile, Uruguay, and Mexico have already received considerable attention in this book. With regard to regime, Cardoso has placed particular emphasis on the fundamental difference between party and military authoritarianism, and several authors, including O'Donnell, have stressed differences in regime, coalition, and policy that relate to the participation of, and the benefits received by, the agricultural sector; the industrialization policies adopted; the degree of emphasis on building, as opposed to dismantling, the state; policies toward foreign capital; and the degree of repression. A great many of the traits essential to the model thus vary greatly across these cases. Other differences important to understanding the long-term dynamics of bureaucratic-authoritarianism might be underlined as well. In Mexico, party and union organizations with a major base in the popular sector have played a central role in supporting the contemporary authoritarian system.[2] The very different relationship between the state and the organizations of the popular sector in Brazil may reasonably be described as involving "state corporatism," whereas in Chile and Uruguay this relationship involves more nearly pure repression.[3] Electoral competition is severely limited in Brazil and Mexico, but the use of elections in these countries reflects a major contrast in terms of the intensity of exclusionary policies in comparison with Chile and Uruguay in the first phase of their current authoritarian experience. This use of elections also points to an element of similarity between Mexico and Brazil and the non-bureaucratic-authoritarian experience of Colombia and Venezuela, which have also recently gone through periods of semi-competitive elections.[4] One is thus dealing with a complex panorama of similarities and differences among these cases.

In the context of this panorama of similarities and differences,

[2] See Susan Kaufman Purcell, *The Mexican Profit-Sharing Decision: Politics in an Authoritarian Regime* (Berkeley and Los Angeles: University of California Press, 1975), Chapter 1.

[3] Ruth B. Collier and David Collier, "Inducements versus Constraints: Disaggregating 'Corporatism,'" *The American Political Science Review* 73, No. 4 (December 1979), forthcoming.

[4] For valuable discussions of Venezuela and Colombia, see Daniel Levine, "The Role of Political Learning in the Restoration and Consolidation of Democracy: Venezuela since 1958" and Alexander W. Wilde, "The Breakdown of Oligarchical Democracy in Colombia," both in Juan J. Linz and Alfred Stepan, eds., *The Breakdown of Democratic Regimes: Latin America* (Baltimore: The Johns Hopkins University Press, 1978).

a disaggregated approach obviates debates about whether a particular case "really is" bureaucratic-authoritarian. The question has been raised with regard to Mexico, and on the basis of classifications of cases presented in this book could be raised about Peru as well. Yet within the framework of a literature in which bureaucratic-authoritarianism has been given so many definitions, I do not think these are interesting questions. There are major similarities and major differences, and the relative importance of these similarities and differences cannot be determined on the basis of definitions, but rather on the basis of a causal analysis concerned with discovering which factors play the most important role in shaping the political evolution of these societies.

This disaggregated approach also permits a more adequate assessment of the degree to which bureaucratic-authoritarianism is, in fact, something new. Though it unquestionably represents a major change from the political patterns that prevailed in Latin America in the late 1950's and early 1960's, arguments presented by scholars such as Thomas Skidmore and Philippe Schmitter make it clear that the degree to which it differs from certain earlier forms of authoritarianism is by no means a closed question.[5] Governments that to varying degrees exclude a previously activated popular sector, pursue orthodox economic policies, have some degree of technocratic orientation, actively seek foreign capital, and at least to some extent promote the production of intermediate and capital goods have appeared at various levels of industrial modernization in Latin America.[6]

[5] Thomas E. Skidmore, "Politics and Economic Policy Making in Authoritarian Brazil, 1937-71" and Philippe C. Schmitter, "The 'Portugalization' of Brazil?" both in Alfred Stepan, ed., *Authoritarian Brazil: Origins, Policies, and Future* (New Haven: Yale University Press, 1973).

[6] One of the contexts in which earlier exclusionary governments have appeared is in cases of "enclave" economies discussed in Cotler's chapter and in the text below. These enclaves produced a very early and intense political activation of organized labor that was a central element in major episodes of incorporating policies and populist-type coalitions—which in turn set in motion ongoing cycles of incorporation and exclusion at a point when these countries were at relatively low levels of industrialization—indeed, much lower than one would expect on the basis of the hypothesis that populism is linked to the initial phase of industrialization. For a discussion of this enclave pattern in Peru, see Peter F. Klaren, *Modernization, Dislocation, and Aprismo: Origins of the Peruvian Aprista Party* (Austin: University of Texas Press, 1973). My *Squatters and Oligarchs: Authoritarian Rule and Policy Change in Peru* (Baltimore: The Johns Hopkins University Press,

Kaufman's chapter points to a series of features of the first Vargas government in Brazil that one might associate with bureaucratic-authoritarianism, and the 1943 military government in Argentina also had some of these traits.

Rather than attempting to determine whether bureaucratic-authoritarianism is really something new, it appears simpler to enumerate the specific traits that are new. Three important traits stressed in this book do appear to be new. They are: (1) The central role in the dominant coalition of a highly internationalized and oligopolized bourgeoisie; (2) Rule by the military as an institution—as opposed to rule by one or a few military leaders; and (3) The relationship with the agricultural sector. This sector is in certain important cases not in the coalition, and when it is, it is more progressive agro-business, rather than the more traditional social and political groupings earlier associated with the export sector, that plays a key role. The question of whether these new traits *lead to* a larger syndrome of new characteristics would appear to be a question best addressed on the basis of empirical demonstration.

Finally, important contrasts in the way different countries entered the current era of authoritarianism also do not come into focus until one considers separately these issues of regime, coalition, and policy. In Brazil in 1964 and Argentina in 1966, important changes in regime helped bring to power political coalitions many elements of which had previously held power. These coalitions returned to many policies which had been tried before.[7] By contrast, a striking characteristic of contemporary

---

1976) discusses these cycles of incorporation and exclusion. For a discussion of the role of technocratic orientations and the concern with intermediate and capital goods industries in what is generally considered to be a principal populist period in Brazil—the 1930-1945 Vargas government—see Thomas Skidmore, *Politics in Brazil, 1930-1964: An Experiment in Democracy* (London: Oxford University Press, 1967), Chapter 1.

[7] O'Donnell refers briefly to these elements of continuity in *Modernization and Bureaucratic-Authoritarianism: Studies in South American Politics* (University of California, Berkeley, Institute of International Studies, Politics of Modernization Series No. 9), pp. 64-65. For a detailed discussion of this continuity with respect to Argentina, see Benjamin Most, "Changing Authoritarian Systems: An Assessment of their Impact on Public Policies in Argentina, 1930-1970" (doctoral dissertation, Department of Political Science, Indiana University, 1978), Chapter 3. Some observers argue that the Brazilian military did not have a well-defined economic model in mind when it took power in 1964. However, the evidence examined by Stepan does not support this contention. See Alfred Stepan, *The*

Mexico is its capacity to carry out a major shift to more orthodox economic policies without a change in regime, as occurred after December 1976, following the inauguration of López Portillo. Hirschman stresses that the transition to orthodox economic policies in Colombia and in the Frei period in Chile occurred not only without a regime change, but under pluralistic regimes. One is thus faced with a spectrum of different types of interaction between regime and policy change that cuts across the bureaucratic-authoritarian/non-bureaucratic-authoritarian distinction, and a more "fine-grained" approach to describing these regime and policy changes appears to be appropriate. Such an approach also appears appropriate in light of the concern voiced by scholars such as Douglas Chalmers and others that both in the rhetoric of Latin American politics and in research on Latin American politics there may be a tendency to exaggerate the degree of policy change that accompanies major regime changes.[8] While there is no doubt that in some areas drastic policy change has occurred, this concern does point to the importance of monitoring policy change quite closely.[9]

With regard to the timing of different aspects of regime change, it is noteworthy that the really extensive use of torture did not begin in Brazil in 1964 with the onset of the military regime, but rather in the late 1960's. Similarly, torture was less important in Argentina under the post-1966 Onganía government than it was during the more competitive period from 1973 to 1976 and during the post-1976 authoritarian period. It has of course been extremely important in Chile and Uruguay. Once these distinctions have been made, one might be led to hypothesize that whereas certain aspects of contemporary authoritarianism were present from the onset of all of these regimes

---

Military in Politics: Changing Patterns in Brazil (Princeton: Princeton University Press, 1971), p. 218, note 6.

[8] Douglas A. Chalmers, "The Politicized State in Latin America," in James M. Malloy, ed., *Authoritarianism and Corporatism in Latin America* (Pittsburgh: University of Pittsburgh Press, 1977). For an extended review of the literature on Latin America that makes this argument, see Most, "Changing Authoritarian Systems."

[9] A major, comparative research project on the stabilization policies adopted by these authoritarian governments is currently being carried out by three major Latin American research centers—CEBRAP in Brazil, CEDES in Argentina, and CIEPLAN in Chile. This project will certainly shed new light on these patterns of policy change.

and derived from the immediate crises that brought them to power, the emergence of torture may in some cases have been part of the reaction of the political right to the widespread urban protest and urban terrorism that occurred beginning in the late 1960's in many countries—not only in Latin America, but also in Europe and the United States. By taking apart these different aspects of regime change, one can thus derive further hypotheses about alternative explanations that may enlarge the understanding of contemporary authoritarianism.

Thus, in terms of three frameworks of comparison—among contemporary authoritarian and competitive regimes; between contemporary authoritarianism and earlier eras of authoritarianism; and between the pattern of authoritarianism that recently emerged in each country and the political patterns that immediately preceded its emergence—one finds a complex spectrum of similarities and differences. Both for the purpose of description, and in order to "set into motion" these similarities and differences in a dynamic explanation of political change, it appears useful to concentrate the analysis at a disaggregated level. This approach would not neglect the idea that it is essential to examine the different constellations or configurations in which distinct patterns of regime, coalition, and policy occur together. The analysis of the interrelationship among these dimensions is a central concern of the analysis. This interrelationship is simply treated as being far more variegated than was suggested by the original classification.

A Crucial Working Assumption

Though this disaggregated approach facilitates these three fundamental comparisons, a further element derived from conceptual discussions of bureaucratic-authoritarianism must be added if this approach is to reflect adequately the underlying ideas in this literature. In light of the arguments presented in this book by Cardoso and particularly by O'Donnell, it is important to build into this disaggregated approach the concerns raised in their discussion of the state and in O'Donnell's argument that bureaucratic-authoritarianism is a type of state, in the abstract sense of the state as the set of political relationships that serve to maintain the social relations of domination. In the context of the capitalist societies that are the focus of this book, this involves maintaining capitalist relations of production.

O'Donnell's argument points to a very important idea—but

one which I would prefer to incorporate into the analysis by some means other than by adding it to an already extremely complex and frequently changing definition. I would instead maintain as a crucial working assumption of the analysis that a principal dynamic force in shaping political and economic change will be the interplay between different constellations of regime, coalition, and policy, on the one hand, and the issues that arise in attempting to maintain or alter capitalist relations of production, on the other. This interaction involves at least three specific causal relationships. First, when severe crises threaten the existing capitalist relations of production, this may cause leaders within the dominant groups to initiate changes in regime, coalition, and/or policy in order better to protect these relations of production. Second, the emergence of new relations of production—for instance, those involved in the internationalization of production—may generate pressure for modifications in regime, coalition, and/or policy in order to maintain or reinforce these new economic relationships. Third, independently of such pressures, modifications in regime, coalition, and/or policy may be initiated with the goal of changing the capitalist relations of production—or, in the case of a socialist revolution, with the goal of eliminating them.

At the same time that these particular causal patterns are extremely important, many other factors must be considered, as all the authors in this book clearly recognize. A wide variety of different economic and non-economic forces affect the evolution of regime, coalition, and policy. Likewise, any given crisis that threatens the relations of production or any given modification in the relations of production does not automatically result in a predetermined set of political transformations. The working assumption of the analysis simply identifies a type of interaction between the economic and the political sphere about which it is particularly fruitful to develop hypotheses.

It seems to me that this working assumption, combined with the disaggregated approach advocated above, provides a useful basis for making the attractive concept of bureaucratic-authoritarianism more useful for comparative analysis.

POPULISM

The concept of populism is central to the bureaucratic-authoritarian model and directly or indirectly plays an important role in most of the chapters in this volume as well, particularly those of Cotler, Kaufman, and Hirschman. Within the framework of the attempt to explain bureaucratic-authoritarianism that is the concern of this book, the discussion of populism has two primary goals: first, to further clarify ways in which bureaucratic-authoritarianism is new and distinctive by contrasting it with an important earlier type of system that is purportedly quite different; and second, to illuminate the origins of the "agenda of salient social problems and developmental bottlenecks"[10] contributing to the emergence of bureaucratic-authoritarianism.

Several authors in this volume have stressed that the experience with populism has varied greatly among countries. Hence, both for the purpose of exploring the descriptive contrast with bureaucratic-authoritarianism and for assessing the importance of different populist experiences in shaping subsequent patterns of change, a disaggregated approach is once again relevant.

It is important to avoid the assumption that populism is a well-defined, coherent political system that exists from the time of the demise of the oligarchic system to the point of the onset of bureaucratic-authoritarianism. Populism does not necessarily involve a "broad coalition" with "no source of fundamental conflict" among its members[11] but often a narrow, fragile, unstable coalition. The popular sector and industrial elites are often not in the coalition at the same time.[12] "Incorporating" periods are commonly brief, and excluding periods often quickly follow.[13] In some instances the initiative for the coalition has come from military or civilian technocrats who are often viewed as being associated primarily with bureaucratic-authoritarianism. In some

[10] Guillermo O'Donnell, *Modernization*, p. 79.

[11] *Ibid.*, pp. 56 and 59.

[12] Eldon Kenworthy in "Did the 'New Industrialists' Play a Significant Role in the Formation of Peron's Coalition, 1943-46?" (in Alberto Ciria et al., *New Perspectives on Modern Argentina* [Indiana University, Latin American Studies Working Papers, 1972, 15-28]) raises serious questions about the role of industrialists in the original Peronist coalition. Another case in point is the split in the Liberal Party in Colombia in the 1930's and 1940's in opposition to the populist "Revolución en Marcha" (see John D. Martz, *Colombia: A Contemporary Political Survey* [Chapel Hill: University of North Carolina Press, 1962], Chapter 3 and Robert H. Dix, *Colombia: The Political Dimensions of Change* [New Haven: Yale University Press, 1967], Chapter 4.)

[13] The tendency for a rapid shift from incorporation to exclusion comes out clearly in the "enclave" cases noted above (see note 6).

cases, such as Brazil, there has been a concern with promoting not just consumer goods production but also the production of intermediate and capital goods, particularly those related to military security.[14] In many instances it is not clear that the governing elites make a self-conscious effort to extend benefits to the popular sector as a means of expanding the domestic market, and in Mexico the initial phase of industrialization coincided with a steady decline in workers' income.[15] This does not mean that the cases classified as populist and bureaucratic-authoritarian are not different. It does suggest that the degree and nature of differences should be the object of continuing analysis.

The diversity of social problems and developmental bottlenecks that is the legacy of populism is also striking. The pattern of industrialization often identified with populist periods—involving a subsidy of industry through the extraction of resources from the export sector—is seen by many analysts as leading to serious economic difficulties and as debilitating, rather than strengthening, the national economy.[16] It has often been suggested, as Hirschman notes, that this attack on the export sector may tend to "kill the goose that lays the golden eggs."[17] Yet, as Hirschman and others have emphasized, the degree to which this occurred has varied greatly among countries. In some contexts this pattern was followed closely, with a consequent weakening of principal sources of foreign exchange: the most conspicuous example is Argentina. In other cases, agrarian policy has been quite different—involving, in the cases of Mexico, Venezuela, Colombia, and Peru (in the post-1968 period) im-

[14] These themes come out clearly in the discussion of the first Vargas period in Skidmore, *Politics in Brazil*, Chapter 1, and appear also to be crucial elements in the orientation of a number of the officers who led the coup in Argentina in 1943 that initially brought Peron into the government (see Robert Potash, *The Army and Politics in Argentina, 1928-1945* [Stanford: Stanford University Press, 1969]).

[15] For evidence of the decline in real wages in Mexico in the 1940's, a decade commonly identified as a crucial early phase of industrial expansion, see James W. Wilkie, *The Mexican Revolution: Federal Expenditure and Social Change since 1910* (Berkeley and Los Angeles: University of California Press, 1967), p. 187.

[16] For an overview of this issue see Werner Baer, "Import-Substitution and Industrialization in Latin America: Experiences and Interpretations," *Latin American Research Review*, VII (Spring 1972), pp. 95-122.

[17] Albert O. Hirschman, *A Bias for Hope* (New Haven: Yale University Press, 1971), p. 12.

portant agrarian reforms. In Mexico and Colombia, this different pattern of "sectoral clash" has been followed by a pattern of
more nearly balanced growth.[18] Hirschman suggests another
possible source of diversity by stressing that the economic crises
that arise toward the end of populist periods derive in considerable measure from massive increases in public spending that occurred in these periods—and hence from public policy, rather
than directly from underlying problems of the type of industrialization being experienced. Major differences in the intensity of
these economic crises may thus be accounted for in considerable
measure by political factors.

Political differences in the populist experience are important
in other ways as well. For instance, differences in the way in
which the initial legal and political incorporation of organized
labor occurs—a transition that often coincides with other transitions identified with populism—appears to set in motion different patterns of change.[19] For instance, one finds important
differences among cases in the degree to which this initial incorporation involved an attempt on the part of elites to link
labor to—as opposed to insulating it from—a political party or
political movement. This variable, along with the coalitional position of other class and sectoral groups, the degree of polarization that occurs in conjunction with populism, and other factors,
plays a role in determining whether a well-institutionalized
multi-class integrative political party emerges from the populist
period—which in turn has important implications for the capacity for political control of the popular sector in later periods.

[18] See Robert R. Kaufman, "Mexico and Latin American Authoritarianism," in
José Luis Reyna and Richard S. Wienert, eds., *Authoritarianism in Mexico* (Phila-
delphia: Institute for the Study of Human Issues, 1977). For an interesting dis-
cussion of the pattern of more nearly balanced growth in Colombia, see Carlos F.
Díaz-Alejandro, *Foreign Trade Regimes and Economic Development: Colombia* (New
York: National Bureau of Economic Research, 1976).

[19] See David Collier and Ruth B. Collier, "Who Does What, to Whom, and
How: Toward a Comparative Analysis of Latin American Corporatism," in Malloy, ed., *Authoritarianism and Corporatism*; Ruth B. Collier and David Collier, "Inducements versus Constraints: Disaggregating Corporatism"; and Ruth B. Collier, "Popular Sector Incorporation and Regime Evolution in Brazil and Mexico"
(paper presented at the Conference on Brazil and Mexico, Center for Inter-
American Relations, New York, 1978). See also Kaufman, "Mexico and Latin
American Authoritarianism," and Marcelo Cavarozzi, "Populismos y 'partidos de
clase media:' Notas comparativas" (Documento CEDES/G.E. CLACSO/No. 3,
Centro de Estudios de Estado y Sociedad, Buenos Aires, 1976).

Other political differences involve the capacity for "conflict-resolution" that appears, or fails to appear, in the wake of populist episodes. In Colombia and Venezuela, where the political crisis associated with populism became most intense in the 1940's, a period of harshly repressive authoritarian rule followed this crisis. Then the principal civilian political parties self-consciously chose to limit party competition and thereby avoid future polarization.[20] Colombia and Venezuela therefore entered the 1960's and 1970's having already experimented with norms for limiting the political expression of the popular sector within a democratic framework. Similarly in Mexico, the populism and the campaign against the church of the 1930's were ended without leaving a massive residue of political antagonisms and polarization.[21] The end of the Perón era in Argentina, by contrast, was characterized by extreme political antagonisms and polarization.[22]

The hypothesized link between the emergence of populism and the initial phase of import substitution requires scrutiny. If one examines the timing of the most frequently discussed populist periods—such as the Cárdenas and Vargas governments, the first Perón government, the "Trienio" in Venezuela from 1945 to 1948, and the Bustamante period in Peru—it becomes clear that this link is at best complex and in some cases non-existent. In some instances such as Argentina, populism appears toward the end of the initial phase of import substitution, whereas in other contexts systems with many populist features appear at the onset or well before the onset of any meaningful degree of import substitution—particularly in Venezuela and Peru and also in Chile. Kaufman's chapter makes a parallel argument. He stresses that the initial phase of import substitution may coincide with "populist pressures," but that populism in fact goes through different phases involving different coalitions and different portions of the popular sector—and

[20] See note 4.

[21] A suggestive analysis of the resolution of the church conflict is presented in Laura N. O'Shaughnessy, "Opposition in an Authoritarian Regime: The Incorporation and Institutionalization of the Mexican National Action Party (PAN)" (doctoral dissertation, Department of Political Science, Indiana University, 1976).

[22] A fascinating analysis of these antagonisms is presented in O'Donnell, *Modernization*, Chapter 4.

that these phases often do not coincide with the first phase of import substitution.

Further insights into these important variations in the experience of different countries with populism can be gained if one considers a broader range of explanations of populism. One such explanation, which has important implications for the larger set of problems that are the legacy of populism, involves the argument that populism does not necessarily occur in response to the resources made available by the "expanding economic pie" that is hypothesized to characterize the initial phase of import substitution. The immediate economic context may in part involve an expansion of available resources that results from major increases in the volume and/or prices of primary product exports. An important example may be the first Perón government in Argentina.[23]

Another explanation of populism stressed by Cotler involves an analysis not of phases of industrialization but of certain patterns of social differentiation and political activation of the popular sector that have appeared in some countries well before the onset of any meaningful degree of industrialization, in contexts characterized by relatively small, undifferentiated modern sectors. In Peru, Chile, Venezuela, and Mexico, some of the aspects of twentieth-century modernization that have shaped the emergence of populism have involved the extraction or production of minerals and agricultural products in isolated "enclaves" of highly capitalized, mechanized, modern economic activity. The isolated concentrations of workers in these areas produced intense political activation of organized labor at a time when the process of import substitution was in a very preliminary phase. This activation was a central element in major episodes of incorporating policies and populist-type coalitions that have had substantial importance in the overall political evolution of these countries. Particularly in Peru, these initial incorporating episodes set in motion ongoing cycles of incorporation and exclusion that have become central features of national politics.[24] It thus appears that the analysis of populism and incorporation (as

[23] For relevant data on export trends in Argentina, see Carlos Díaz-Alejandro, *Essays on the Economic History of the Argentine Republic* (New Haven: Yale University Press, 1970).

[24] With reference to Peru, see note 6 above and Cotler's chapter.

well as of exclusion) has been too narrowly tied to the process of industrialization.

Rather than to view populism as a relatively similar transition through which all countries go, it appears most useful to view it as a major point of differentiation among countries, both in terms of its causes and its consequences. It thus becomes a major "background variable" that contributes to shaping differences in the subsequent experience of these countries. As with the concept of bureaucratic-authoritarianism, it seems best to carry out the comparison of populist periods at a relatively disaggregated level, considering separately issues of regime, policy, and coalition—as well as employing the working assumption noted above. At the same time, as with the concept of bureaucratic-authoritarianism, it seems perfectly appropriate to retain the term populism (or populist) for periods in which the popular sector plays a significant role in national politics.

EXPLAINING THE RISE OF AUTHORITARIANISM

The chapters in this book have attempted to explain more adequately the recent rise of authoritarianism in Latin America. The results of this effort have been, in one sense, quite frustrating, and yet in another sense quite useful. The frustration has two sources. First, though considerable effort has been made to test alternative explanations, this is not a subject-matter that readily lends itself to the definitive disconfirmation of hypotheses—or to definitive failures to disconfirm that greatly strengthen the plausibility of a given line of argument. Second, many new explanations have been proposed. Because relatively few hypotheses have been decisively rejected and a number of potential explanations have been added, one is now confronted with well over a dozen alternative explanatory factors.[25]

[25] An inventory of alternative explanations of the rise of authoritarianism (and of its non-appearance in certain countries) which are touched upon in this volume might include: the problems associated with different phases of industrialization; the rise of transnational corporations and the internationalization of production; differences among countries in the long-term prosperity of the primary product export sector; short-term fluctuations in the prosperity of this sector; the scope of the resources that the state is able to derive from taxing this sector; the growing political importance of certain social sectors and social roles, such as the popular sector, technocrats, and "nationals" within each country who

At the same time, there has been an advance in understanding. First, new ways of thinking about the problem of explaining the rise of authoritarianism have been proposed that will make it easier to avoid mistakes or misunderstandings that have previously occurred in conjunction with this literature. Second, certain explanatory factors, while not totally disconfirmed, have at least been placed in a more appropriate perspective. Third, though a multitude of explanations has been discussed, there is a logical ordering among them. Once this ordering is made explicit, the variety of explanations appears less bewildering.

Considerable progress can be made in imposing some order on these alternative explanations by placing them into two groups. On the one hand, the rise of authoritarianism occurred in the context of relatively severe economic and political crises which, as O'Donnell put it in his chapter, to varying degrees threatened the capitalist parameters of society. A number of lines of argument involve general explanations for why these crises occurred. Prominent among these are, of course, the arguments about problems of Latin American industrialization and related changes in international capitalism. Other explanations concern characteristics of particular countries that may have intensified these crises or made it easier to deal with the crises without drastic regime change. Many of the explanations in this second group involve differences between the cases in which contemporary authoritarianism emerged in its most repressive form and the contrasting experience of countries such as Mexico, Venezuela, Colombia, and Peru. For the sake of

are closely tied to transnational corporations; the emergence of "new professionalism" in the military and of new military ideologies about intervention in politics; the nature of the earlier political incorporation of important class groups in society, for instance, the urban popular sector and industrialists; the closely related issues of the degree to which social conflict is mitigated by the existence of multi-class, integrative parties and the degree of effective state control of organized labor; the political strength of the popular sector (which may be affected by the nature of this incorporation, but which is also shaped by other factors); U.S. intervention; the revolutionary and counterrevolutionary reaction to the Cuban revolution; military competition among Latin American nations; differences among countries in political ideology and political culture; political leadership, and the presence (or absence) of deliberate "preemptive" political action that leads to political compromises that help to mitigate the crises that tend to trigger the rise of authoritarianism; and a pattern of "tentativeness" of Latin American political institutions that makes regime change more likely to occur in the context of crisis.

convenience, these explanations may be referred to as "background" variables.[26]

Explaining the General Context of Crisis

Because several of the principal explanations for these crises involve economic factors and because some confusion has arisen regarding the relative importance of economic and political explanations in this literature, it is appropriate to begin by briefly reviewing this issue. Though it is certainly true that economic variables play a large role in explanations of the rise of authoritarianism, various authors have stressed that these economic factors can only be properly understood by carefully examining the way in which they have interacted with political factors. Cardoso has stressed this point for many years,[27] and devotes considerable attention to it in this book. Hirschman also gives it central attention, both in his critique of the argument about increased income inequality in Brazil and in the new explanations of the rise of authoritarianism that he proposes. Other authors stress this theme as well, particularly Serra.

This theme is also essential to the understanding of O'Donnell's analysis. While O'Donnell places central emphasis on economic factors, he is also centrally concerned with the impact of changes in social structure and with the conflicts that emerge among actors whose roles are defined as much in social and political terms as in economic terms.[28] Thus, his analysis of the rise of authoritarianism focused on the interaction between the popular sector and the technocrats, and his analysis in this book of the dynamics of authoritarianism focuses on interactions such as that between the nationalism of the military and the internationalism of the upper bourgeoisie. As a result, the actual links between economic variables and political outcomes are ex-

[26] These two groups may in a sense overlap to some degree. For instance, the direct impact on particular countries of the factors in the first group may differ somewhat (or even considerably), leading to the kinds of differences among cases that I have attributed to the factors in the second group. Nonetheless, this distinction appears useful for organizing the discussion.

[27] See, for instance, Fernando Henrique Cardoso and Enzo Faletto, *Dependencia y desarrollo en América Latina* (Mexico City: Siglo Veintiuno Editores, 1969), pp. 162-63; and Cardoso, "Associated Dependent Development: Theoretical and Practical Implications," in Alfred Stepan, ed., *Authoritarian Brazil*, p. 143.

[28] I acknowledge helpful conversations I have had regarding this point with Louis Goodman and Barbara Geddes.

tremely complex, as can readily be seen in Figure 1 of Chapter 1. His stress on the idea of "elective affinities" reflected a similar concern with the role of political factors. Hence, even when one is examining the economic arguments about this period of crisis in Latin America, it is important to recognize that what is involved are in part political explanations of the reaction of these countries to economic problems.

Keeping these caveats in mind, we may now review the findings of this book regarding the principal economic arguments. Perhaps the clearest finding concerns the hypothesis that the emergence of the new authoritarianism occurred in important measure in response to problems that arise in conjunction with the deepening of industrialization, involving the vertical integration of production to include the domestic manufacture or processing of intermediate and capital goods. Hirschman, Serra, and Kaufman find that, except for the case of Argentina, there is little support for this hypothesis. A concern with deepening was not on the agenda of the international debate on problems of industrialization, and with reference to the crucial Brazilian case, Serra shows that what initially occurred was in fact a process of "undeepening," though an emphasis on deepening did emerge in the 1970's. In the Southern Cone today, a central development priority appears not to be deepening but rather, among other things, a "reagrarianization" of the economy.

Three qualifying observations must be made, however, with reference to this rejection of the deepening hypothesis. First, deepening was important in Argentina, and later did become important in Brazil. Second, O'Donnell stresses that in cases in which high rates of inflation continue under authoritarian rule, capital accumulation will occur more through financial speculation than through investment in new productive activities, thus inhibiting the effective promotion of new forms of production. He suggests that when and if this problem is overcome, a stronger emphasis on deepening may emerge—particularly in the larger countries. Third, in his analysis of Argentina from 1970 to 1976, Kaufman shows that the loosening of authoritarian controls appeared to have a much greater negative impact on new investment in areas of production that involved deepening, and much less of an impact on investment in the production of manufactured goods for export. This finding supports the hypothesis that providing a long-term guarantee of economic and political stability is particularly important for investments in deepening.

Nonetheless, the concern with deepening was at most only one element within a broad spectrum of policy concerns, and in some cases it was completely irrelevant—or in fact represented an opposite priority from that reflected in the economic policies that emerged immediately after the military coups.

Though the deepening hypothesis must in important measure be rejected, it was only one of the elements in O'Donnell's original argument about the links between the problems of import-substitution and political change (see Figure 1 in Chapter 1). Other evidence presented in this book is more nearly consistent with other parts of the original argument. Thus, both Kaufman and Hirschman argue that the more recent period of economic growth in Latin America has in important ways been more difficult than the initial phase of industrialization and that these new difficulties have had important political implications.

Kaufman's analysis, like my own discussion above, suggests that the initial phase of industrialization was not consistently associated with populism. Indeed, drawing on the insightful earlier research of Charles Anderson, Kaufman emphasizes that what is striking about this earlier phase is that it occurred under a variety of different political conditions. There is a *lack* of any consistent association with a particular type of political system. In this sense, the initial, "easy" phase of import substitution really was easier. By contrast, while there is certainly some important variation among the types of political systems that have appeared in the industrially more advanced countries of Latin America, Kaufman suggests that because of the trade-offs and tensions that arise in conjunction with the alternative economic growth policies that are presently relevant in these countries, there has been a reduction in the range of political conditions under which these dependent, capitalist economies can now prosper.

A parallel, but distinct, argument about phases of industrialization is made by Hirschman, who stresses the consequences of the initial phase of industrial expansion for public policy and for the attitudes of political leaders about the use of economic resources. He suggests that major political leaders in this period "could all be considered victims of the delusions of economic invulnerability fostered by the surprising early successes and rapid penetration of industry into a supposedly hostile environment."[29] This may have contributed to a pattern of "unorthodox" economic policies that played an important role in subsequent economic difficulties. The combination of the slowing of industrial expansion after the initial phase of growth, the changing demands of international capital regarding an appropriate "investment climate," and the legacy of the earlier economic policies created major pressure for a shift to orthodox economic policies. He sees the need to make this transition as placing new demands on the political system. Like Kaufman and O'Donnell, however, he does not view the need to make this transition as imposing any absolute "requirements" in terms of the form of the political regime, and he stresses that in two cases it has been carried out under competitive regimes.

The original explanation of bureaucratic-authoritarianism was not, of course, exclusively tied to the idea of phases of industrialization. With regard to the argument about the increasing political activation of the popular sector, the growing political role of this sector appears to have been, in conjunction with these other economic problems, an important element in the crises that occurred and in the reaction to them. However, there also appear to be major, long-term differences among countries in the strength of the popular sector that will be stressed below in discussion of background variables.

With regard to another underlying change in social structure, the spread of technocratic roles, Kaufman's analysis of Uruguay—where he found a technocratic policy orientation in a context in which there was only a modest development of technocratic occupational roles—led him to be skeptical about the importance of this factor. O'Donnell's own more recent discussion may suggest a basis for reconciling this finding regarding Uruguay with the larger argument. Whereas his initial discussion of technocrats placed substantial emphasis on the significance of their growing numerical importance, his subsequent analysis places greater stress on the idea that the technocrats serve to transmit the norms of the international business and financial community. The case of Uruguay suggests that such external influences may play as large a role in producing a

[29] See Hirschman's chapter in this volume, p. 67.

technocratic policy orientation as the actual number of technocrats in any particular country.

This argument about the role of technocrats in transmitting external norms points to just one of a series of factors in the international system that require more systematic attention. Discussions of bureaucratic-authoritarianism frequently refer to such factors as changes in international capitalism, the Cuban Revolution, and United States' intervention, but it is not clear whether these are additional necessary conditions for the emergence of bureaucratic-authoritarianism, "supportive" conditions, or conditions of only marginal relevance.

The expansion of the foreign role in Latin American industrialization that has occurred in the past couple of decades may have taken place in part in response to internal changes in industry—i.e., due to the levels of technology, managerial expertise, and capital needed to sustain the growth of more advanced forms of industrial production. It is also the case, however, that international capital was seeking new outlets for investments in the Third World in the 1950's and 1960's. As a result of this external "pressure for new investment,"[30] this was a period of a major increase in foreign investment in a number of Latin American countries at a variety of levels of industrialization. It was also the period of the rise of multinational corporations and of an increasing internationalization of industrial production in Latin America. The complex implications of this externally initiated internationalization of production for domestic coalitional patterns and for the collapse of populism has been stressed from the very beginning of the populist/post-populist literature.[31] Within this book, the nature of the arguments about these implications are well illustrated in O'Donnell's chapter, which extends this line of analysis in order to gain new insights into the dilemmas that emerge once authoritarianism has been established. Indeed, O'Donnell views the central role in the dominant coalition of a highly internationalized bourgeoisie as such an important shared trait of these cases of contemporary authoritarianism that he has treated this trait as a defining characteristic of bureaucratic-authoritarianism.[32]

---

[30] Cardoso and Faletto, pp. 140-41.   [31] *Ibid.*, Chapter 6.

[32] I should stress that, to the extent that the goal of the analysis is to explain bureaucratic-authoritarianism, I find it problematic to include in the definition one of the traits that is also a principal explanation, since this makes it logically

   Another external factor that various authors have mentioned
is the reaction to the Cuban Revolution. In Chile, Brazil, and
Uruguay in the period prior to the rise of authoritarianism, a
radical populist or socialist movement attempted to move the
political system to the left, as a very different means of dealing
with the social and economic problems of these societies from
that which has subsequently been adopted by the military governments. These moves to the left were of course followed by a
sharp move to the right and the rise of authoritarianism. In explaining this sequence of events, as well as the patterns of
change followed in Argentina,[33] it is essential to consider the
demonstration effect of the Cuban Revolution. The success of
the Cuban Revolution unquestionably increased the plausibility
of attempting a move to the left in these countries. Similarly,
both in the military and in other sectors of society, the concern
with preventing a "second Cuba" greatly intensified the reaction
of the political right in each country to these attempted moves to
the left. The short- and medium-term consequences for neighboring countries of some of the most important revolutions in
modern history have been counterrevolutionary rather than
revolutionary. Correspondingly, the present period of military
rule in Latin America may involve in part the working out of the
counterrevolutionary implications of the Cuban Revolution.
   All of this of course occurred in a regional setting in which a
second Cuba was likewise unacceptable to the United States. The
United States reaction encouraged this move to the right in several ways, both through direct intervention, overt and covert,
and through strong U.S. support for the emergence of the new
technocratic, interventionist orientation within the Latin American military. U.S. intervention played an important role in part
during the period immediately prior to the emergence of authoritarianism. On a broader level, an increasingly thorough
documentation is now available of the sustained effort over

---

impossible to falsify the explanation by discovering cases of bureaucratic-
authoritarianism in which this explanatory factor is not present. Because
O'Donnell's chapter in this book is not concerned with explaining the rise of
bureaucratic-authoritarianism, this problem does not arise in connection with his
present analysis. However, this usage does once again point to the problem of
the confusion that may arise because different definitions are proposed in response to the particular concerns of each analyst.

[33] O'Donnell, *Modernization*, p. 72, refers to the impact of Cuba in Argentina.

many years by the U.S. government and by private groups in the United States to weaken the left in a number of Latin American countries.[34] This may have had an important effect on the relative strength of the political left and the political right in the context of these recent crises, and hence possibly on the outcome of these crises. An important priority in achieving a more complete explanation of the recent rise of authoritarianism is to assess more adequately the importance of this complex set of external and internal reactions and counter-reactions to Cuba—as well as to the larger context of the Cold War. Likewise, though these reactions and counter-reactions unquestionably became intertwined with the issues of economic development discussed above, it must be recognized that this reaction to international political forces may possibly represent an additional necessary condition for the rise of authoritarianism.[35]

Background Variables

Other explanatory factors that must be considered involve background variables that contribute to the understanding of major differences among countries in the political reaction to this larger context of crisis. One of the principal means employed to bring these explanations into focus has been to explore the contrasts between the experience of Argentina, Brazil, Chile, and Uruguay and that of cases such as Mexico, Peru, Venezuela, and Colombia where contemporary authoritarianism has emerged in a different form—or not at all.

Several chapters adopt this research strategy. Kaufman attempts to account for different patterns of change by adding Mexico to the comparison of Argentina, Brazil, Chile, and Uruguay in a comparative analysis of the interplay between

---

[34] For a valuable study that provides useful documentation of U.S. intervention over several decades in Chile and Brazil, at the same time that it uses elements of O'Donnell's analysis, see Kenneth P. Erickson and Patrick V. Peppe, "Dependent Capitalist Development, U.S. Foreign Policy, and Repression of the Working Class in Chile and Brazil," *Latin American Perspectives* 3, No. 1 (Winter 1976), 19-44.

[35] The importance of the international diffusion of urban protest and terrorism in the late 1960's that was mentioned above might be examined as well, though this would, in part, involve the explanation of slightly different outcomes—including the intensification of repression under an existing authoritarian regime in Brazil, a major episode of repression in Mexico, and the *collapse* of authoritarianism in Argentina.

growth rates, rates of inflation, and the strength of populist
political pressures. His analysis points to the importance of a
long tradition of intense popular sector pressures in Argentina,
Chile, and Uruguay as a background factor that appears to have
intensified the crises in these three cases. Hirschman suggests
that part of the explanation for the survival of competitive regimes in Colombia and Venezuela may be found in the way in
which the interplay between the entrepreneurial and reform
functions occurred in these countries and in their isolation from
the pattern of ideological escalation that was more central to the
political debate in other countries. He thus sees the different way
in which the interplay between these two functions occurred in
the Southern Cone countries and their greater centrality within
the hypothesized pattern of ideological escalation as an important feature of the larger political context in these countries
within which the political implications of the recent period of
crisis were worked out. Cotler explores the patterns of change
followed in the Southern Cone plus Brazil, as opposed to Peru
and Mexico. He traces out the consequences for the character of
populism of an earlier pattern of export growth that was in
greater measure nationally controlled, as in the southern countries, as opposed to one that was to a greater degree organized
around foreign controlled export enclaves, as in Peru and
Mexico. These enclave cases experienced a type of populism
characterized by a greater degree of nationalism and by a far
greater agrarian component. Cotler then describes the collapse
of populism in Peru and Mexico, and speculates about the possibility that they will converge with the more harshly repressive
patterns of the other countries. Thus, while other chapters point
to the possibility of the collapse of authoritarianism in the
Southern Cone, Cotler suggests that Peru and Mexico may be
about to enter a more harsh phase of authoritarianism.

In sorting through the similarities and differences among
these countries, it is interesting to speculate whether it would be
possible to identify a parsimonious set of variables that could
contribute to the understanding of all these cases together. A
useful step toward accounting for differences among countries
in the rise and initial consolidation of authoritarianism could be
taken by focusing on two background variables that have been
discussed in other chapters in this book and also in my discussion of populism above: (1) Major differences among countries

in the availability of economic resources, which has important implications for the "demands-performance gap" that is a central feature of the period of economic and political crisis prior to the emergence of authoritarianism; and (2) The political strength of the popular sector. A third, "intervening" variable derived from O'Donnell's original analysis may be added that will further contribute to tracing out the different patterns of change followed by the different countries: The degree of perception of threat on the part of established elites in the face of the crises and polarization that occurred in the 1960's and 1970's. Figure 1 tentatively presents an argument that can be made on the basis of these three variables. It should be emphasized that the classification of cases reflected in this figure is illustrative rather than definitive; that the implied causal argument remains incomplete and at the stage of hypothesis; and that the argument simply assumes, and is not intended to explain, the existence of the larger context of crises discussed above. The argument may be organized into the following steps:

1. *Availability of Diversified or Special Economic Resources and the Demands-Performance Gap.* The special role of oil revenues in Venezuela, and the pattern of moderately balanced growth in Colombia and Mexico, which is in part the *economic* legacy of the populism they experienced, appear to have led to more moderate gaps between demands and performance. The other four countries appear to have benefited from diversified or alternative resources to a considerably lesser degree, and therefore to have had more severe gaps between demands and performance.

2. *Political Strength of Popular Sector and Political and Economic Crisis.* The strength of the popular sector,[36] which is in part a *political* legacy of the type of populism experienced in each country, may have a crucial impact on whether the gap between demands and performance leads to severe crisis. In Venezuela, Colombia, and Brazil, the strength of the popular sector might be classified as moderate to low. The resulting level of political and economic crisis is more moderate, with differences among these cases perhaps being due at least in part to differences in economic resources. In Argentina, Chile, and Uruguay the

[36] The placement of this second variable after economic resources both in the text and in the figure is not intended to imply that one is the result of the other. They may vary independently.

FIGURE 1

HYPOTHETICAL INTERACTION AMONG
ECONOMIC RESOURCES, POPULAR SECTOR
STRENGTH, AND PERCEPTION OF THREAT

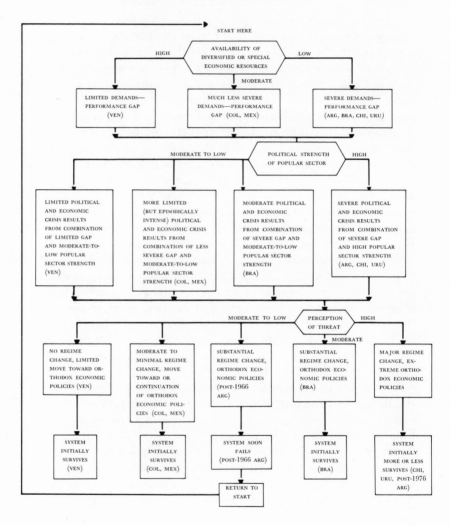

combination of a strong popular sector and more limited resources led to particularly severe political and economic crisis.

3. *Perception of Threat, Regime and Policy Change, and Initial Survival of System.* The degree to which technocrats, members of the business community, and the middle class perceive the political and economic crisis as a threat to the existing economic and political order has a crucial impact on the formation of a new, technocratically oriented coalition; on the degree of subsequent regime and policy change; and on the degree to which the new coalition is able to sustain this regime and policy change. In Venezuela, Colombia, and Mexico the moderate to low perception of threat has led to shifts in economic policy, tightening of repression and political control, and efforts to sustain some form of agreement among the principal political parties (or within the PRI, in the case of Mexico) to limit competition and polarization. So far, however, the military coups and more dramatic discontinuities of regime, coalition, and policy of the other countries have not occurred.

Argentina in 1966 is the other case of moderate to low perception of threat. In this instance the history of political and economic crisis was sufficiently intense that the military carried out a coup and initiated substantial regime change. The lower degree of immediate perception of threat and of elite cohesion, however, left the new coalition without sufficient unity to withstand extreme pressures from disaffected social sectors, particularly the powerful popular sector. In part because of this "mismatch" between underlying popular sector strength and immediate perception of threat, the new coalition soon disintegrated.

Although Argentina obviously changed profoundly between the mid-1960's and the 1970's, within the framework of the present discussion in a sense it has "returned to the start" (see Figure 1) after the failure of the post-1966 government. Once again Argentina faced the problem of availability of resources, combined with the issues that arise from having an extremely strong popular sector. In response to the severe political and economic crisis of the mid-1970's, however, Argentina followed a pattern more similar to Chile and Uruguay. A high perception of threat was followed by major regime change and a shift to extreme orthodox economic policies. Although in all three cases the coalition experienced severe internal and political strains, the high degree of perceived threat has made it possible so far to maintain the new systems.

Brazil may be roughly categorized as intermediate with regard to perception of threat. The trajectory of this case differs sharply from that of the post-1966 Argentina system in that the new dominant coalition faced a popular sector of only low to moderate strength, as opposed to the exceptionally strong popular sector in Argentina. The new Brazilian system therefore not only initially survived, but in many ways has been more or less "successful" in its own terms.

How does Peru fit into this analysis? While the eight countries considered in this book may be classified as the most industrially advanced nations of Latin America, Peru is the least industrially advanced nation within this group. In important ways, Peru is historically "behind" the other seven countries in the timing of a number of fundamental economic, social, and political transformations. Further, even if one recognizes the need to disaggregate the idea of populism and examine differences among cases, there is unquestionably a basic "agenda" of reforms associated with populism. Prior to the military coup of 1968, many of these reforms had not been carried out in Peru.

The existence of this inviting "reform space," combined with the lower level of urban and industrial development, helps to account for many of the important contrasts analyzed in detail by Cotler and noted by Cardoso and O'Donnell, between the institutional military government in Peru and those that appeared in Argentina, Brazil, Chile, and Uruguay.[37] Though Peru's history of "enclave" development and the tradition of militant unionism it produced have led to a contemporary pattern of vigorous labor protest, the intensity of conflict in the urban political system in this somewhat less industrial, relatively less urbanized, society was far more limited in the 1960's than in many of the other countries considered in this book. Rural conflict was intense, and it has been argued that a high degree of perception of threat in the face of this conflict contributed to the initial cohesiveness of the Peruvian military government.[38] Yet in con-

[37] In addition to the discussions of Peru in Cotler's and Cardoso's chapters in this volume, see O'Donnell, *Modernization*, pp. 111-12, where he presents a valuable assessment of the relation of the Peruvian case to his larger argument.

[38] See Alfred Stepan, *The State and Society: Peru in Comparative Perspective* (Princeton: Princeton University Press), Chapter 4.

trast to the situation in the more advanced nations to the south, there was a much easier way of dealing with this conflict, involving a policy innovation that had already played a central role in the development of other enclave cases such as Mexico and Venezuela: agrarian reform.

These multiple factors help to account for the initial reformist stance of the institutional military government that came to power in Peru in 1968. These factors are related to, but obviously go far beyond, the variables stressed in Figure 1 above. The full integration of these factors into the analysis requires a far larger model that brings together the explanations of populism and of bureaucratic-authoritarianism. The task of constructing this model is obviously well beyond the scope of this chapter.

The recent turn to the right and shift to orthodox economic policies in Peru have occurred in part in response to problems of populism already stressed in several analyses in this volume, particularly rising inflation, balance-of-payments problems, and massive increases in foreign indebtedness that have resulted from the spending and investment policies of the military government and from the serious deterioration of primary product export revenues. Though these orthodox policies have been implemented by a military-authoritarian regime that was already in power, the coherence and stability of these policies and of this regime is hardly assured. This may be due in part to the fact that by the mid-1970's the military government had already been seriously discredited, and in part due to two factors stressed in Figure 1 above—the important increase in the size and militancy of the urban popular sector that appears to have occurred in the nearly ten years since the military government first came to power, and the relatively low perception of internal threat at the time of the initial shift to orthodox economic policies in 1976. As a result, it may be the case that in Peru, as in the post-1966 period in Argentina, the military will soon be seeking ways of extricating itself from power.

This brief discussion of Peru suggests two reasons why attempts to extend the model to additional cases are instructive. First, they may provide fresh insights into these new cases. Second, they may stimulate the researcher to modify the original model in such a way that it not only accounts more adequately for new cases, but perhaps also accounts more adequately for the cases with reference to which the model was originally constructed.

After this extended discussion of alternative explanations of the rise of authoritarianism and its non-appearance in some countries, what conclusions can we reach about its causes? Considerable progress has been made in refining several major lines of argument and in gaining a deeper understanding of the larger context out of which authoritarianism emerged. However, these chapters do not reach rigorous conclusions regarding the necessary and sufficient conditions for its emergence, and are not intended to end the debate regarding what these conditions in fact are. On the contrary, our hope is to stimulate further critical examination of the origins of the new authoritarianism in Latin America.

The Evolution of Authoritarianism

The analysis of change under authoritarian rule has been a central concern since the earliest phase of the literature on the new authoritarianism, and the chapters in this book have taken important further steps in exploring this topic. A central theme that emerges, particularly in the analyses of Cardoso, Serra, and O'Donnell, is that though these governments employ high levels of coercion in dealing with opposition, though they presumably apply high levels of technical expertise in the selection of economic policies, and though they enjoy or potentially can enjoy massive financial support from international capitalism, their rule is characterized by major internal tensions and contradictions. These governments are in many ways fragile and vulnerable.

These tensions and contradictions in part involve economic issues, and, as Serra stresses, these authoritarian governments may be just as vulnerable to major failures and errors of economic policy as are more competitive systems. The tensions and contradictions also derive from fundamental political problems. The effective application of stabilization policies may sharply reduce the size of the coalition that supports the government as initial supporters of the coup in broad sectors of the middle class discover that they are not among the major beneficiaries of these policies. The extreme exclusionary character of these systems either undermines or involves the outright elimination of institutions of representation and of important political symbols that might otherwise serve to legitimate the state and to link it to society. The disappearance of the threat of "subversion" eliminates one of the important justifications for the repression that may be needed to maintain political control of the popular sector. There may be a sharp conflict between the internationalism and profit orientation of the elements of the bourgeoisie that are among the most crucial supporters of the coalition, and the nationalism and the tendency toward a distrust of the profit orientation on the part of important elements of the military. Many technocrats and other elements of the upper bourgeoisie are, in turn, made uncomfortable by their proximity within the dominant coalition to the elements of the military most closely identified with the repression.

The thesis of O'Donnell's analysis is that tensions and contradictions such as these will ultimately create enormous pressure that pushes these systems toward some form of political opening or democratization, and the conclusions to Cardoso's and Hirschman's chapters, in somewhat different ways, point in the same direction. It is of course possible that additional countries will succumb to repressive military rule. Colombia periodically appears to be a candidate, and Cotler's analysis points to the possibility of a major intensification of repression in Peru and Mexico. Likewise, the possibility of war in the Southern Cone poses grave risks for any effort to predict future patterns of change—and could represent the ultimate, pathetic response of these governments to the problem of evoking symbols of identification with the state, such as nationalism. Yet there is substantial ground for believing that at least some of the present authoritarian governments in Latin America will be replaced in the coming years by more competitive regimes. Experimentation with different types of controlled elections and with the partial restoration of the party system have already played, or will play, an important role in attempts to legitimate authoritarian rule. In the longer run, this experimentation could lead to attempts to find a new political formula that could eventually lead to the restoration of some form of democracy.

To the extent that these changes occur, they will open interesting new avenues for research on Latin American politics.[39] On

[39] Philippe C. Schmitter and Guillermo O'Donnell are currently coordinating

one level, what will be called for will be intensive, detailed analyses of these attempted restorations as they take place in the coming years. On another level, it will be essential to consider the possibility that such a restoration of democracy would be part of a long-term cycle of authoritarianism and democracy within the region and that attempts to understand the prospects for democratization should be linked to attempts to explain this long-term cycle of change. This involves several different lines of inquiry.

First, since the achievement of some form of democratization in Latin America in the coming decade in important measure involves resolving the tensions and problems that contributed to the recent rise of authoritarianism, the understanding of this coming period of democratization must be built on the best possible understanding of the causes of these earlier tensions, as well as the reasons why they were less intense in some countries and in some cases did not lead to authoritarianism. Hence, further progress in advancing the understanding of the current era of authoritarianism remains a central priority.

Second, the perspective of analyzing the current prospects for democratization within the framework of a long-term cycle of political change suggests certain historical comparisons which may contribute to understanding these future patterns of change. For instance, an obvious point of comparison would be with the period of authoritarianism in the late 1940's and early 1950's in several countries and the subsequent period of democratization in the mid- to late-1950's. Such a comparison would provide a basis for testing the argument about long-term causal patterns such as that suggested by the hypothesis that the way in which democracy is restored at one point in time affects the likelihood of the rise of authoritarianism at a subsequent point, which in turn may shape opportunities for democratization at a still later point in time. The experience of Colombia and Venezuela in the 1940's and 1950's of extreme polarization; followed by repressive military rule; followed in turn by a restoration of a type of democracy based on a formal or informal pact among political parties to limit future competition and polarization would provide an interesting starting point for such an analysis. The partially parallel experience of Peru in this same

a series of studies supported by Latin American Program of the Woodrow Wilson International Center for Scholars in Washington, D.C. that will play an important role in addressing these topics.

period, and the extremely different resolution of similar issues in Argentina, would provide other useful points of comparison.

Third, this perspective encourages one to step back and ask the more generic question of why this cycle has occurred. On this level, it is possible that the rise and collapse of authoritarian regimes have, in part, the same explanation. Douglas Chalmers' analysis of the "politicized state" in Latin America, Charles Anderson's analysis of the "tentativeness" of Latin American political institutions, and Hirschman's discussion in this book of the problems of legitimation that arise when the accumulation function is in important measure in foreign hands appear to be of great relevance here.[40] They offer a starting point for exploring a pattern of greater fragility of political institutions that increases the likelihood that in the context of crisis regime change will occur—whether it be from democratic to authoritarian or from authoritarian to democratic. Such a perspective would in no sense eclipse the kinds of concerns raised in this book—it would serve instead as an important supplement to them.

EXTENDING THE ANALYSIS TO OTHER REGIONS

Kurth's chapter, which introduces ideas derived from the bureaucratic-authoritarian model into a discussion of European development, represents quite a different approach to extending the scope of the analysis. Attempts to extend the analysis to other regions, much like the extension of the analysis to additional Latin American countries, can contribute to several useful goals. Such attempts provide new explanations for patterns of industrial and political change in these other regions. They may stimulate attempts to link models developed with reference to Latin America to other theories of industrial and political change. They encourage scholars to assess the generality of the patterns found in Latin America, which may in turn aid Latin American specialists in identifying more explicitly and generically the contextual characteristics responsible for the political patterns that have emerged within Latin America. Finally, attempts to elaborate the model within the traditions of scholarship on other regions may suggest to Latin American specialists new approaches to analyzing their own region.

[40] Chalmers, "The Politicized State"; Charles W. Anderson, *Politics and Economic Change in Latin America: The Governing of Restless Nations* (Princeton: D. Van Nostrand Co., 1967); and Hirschman, pp. 90-92 in this book.

These opportunities to gain new insights and improve theory are well illustrated in Kurth's chapter. The approach to analyzing the politics of industrialization that he draws in part from research on Latin America appears to provide an interesting new perspective on political change in Europe. His effort to explore further the links between the analysis of different sectors of industry that is crucial to the bureaucratic-authoritarian model and arguments developed in research on Europe regarding the timing of industrialization points to important ways in which the theoretical scope of the Latin American model can be enlarged. Kurth's analysis of a series of different historical and regional patterns of industrialization brings into sharper focus the characteristics of the Latin American setting that have contributed to recent patterns of national political evolution in Latin America, leading him to interesting speculations about future patterns of change in such countries as Brazil. Finally, Kurth's sensitivity to the continuous interplay among four different levels of analysis—involving domestic political factors, domestic economic factors, international political and military relations, and international economic relations—reflects an analytic perspective that merits imitation in research on Latin America. Though the other authors in this volume frequently note the impact of international political, military, and economic relations on patterns of change within Latin American countries, none of them attempts as multi-faceted an analysis of the continuous interaction among these different factors as is presented in Kurth's chapter.

Application of the bureaucratic-authoritarian model to other Third World regions may also prove fruitful. One recent study has explicitly applied the model to South Korea.[41] Extension of the analysis to a region such as Africa could provide further evidence to support the argument that the model should be less closely tied to phases of industrialization and more oriented around changes in the international economic system. Some of the important features of the political economy of many African countries may simply represent variations within the category of "oligarchic systems" described in the Latin American literature. These African countries are generally pre-industrial, oriented around agricultural and mineral exports, with relatively low

[41] Sungjoo Han, "Power, Dependency, and Representation in South Korea" (paper presented at the 1977 annual meeting of the American Political Science Association, Washington, D.C.).

levels of popular sector activation. But the status of being extremely "late" developers may produce new and distinctive constellations of regime, coalition, and policy. Many of these countries seem to be experiencing complex problems in their relationships with the international capitalist system, problems that have important traits in common with those experienced in the more advanced countries of Latin America. Many are experiencing severe problems of foreign indebtedness, balance of payments, and inflation, as well as restrictions on domestic economic policy imposed by international lending agencies, that would sound familiar to students of the advanced Latin American countries. Extensions of the argument to cases such as these could provide a valuable opportunity to explore the possibility that the pervasive impact of the contemporary international economic system may affect the relatively non-industrial countries of Africa and the more industrially advanced countries of Latin America in ways that are more similar than one might expect on the basis of the bureaucratic-authoritarian model.

In addition to the contribution of such extensions of the analysis to social science theory, their practical implications should be stressed as well. At several points it has been emphasized that the need to analyze bureaucratic-authoritarianism derives in part from the possibility that a better understanding of the economic, social, and political problems that gave rise to this authoritarianism can contribute to the discovery of more humane solutions to these same problems. Within the Latin American setting, this involves in part the effort in a number of countries to bring to an end the current era of harsh authoritarianism. It also involves a concern with stimulating a process of political learning that may make it easier for additional countries—for instance, Colombia—to avoid these forms of authoritarianism.

Scholars and political leaders from other Third World regions often look with concern at recent events in the southern countries of South America, out of an awareness that these events may have important implications for the future evolution of their own nations. These scholars and political leaders certainly share with the authors in this book the hope that an understanding of bureaucratic-authoritarianism can contribute to a further process of political learning that may make it easier for still other countries to avoid the forms of political oppression that have recently emerged in Latin America.

Glossary

The chapters in this book are written in such a way that the meaning of the terms employed should at most points be evident from the context. However, because a few terms may be unfamiliar to some readers, and because there are a few differences in usage among authors, it is appropriate to present here for some of the most important terms the definitions employed in this book.

Authoritarianism: Following Linz, one may view authoritarianism as a type of political regime that is distinct from both democracy and totalitarianism and that in certain respects, particularly with regard to the degree of limitation of political pluralism, is an intermediate type. Linz defines authoritarian regimes as "political systems with limited, not responsible, political pluralism; without elaborate and guiding ideology (but with distinctive mentalities); without intensive or extensive political mobilization (except at some points in their development); and in which a leader (or occasionally a small group) exercises power within formally ill-defined limits but actually quite predictable ones."[1]

Bureaucratic-Authoritarianism: As a first approximation, this may be thought of as a type of authoritarianism characterized by a self-avowedly technocratic, bureaucratic, non-personalistic approach to policy making and problem solving. Beyond this, there is some variation among the authors in this book in the use of the term. O'Donnell's original usage, based on a large number of defining characteristics that involve issues of regime, coalition, and policy, is summarized in Chapter 1, p. 24. His more recent, slightly modified, definition is presented in Chapter 7, pages 291-94. His definition embraces contemporary Argentina, Brazil, Chile and Uruguay, as well as Argentina from 1966 to 1973. Though in earlier writings he has called attention to important commonalities between

[1] Juan J. Linz, "An Authoritarian Regime: Spain," in Erik Allardt and Yrjo Littunen, eds., *Cleavages, Ideologies, and Party Systems* (Helsinki: Academic Bookstore, 1964).

these cases and contemporary Mexico, he does not in his present analysis define Mexico as bureaucratic-authoritarian.

Cardoso (Chapter 2, pp. 34-38) advocates a much more restricted usage that refers only to the type of political regime, and he limits it to regimes characterized by institutional military rule. He thereby explicitly excludes Mexico from this category, but includes Peru in the post-1968 period within it. Kaufman (Chapter 5, pp. 187-90) also uses the term to refer to the type of political regime, and his chapter has likewise not included Mexico. See also Collier's discussion of this concept in Chapter 9, pp. 364-71.

Capital Goods: Machinery and equipment used in industrial production.

Corporatism: As used in this volume (there are important, alternative definitions), this is a pattern of relationships between the state and interest groups that involves such elements as state structuring of representation that produces a system of officially sanctioned, noncompetitive interest associations organized into legally prescribed functional groupings; state subsidy of these associations; and direct state control over their leadership, demand-making, and internal governance.

Deepening of Industrialization: Expansion of industrial production beyond consumer goods to include the intermediate and capital goods used in the production process. This is also referred to as the "vertical" integration of production through "backward linkages" from consumer goods production to the production of the intermediate and capital goods employed in consumer goods production.

Easy Phase of Import Substitution: The rapid expansion of consumer goods production which may occur when this production is aimed at satisfying an already existing domestic market that is newly protected by the imposition of tariffs or import controls and/or by the collapse of foreign trade.

Exhaustion of (Easy Phase of) Import Substitution: Completion of the initial phase of industrial expansion oriented toward satisfying the domestic market for consumer goods previously supplied by imported products. See the discussions presented by Hirschman (Chapter 3, pp. 70 ff.) and Serra (Chapter 5, pp. 118 ff.).

Exclusion (of the Popular Sector): "Consistent governmental refusal to meet the political demands made by the leaders of [the popular] sector . . . [and denial] to this sector and its leaders [of] access to positions of political power from where they can have direct influence on national policy decisions. . . . The concept of 'exclusion' . . . assumes previous 'presence' in the national political arena: an excluded sector is a politically activated sector."[2] This is also discussed by O'Donnell in Chapter 7, pp. 292-93. See also Incorporation.

Import-Substituting Industrialization: Expansion of industrial production to supply a domestic market previously supplied by imported goods. See also Easy Phase of Import Substitution.

Incorporation (of the Popular Sector): Deliberate government effort to activate the popular sector and to allow it some voice in national politics. This also includes cases in which the government, without deliberate efforts at either exclusion or incorporation, adapts itself to the existing levels of political activation and the given set of political actors.[3] See also "Exclusion."

Intermediate goods: Inputs used in industrial production, such as fuels, metals, and petrochemicals.

Internationalization of Production: This transition, which is associated with the rise of multinational corporations, involves: 1. An increasing linkage or fusion of "local" and "foreign" factors of production—i.e., investment, credit, technology, management, etc.; and 2. An increasing linkage or fusion in the relations of production through growing formal and informal association of the domestic and international bourgeoisie. Also referred to as the Transnationalization of Production.

Monetarist Economic Policies: See Orthodox Economic Policies.

Normalization Policies: See Orthodox Economic Policies.

Orthodox Economic Policies: Policies that emphasize market mechanisms through such measures as the devaluation of the currency, adoption of floating exchange rates, tariff reduction,

---

[2] Guillermo O'Donnell, *Modernization and Bureaucratic-Authoritarianism: Studies in South American Politics* (Institute of International Studies, University of California, Berkeley, Politics of Modernization Series No. 9, 1973), p. 55.

[3] *Loc. cit.*

abolition of import and price controls, and increases in the charges for public services to reflect their cost. However, strict wage controls are often introduced at the same time that these other controls are abolished. Also referred to as Monetarist Economic Policies, Normalization Policies, and Stabilization Policies.

Political System: In Chapter 1, following O'Donnell's usage in *Modernization and Bureaucratic-Authoritarianism* (which refers to "bureaucratic-authoritarian *political systems*"), Collier uses this term to refer to the overall configuration of regime, dominant coalition, and public policy that characterizes a national polity. More recently, O'Donnell has instead employed the expression "bureaucratic-authoritarian *state*" (see State).

Popular Sector: The urban and rural lower class and lower middle class.

Populism: In O'Donnell's original analysis, and in the populist/post-populist literature more generally (see Chapter 1, pp. 19-20), this term is commonly used to refer to a type of political system (or state) characterized by a number of traits, including the following: (1) It is based on a multi-class coalition of urban-industrial interests, including industrial elites and the urban popular sector; (2) It is politically "incorporating" vis-à-vis the urban (and sometimes also rural) popular sector; and (3) It promotes the initial phase of import-substituting industrialization oriented around consumer goods. Populism is commonly seen as the type of political system that emerges with the demise of the earlier oligarchic system and that is subsequently superseded by bureaucratic-authoritarianism. See the extended analysis of populism in Cotler's chapter; in Chapter 5, pp. 196-203; and in Chapter 9, pp. 371-77.

Primary Products: Products derived from agriculture, forestry, or mining. These contrast with the products of the secondary sector (manufacturing and industry) and the tertiary sector (services).

Producers' Goods: See Capital Goods.

Regime: The formal and informal structure of governmental roles and processes. The regime thus includes such things as the method of selection of the government (election, coup, selection process within the military, etc.), formal and informal mechanisms of representation, and patterns of repression. The regime is typically distinguished from the particular incumbents who occupy governmental roles, the political coalition that supports these incumbents, and the public policies they adopt (except of course policies that define or transform the regime itself).

Stabilization Policies: See Orthodox Economic Policies.

State: Cardoso uses this term to mean "the basic 'pact of domination' that exists among social classes or fractions of dominant classes and the norms which guarantee their dominance over the subordinate strata" (Chapter 2, p. 38). O'Donnell employs a similar usage, but stresses that the term must be understood on two levels. On an analytic level, it is the "political aspect of the social relations of domination" (Chapter 7, p. 287). It "supports and organizes these relations of domination . . ." (p. 287). On a concrete level, it consists of a set of institutions and the laws which carry out this function (p. 287).

At certain points in other chapters, one occasionally finds a usage in which the state consists of the institutional structure, the incumbents within this structure, and body of law that make up the public sector. It thus includes the government (in the sense of the head of state and the immediate political leadership that surrounds the head of state), the public bureaucracy, the legislature, the judiciary, public and semi-public corporations, and the legal system. See also Chapter 5, pp. 249-50 and Chapter 9, pp. 370-71.

Technocrats: Individuals with a high level of specialized academic training which serves as a principal criterion on the basis of which they are selected to occupy key decision-making or advisory roles in large, complex organizations—both public and private.

Transnationalization of Production: See Internationalization of Production.

Upper Bourgeoisie: The managerial, professional, and ownership elite that exercises control over economic production or is closely associated with the control of production.

Bibliography

This bibliography provides an overview of the larger literature of which the chapters in this book form a part. It includes the sources cited in the individual chapters and a limited number of additional references. The sources on Latin America are first presented under seven subject headings: authoritarianism, industrialization and economic development, international political and economic context, populism, the military, insurgency and repression, and political parties. A partially overlapping set of sources grouped by country is then presented for Argentina, Brazil, Chile, Colombia, Mexico, Peru, Uruguay, and Venezuela. Finally, there is a listing of the sources on European industrialization and development and of the other general sources that are cited in this book. Each section of the bibliography includes a list of cross-references to other sections.

Since this edition of the book is intended primarily for a North American audience, the emphasis is on sources available in the United States. If a book or article has been published both in Spanish or Portuguese and in English, the English version is usually cited. Needless to say, in covering both the general literature and references on individual countries within the framework of a relatively brief bibliography, it was necessary to exclude many excellent studies.

I. Sources on Latin America: Subject Listing

A. *Authoritarianism*

(1) Anderson, Charles W. *Politics and Economic Change in Latin America.* Princeton: Van Nostrand Co., 1967.

(2) Brodersohn, Mario S. "Sobre 'modernización y autoritarismo' y el estancamiento inflacionario argentino." *Desarrollo Económico* 13, No. 51 (October/December, 1973), pp. 591-605.

(3) Cardoso, Fernando Henrique and Enzo Faletto. *Dependencia y desarrollo en América Latina.* Mexico City: Siglo Veintiuno Editores, 1969. Recently published in English as

406　　　　　　　　　　　*Bibliography*

Dependency and Development in Latin America. Berkeley and Los Angeles: University of California Press, 1978.

(4) ———. *Ideologías de la burguesía industrial en sociedades dependientes (Argentina y Brasil).* Mexico City: Siglo Veintiuno Editores, 1971.

(5) ———. *Estado y sociedad en América Latina.* Buenos Aires: Ediciones Nueva Visión, 1972.

(6) ———. "Associated-Dependent Development: Theoretical and Practical Implications." In Alfred Stepan, ed., *Authoritarian Brazil: Origins, Policies and Future.* New Haven: Yale University Press, 1973.

(7) ———. "Estadização e autoritarismo esclarecido: Tendencias e limites." Unpublished paper, São Paulo, 1975.

(8) ———. *Autoritarismo e Democratização.* Rio de Janeiro: Editora Paz e Terra, 1975.

(9) Chalmers, Douglas A. "The Politicized State in Latin America." In James M. Malloy, ed., *Authoritarianism and Corporatism in Latin America.* Pittsburgh: University of Pittsburgh Press, 1977.

(10) Collier, David and Ruth Berins Collier. "Who Does What, to Whom, and How: Toward a Comparative Analysis of Latin American Corporatism." In James M. Malloy, ed., *Authoritarianism and Corporatism in Latin America.* Pittsburgh: University of Pittsburgh Press, 1977.

(11) Collier, Ruth Berins. "Popular Sector Incorporation and Regime Evolution in Brazil and Mexico." Paper presented at the Conference on Brazil and Mexico, Center for Inter-American Relations, New York, 1978.

(12) ——— and David Collier. "Inducements Versus Constraints: Disaggregating Corporatism." *The American Political Science Review* 73, No. 4 (December 1979), forthcoming.

(13) Dos Santos, Theotonio. *Socialismo o fascismo: Dilema Latinoamericano.* Santiago: Prensa Latinoamericana (2nd edition), 1972.

(14) Germani, Gino. *Authoritarianism, National Populism, and Fascism.* New Brunswick, N.J.: Transaction Books, 1977.

(15) Jaguaribe, Helio. *Crisis y alternativas de América Latina.* Buenos Aires: Editorial Paidós, 1972.

(16) Kaufman, Robert R. *Transitions to Stable Authoritarian-Corporate Regimes: The Chilean Case?* Sage Professional

Papers, Comparative Politics Series 1, No. 01-060, 1976.

(17) ———. "Notes on the Definition, Genesis, and Consolidation of Bureaucratic-Authoritarian Regimes." Unpublished paper, Department of Political Science, Douglass College, New Brunswick, N.J., 1975.

(18) ———. "Mexico and Latin American Authoritarianism." In José Luis Reyna and Richard S. Weinert, eds., *Authoritarianism in Mexico*. Philadelphia: Institute for the Study of Human Issues, 1977.

(19) Kling, Merle, "Toward a Theory of Power and Political Instability in Latin America." In James Petras and Maurice Zeitlin, eds., *Latin America: Reform or Revolution?* Greenwich, Conn.: Fawcett World Library, 1968.

(20) Linz, Juan J. "The Future of an Authoritarian Situation or the Institutionalization of an Authoritarian Regime: The Case of Brazil." In Alfred Stepan, ed., *Authoritarian Brazil: Origins, Policies, and Future*. New Haven: Yale University Press, 1973.

(21) ——— and Alfred Stepan, eds. *The Breakdown of Democratic Regimes: Latin America*. Baltimore: The Johns Hopkins University Press, 1978.

(22) Malloy, James M. "Authoritarianism and Corporatism in Latin America: The Modal Pattern." In James M. Malloy, ed., *Authoritarianism and Corporatism in Latin America*. Pittsburgh: University of Pittsburgh Press, 1977.

(23) ———, ed. *Authoritarianism and Corporatism in Latin America*. Pittsburgh: University of Pittsburgh Press, 1977.

(24) Morse, Richard M. "The Heritage of Latin America." In Louis Hartz, *The Founding of New Societies*. New York: Harcourt, Brace, & World, Inc., 1964.

(25) O'Donnell, Guillermo A. *Modernization and Bureaucratic-Authoritarianism: Studies in South American Politics*. Berkeley: Institute of International Studies, University of California, 1973.

(26) ———. "Reflections on the Patterns of Change in the Bureaucratic-Authoritarian State." *Latin American Research Review* 12, No. 1 (Winter 1978), pp. 3-38. Also published in Spanish as "Reflexiones sobre las tenden-

cias generales de cambio en el estado burocrático-autoritario." Documento CEDES/G.E. CLACSO No. 1, Centro de Estudios de Estado y Sociedad, Buenos Aires, 1975.

(27) ————. "Corporatism and the Question of the State." In James M. Malloy, ed., *Authoritarianism and Corporatism in Latin America.* Pittsburgh: University of Pittsburgh Press, 1977. Also published in Spanish as "Sobre el 'corporativismo' y la cuestión de Estado." Documento CEDES/G.E. CLACSO No. 2, Centro de Estudios de Estado y Sociedad, Buenos Aires, 1976.

(28) ————. "Apuntes para una teoría del Estado." Documento CEDES/G.E. CLACSO No. 9, Centro de Estudios de Estado y Sociedad, Buenos Aires, 1977.

(29) Petras, James F. "L'Amerique Latine, Banc d'Essai d'un Nouveau Totalitarisme." *Le Monde Diplomatique* (Paris) April, 1977.

(30) Purcell, Susan Kaufman. *The Mexican Profit-Sharing Decision: Politics in an Authoritarian Regime.* Berkeley and Los Angeles: University of California Press, 1975.

(31) Reyna, José Luis and Richard S. Weinert, eds. *Authoritarianism in Mexico.* Philadelphia: Institute for the Study of Human Issues, 1977.

(32) Schmitter, Philippe C. *Interest Conflict and Political Change in Brazil.* Stanford: Stanford University Press, 1971.

(33) ————. "Paths to Political Development in Latin America." In Douglas A. Chalmers, ed., *Changing Latin America: New Interpretations of its Politics and Society.* New York: The Academy of Political Science, Columbia University, 1972.

(34) ————. "Still the Century of Corporatism." *The Review of Politics* 36, No. 1 (January 1974), pp. 85-121.

(35) Stavenhagen, Rodolfo. "The Future of Latin America: Between Underdevelopment and Revolution." *Latin American Perspectives* 1, No. 1 (Spring 1974), pp. 124-49.

(36) Stepan, Alfred. *The State and Society: Peru in Comparative Perspective.* Princeton: Princeton University Press, 1978.

(37) Véliz, Claudio. *The Centralist Tradition of Latin America.* Princeton: Princeton University Press, 1979.

(38) Wiarda, Howard J. "Toward a Framework for the Study of Political Change in the Iberic-Latin Tradition: The

Corporative Model." *World Politics* 25, No. 2 (January 1973), pp. 206-35.

See also 170, 183, 204, 209, 220, 230, 251, 261, 263, 298, 318, 353, 421, 470, 474, 475, 476.

B. *Industrialization and Economic Development*

(39) Anderson, Charles W. "Political Factors in Latin American Economic Development." *Journal of International Affairs* 20, No. 2 (1966), pp. 235-53.

(40) Ayza, Juan, Gerard Fichet and Norberto Gonzales. *América Latina: Integración económica y sustitución de importaciones*. México, D.F.: ECLA, Fondo de Cultura Económica, 1976.

(41) Baer, Werner. "Import Substitution and Industrialization in Latin America: Experiences and Interpretations." *Latin American Research Review* 7, No. 1 (Spring 1972), pp. 95-122.

(42) ———. "The Economics of Prebisch and ECLA." *Economic Development and Cultural Change* 10, No. 2 (January 1972), pp. 169-82.

(43) Balassa, Bela et al. *The Structure of Protection in Developing Countries*. Baltimore: The Johns Hopkins University Press, 1971.

(44) Cardoso, Fernando Henrique and José Luis Reyna. "Industrialization, Occupational Structure, and Social Stratification in Latin America." In Cole Blasier, ed., *Constructive Change in Latin America*. Pittsburgh: University of Pittsburgh Press, 1968.

(45) ———. "The Industrial Elite." In Seymour Martin Lipset and Aldo Solari, eds., *Elites in Latin America*. New York: Oxford University Press, 1967.

(46) Corden, Max. "The Structure of a Tariff System and the Effective Protection Rate." *Journal of Political Economy* 74, No. 3 (June 1966), pp. 221-37.

(47) Diamand, Marcelo. *Doctrinas económicas: Desarrollo e independencia*. Buenos Aires: Editorial Paidós, 1973.

(48) Díaz-Alejandro, Carlos F. "On the Import Intensity of Import Substitution." *Kyklos* 18, No. 3 (1965), pp. 495-509.

(49) Dos Santos, Theotonio. "The Changing Structure of

Foreign Investments in Latin America." In James Petras and Maurice Zeitlin, eds., *Latin America: Reform or Revolution?* Greenwich, Conn.: Fawcett Publications, 1968.

(50) Economic Commission for Latin America. *Economic Survey of Latin America* (Published annually since 1948). New York: United Nations.

(51) ————. *The Economic Development of Latin America and its Principal Problems.* Lake Success, New York: United Nations, 1950.

(52) ————. *El proceso de industralización en América Latina.* New York: United Nations, 1965.

(53) ————. *El proceso de industrialización en América Latina en los primeros años del segundo decenio para el desarrollo.* Santiago, 1971.

(54) ————. "La industrialización latinoamericana en los años setenta." *Cuadernos de la CEPAL*, 1975.

(55) ————. *Las exportaciones de manufacturas en América Latina: Informaciones estadísticas y algunas consideraciones generales.* Santiago: United Nations (E/CEPAL/L.128: 22 de enero de 1976), 1976.

(56) ————. "En torno a las ideas de la CEPAL: Desarrollo, industrialización, y comercio externo." *Cuadernos de la CEPAL*, 1977.

(57) ————. "En torno a las ideas de la CEPAL: Problemas de la industrialización en América Latina." *Cuadernos de la CEPAL*, 1977.

(58) Epstein, Edward C. "Anti-Inflation Policies in Argentina and Chile or Who Pays the Cost." *Comparative Political Studies* 11, No. 2 (July 1978), pp. 211-30.

(59) Felix, David. "Monetarists, Structuralists, and Import-Substituting Industrialization: A Critical Approach." *Studies in Comparative International Development* 1, No. 10 (1965).

(60) ————. "Technological Dualism in Late Industrializers." *Journal of Economic History* 34, No. 1 (March 1974), pp. 194-238.

(61) Fishlow, Albert. "Development Policy: Some Lessons from the Past." Paper presented at the Annual Meeting of the American Economic Association, New York, 1977.

(62) Frank, Andre Gunder. *Lumpenbourgeoisie: Lumpendevelopment.* New York: Monthly Review Press, 1972.

(63) ———. "Latinoamérica: Subdesarrollo capitalista o revolución socialista." *Pensamiento Crítico* No. 13 (February 1968), pp. 3-41.

(64) Furtado, Celso. *Economic Development of Latin America.* New York: Cambridge University Press, First edition, 1970. Second edition, 1976.

(65) Glade, William P. *The Latin American Economies: A Study of Their Institutional Evolution.* New York: American Book Company, 1969.

(66) Grunwald, Joseph. "Some Reflections on Latin American Industrialization Policies." *Journal of Political Economy* 78, No. 4 (August 1970), pp. 826-56.

(67) Hirschman, Albert O. *The Strategy of Economic Development.* New Haven: Yale University Press, 1958.

(68) ———. *Latin American Issues: Essays and Comments.* New York: The Twentieth Century Fund, 1961.

(69) ———. *Journeys Toward Progress: Studies of Economic Policy-Making in Latin America.* New York: Anchor Books, 1965.

(70) ———. "The Political Economy of Import-Substituting Industrialization in Latin America." *Quarterly Journal of Economics* 82, No. 1 (February 1968), pp. 2-32.

(71) ———. "Ideologies of Economic Development in Latin America." In Albert Hirschman, ed., *A Bias for Hope.* New Haven: Yale University Press, 1971.

(72) ———, ed. *A Bias for Hope: Essays on Development and Latin America.* New Haven: Yale University Press, 1971.

(73) ———. "The Changing Tolerance for Income Inequality in the Course of Economic Development." *Quarterly Journal of Economics* 87, No. 4 (November 1973), pp. 543-66.

(74) ———. "A Generalized Linkage Approach to Development, with Special Reference to Staples." *Economic Development and Cultural Change* 25, Supplement: Essays in Honor of Bert F. Hoselitz (1977), pp. 67-98.

(75) ———. "The Social and Political Matrix of Inflation: Elaborations of the Latin American Experience." Mimeographed. Princeton: Institute for Advanced Study, 1978.

(76) Iglesias, Enrique V. "Situation and Prospects of the Latin American Economy in 1975." *CEPAL Review*, First semester 1976, pp. 211-30.

(77) Jaguaribe, Helio. "Dependencia y autonomía en América Latina." *Panorama Económico* No. 243 (April 1969).

(78) Johnson, Harry G. *Economic Policies Toward Less Developed Countries*. Washington, D.C.: Brookings Institution, 1967.

(79) Kahl, Joseph A., ed. *La industrialización en América Latina*. México, D.F.: Fondo de Cultura Económica, 1965.

(80) Kenworthy, Eldon. "Argentina: The Politics of Late Industrialization." *Foreign Affairs* 47, No. 3 (April 1967), pp. 465-76.

(81) King, Timothy, *Mexico: Industrialization and Trade Policies since 1940*. New York: Oxford University Press, 1970.

(82) Leal Buitrago, Francisco. "Desarrollo, subdesarrollo y ciencias sociales." In F. Leal Buitrago et al., *El agro en el desarrollo colombiano*. Bogotá: Punta de Lanza, 1977.

(83) Leiserson, Alcira. *Notes on the Process of Industrialization in Argentina, Chile, and Peru*. Politics of Modernization Series, No. 3. Berkeley: Institute of International Studies, University of California, 1966.

(84) Little, Ian, Tibor Scitovsky, and Maurice Scott. *Industry and Trade in some Developing Countries*. New York: Oxford University Press, 1970.

(85) Marini, Rui M. *Subdesarrollo y revolución*. Mexico City: Siglo Veintiuno Editores, 1969.

(86) ———. *Dialéctica de la dependencia*. Mexico City: Nueva Era, 1973.

(87) Morley, Samuel and Gordon W. Smith. "On the Measurement of Import Substitution." *American Economic Review* 60, No. 4 (September 1970), pp. 728-35.

(88) Schydlowsky, Daniel M. "Industrialization and Growth." In Luigi R. Einaudi, ed., *Beyond Cuba: Latin America Takes Charge of Its Future*. New York: Crane, Russak and Co., 1974.

(89) ———. "Latin American Trade Policies in the Seventies: A Prospective Appraisal." *Quarterly Journal of Economics* 86, No. 2 (May 1972), pp. 263-89.

(90) Serra, José. "El estilo reciente de desarrollo de América

Latina—notas introductorias." *Trimestre Económico* (no. 174) Vol. 44, No. 2 (April-June 1977), pp. 427-54.

(91) —— and Fernando Henrique Cardoso. "As desventuras da dialética da dependencia." Mimeographed. Princeton: Institute for Advanced Study, 1978.

(92) Sheahan, John. "Market-Oriented Economic Policies and Political Repression in Latin America." *Economic Development and Cultural Change*, forthcoming.

(93) Skidmore, Thomas E. "The Politics of Economic Stabilization in Post War Latin America." In James M. Malloy, ed., *Authoritarianism and Corporatism in Latin America*. Pittsburgh: University of Pittsburgh Press, 1977.

(94) Weaver, Frederick S. *The Industrialization of South America*. New York: Urizon Press, forthcoming.

(95) Wynia, Gary W. *The Politics of Latin American Development*. Cambridge: Cambridge University Press, 1978.

See also 2, 142, 190, 195, 196, 197, 201, 212, 214, 215, 216, 217, 218, 219, 221, 226, 228, 229, 234, 235, 236, 237, 241, 242, 245, 246, 247, 248, 253, 258, 259, 260, 265, 267, 268, 269, 270, 272, 276, 277, 278, 285, 286, 287, 290, 296, 301, 303, 307, 308, 310, 320, 323, 325, 327, 329, 331, 335, 347, 350, 358, 359, 371.

C. International Political and Economic Context

(96) Anderson, Charles W. "The Changing International Environment of Development and Latin America in the 1970s." *Inter-American Economic Affairs* 24, No. 2 (Fall 1970), pp. 65-87.

(97) Apter, David E. and Louis Wolf Goodman, eds. *The Multinational Corporation and Social Change*. New York: Praeger Publishers, 1976.

(98) Atkins, G. Pope. *Latin America in the International Political System*. New York: The Free Press, 1977.

(99) Barnet, Richard J. and Ronald E. Mueller. *Global Reach: The Power of the Multinational Corporations*. New York: Simon and Schuster, 1974.

(100) Bath, C. Richard and Dilmus D. James. "Dependency Analysis of Latin America." *Latin American Research Review* 11, No. 3 (1976), pp. 3-54.

(101) Bergsten, C. Fred and Thomas Horst. *American Multinationals and American Interests.* Washington, D.C.: Brookings Institution, 1978.

(102) ————. *The Dilemmas of the Dollar: The Economics and Politics of the United States International Policy.* New York: New York University Press, 1975.

(103) Blasier, Cole. *The Hovering Giant: U.S. Responses to Revolutionary Change in Latin America.* Pittsburgh: University of Pittsburgh Press, 1976.

(104) Caporaso, James A., ed. *Dependence and Dependency in the Global System.* Special issue of *International Organization* 32, No. 1 (Winter 1978).

(105) Cardoso, Fernando Henrique. "The Consumption of Dependency Theory in the United States." *Latin American Research Review* 12, No. 3 (1977), pp. 7-24.

(106) Chilcote, Ronald H. "A Question of Dependency." *Latin American Research Review* 13, No. 2 (1978), pp. 55-68.

(107) Commission on United States-Latin American Relations. *The Americas in a Changing World.* New York: Quadrangle Books, 1975.

(108) Cotler, Julio and Richard R. Fagen, eds. *Latin America and the United States: The Changing Political Realities.* Stanford: Stanford University Press, 1974.

(109) Domínguez, Jorge I. "Consensus and Divergence: The State of the Literature on Inter-American Relations in the 1970s." *Latin American Research Review* 13, No. 1 (1978), pp. 87-126.

(110) Dos Santos, Theotonio. "The Changing Structure of Foreign Investments in Latin America." In James Petras and Maurice Zeitlin, eds., *Latin America: Reform or Revolution?* Greenwich, Conn.: Fawcett Publications, 1968.

(111) Erickson, Kenneth P. and Patrick V. Peppe. "Dependent Capitalist Development, U.S. Foreign Policy, and Repression of the Working Class in Chile and Brazil." *Latin American Perspectives* 3, No. 1 (Winter 1976), pp. 19-44.

(112) Fagen, Richard R., ed. *U.S. Foreign Policy and Latin America.* Stanford: Stanford University Press, 1979.

(113) ————. "Studying Latin American Politics: Some Implica-

tions of a Dependencia Approach." *Latin American Research Review*, 12, No. 2 (1977), pp. 3-27.

(114) Fishlow, Albert et al. *Rich and Poor Nations in the World Economy.* New York: McGraw Hill, 1977.

(115) Furtado, Celso. "U.S. Hegemony and the Future of Latin America." In Irving L. Horowitz, ed., *Latin American Radicalism.* New York: Vintage Books, 1969.

(116) Gilpin, Robert. *U.S. Power and the Multinational Corporation: The Political Economy of Direct Foreign Investment.* New York: Basic Books, 1975.

(117) Grunwald, Joseph, ed. *Latin America and World Economy: A Changing International Order.* Beverly Hills: Sage Publications, 1978.

(118) Hellman, Ronald and H. Jon Rosenbaum, eds. *Latin America: The Search for a New International Role.* New York: Sage Publications, 1975.

(119) Kindleberger, Charles P. *Economic Response: Comparative Studies in Trade, Finance, and Growth.* Cambridge, Mass.: Harvard University Press, 1978.

(120) Kurth, James R. "United States Foreign Policy and Latin American Military Rule." In Philippe C. Schmitter, ed., *Military Rule in Latin America: Functions Consequences, and Perspectives.* Beverly Hills: Sage Publications, 1973.

(121) Leontief, Wassily. *The Future of the World Economy.* New York: Oxford University Press, 1977.

(122) Lewis, W. Arthur. *The Evolution of the International Economic Order.* Princeton: Princeton University Press, 1978.

(123) Lowenthal, Abraham. "The United States and Latin America: Ending the Hegemonic Presumption." *Foreign Affairs* 55, No. 1 (October 1976), pp. 199-213.

(124) ———. "United States Policy Toward Latin America: 'Liberal,' 'Radical,' and 'Bureaucratic' Perspectives." *Latin American Research Review* 8, No. 3 (Fall 1973), pp. 3-25. Also published in Julio Cotler and Richard R. Fagen, eds., *Latin America and the United States.* Stanford: Stanford University Press, 1974.

(125) Martins, Luciano. *Nação e Corporação Multinacional.* Rio de Janeiro: Paz e Terra, 1975.

(126) Sunkel, Osvaldo. *Capitalismo transnacional y disintegración*

nacional en América Latina. Buenos Aires: Ediciones Nueva Visión, 1973.

(127) Vaitsos, Constantine. *Intercountry Income Distribution and Transnational Enterprises*. Oxford: Oxford University Press, 1974.

(128) Vernon, Raymond. *Sovereignty at Bay: The Multinational Spread of U.S. Enterprises*. New York: Basic Books, 1971.

(129) Whitaker, Arthur P. *The United States and the Southern Cone: Argentina, Chile and Uruguay*. Cambridge, Mass.: Harvard University Press, 1976.

See also 3, 232, 288.

D. Populism

(130) Alvaro, Moisés, Liisa North, and David Raby. "Conflicts within Populist Regimes, Brazil and Mexico." *Latin American Research Unit Studies* Vol. 2, No. 1 (October 1977).

(131) Cavarozzi, Marcelo. "Populismos y 'partidos de clase media': Notas comparativas." Documento CEDES/G.E. CLACSO/No. 3, 1976.

(132) Di Tella, Torcuato S. "Populism and Reform in Latin America." In Claudio Véliz, ed., *Obstacles to Change in Latin America*. New York: Oxford University Press, 1966.

(133) Erickson, Kenneth P. "Populism and Political Control of the Working Class in Brazil." *Proceedings of the Pacific Coast Council of Latin American Studies*, Vol. 4, 1975.

(134) Ianni, Octavio. *A Formação do Estado Populista na América Latina*. Rio de Janeiro: Editora Civilização Brasileira S.A., 1975.

(135) Jaguaribe, Helio. *Political Development: A General Theory and a Latin American Case Study*. New York: Harper & Row Publishers, 1973.

(136) Kenworthy, Eldon. "The Function of the Little Known Case in Theory Formation or What Peronism Wasn't." *Comparative Politics* 6, No. 1 (October 1973), pp. 17-46.

(137) ———. "Did the 'New Institutionalists' Play a Significant Role in the Formation of Peron's Coalition, 1943-46?" In James Scobie, ed., *New Perspectives on Modern Argentina*. Bloomington, Indiana: Latin American Studies, Indiana University, 1971.

(138) Weffort, Francisco C. "Le Populisme dans la Politique Bresilinne." *Les Temps Modernes* 23, No. 257 (October 1967), pp. 624-49.

(139) ———. "State and Mass in Brazil." In Irving Louis Horowitz, ed., *Masses in Latin America.* New York: Oxford University Press, 1970.

See also 3, 11, 12, 14, 18, 22, 25, 27, 94, 200, 207, 208, 240, 257, 258, 316, 317, 342.

E. The Military

(140) Burggraff, Winfield J. *The Venezuelan Armed Forces in Politics, 1933-1953.* Columbia: University of Missouri Press, 1972.

(141) Cantón, Darío. "Military Intervention in Argentina: 1900-1966." Instituto Torquato Di Tella, Centro de Investigaciones Sociales Documento de Trabajo No. 39, 1968.

(142) Dean, Warren. "Latin American Golpes and Economic Fluctuations, 1823-1966." *Southwestern Social Science Quarterly* 51, No. 1 (June 1970), pp. 70-80.

(143) Einaudi, Luigi R. and Alfred C. Stepan. "Latin American Institutional Development: Changing Military Perspectives in Peru and Brazil." Report prepared for The Office of External Research, Department of State. Rand Corporation, R-586-DOS.

(144) Fitch, John S. "Toward a Model of the Coup d'Etat in Latin America." In Garry D. Brewer and Ronald D. Brunner, eds., *Political Development and Change: A Policy Approach.* New York: The Free Press, 1975.

(145) Germani, Gino and Kalman Silvert. "Politics, Social Structure and Military Intervention in Latin America." *European Journal of Sociology* 1, No. 1 (1961), pp. 62-81.

(146) Horowitz, Irving L. and Ellen K. Trimberger. "State Power and Military Nationalism in Latin America." *Comparative Politics* 8, No. 2 (January 1976), pp. 223-44.

(147) Loveman, Brian and Thomas M. Davies, Jr., eds. *The Politics of Antipolitics: The Military in Latin America.* Lincoln: University of Nebraska Press, 1978.

(148) Lowenthal, Abraham F., ed. *Armies and Politics in Latin America.* New York: Holmes & Meier Publishers, 1976.

(149) North, Liisa. *Civil-Military Relations in Argentina, Chile, and Peru.* Berkeley: Institute of International Studies, University of California, 1966.

(150) Nun, José. *Latin America: The Hegemonic Crisis and the Military Coup.* Berkeley: Institute of International Studies, University of California, 1969.

(151) Nunn, Frederick M. "New Thoughts on Military Intervention in Latin American Politics: The Chilean Case 1973." *Journal of Latin American Studies* 7, No. 2 (November 1975), pp. 271-304.

(152) O'Donnell, Guillermo A. "Modernization and Military Coups: Theory, Comparisons, and the Argentine Case." In Abraham F. Lowenthal, ed., *Armies and Politics in Latin America.* New York: Holmes & Meier Publishers, 1976.

(153) Potash, Robert A. "The Military and the Policy Making Process, 1946-1958 (Perón to Aramburu)." In James R. Scobie, ed., *New Perspectives on Modern Argentina.* Bloomington, Indiana: Latin American Studies, Indiana University, 1977.

(154) ———. *The Army and Politics in Argentina, 1928-1945: Yrigoyen to Perón.* Stanford: Stanford University Press, 1969.

(155) Roveldi, David F. "The Mexican Army and Political Order since 1940." In Abraham F. Lowenthal, ed., *Armies and Politics in Latin America.* New York: Holmes & Meier Publishers, 1976.

(156) Schmitter, Philippe C., ed. *Military Rule in Latin America: Function, Consequences and Perspectives.* Beverly Hills: Sage Publications, 1973.

(157) Stepan, Alfred. "The New Professionalism of Internal Warfare and Military Role Expansion." In Alfred Stepan, ed., *Authoritarian Brazil: Origins, Policies, and Future.* New Haven: Yale University Press, 1973.

(158) Villanueva, Victor. *Nueva mentalidad militar en el Perú?* Buenos Aires: Editorial Replanteo, 1969.

(159) ———. *El CAEM y la revolución de la fuerza armada.* Lima: Instituto de Estudios Peruanos, 1972.

See also 120, 157, 170, 199, 209, 211, 250, 263, 298, 342, 351, 352.

F. *Insurgency and Repression*

(160) Alarcón, Rodrigo. *Brasil: Represión y tortura.* Santiago: Editorial Orbe, 1971.

(161) Alves, Marcio Moreira. *A Grain of Mustard Seed. The Awakening of the Brazilian Revolution.* New York: Anchor Books, 1973.

(162) Amnesty International. *Amnesty International Newsletter* (Published Monthly).

(163) ———. *Amnesty International Report on Torture 1975* (with a Special Report on Chile by Rose Styron). New York: Farrar, Straus and Giroux, 1975.

(164) ———. *Amnesty International Report 1977.* London: Amnesty International Publications, 1977.

(165) Bájar, Hector. *Peru 1965: Notes on a Guerrilla Experience.* New York: Monthly Review Press, 1970.

(166) Cristianos Frente a los Hechos Resistencia y Solidaridad. *Chile: Masacre de un pueblo.* Lima: Centro de Estudios y Publicaciones, 1974.

(167) Debray, Regis. *Revolution in the Revolution?* New York: Grove Press, 1976.

(168) Duff, Ernest and John McCamant. *Violence and Repression in Latin America.* New York: The Free Press, 1976.

(169) Gott, Richard. *Guerrilla Movements in Latin America.* Garden City, N.Y.: Anchor Books, 1970.

(170) International Commission of Jurists. "Military Regimes in Latin America." *The Review of the International Commission of Jurists* No. 17 (December 1976), pp. 13-26.

(171) Kohl, James and John Litt. *Urban Guerrilla Warfare in Latin America.* Cambridge, Mass.: The MIT Press, 1974.

(172) Latin American Newsletters, Ltd. "Torture in Latin America." *Latin America* 10, No. 12 (19 March 1976), p. 91.

(173) Núcleo de Estudios Nacionales de Ediciones Grito de Asencio. *Torturas: Uruguay 70.* Montevideo, 1970?

(174) Petras, James. "Revolution and Guerrilla Movements in Latin America: Venezuela, Guatemala, Colombia, and Peru." In James Petras and Maurice Zeitlin, eds., *Latin America: Reform or Revolution?* Greenwich, Conn.: Fawcett Publications, 1968.

(175) Ramsey, Russell W. "Critical Bibliography on La Violencia

in Colombia." *Latin American Research Review* 8, No. 1 (1973), pp. 3-44.

(176) Russell, Charles A., James A. Miller, and Robert E. Hildner. "The Urban Guerrilla in Latin America: A Select Bibliography." *Latin American Research Review* 9, No. 1 (1974), pp. 37-80.

(177) ———, James F. Schenkel, and James A. Miller. "Urban Guerrillas in Argentina: A Select Bibliography." *Latin American Research Review* 9, No. 3 (1974), pp. 53-92.

See also 92, 111, 157, 231, 263, 362, 364.

G. Political Parties

(178) Cantón, Darío. *Elecciones y partidos políticos en la Argentina, historia, interpretación y balance, 1910-1966.* Buenos Aires: Siglo Veintiuno Editores, 1973.

(179) Chalmers, Douglas A. "Parties and Society in Latin America." *Studies in Comparative International Development* 7, No. 2 (1972), pp. 102-30.

(180) Fitzgibbon, Russell H. "The Party Potpourri in Latin America." *Western Political Quarterly* 10, No. 1 (March 1957), pp. 3-22.

(181) ———. *A Directory of Latin American Political Parties.* Tempe: Center for Latin American Studies, Arizona State University, 1970.

(182) Gott, Richard, ed. *Guide to the Political Parties of South America.* Middlesex, England: Penguin Books Ltd., 1973.

(183) Kaufman, Robert R. "Corporatism, Clientelism, and Partisan Conflict: A Study of Seven Countries." In James M. Malloy, ed., *Authoritarianism and Corporatism in Latin America.* Pittsburgh: University of Pittsburgh Press, 1977.

(184) Martz, John D. "Dilemmas in the Study of Latin American Political Parties." *Journal of Politics* 26, No. 3 (August 1964), pp. 509-31.

(185) McDonald, Ronald H. *Party Systems and Elections in Latin America.* Chicago: Markham Publishing Co., 1971.

(186) Needler, Martin C. "The Closeness of Elections in Latin America." *Latin American Research Review* 12, No. 1 (1977), pp. 115-21.

(187) Ranis, Peter. "A Two-Dimensional Typology of Latin

American Political Parties." *Journal of Politics* 38, No. 3 (August 1968), pp. 798-832.

(188) Scott, Robert E. "Political Parties and Policy-Making in Latin America." In Joseph LaPalombara and Myron Weiner, eds., *Political Parties and Political Development.* Princeton: Princeton University Press, 1966.

(189) Stevens, Evelyn P. "Mexico's PRI: The Institutionalization of Corporatism?" In James M. Malloy, ed., *Authoritarianism and Corporatism in Latin America.* Pittsburgh: University of Pittsburgh Press, 1977.

See also 11, 25, 131, 132, 199, 302, 305, 313, 330, 349, 398, 380.

II. Sources on Latin America—Country Listing

A. Argentina

(190) Ayres, Robert L. "The 'Social Pact' as Anti-Inflationary Policy: The Argentine Experience since 1973." *World Politics* 28, No. 4 (July 1976), 473-501.

(191) Brodersohn, Mario S., ed. *Estrategias de industrialización para la Argentina.* Buenos Aires: Editorial del Instituto, 1970.

(192) Corradi, Juan Eugenio. "Argentina." In Ronald Chilcote and Joel Edelstein, eds., Latin America: *The Struggle with Dependency and Beyond.* Cambridge, Mass.: Schenkman Publishing Co., 1974.

(193) Delich, Francisco J. *Crisis y protesta social: Córdoba, 1969-1973.* Bueno Aires: Siglo Veintiuno Editores, 1974.

(194) Di Tella, Torcuato S. *El sistema político argentino y la clase obrera.* Buenos Aires: Editorial Universitario de Buenos Aires, 1964.

(195) Díaz-Alejandro, Carlos F. *Essays on the Economic History of the Argentine Republic.* New Haven: Yale University Press, 1970.

(196) Economic Commission for Latin America. *Análisis y proyecciones del desarrollo económico, 5: El desarrollo económico de la Argentina, Parte 1. Los problemas y perspectivas del crecimiento económico argentino, y Parte II, Los sectores de la producción.* Mexico City: United Nations, 1959.

(197) Ferrer, Aldo. *La economía argentina: Las etapas de su desar-*

rollo y problemas actuales. México, D.F.: Fondo de Cultura Económica, 1963.

(198) Germani, Gino. *Authoritarianism, National Populism, and Fascism*. New Brunswick, N.J.: Transaction Books, 1977.

(199) de Imaz, José Luis. *Los que mandan*. Albany: State University of New York Press, 1970.

(200) Kenworthy, Eldon. "The Formation of the Peronist Coalition." Doctoral Dissertation, Department of Political Science, Yale University, 1970.

(201) Mallon, Richard D. and Juan V. Sourrouville. *Economic Policymaking in a Conflict Society: The Argentine Case*. Cambridge, Mass.: Harvard University Press, 1975.

(202) Merkx, Gilbert W. "Sectoral Clashes and Political Change: The Argentine Experience." *Latin American Research Review* 4, No. 3 (Fall 1969), pp. 89-114.

(203) Most, Benjamin A. "Changing Authoritarian Systems: An Assessment of Their Impact on Public Policy in Argentina, 1930-1970." Doctoral Dissertation, Department of Political Science, Indiana University, 1978.

(204) O'Donnell, Guillermo A. "Estado y alianzas en la Argentina, 1956-1976." *Desarrollo Económico* 16, No. 64 (enero-marzo 1977), pp. 523-24.

(205) *Review of the River Plate*. (Various dates.)

(206) Rock, David, ed. *Argentina in the Twentieth Century*. Pittsburgh: University of Pittsburgh Press, 1975.

(207) Smith, Peter H. "The Social Bases of Peronism." *Hispanic American Historical Review* 32, No. 1 (February 1972), pp. 53-73.

(208) ———. *Argentina and the Failure of Democracy: Conflict Among Political Elites, 1904-1955*. Madison: University of Wisconsin Press, 1974.

(209) Smith, William C. "The Armed Forces and the Authoritarian-Bureaucratic State in Argentina." Paper presented at the Inter-University Seminar on Armed Forces in Society, Tempe, Arizona, 1976.

(210) Wynia, Gary W. *Argentina in the Postwar Era: Politics and Economic Policy Making in a Divided Society*. Albuquerque: University of New Mexico Press, 1978.

See also 2, 18, 25, 58, 80, 83, 93, 129, 136, 137, 141, 149, 152, 153, 154, 177, 178, 183.

B. Brazil

(211) Ames, Barry. *Rhetoric and Reality in a Militarized Regime: Brazil Since 1964.* Sage Professional Papers, Comparative Politics Series 4, No. 01-042 (1970).

(212) Bacha, Edmar. "Issues and Evidence on Recent Brazilian Economic Growth." *World Development* 5, Nos. 1 & 2 (January-February 1977), pp. 47-68.

(213) ———— and L. Taylor. "Brazilian Income Distribution in the 1960s: Facts, Models, Results, and the Controversy." Mimeographed. Cambridge, Mass., 1977.

(214) Baer, Werner. *Industrialization and Economic Development in Brazil.* Homewood, Illinois: The Economic Growth Center, Yale University, 1965.

(215) ———— and A. Maneschi. "Import-Substitution, Stagnation, and Structural Change: An Interpretation of the Brazilian Case," *Journal of the Developing Areas* 6, No. 2 (January 1971), pp. 177-92.

(216) Bergsman, Joel. *Brazil: Industrialization and Trade Policies.* New York: Oxford University Press, 1970.

(217) ———— and Samuel Morley. "Import Constraints and Development: Causes of the Recent Decline of Brazilian Economic Growth. A Comment." *Review of Economics and Statistics* 51, No. 1 (February 1969), pp. 101-04.

(218) Bonelli, Regis and Pedro S. Malan. "Os limites do possível: Notas sobre balanço de pagamentos e indústria nos anos 70." *Pesquisa e Planejamento Econômico* 6, No. 2 (1976).

(219) ————. "Growth and Technological Change in Brazilian Manufacturing Industries during the Sixties." Doctoral Dissertation, Department of Economics, University of California, Berkeley, 1975.

(220) Cardoso, Fernando Henrique. *Autoritarismo e Democratização.* Rio de Janeiro: Editora Paz e Terra, 1975.

(221) ————. *Empresario Industrial e Desenvolvimento Econômico no Brasil.* São Paulo: Difusão Europeia do Livro, 1964.

(222) ————. *Ideologías de la burgesía industrial en sociedades dependientes (Argentina y Brasil).* Mexico City: Siglo Veintiuno Editores, 1971.

(223) ————. *O Modêlo Político Brasileiro.* São Paulo: Difel, 1972.

(224) Departamento Intersindicial de Estatísticas e Estudos

Sócio-Econômicos. "Família Assalariada: Padrão e Custo de Vida." *Estudos Sócio-Econômicos* 2 (January 1974).

(225) ———. "Dez anos de política salarial." *Estudos Sócio-Econômicos* 3 (August 1975).

(226) Dos Santos, Theotonio. "Foreign Investment and the Large Enterprise in Latin America: The Brazilian Case." In James Petras and Maurice Zeitlin, eds., *Latin America: Reform or Revolution?* Greenwich, Conn.: Fawcett Publications, 1968.

(227) ———. "Brazil: The Origins of a Crisis." In Ronald Chilcote and Joel Edelstein, eds., *Latin America: The Struggle with Dependency and Beyond.* Cambridge, Mass.: Schenkman Publishing Co., 1974.

(228) Economic Commission for Latin America. "Growth and Decline of Import Substitution in Brazil." *Economic Bulletin for Latin America* 9, No. 1 (March 1964), pp. 1-59.

(229) ———. *Análisis y proyecciones del desarrollo económico, 2: El desarrollo económico del Brasil.* Mexico City: United Nations, 1956.

(230) Erickson, Kenneth P. *The Brazilian Corporative State and Working Class Politics.* Berkeley and Los Angeles: University of California Press, 1977.

(231) ——— and Patrick V. Peppe. "Dependent Capitalist Development, U.S. Foreign Policy, and Repression of the Working Class in Chile and Brazil." *Latin American Perspectives* 3, No. 1 (Winter 1976), pp. 19-44.

(232) Evans, Peter. *Dependent Development: The Alliance of Multinational, State, and Local Capital in Brazil.* Princeton: Princeton University Press, 1979.

(233) Fernandes, Florestan. *A Revolução Burguêsa no Brasil.* Rio de Janeiro: Zahar, 1975.

(234) Fishlow, Albert. "Some Reflections on Post-1964 Brazilian Economic Policy." In Alfred Stepan, ed., *Authoritarian Brazil: Origins, Policies, and Future.* New Haven: Yale University Press, 1973.

(235) Furtado, Celso. *Diagnosis of the Brazilian Crisis.* Berkeley and Los Angeles: University of California Press, 1965.

(236) ———. *The Economic Growth of Brazil: A Survey from Colonial to Modern Times.* Berkeley and Los Angeles: University of California Press, 1971.

(237) ———. *Análise do "Modêlo" Brasileiro*. Rio de Janeiro: Civilização Brasileira, 1972.

(238) Gall, Norman. "The Rise of Brazil." *Commentary* 63, No. 1 (January 1977), pp. 49-50.

(239) Gudín, Eugenio. *Análise de Problemas Brasileiros*. Rio de Janeiro: Agir, 1965.

(240) Ianni, Octavio. *Crisis in Brazil*. New York: Columbia University Press, 1970.

(241) Instituto do Planejamento Econômico e Social do Ministerio do Planejamento. *Diagnostico da Industrialização Brasileira*. Rio de Janeiro: IPEA, 1968.

(242) ———. *Crescimento Industrial no Brasil*. Rio de Janeiro: Relatório de Pesquisa, No. 26, 1974.

(243) Jaguaribe, Helio. *Economic and Political Development: A Theoretical Approach and a Brazilian Case Study*. Cambridge, Mass.: Harvard University Press, 1968.

(244) Lafer, Celso. *O Sistema Político Brasileiro*. São Paulo: Perspectiva, 1975.

(245) Leff, Nathaniel H. *The Brazilian Capital Goods Industry, 1929-1964*. Cambridge, Mass.: Harvard University Press, 1968.

(246) ———. "Export Stagnation and Autarkic Development in Brazil." *Quarterly Journal of Economics* 81, No. 2 (May 1967), pp. 286-301.

(247) ———. "Import Constraints and Development: Causes of the Recent Decline of Brazilian Growth." *The Review of Economics and Statistics* 49, No. 4 (November 1967), pp. 494-501.

(248) Morley, Samuel A. and Gordon W. Smith. "The Effect of Changes in the Distribution of Income on Labor, Foreign Investment, and Growth in Brazil." In Alfred Stepan, ed., *Authoritarian Brazil: Origins, Policies and Future*. New Haven: Yale University Press, 1973.

(249) Roett, Riordan. *Brazil: Politics in a Patrimonial Society*. Revised edition. New York: Praeger Publishers, 1978.

(250) ———. "A Praetorian Army in Politics: The Changing Role of the Brazilian Military." In Riordan Roett, ed., *Brazil in the Sixties*. Nashville: Vanderbilt University Press, 1972.

(251) Schmitter, Philippe C. "The Portugalization of Brazil." In Alfred Stepan, ed. *Authoritarian Brazil: Origins, Policies,*

and Future. New Haven: Yale University Press, 1973.

(252) Schneider, Ronald M. *The Political System of Brazil: Emergence of a "Modernizing" Authoritarian Regime, 1964-1970*. New York: Columbia University Press, 1971.

(253) Serra, José. "El milagro económico brasileño: realidad o mito?" *Revista Latinoamericana de Ciencias Sociales* 1, No. 3.

(254) Simonsen, Mario Henrique. *Brasil 2001*. Rio de Janeiro: APEC, 1969.

(255) ———. "Brasil e suas perspectivas econômicas." Mimeographed. Ministerio de Fazenda, 1976.

(256) ——— and Roberto Campos. *A Nova Economia Brasileira*. Rio de Janeiro: Livraria Jose Olimpio Editora, 1974.

(257) Skidmore, Thomas E. *Politics in Brazil, 1930-1964*. New York: Oxford University Press, 1967.

(258) ———. "Politics and Economic Policy Making in Authoritarian Brazil, 1937-71." In Alfred Stepan, ed., *Authoritarian Brazil*. New Haven: Yale University Press, 1973.

(259) Soares, Glaucio Dillon. "The New Industrialization and the Brazilian Political System." In James Petras and Maurice Zeitlin, eds., *Latin America: Reform or Revolution?* Greenwich, Conn.: Fawcett World Library, 1968.

(260) Stein, Stanley J. *The Brazilian Cotton Manufacture: Textile Enterprise in Underdeveloped Area, 1850-1950*. Cambridge, Mass.: Harvard University Press, 1957.

(261) Stepan, Alfred, ed. *Authoritarian Brazil: Origins, Policies, and Future*. New Haven: Yale University Press, 1973.

(262) ———. "Political Leadership and Regime Breakdown: Brazil." In Juan J. Linz and Alfred Stepan, eds., *The Breakdown of Democratic Regimes: Latin America*. Baltimore: The Johns Hopkins University Press, 1978.

(263) ———. *The Military in Politics: Changing Patterns in Brazil*. Princeton: Princeton University Press, 1971.

(264) Suplicy, E. "A Política Salarial e o Indice de Preços." Brasilia: Comissão de Economia do Senado, 1977.

(265) Suzigan, Wilson et al. *Crescimento industrial no brasil, incentivos e desempenho recente*. Rio de Janeiro: IPEA/INPES, 1974.

(266) ———. "Contas nacionais do brasil, conceitos e metodologia—Um comentario." *Pesquisa e Planejamento* 3, No. 2 (1973), pp. 389-405.

(267) Tavares, María de Conceição. "Growth and Decline of Import Substitution in Brazil." *Economic Bulletin for Latin America* 9 (March 1964), pp. 1-65.

(268) ———. *De Substitução de Importacões ao Capitalismo Financeiro*. Rio de Janeiro: Zahar, 1972.

(269) ———. "Acumulação de Capital e Industrialização no Brasil." Mimeographed. Rio de Janeiro: Faculdade de Enconômia e Administraçao de UFRJ, 1975.

(270) ——— and José Serra. "Más allá de la estagnación: Una discusión sobre el estilo de desarrollo reciente de Brasil." *El Trimestre Económico* 34, No. 4 (October-December 1971), pp. 905-50.

(271) Weffort, Francisco. "Los trabajadores callados." *Sociedad y Política* 1, No. 3 (Mayo 1973), pp. 52-53.

See also 6, 8, 18, 20, 25, 32, 69, 84, 93, 111, 130, 133, 138, 139, 143, 157, 160, 161, 183, 231.

C. Chile

(272) Ayres, Robert L. "Economic Stagnation and the Emergence of the Political Ideology of Chilean Underdevelopment." *World Politics* 25, No. 1 (October 1972), pp. 34-61.

(273) Cavarozzi, Marcelo J. and James F. Petras. "Chile." In Ronald Chilcote and Joel Edelstein, eds., *Latin America: The Struggle with Dependency and Beyond*. Cambridge, Mass.: Schenkman Publishing Co., 1974.

(274) Cavarozzi, Marcelo José. "The Government and the Industrial Bourgeoisie in Chile: 1938-1964." Doctoral Dissertation, Department of Political Science, University of California, Berkeley, 1975.

(275) Cleaves, Peter S. *Bureaucratic Politics and Administration in Chile*. Berkeley and Los Angeles: University of California Press, 1974.

(276) Economic Commission for Latin America. "Chile." Separata del Estudio Económico de América Latina, 1976. United Nations (E/CEPAL/1026/ADD. 1), 1976.

(277) Ellsworth, P. T. *Chile: An Economy in Transition*. New York: MacMillan Publishing Co., 1945.

(278) Felix, David. "Chile." In A. Pepelasis et al., eds., *Economic Development, Analysis and Case Studies*. New York: Harper and Row, 1961.

(279) Fleet, Michael H. "Chile's Democratic Road to Socialism." *Western Political Quarterly* 26, No. 4 (December 1973), pp. 766-86.

(280) Garretón, Manuel A. et al. "Ideología y procesos sociales en la sociedad chilena, 1970-1973: Informe y materiales de trabajo." 2 Volumes. Santiago: Facultad Latinoamericana de Ciencias Sociales—FLACSO, 1976.

(281) ———. "Ideología y procesos sociales en la sociedad chilena, 1970-1973." Documentos de Trabajo: junio, 1976-marzo, 1977, 2 Volumes. Santiago: Facultad Latinoamericana de Ciencias Sociales—FLACSO, 1977.

(282) International Labour Office. *The Trade Union Situation in Chile.* Report of the Fact Finding and Conciliation Commission on Freedom of Association, 1975.

(283) Kaufman, Robert R. "The Chilean Political Right and Agrarian Reform: Resistance and Moderation." Institute for the Comparative Study of Political Systems, Washington, D.C., Operations and Policy Research, Inc., 1967.

(284) ———. *The Politics of Chilean Land Reform, 1950-1970.* Cambridge, Mass.: Harvard University Press, 1973.

(285) Lagos, Ricardo and Oscar A. Rufatt. "Military Governments and Real Wages in Chile." *Latin American Research Review* 10, No. 2 (Summer 1975), pp. 139-47.

(286) Mamalakis, Markos J. *The Growth and Structure of the Chilean Economy, from Independence to Allende.* New Haven: Yale University Press, 1976.

(287) ——— and Clark W. Reynolds. *Essays on the Chilean Economy.* Homewood, Illinois: Irwin Publishers, 1965.

(288) Moran, Theodore H. *Multinational Corporations and the Politics of Dependence: Copper in Chile.* Princeton: Princeton University Press, 1974.

(289) Morris, James D. *Elites, Intellectuals, and Consensus: A Study of the Social Question and the Industrial Relations System in Chile.* Ithaca, New York: New York State School of Industrial and Labor Relations, Cornell University, 1966.

(290) Muñoz, Oscar. "An Essay on the Process of Industrialization in Chile since 1914." Yale Economic Essays, Yale University, 1968.

(291) Peppe, Patrick V. "Working Class Politics in Chile." Doctoral Dissertation, Department of Political Science, Columbia University, 1971.

(292) Pinto, Aníbal. *Tres ensayos sobre Chile y América Latina*. Buenos Aires: Solar, 1971.

(293) Plastrik, Stanley. "A First Word on the Chilean Tragedy." *Dissent* 21, No. 1 (Winter 1974), pp. 7-11.

(294) Serra, José. "Economic Policy and Income Distribution in Chile, 1970-1973." Doctoral Dissertation, Department of Economics, Cornell University, 1976.

(295) Sigmund, Paul. "Seeing Allende Through the Myths." *Worldview* 17, No. 4 (April 1974), pp. 16-21.

(296) Sunkel, Osvaldo. "Change and Frustration in Chile." In Claudio Véliz, ed., *Obstacles to Change in Latin America*. New York: Oxford University Press, 1965.

(297) Sweezy, Paul M. "Chile, The Question of Power." *Monthly Review* 25, No. 7 (December 1973), pp. 1-11.

(298) Valenzuela, Arturo. *The Breakdown of Democratic Regimes: Chile*. Baltimore: The Johns Hopkins University Press, 1978.

(299) ———— and J. Samuel Valenzuela, eds. *Chile: Politics and Society*. New Brunswick, N.J.: Transaction Books, 1976.

See also 16, 58, 69, 83, 111, 129, 149, 151, 166, 183, 231.

D. Colombia

(300) Bailey, John J. "Pluralist and Corporatist Dimensions of Interest Representation in Colombia." In James M. Malloy, ed., *Authoritarianism and Corporatism in Latin America*. Pittsburgh: University of Pittsburgh Press, 1976.

(301) Díaz-Alejandro, Carlos F. *Foreign Trade Regimes and Economic Development: Colombia*. New York: Columbia University Press, 1976.

(302) Dix, Robert H. *Colombia: The Political Dimension of Change*. New Haven: Yale University Press, 1967.

(303) Economic Commission for Latin America. *Analyses and Projections of Economic Development, 3: The Economic Development of Colombia*. Geneva: United Nations, 1957.

(304) Fluharty, Vernon Lee. *Dance of the Millions*. Pittsburgh: University of Pittsburgh Press, 1957.

(305) Hartlyn, Jonathan. "Accommodation and Confrontation in Colombian Politics: The Dismantling of the National Front." Dissertation Prospectus, Department of Political Science, Yale University, 1976.

(306) Martz, John D. *Colombia: A Contemporary Political Survey.* Chapel Hill: University of North Carolina Press, 1962.

(307) Nelson, Richard R., T. Paul Schultz and Robert L. Slighton. *Structural Change in a Developing Economy, Colombia's Problems and Prospects.* Princeton: Princeton University Press, 1971.

(308) Nieto Arteta, Luis Eduardo. *El café en la sociedad colombiana.* Bogotá: Breviarios de Orientación Colombiana, 1958.

(309) Ocampo, José F. "The Present Stage of the Colombian Revolution." *Latin American Perspectives* 2, No. 3 (Fall 1975), pp. 5-18.

(310) Ospina Vásquez, Luis. *Industria y protección en Colombia, 1810-1930.* Medellín, Colombia: E.S.F., 1955.

(311) Sharpless, Richard E. *Gaitán of Colombia: A Political Biography.* Pittsburgh: University of Pittsburgh Press, 1978.

(312) Urrutia, Miguel and Mario Arrubla. *Compendio de estadísticas históricas de Colombia.* Bogotá: Dirección de Divulgación Cultural, Universidad Nacional de Colombia, 1970.

(313) Wilde, Alexander W. "Conversations Among Gentlemen: Oligarchical Democracy in Colombia." In Juan J. Linz and Alfred Stepan, eds., *The Breakdown of Democratic Regimes: Latin America.* Baltimore: The Johns Hopkins University Press, 1978.

See also 69, 175, 183.

E. Mexico

(314) Anderson, Bo and James D. Cockroft. "Control and Cooptation in Mexican Politics." *International Journal of Comparative Sociology* 7, No. 1 (March 1966), pp. 11-28.

(315) Coleman, Kenneth M. *Diffuse Support in Mexico: The Potential for Crisis.* Sage Professional Papers, Comparative Politics Series 5, No. 01-057, 1976.

(316) Córdova, Arnaldo. *La política de masas del cardenismo.* México, D.F.: Ediciones Era, 1974.

(317) Cornelius, Wayne A. "Nation Building, Participation, and Distribution: The Politics of Social Reform Under Cárdenas." In Gabriel Almond et al., eds., *Crisis, Choice and Change: Historical Studies of Political Development.* Boston: Little, Brown Co., 1973.

(318) Davis, Charles L. "The Mobilization of Public Support for

an Authoritarian Regime: The Case of the Lower Class in Mexico City." *American Journal of Political Science* 20, No. 4 (November 1976), pp. 653-70.

(319) Eckstein, Susan J. *The Poverty of Revolution: The State and the Urban Poor in Mexico.* Princeton: Princeton University Press, 1977.

(320) FitzGerald, E. V. K. "The State and Capital Accumulation in Mexico." Paper presented at the Conference of the Society for Latin American Studies, 1977.

(321) González Casanova, Pablo. *Democracy in Mexico.* New York: Oxford University Press, 1970.

(322) Hamilton, Nora. "The State and Class Formation in Post-Revolutionary Mexico." Paper presented at the joint meeting of the Latin American Studies Association and the African Studies Association, Houston, 1977.

(323) Hansen, Roger D. *The Politics of Mexican Development.* Baltimore: The Johns Hopkins University Press, 1971.

(324) Johnson, Kenneth F. *Mexican Democracy: A Critical View.* Revised edition. New York: Praeger Publishers, 1978.

(325) King, Timothy. Mexico: *Industrialization and Trade Policies Since 1940.* New York: Oxford University Press, 1970.

(326) Koslow, Lawrence E., ed. *The Future of Mexico.* Tempe: Center for Latin American Studies, University of Arizona, 1977.

(327) Mosk, Sanford A. *Industrial Revolution in Mexico.* Berkeley and Los Angeles: University of California Press, 1950.

(328) O'Shaugnessy, Laura Nuzzi. "Opposition in an Authoritarian Regime: The Incorporation and Institutionalization of the Mexican National Action Party (PAN)." Doctoral Dissertation, Department of Political Science, Indiana University, 1976.

(329) Reynolds, Clark W. *The Mexican Economy: Twentieth-Century Structure of Growth.* New Haven: Yale University Press, 1970.

(330) Scott, Robert E. *Mexican Government in Transition.* Urbana: University of Illinois Press, 1964.

(331) Singer, Morris. *Growth, Equality and the Mexican Experience.* Austin: University of Texas Press, 1969.

(332) Smith, Peter H. *Labyrinths of Power: Political Recruitment in Twentieth Century Mexico.* Princeton: Princeton University Press, 1978.

(333) Stevens, Evelyn P. *Protest and Response in Mexico.* Cambridge, Mass.: The MIT Press, 1974.

(334) Vernon, Raymond. *The Dilemma of Mexico's Development: The Roles of the Private and Public Sectors.* Cambridge, Mass.: Harvard University Press, 1965.

(335) Villareal, René. "The Policy of Import-Substituting Industrialization, 1929-1975." In José Luis Reyna and Richard S. Weinert, eds., *Authoritarianism in Mexico.* Philadelphia: Institute for the Study of Human Issues, 1977.

(336) Wilkie, James W. *The Mexican Revolution.* Berkeley and Los Angeles: University of California Press, 1970.

See also 18, 30, 31, 84, 93, 155, 183, 189.

F. Peru

(337) Alberti, Giorgio, Jorge Santistevan and Luis Pasara. *Estado y clase: La comunidad industrial en el Perú.* Lima: Instituto de Estudios Peruanos, 1977.

(338) Astiz, Carlos A. *Pressure Groups and Power Elites in Peruvian Politics.* Ithaca: Cornell University Press, 1969.

(339) Bourricaud, François. *Power and Society in Contemporary Peru.* New York: Praeger Publishers, 1970.

(340) ———, Jorge Bravo Bresani, Henri Favre and Jean Piel. *La oligarquía en el Perú: Tres ensayos y una polémica.* Instituto de Estudios Peruanos, 1969.

(341) Collier, David. *Squatters and Oligarchs: Authoritarian Rule and Policy Change in Peru.* Baltimore: The Johns Hopkins University Press, 1976.

(342) Cotler, Julio. "Political Crisis and Military Populism in Peru." *Studies in Comparative International Development* 6, No. 5 (1971), pp. 95-113.

(343) ———. "The Mechanics of Internal Domination and Social Change in Peru." *Studies in Comparative International Development* 3, No. 12 (1968), pp. 229-46.

(344) ———. "The New Mode of Political Domination in Peru." In Abraham Lowenthal, ed., *The Peruvian Experiment: Continuity and Change Under Military Rule.* Princeton: Princeton University Press, 1975.

(345) ———. "A Structural-Historical Approach to the Breakdown of Democratic Institutions: Peru." In Juan J. Linz and Alfred Stepan, eds., *The Breakdown of Democratic*

Regimes: Latin America. Baltimore: The Johns Hopkins University Press, 1978.

(346) ———. *Clases, estado y nación en el Perú.* Lima: Instituto de Estudios Peruanos, 1978.

(347) Economic Commission for Latin America. *Analyses and Projections of Economic Development, 6: The Industrial Development of Peru.* Mexico City: United Nations, 1959.

(348) Haya de la Torre, Víctor Raúl. *El antiimperialismo y el APRA.* Lima: Editorial Amanta, 1972.

(349) Klaren, Peter F. *Modernization, Dislocation, and Aprismo: Origins of the Peruvian Aprista Party, 1870-1932.* Austin: University of Texas Press, 1973.

(350) Kuczynski, Pedro Pablo. *Economic Stress Under Peruvian Democracy.* Princeton: Princeton University Press, 1977.

(351) Lowenthal, Abraham F., ed. *The Peruvian Experiment: Continuity and Change Under Military Rule.* Princeton: Princeton University Press, 1975.

(352) ———. "Peru's Ambiguous Revolution." In Abraham Lowenthal, ed., *The Peruvian Experiment: Continuity and Change Under Military Rule.* Princeton: Princeton University Press, 1975.

(353) Malloy, James M. "Authoritarianism, Corporatism, and Mobilization in Peru." *The Review of Politics* 36, No. 1 (January 1974), pp. 52-84.

(354) Mariátegui, José Carlos. *Seven Interpretive Essays on Peruvian Reality.* Austin: University of Texas Press, 1971.

(355) ———. *Ideología y política.* Lima: Editorial Amanta, 1972.

(356) Quijano, Aníbal. "Nationalism and Capitalism in Peru: A Study in Neo-Imperialism." *Monthly Review* 23, No. 3 (July 1971), entire issue.

(357) Sulmont, Denis. *El movimiento obrero en el Perú, 1900-1956.* Lima: Pontífica Universidad Católica del Perú, Fondo Editorial, 1975.

(358) Webb, Richard C. *Government Policy and the Distribution of Wealth in Peru, 1963-1973.* Cambridge, Mass.: Harvard University Press, 1978.

See also 36, 83, 143, 149, 157, 158, 159.

G. *Uruguay*

(359) Economic Commission for Latin America. "Uruguay." Separata del Estudio Económico de América Latina, 1976. United Nations (E/CEPAL/1026/ADD. 2), 1976.

434 *Bibliography*

(360) Errandonea: Alfredo and Daniel Constabile. *Sindicato y sociedad en el Uruguay*. Montevideo: Biblioteca de Cultura Universitaria, 1968.

(361) Graillot, Helene. "Uruguay." In Richard Gott, ed., *Guide to the Political Parties of South America*. Middlesex, England: Penguin Books Ltd., 1973.

(362) Handelman, Howard. "Uruguayan Journal." *Worldview* 20, No. 10 (October 1977), pp. 16-24.

(363) ———. "Class Conflict and the Repression of the Uruguayan Working Class." Paper presented at the University of New Mexico Conference on "Contemporary Trends in Latin American Politics," 1977.

(364) Kaufman, Edy. *Uruguay in Transition*. New Brunswick: Transaction Books, 1978.

(365) Pintos, Francisco R. *Historia del movimiento obrero del Uruguay*. Montevideo: Editorial "Gaceta de Cultura," 1960.

(366) Taylor, Philip B., Jr. "Interests and Institutional Dysfunction in Uruguay." *The American Political Science Review* 43, No. 1 (March 1963), pp. 62-74.

(367) ———. *Government and Politics of Uruguay*. New Orleans: Tulane University Press, 1960.

(368) Van Der Wolf, Bernard. "La programación monetario-financiera en el Uruguay, 1955-1970." Cuadernos del Instituto Latinoamericano de Planificación Económica y Social, Serie II, No. 22, 1974.

(369) Weinstein, Martin. *Uruguay: The Politics of Failure*. Westport, Conn.: Greenwood Press, 1975.

(370) Whitaker, Arthur P. *The United States and the Southern Cone: Argentina, Chile, and Uruguay*. Cambridge, Mass.: Harvard University Press, 1976.

(371) Wonsewer, Israel et al. *Aspectos de la industrialización en el Uruguay*. Montevideo: Publicaciones de la Universidad, 1959.

See also 129, 173, 183.

H. Venezuela

(372) Alexander, Robert J. *The Venezuelan Democratic Revolution*. New Brunswick, N.J.: Rutgers University Press, 1964.

(373) Blank, David Eugene. *Politics in Venezuela*. Boston: Little, Brown Co., 1973.

(374) Bonilla, Frank and José A. Michelena. *The Illusion of Democracy in Dependent Nations*. Vol. 3 of *The Politics of Change in Venezuela*. Cambridge, Mass.: The MIT Press, 1971.

(375) Bonilla, Frank. *The Failure of Elites*. Cambridge, Mass.: The MIT Press, 1970.

(376) Chen, Chi-Yi. *Economía social del trabajo: Caso de Venezuela*. Caracas: Librería Editorial Salesiana, 1969.

(377) Gil, José Antonio. "Entrepreneurs and Regime Consolidation." In John D. Martz and David J. Myers, eds., *Venezuela: The Democratic Experience*. New York: Praeger Publishers, 1977.

(378) Levine, Daniel H. *Conflict and Political Change in Venezuela*. Princeton: Princeton University Press, 1973.

(379) ———. "Venezuela since 1958: The Consolidation of Democratic Politics." In Juan J. Linz and Alfred Stepan, eds., *The Breakdown of Democratic Regimes: Latin America*. Baltimore: The Johns Hopkins University Press, 1978.

(380) Martz, John D. *Acción Democrática: Evolution of a Modern Political Party in Venezuela*. Princeton: Princeton University Press, 1966.

(381) ——— and David J. Myers, eds. *Venezuela: The Democratic Experience*. New York: Praeger Publishers, 1977.

(382) Powell, John Duncan. *Political Mobilization of the Venezuelan Peasant*. New York: Cambridge University Press, 1971.

(383) Ray, Talton F. *The Politics of the Barrios of Venezuela*. Berkeley and Los Angeles: University of California Press, 1969.

(384) Tugwell, Franklin. *The Politics of Oil in Venezuela*. Stanford: Stanford University Press, 1975.

See also 140, 183.

III. European Industrialization and Development

(385) Abraham, David. "Inter-Class Conflict and the Formation of Ruling Class Consensus in Late Weimar Germany." Doctoral Dissertation, Department of History, University of Chicago, 1977.

(386) Anderson, Charles W. *The Political Economy of Modern*

Spain: Policy-Making in an Authoritarian System. Madison: University of Wisconsin Press, 1970.

(387) Artz, Frederick B. *Reaction and Revolution, 1814-1832.* New York: Harper and Row, 1963.

(388) Berghahn, V. R. *Germany and the Approach of War in 1914.* New York: St. Martin's Press, 1973.

(389) Biucchi, B. M. "The Industrial Revolution in Switzerland." In Carlo M. Cipolla, ed., *The Emergence of Industrial Societies.* London: Collins/Fontana, 1973.

(390) Borchandt, Knut. "The Industrial Revolution in Germany 1700-1914." In Carlo M. Cipolla, ed., *The Emergence of Industrial Societies.* London: Collins/Fontana, 1973.

(391) Borkin, Joseph. *The Crime and Punishment of I. G. Farben.* New York: The Free Press, 1978.

(392) Bracher, Karl Kietrich. *The German Dictatorship: The Origins, Structure, and Effects of National Socialism.* New York: Praeger Publishers, 1970.

(393) Brenan, Gerald. *The Spanish Labyrinth: An Account of the Social and Political Background of the Civil War.* Cambridge: Cambridge University Press, 1950.

(394) Bullock, Alan. *Hitler: A Study in Tyranny.* Revised edition. New York: Harper and Row, 1964.

(395) Burn, Duncan. *The Economic History of Steelmaking, 1867-1939: A Study in Competition.* Cambridge: Cambridge University Press, 1961.

(395) Cameron, Rondo E. *France and the Economic Development of Europe, 1800-1914, Conquests of Peace and Seeds of War.* Princeton: Princeton University Press, 1961.

(397) Catagna, Luciano. "The Industrial Revolution in Italy 1830-1914." In Carlo M. Cipolla, ed., *The Emergence of Industrial Societies.* London: Collins/Fontana, 1973.

(398) Cipolla, Carlo M., ed. *The Emergence of Industrial Societies.* London: Collins/Fontana, 1973.

(399) Dahrendorf, Ralf. *Society and Democracy in Germany.* Garden City, New York: Doubleday Anchor, 1969.

(400) Earle, Edward M., ed. *Modern France.* Princeton: Princeton University Press, 1951.

(401) Elwitt, Sanford. *The Making of the Third Republic: Class and Politics in France, 1868-1884.* Baton Rouge: Louisiana State University Press, 1975.

(402) Feldman, Gerald D. *Iron and Steel in the German Inflation, 1916-1923.* Princeton: Princeton University Press, 1977.

(403) Fieldhouse, D. K. *Economics and Empire.* Ithaca, New York: Cornell University Press, 1971.

(404) Gerschenkron, Alexander. *Economic Backwardness in Historical Perspective.* Cambridge, Mass.: Harvard University Press, 1962.

(405) ———. *Continuity in History and Other Essays.* Cambridge, Mass.: Harvard University Press, 1968.

(406) ———. *Bread and Democracy in Germany.* Berkeley: University of California Press, 1943.

(407) Gourevitch, Peter. "International Trade, Domestic Coalitions, and Liberty: Comparative Responses to the Crisis of 1876-1896." *The Journal of Interdisciplinary History,* Volume 8 (Autumn 1977), pp. 281-313.

(408) Gross, N. T. "The Industrial Revolution in the Habsburg Monarchy, 1750-1914." In Carlo M. Cipolla, ed., *The Emergence of Industrial Societies.* London: Collins/Fontana, 1973.

(409) Henderson, W. O. *Britain and Industrial Europe: 1750-1870: Studies in British Influence on the Industrial Revolution in Western Europe.* Third Edition, London: Leicester University Press, 1972.

(410) Hirschman, Albert O. *The Passions and the Interests, Political Arguments for Capitalism before its Triumph.* Princeton: Princeton University Press, 1977.

(411) Hobsbawm, Eric. *Industry and Empire: The Making of Modern Society, Vol. II, 1759 to the Present Day.* New York: Pantheon, 1968.

(412) ———. *The Age of Capital, 1848-1875.* New York: Charles Scribner's Sons, 1975.

(413) ———. *The Age of Revolution: Europe 1789-1848.* London: Weidenfeld and Nicolson, 1962.

(414) Howard, Frank A. *Buna Rubber: The Birth of an Industry.* New York: The Free Press, 1978.

(415) Kehr, Eckart. *Battleship Building and Party Politics.* Chicago: University of Chicago Press, 1975.

(416) Kemp, Tom. *Industrialization in Nineteenth Century Europe.* London: Longman, 1969.

(417) Kurth, James A. "The Political Consequences of the

Product Cycle: Industrial History and Political Outcomes." *International Organization*, forthcoming.

(418) Landes, David S. *The Unbound Prometheus: Technological Change and Industrial Development in Western Europe from 1750 to the Present.* Cambridge: Cambridge University Press, 1969.

(419) Langer, William L. *Political and Social Upheaval, 1832-1852.* New York: Harper and Row, 1969.

(420) Lieberman, Sima. *The Growth of European Mixed Economies, 1945-1970.* New York: Oxford University Press, 1969.

(421) Linz, Juan J. *Crisis, Breakdown, and Reequilibration.* Baltimore: The Johns Hopkins University Press, 1978.

(422) ———— and Alfred Stepan, eds. *The Breakdown of Democratic Regimes: Europe.* Baltimore: The Johns Hopkins University Press, 1978.

(423) Maier, Charles S. *Recasting Bourgeois Europe: Stabilization in France, Germany, and Italy in the Decade After World War I.* Princeton: Princeton University Press, 1975.

(424) Marder, Arthur J. *The Anatomy of British Sea Power: A History of British Naval Policy in the Pre-Dreadnought Era, 1880-1905.* New York: Alfred A. Knopf, 1940.

(425) Milward, Alan S. and S. B. Saul. *The Economic Development of Continental Europe, 1780-1870.* Totowa, New Jersey: Rowman and Littlefield, 1973.

(426) Mitchell, B. R. *European Historical Statistics, 1750-1970.* New York: Columbia University Press, 1976.

(427) Morazé, Charles. *The Triumph of the Middle Classes.* Garden City, New York: Anchor Books, 1968. First published in France under the title of *Les Bourgeois Conquerants.*

(428) Nadal, Jordi. "The Failure of the Industrial Revolution in Spain 1830-1914." In Carlo M. Cipolla, ed., *The Emergence of Industrial Societies.* London: Collins/Fontana, 1973.

(429) Neumann, Franz. *Behemoth: The Structure and Practice of National Socialism.* New York: Oxford University Press, 1942.

(430) Nolte, Ernst. *Three Faces of Fascism: Action Francaise, Italian Fascism, National Socialism.* New York: Holt, Rinehart, and Winston, 1966.

(431) Ortega y Gasset, José. *Invertebrate Spain.* New York: W. W. Norton, 1937.

(432) Overy, R. J. "Cars, Roads, and Economic Recovery in

Germany, 1932-1938." *The Economic History Review*, 27, No. 3 (1975), pp. 466-83.

(433) Owen, Roger and Bob Sutcliffe, eds. *Studies in the Theory of Imperialism.* London: Longman, 1972.

(434) Paine, Stanley. "Spain." In Hans Rogger and Eugen Weber, eds., *The European Right: A Historical Profile.* Berkeley: University of California Press, 1965.

(435) Palmade, Guy P. *French Capitalism in the Nineteenth Century.* Newton Abbot, Devon: David and Charles, 1972.

(436) Polyani, Karl. *The Great Transformation: The Political and Economic Origins of Our Time.* Boston: Beacon Press, 1957.

(437) Postan, M. M. *An Economic History of Western Europe, 1945-1964.* London: Meuthen, 1967.

(438) Rogger, Hans and Eugen Weber, eds. *The European Right: A Historical Profile.* Berkeley and Los Angeles: University of California Press, 1965.

(439) Rosenberg, Hans. "Political and Social Consequences of the Great Depression of 1873-1896 in Central Europe." *Economic History Review*, 13 (1943).

(440) Rostow, Walt W. *British Economy in the 19th Century.* Cambridge: Cambridge University Press, 1948.

(441) Sarti, Roland. *Fascism and the Industrial Leadership in Italy, 1919-1940.* Berkeley: University of California Press, 1971.

(442) Schweitzer, Arthur. *Big Business in the Third Reich.* Bloomington, Indiana: Indiana University Press, 1964.

(443) Seton-Watson, Hugh. *Eastern Europe Between the Wars, 1918-1941.* Third Edition, revised. New York: Harper and Row, 1967.

(444) Smith, Dennis Mack. *Italy: A Modern History.* Revised Edition. Ann Arbor: University of Michigan Press, 1969.

(445) Stern, Fritz: *Gold and Iron: Bismarck, Bleichroder, and the Building of the German Empire.* New York: Alfred A. Knopf, 1977.

(446) Stolper, Gustav, Karl Häuser, and Knut Borchardt. *The German Economy, 1870 to the Present.* New York: Harcourt, Brace, and World, 1967.

(447) Svennilson, Ingvar. *Growth and Stagnation in the European Economy.* Geneva: United Nations Economic Commission for Europe, 1954.

(448) Ullman, Joan Connelly. *The Tragic Week: A Study of Anti-*

clericalism in Spain, 1875-1912. Cambridge, Mass.: Harvard University Press, 1968.

(449) Vernon, Raymond, ed. *Big Business and the State: Changing Relations in Western Europe.* Cambridge, Mass.: Harvard University Press, 1974.

(450) Webster, R. A. *Industrial Imperialism in Italy, 1908-1915.* Berkeley: University of California Press, 1975.

(451) Whyte, Arthur James. *The Evolution of Modern Italy.* New York: W. W. Norton, 1965.

(452) Woodruff, William. "The Emergence of an International Economy, 1700-1914." In Carlo M. Cipolla, ed., *The Emergence of Industrial Societies.* London: Collins/Fontana, 1973.

IV. OTHER GENERAL SOURCES CITED IN THIS VOLUME

(453) Afanas'ev, A. *Russian Fairy Tales.* New York: Pantheon, 1973.

(454) Anderson, Perry. "The Antinomies of Antonio Gramsci." *New Left Review,* No. 100 (November 1976 to January 1977), pp. 5-80.

(455) Bates, Thomas R. "Gramsci and the Theory of Hegemony." *Journal of the History of Ideas* 36, No. 2 (April-May 1975), pp. 351-66.

(456) Bayari, Jean-François. "L'Analyse des Situations Autoritaires: Etude Bibliographique." *Revue Française de Science Politique* 26, No. 3 (June 1976), pp. 483-520.

(457) Bendix, Reinhard. *Max Weber: An Intellectual Portrait.* Garden City, N.Y.: Anchor Books, 1962.

(458) ———. "Tradition and Modernity Reconsidered." *Comparative Studies in Society and History* 9 (April 1967), pp. 292-346.

(459) Coleman, James S. "Conclusion: The Political Systems of the Developing Areas." In Gabriel A. Almond and James S. Coleman, eds., *The Politics of the Developing Areas.* Princeton: Princeton University Press, 1960.

(460) Cutright, Phillips. "National Political Development: Measurement and Analysis." *The American Sociological Review* 28, No. 2 (April, 1963), pp. 253-64.

(461) Dahl, Robert A. *Polyarchy: Participation and Opposition.* New Haven: Yale University Press, 1971.

(462) Easton, David. *A Systems Analysis of Political Life*. New York: John Wiley & Sons, 1965.

(463) Gerschenkron, Alexander. *Continuity in History and Other Essays*. Cambridge, Mass.: Harvard University Press, 1968.

(464) ———. *Economic Backwardness in Historical Perspective*. Cambridge, Mass.: Harvard University Press, 1962.

(465) ———. "The Typology of Industrial Development as a Tool of Analysis." In Alexander Gerschenkron, *Continuity in History and Other Essays*. Cambridge, Mass.: Harvard University Press, 1968.

(466) Glaser, Barney and Anselm Strauss. *The Discovery of Grounded Theory: Strategies for Qualitative Research*. Chicago: Aldine Publishing Company, 1967.

(467) Gusfield, Joseph R. "Tradition and Modernity: Misplaced Polarities in the Study of Social Change." *American Journal of Sociology* 72 (January 1967), pp. 351-62.

(468) Han, Sungjoo, "Power, Dependency, and Representation in South Korea." Paper presented at the Annual Meeting of the American Political Science Association, Washington, D.C., 1977.

(469) Hartz, Louis. *The Liberal Tradition in America*. New York: Harcourt, Brace, 1955.

(470) ———. *The Founding of New Societies: Studies in the History of the United States, Latin America, South Africa, Canada, and Australia*. New York: Harcourt, Brace & World, Inc., 1964.

(471) Huntington, Samuel P. "Political Development and Political Decay." *World Politics* 18, No. 3 (April 1965), pp. 386-430.

(472) ———. *Political Order in Changing Societies*. New Haven: Yale University Press, 1968.

(473) ——— and Clement H. Moore, eds. *Authoritarian Politics in Modern Society: The Dynamics of Established One-Party Systems*. New York: Basic Books, 1970.

(474) Linz, Juan J. "An Authoritarian Regime: Spain." In Erik Allardt and Yrjo Littunen, eds., *Cleavages, Ideologies and Party Systems*. Helsinki: Academic Bookstore, 1964.

(475) ———. "Notes Toward a Typology of Authoritarian Regimes." Paper presented at the Annual Meeting of the American Political Science Association, Washington, D.C., 1972.

442 *Bibliography*

(476) ———. "Totalitarianism and Authoritarian Regimes." In Fred Greenstein and Nelson Polsby, eds., *Handbook of Political Science*, Vol. 3, Macropolitical Theory. Reading, Mass.: Addison-Wesley Press, 1975.

(477) Lipset, Seymour Martin. "Some Social Requisites of Democracy: Economic Development and Political Legitimacy." *The American Political Science Review* 53, No. 1 (March 1959), pp. 69-105.

(478) Moore, Barrington, Jr. *Social Origins of Dictatorship and Democracy: Lord and Peasant in the Making of the Modern World*. Boston: Beacon Press, 1966.

(479) O'Connor, James. *The Fiscal Crisis of the State*. New York: St. Martin's Press, 1973.

(480) Organski, A. F. K. *The Stages of Political Development*. New York: Alfred A. Knopf, 1965.

(481) Packenham, Robert A. *Liberal America and the Third World*. Princeton: Princeton University Press, 1973.

(482) Pride, Richard A. "Origins of Democracy: A Cross National Study of Mobilization, Party Systems and Democratic Stability." Sage Professional Papers, Comparative Politics Series 1, No. 02-012 (1970).

(483) Przeworski, Adam and Henry Teune. *The Logic of Comparative Social Inquiry*. New York: John Wiley and Company, 1970.

(484) Rostow, Walt W. *The Stages of Economic Growth*. Cambridge: Cambridge University Press, 1960.

(485) ———. *Politics and the Stages of Growth*. Cambridge: Cambridge University Press, 1971.

(486) Roth, Guenther. "Personal Rulership. Patrimonialism, and Empire-Building in the New States." *World Politics* 20, No. 2 (January 1968), pp. 194-206.

(487) Rothschild, Emma. *Paradise Lost: The Decline of the Auto-Industrial Age*. New York: Random House, 1973.

(488) Rudolph, Lloyd I. and Susan Hoeber Rudolph. *The Modernity of Tradition: Political Development in India*. Chicago: University of Chicago Press, 1967.

(489) Schmitter, Philippe C. *Corporatism and Public Policy in Authoritarian Portugal*. Sage Professional Papers, Contemporary Political Sociology Series, Vol. 1, No. 06-011 (1975).

(490) ———. "Liberation by Golpe: Retrospective Thoughts on

the Demise of Authoritarian Rule in Portugal." In Henry Bienen and David Morell, eds., *Political Participation Under Military Regimes*. Beverly Hills: Sage Publications, 1976.

(491) Shonfield, Andrew. *Modern Capitalism: The Changing Balance of Public and Private Power*. New York: Oxford University Press, 1969.

(492) Tipps, Dean C. "Modernization Theory and the Comparative Study of Societies." *Comparative Studies in Society and History* 15 (March 1973), pp. 199-226.

(493) Weber, Max. *The Theory of Social and Economic Organization*, edited by Talcott Parsons. New York: The Free Press, 1964.

(494) Whitaker, C. S. "A Dysrhythmic Process of Political Change." *World Politics* 19, No. 2 (January 1967), pp. 190-217.

(495) Woytinsky, W. S. and E. S. Woytinsky. *World Population and Production: Trends and Outlook*. New York: The Twentieth Century Fund, 1953.

Index

Contributors

Fernando Henrique Cardoso is Director of CEBRAP (Centro Brasileiro de Análise e Planejamento) in São Paulo. His numerous publications include *Dependencia y desarrollo en América Latina* (with Enzo Faletto), *Política e desenvolvimento em sociedades dependentes: ideologias do empresariado industrial argentino e brasileiro, O modelo político brasileiro, Autoritarismo e democratização*, and *Democracia para mudar*.

David Collier is Associate Professor of Political Science and Chair of the Center for Latin American Studies at the University of California, Berkeley. He is the author of *Squatters and Oligarchs: Authoritarian Rule and Policy Change in Peru* and of articles on the timing and sequence of political change, on corporatism, and on the relationship between the state and organized labor in Latin America.

Julio Cotler is a Senior Researcher at the Instituto de Estudios Peruanos, in Lima, and Professor at the University of San Marcos. Between 1974 and 1976 he was Professor at the National Autonomous University in Mexico. He is the author of *Clases, estado y nación en el Perú*; is co-editor, with Richard Fagen, of *Latin America and the United States: The Changing Political Realities*; and has published extensively on peasant movements, corporatism, military populism, internal domination, and dependency.

Albert O. Hirschman is Professor of Social Science at the Institute for Advanced Study in Princeton. He has taught at Yale, Columbia and Harvard, and spent five years in Colombia as economic adviser and consultant. He is author of *National Power and the Structure of Foreign Trade, The Strategy of Economic Development, Journeys Toward Progress, Development Projects Observed, Exit, Voice, and Loyalty, A Bias for Hope: Essays on Development and Latin America*, and *The Passions and the Interests*.

Robert R. Kaufman is Professor and Chairman of the Department of Political Science at Douglass College, Rutgers University. His publications include *The Politics of Chilean Land Reform; Transitions to Stable Authoritarian Rule: The Chilean Case*; and "Authoritarianism and Industrial Change in Mexico, Argentina, and Brazil."

James R. Kurth is Professor of Political Science at Swarthmore College. He has been a visiting member of the Institute for Advanced Study in

Princeton. His publications have focused on the interrelationship between domestic and international political change, especially with reference to United States' foreign policy and to Latin Europe. He is currently completing a book on the relationship between industrial structure and political change in North Atlantic countries. He is co-editor of *Testing Theories of Economic Imperialism*.

Guillermo O'Donnell is the founder and former Director of CEDES (Centro de Estudios de Estado y Sociedad) in Buenos Aires, and is presently a Senior Researcher at CEDES. He has been a Visiting Professor at the University of Michigan and a Visiting Member of the Institute for Advanced Study, Princeton. His publications include *Modernization and Bureaucratic-Authoritarianism: Studies in South American Politics*, and, with Delfina Linck, *Dependencia y autonomía*. He has recently completed a book on the "bureaucratic-authoritarian" period in Argentina between 1966 and 1973.

José Serra is Professor of Economics at the University of Campinas in Brazil. He is a consultant at CEBRAP (Centro Brasileiro de Análise e Planejamento) in São Paulo and has been a visiting member of the Institute for Advanced Study, Princeton. He is the author of *Economic Policy and Income Distribution in Chile, 1970-73* and of articles on economic development and on the Chilean and Brazilian economies.

Library of Congress Cataloging in Publication Data

The new authoritarianism in Latin America.
 Bibliography: p.
 Includes index.
  1. Latin America—Politics and government—1948-
Addresses, essays, lectures.   2.   Authoritarianism—
Addresses, essays, lectures.   3.   Bureaucracy—Addresses,
essays, lectures.   4.   Latin America—Armed Forces—Polit-
ical activity—Addresses, essays, lectures.   I. Collier,
David, 1942-   II. Cardoso, Fernando Henrique.
III.   Joint Committee on Latin American Studies.
JL960.N48   320.9′8′003   79-83982
ISBN 0-691-07616-2
ISBN 0-691-02194-5 pbk.